The Professional Kitchen Manager

Jack D. Ninemeier

The School of Hospitality Business, Michigan State University

David K. Hayes

Panda Pros Hospitality Management and Training

Allisha A. Miller

Panda Pros Hospitality Management and Training

Prentice Hall

Boston   Columbus   Indianapolis   New York   San Francisco   Upper Saddle River
Amsterdam   Cape Town   Dubai   London   Madrid   Milan   Munich   Paris   Montreal   Toronto
Delhi   Mexico City   São Paulo   Sydney   Hong Kong   Seoul   Singapore   Taipei   Tokyo

Editorial Director: Vernon Anthony
Senior Acquisitions Editor: William Lawrensen
Editorial Assistant: Lara Dimmick
Director of Marketing: David Gesell
Campaign Marketing Manager: Leigh Ann Sims
Curriculum Marketing Manager: Thomas Hayward
Senior Marketing Coordinator: Alicia Wozniak
Marketing Assistant: Les Roberts
Associate Managing Editor: Alex Wolf
Operations Specialist: Laura Messerly
Art Director: Jayne Conte
Cover Designer: Axell Designs
Cover Art: Fotolia
Lead Media Project Manager: Karen Bretz
Full-Service Project Management: Kailash Jadli/Apatara®, Inc.
Composition: Aptara®, Inc.
Printer/Binder: Edwards Brothers
Cover Printer: Lehigh-Phoenix Color/Hagerstown
Text Font: Minion

Credits and acknowledgments for material borrowed from other sources and reproduced, with permission, in this textbook appear on appropriate page within text.

Library of Congress Cataloging-in-Publication Data

Hayes, David K.
  The professional kitchen manager / David K. Hayes, Jack D. Ninemeier, Allisha A. Miller.
    p. cm.
  Includes bibliographical references and index.
  ISBN-13: 978-0-13-139174-1
  ISBN-10: 0-13-139174-7
  1. Food service management.   2. Kitchens.   I. Ninemeier, Jack D.   II. Miller, Allisha.   III. Title.

  TX911.3.M27H394 2012
  647.95068—dc22   2011003016

10 9 8 7 6 5 4 3 2 1

Prentice Hall
is an imprint of

www.pearsonhighered.com

ISBN 10:   0-13-139174-7
ISBN 13: 978-0-13-139174-1

CONTENTS

PREFACE

HELP WANTED!

Exciting opportunities for a professional kitchen manager to assume all responsibilities for the management and operation of food production in a fast-paced and labor-intensive operation serving hundreds of high-quality meals per day. Challenges include planning and designing menus, selecting the very best employees, and training and facilitating their work for optimal performance. If you can control the purchasing, receiving, storing, and issuing of foods, develop and cost standard recipes, and analyze sales and revenue information we want you! You'll join a young and aggressive team with a focus on ensuring that all of our guests are completely satisfied with their dining experience and that our budgeted profit goals are met.

Every quantity food production operation requires someone to "be in charge" regardless of whether he or she is called a cook, chef, kitchen manager, or another term. This person must have a wide array of knowledge and skills to meet all necessary production management responsibilities. This individual may have received formal training in a well-planned hospitality management or culinary education program in which the management of human resources, food and beverage products, and financial assets, among other resources, were discussed along with the "art and science" of food production.

Every successful food service operation serves "good" food. However, the concept of "good" relates to the taste, aroma, presentation, portion size, value, and other factors seen from the perspectives of those being served. Our definition, then, relates to much more than just compliance with standard recipes. Those in charge of today's kitchens must know how to plan and design menus, and they are an important member of the management team. Their goal: to consistently use on-going sanitation, safety, and human resources practices to make their operation an "employer of first choice" rather than an "employer of last resort."

Contemporary kitchen managers frequently work in labor-intensive operations because technology has not found a way to replace people with equipment or use of convenience foods. Even if this was possible, guests in many food service operations think that "fresh is best" and want freshly prepared meals. How are food production employees selected and trained? How are they supervised and motivated? How are labor costs managed to remain within budgetary restraints? Kitchen managers must know the answers to these questions and apply their knowledge and practice their skills daily.

There are management-related aspects to menu planning, design, and evaluation and to the development and implementation of standard recipes to consistently deliver food meeting guests' expectations. Management control procedures are required for purchasing, receiving, storing, and issuing food products, and the input of trained kitchen managers is required to minimize expenses while maximizing the quality of food products before they are prepared and portioned onto the guests' plates. Kitchen managers also help their property's management team by providing insight into "what the numbers say" about historical sales and revenue information.

It is easy to defend, then, the need for this specialized resource, *The Professional Kitchen Manager*. Our text addresses the broad spectrum of the critical decisions a kitchen manager makes.

WHO WILL BENEFIT FROM THIS BOOK?

Hospitality management and culinary education students, their faculty members, and practicing industry professionals will benefit from reading and using the concepts discussed in this book.

Students will learn a basic foundation of food production management information as they read and study the information in this book, as they work through end-of-section activities throughout each chapter, and if they use the specially-designed kitchen management simulations that have been specifically developed for each chapter. As importantly, this book is a resource that can help them answer questions on the job and plan training programs for their own staff after they assume management positions.

Faculty members want their students to succeed and know that their students' educational background is integral to that success. Class resources must meet their standards for the delivery of quality educational opportunities. Instructors will find this book to be well-organized, present important information, and be delivered in a way that retains their students' interest and helps students to enhance their learning.

Those already working in the industry know that their education didn't end on the last day they attended class. The culinary world changes continuously and quickly, and ongoing professional development activities are needed to keep current. Experienced kitchen managers may be confronted with operating problems, and this text can be reviewed to provide information that might address and resolve operating challenges.

BOOK ORGANIZATION

Chapter information in this book is divided into logical and sequential phases that answer five basic questions:

- *Question 1: What must kitchen managers know before any food production begins?* This question is answered in Chapter 1 that provides an overview of the industry, kitchen managers' professional obligations, and basic information about sanitation and safety.
- *Question 2: What must kitchen managers know about facilitating the work of production employees?* Chapter 2 discusses tactics for selecting and training food production employees, and Chapter 3 provides basic information about motivating and supervising employees and controlling labor costs by developing effective schedules.
- *Question 3: What must kitchen managers know about menus and standard recipes?* Chapters 4 and 5 discuss, respectively, menu planning and design, and Chapters 6 and 7 provide information about using and costing standard recipes.
- *Question 4: What must kitchen managers know and do to control food costs and quality?* This question is answered in Chapters 8 and 9 as basic information about purchasing, receiving, storing, and issuing practices are presented.
- *Question 5: What are the responsibilities of kitchen managers after food production?* Chapter 10 discusses the kitchen managers' role in menu analysis, and Chapter 11 reviews information helpful for kitchen managers when they analyze sales and revenue information.

CHAPTER FEATURES

Each chapter component should complement the topic, help to maintain readers' interest, alert readers to additional information, and/or allow them to apply knowledge learned from study of the chapter. The following components in each chapter help to attain one or more of these goals.

Chapter Ingredients Outline

Chapter content is previewed in a two-level outline to allow readers to preview content and help busy readers locate information of interest.

Chapter Objectives

This part in each chapter identifies the specific reason (objective) for including and developing each section of the chapter. It identifies what the reader will be able to do after successfully completing the chapter.

Coming Right Up Overview

This part is an introduction which provides a preview of chapter information and explains and defends why its content is important for the kitchen manager.

Overheard In the Kitchen

This boxed feature defines key terms discussed throughout the chapter, and all key terms are listed in alphabetical order and are defined at the end of the book.

"Information On the Side"

Several boxed highlights are included throughout each chapter and provide information of supportive interest to the topics being discussed. Many are anecdotal and provide interesting sidebars of information designed to keep the reader interested in the chapter content.

Managerial Tools

Each chapter contains, as applicable, figures, checklists, samples of forms discussed in the reading, and other information to help readers better understand the information being presented.

End-of-Section Application Activities

Two learning features are included at the end of each major section in each chapter. The Internet-related ("A Pinch of the Internet") and discussion questions ("Completing the Plate Questions") allow readers to, respectively, discover other related information and apply information learned in the chapter. Additionally, there are two "mini" case studies ("Kitchen Challenge Du Jour Case Study") in each chapter with discussion questions that can drive the students' analysis and discussion of the case study.

Chapter Photos

Each chapter contains several photos that depict common themes with which restaurant managers must be familiar. They supplement the text information by allowing readers to actually see the world of kitchen management and help to retain the readers' interest in the chapter's topic.

To access supplementary materials online, instructors need to request an instructor access code. Go to **www.pearsonhighered.com/irc**, where you can register for an instructor access code. Within 48 hours after registering, you will receive a confirming e-mail, including an instructor access code. Once you have received your code, go to the site and log on for full instructions on downloading the materials you wish to use.

ACKNOWLEDGEMENTS AND FINAL THOUGHTS

Many persons contributed to the process that yielded this book, and the authors first wish to thank Mr. Vernon Anthony, *Editorial Director,* and Mr. William Lawrensen, *Senior Acquisitions Editor,* for their cooperation and support. We have worked with these gentlemen on several books over the last several years, and they are great "cheerleaders" for our efforts.

We are also wish to acknowledge the help of our book reviewers: Dirk Boon, Oxnard College; Dan Creed, Normandale Community College; George Harris, Mohave Community College; Robert Hertel, St. Louis Community College; Dean Louie, University of Hawaii Maui College; Prema Monteiro, J F Drake State Technical College; Anthony Pisacano, Ogeechee Technical College; Greg Quintard, Nash Community College; Gary Ward, University of Phoenix; and Diane Withrow, Cape Fear Community College. Each of these experts contributed numerous suggestions that were incorporated into and make this book more helpful to hospitality educators and their students.

Finally, the authors recognize that kitchen managers and their staff perform very challenging work, and we are in constant awe of the outcomes of their efforts. We dedicate this book to those who do and will manage food production operations in businesses of all types and sizes in today's truly global food service industry. We understand that it is much easier for happy and anticipative guests to exclaim, "Bon appétit!" than it is to undertake the ongoing and challenging activities involved in planning, implementing, and actually delivering on the promises that the hospitality profession makes to its consumers. "Our salute to the ladies and gentlemen of the culinary profession!"

Jack D. Ninemeier, Ph.D
Hilo, Hi

David K. Hayes, Ph.D
Okemos, Mi

Allisha A. Miller
Lansing, Mi

Kitchen Managers Get Ready for Food Production

Chapter Ingredients Outline

Learning Objectives

After studying this chapter, you will be able to:

1. Provide an overview of the food service industry.
2. Explain that kitchen managers are professionals.
3. Discuss basic sanitation practices that are important in the kitchen.
4. Describe basic safety practices.

COMING RIGHT UP OVERVIEW

The world of food service holds many challenges. It is made up of many types of operations serving different types of people. The good news is that there are some basic principles useful when operating every food service organization, and these principles will be explored throughout this chapter and the entire book.

Since food service operations differ, there is no standard list of tasks that a kitchen manager performs. However, most are responsible for several food production and management-related activities, and these will be previewed in this chapter.

Every employee in every food service operation must please consumers who might be referred to as guests, students, patients, residents, members, or whether it is someone else for whom the food service is intended. Some people may think that only the counter attendants, hosts and hostesses, or servers who have contact with consumers need to be concerned about this responsibility. They are wrong, and we will explore this idea in this chapter.

Today, with people just like you wanting more for the money they spend while eating away from home, quality is very important. "That's good enough" was never an idea that leads to success, and it is certainly not a good business principle today.

This chapter concludes with overview of sanitation and safety principles that must be consistently practiced by kitchen managers and their employees. Failing to do so can harm or even kill employees and guests, and it is good to know that the use of some basic and simple practices can reduce these risks.

There is a lot to cover as we begin our study of what kitchen managers do, so let's begin right now.

FOOD SERVICE: A BIG INDUSTRY

O B J E C T I V E

1. Provide an overview of the food service industry:
   - Types of food service operations
   - Organization of food service operations
   - Overview of kitchen activities
   - Role of kitchen manager in food service operation

The first part of this chapter provides a "big picture" overview of the food service industry and how a typical food service operation is organized. Then we'll look at common kitchen activities and learn about the kitchen manager's important role in the operation. What do kitchen managers do? You'll know by the time you complete this chapter.

Types of Food Service Operations

Food service operations are a part of the broader **hospitality industry**. All organizations in the hospitality industry have something in common: They provide lodging and/or food services to people when they are away from their homes. Some food services are businesses such as restaurants and hotels who want to make a **profit**, and they are called **commercial food service operations**. Other food services such as those in schools, colleges, hospitals, and on military bases exist primarily for other reasons but still must provide food services. These are called **noncommercial food service operations** because they do not exist to make a profit. Some noncommercial food service operations use their own employees, and they are called **self-operated** food service operations. Others hire a company to operate the food service, and they are called **management company-operated** food services.

OVERHEARD IN THE KITCHEN

Hospitality industry—Organizations that provide lodging and/or food services to people when they are away from their homes.

Profit—The difference between the amount of money that a food service operation earns and spends.

Commercial food service operations—Food services in hotels, restaurants, and other businesses that want to make a profit.

Noncommercial food service operations—Food service operations whose financial goal does not involve making profit from the sale of food and beverage products.

Self-operated (noncommercial food services)—A noncommercial food service operation that is managed and operated by the organization's employees.

Management company-operated (noncommercial food services)—A noncommercial food service operation that is managed and operated by a food service management company.

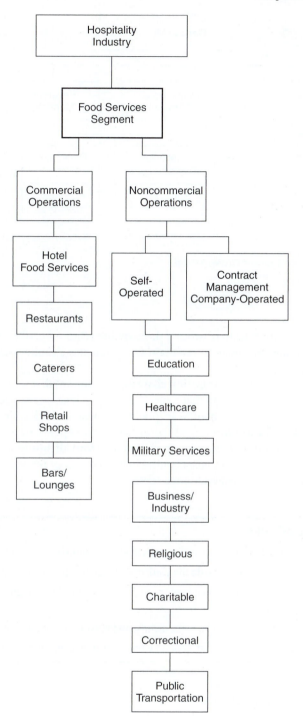

FIGURE 1.1   Some Types of Food Service Operations

Figure 1.1 shows how the food service industry is organized. Remember the good news: The basic principles of managing and operating any type of food service operation, including all those in Figure 1.1 are the same, and they are explained in this book.

Organization of Food Service Operations

Food service organizations can be complex with many specialized positions in large-volume operations, or they can be very simple with few positions in low-volume operations. However, all

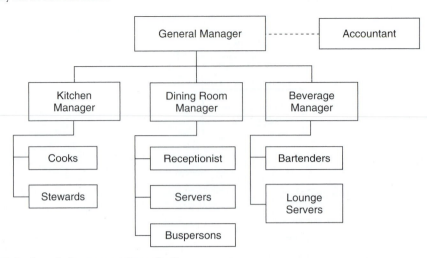

FIGURE 1.2   Sample Restaurant Organization

food service operations are organized around the activities required to obtain, produce, and serve quality food and beverage products, to maintain sanitation and cleanliness, and to support these activities.

Figure 1.2 shows a simple **organization chart** for a restaurant that serves alcoholic beverages.

As you review Figure 1.2, note that general managers have overall **responsibility** for the operation, and they have an accountant to help with financial activities. The kitchen manager is responsible for **back-of-house** food production tasks and supervises the work of cooks and **stewards**. The dining room manager is responsible for **front-of-house** activities and requires help from receptionists, servers, and buspersons. Finally, a beverage manager supervises alcoholic beverage service using bartenders and lounge servers.

OVERHEARD IN THE KITCHEN

Organization chart—A chart that shows how positions in an organization relate to each other.

Responsibility—The need for a person to do the work that is included in a specific position.

Back-of-house—An industry term for employees, positions, and/or departments that have little direct guest contact.

Steward—An employee who washes pots, pans, dishes, and cleans the food and beverage facility.

Front-of-house—An industry term for guest-contact employees, positions, and/or departments.

Overview of Kitchen Activities

Professional kitchen managers have a saying that, "It all starts with the menu!" **Menus** must offer items desired by those being served. After the menu is planned, the **menu items** and **ingredients** needed to "deliver" the menu will be known. Then, these items can be obtained through the **purchasing** process.

After products are purchased, **receiving** is important to make sure the right products in the right quantities and qualities are delivered. **Storing** involves holding products in the best condition until they are needed for **production**. **Issuing** involves moving products from storage areas to the place of production.

Production is the process of getting the products ready for consumption. Many items involve **preparation** as a first step in **cooking**. A final step, **holding** at the proper temperature, may be necessary until items are served.

Figure 1.3 shows the basic activities that, depending upon how the specific food service operation is organized, are common responsibilities of kitchen managers.

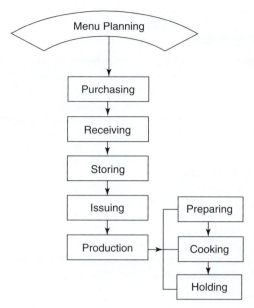

FIGURE 1.3 Food Service Operation

OVERHEARD IN THE KITCHEN

Menu—A list of all the food items that a food service operation has available for consumers.

Menu items—Specific food items that are available at the food service operation.

Ingredients—The individual elements in a menu item. For example, flour and sugar are two ingredients in bread (a menu item).

Purchasing—The process of deciding the right quality and quantity of items that should be purchased and selecting a supplier who can provide them at the right price and right time.

Receiving—The transfer of ownership from a supplier to the food service operation which occurs when products are delivered.

Storing—The process of holding products under the best storage conditions until they are needed.

Production—The process of getting food products ready for service.

Issuing—The process of moving products from storage areas to the place of production.

Preparation—The steps involved in getting an ingredient ready for cooking or serving. For example, celery is cleaned and chopped before cooking in a stew.

Cooking—Applying heat to food to make it more enjoyable.

Holding—The task of keeping food items at the proper serving temperature until they are prepared.

Role of Kitchen Manager in Food Service Operation

When you studied Figure 1.2 above, you learned that the kitchen manager is responsible for food production. While this is true, the activities of a kitchen manager can vary greatly.

For example, the American Culinary Federation (ACF) offers several certification programs for positions with food production responsibilities. These include Culinarian, Sous Chef, Chef de Cuisine, Executive Chef, Culinary Administrator, and Master Chef/Master Pastry Chef. Other terms commonly used in the industry include chef, cook, and back-of-house manager.

While most kitchen manager positions involve food production and supervision of kitchen employees, the exact management tasks that are part of the position can differ. For example, in this book you'll learn about controlling labor costs, planning and designing menus, costing standard recipes, managing purchasing and inventory practices, and analyzing menus and sales information. These are responsibilities of many kitchen managers. Also, persons with this job title may have other responsibilities such as testing recipes, food distribution from a central kitchen to remote serving units, and interacting with **catering** personnel for **banquet** functions.

Kitchen Manager

Part I: Reports to: Restaurant Manager

Part II: Overview of Position: Supervises all kitchen-related operations. Selects, discharges, supervises, trains, and evaluates all food production employees to ensure quality and cleanliness standards are consistently attained. Purchases/issues food items and supplies. Serves on the menu planning team and manages product costs according to budget requirements.

Part III: Job Tasks
1. Supervises all kitchen-related activities.
2. Selects, discharges, supervises, trains and evaluates food preparation personnel to assure quality and cleanliness standards are consistently attained.
3. Purchases/issues food items and supplies.
4. Plans or participates in menu planning.
5. Manages product costs according to budget requirements.
6. Communicates with service personnel about menu changes and specials.
7. Meets with staff and guests about menu/food production concerns and issues.

Part IV: Job Specification

Education: High school graduate or equivalent.

Skills: Able to effectively communicate with employees and read/write recipes, calculate costs and plan menus, employee schedules, and budgets.

Experience: A minimum of three years as a cook or chef. Basic knowledge of kitchen equipment and procedures, safety and sanitation regulations, and food production techniques.

Physical: Must be able to work in fast-paced environment for up to eight hours and be able to lift at least fifty pounds.

FIGURE 1.4   Sample Job Description for Kitchen Manager

OVERHEARD IN THE KITCHEN

Catering—The process of selling a banquet event and interacting with the banquet client.

Banquet—An event in which all or most guests are served items on a pre-selected menu.

What are examples of activities performed by kitchen managers? The sample **job description** shown in Figure 1.4 helps answer this question.

OVERHEARD IN THE KITCHEN

Job description—A list of the tasks that must be performed by a person working in a specific position.

Kitchen managers have three basic types of responsibilities. These involve leadership, food management, and food production:

- *Leadership responsibilities:*
  - Interviews, hires, and supervises kitchen employees.
  - Schedules, disciplines, and conducts performance appraisals for assigned staff.
  - Provides ongoing training for kitchen personnel.
  - Assures that managers are aware of kitchen-related problems.

- *Food Management Responsibilities:*
  - Attains food and labor cost goals specified in the budget.
  - Recommends kitchen equipment, layout, and process improvement changes.
  - Maintains inventory.
  - Helps design and control procedures for food purchasing, receiving, storing, issuing, preparation, and production.
  - Plans and evaluates menus.

Kitchen managers must work closely with their property manager to assure that all procedures are implemented so quality standards will be met.

- *Food Production Responsibilities:*
  - Develops and maintains food quality standards.
  - Produces and/or supervises the production of menu items.
  - Conducts ongoing food quality control checks.
  - Conducts scheduled and unscheduled inspections for sanitation and safety standards.
  - Implements changes as required by health and safety department inspectors.
  - Develops, tests, and modifies standard recipes as required.
  - Costs recipes and uses this information for menu planning, evaluation purposes and for establishing daily specials.

NOW IT'S YOUR TURN

A PINCH OF THE INTERNET (1.1)

1. Are you interested in working in a restaurant? To find out about employment opportunities, look on the home pages of companies in which you may be interested. For example, check out Olive Garden (www.olivegarden.com) and Pizza Hut (www.pizzahut.com).

   Helpful idea: Always review the home page of any company with whom you plan to interview or before taking a field trip to or attending a class lecture in which company representative will be in attendance.

2. Check out the home page for the National Restaurant Association (www.restaurant.org) and the American Culinary Federation (www.acfchefs.org) to learn how these associations help food production professionals.

3. Do you want to learn more about what a kitchen manager does? If so, type "job description for kitchen manager" in your favorite search engine.

COMPLETING THE PLATE QUESTIONS (1.1)

1. What are advantages and disadvantages to being a kitchen manager in some of the types of food service operations shown in Figure 1.1?

2. Assume you had worked in an entry-level position at the Anytown Restaurant for two years and have now been promoted to kitchen manager. How would your relationship with the entry-level persons with whom you worked change now that you are their supervisor? What would you do if one of these persons wanted you to break a policy for him since you had been "shoulder-to-shoulder" coworkers in the past?

3. Which do you think is most important to the success of the food service operation: the kitchen manager responsible for food production or the dining room manager responsible for service?

KITCHEN MANAGERS ARE PROFESSIONALS

OBJECTIVE

2. Explain that kitchen managers are professionals:
   - What is a professional?
   - Professionals please the guests
   - Professionals are concerned about quality

What Is a Professional?

Professionals are persons who work in positions that require much knowledge and skills. When you hear the term "professional," you might think about doctors, lawyers, accountants, and teachers, and they are professionals who have formal education in their field.

OVERHEARD IN THE KITCHEN

Professionals—Persons working in an occupation that requires extensive knowledge and skills.

Kitchen managers can also be considered professionals because specialized knowledge and skills are required for them to work effectively. Also, they can be certified by professional associations such as the National Restaurant Association (www.restaurant.org.), the American Culinary Federation (www.acfchefs.org), and the Dietary Managers Association (www.DMAonline.org) among others.

Professionals are proud of themselves. They do their jobs correctly all the time, and they always try to do better. Professional kitchen managers "go the extra mile," are part of a team, and always try to please their guests and meet their operation's goals.

Professional kitchen managers know what their supervisor expects of them, and they consistently meet these standards. They are good communicators, they are courteous, and they are concerned about problems that confront other staff members.

INFORMATION ON THE SIDE
What Do Kitchen Managers Expect From Their Employers?

Professional kitchen managers expect important things from their employers, including

- Fair pay for the work they do.
- Safe working conditions.
- Training to meet job standards and then ongoing training to improve their performance and advance to more responsible positions.
- Help ensure that all employees work together.
- Information about all policies, rules, and regulations that affect their work.
- A fair evaluation of their performance.

Professional kitchen managers share some things in common that are appreciated by their boss. They:

- Have a positive attitude and are proud of themselves and the important work they do.
- Possess the knowledge and skills required for excellence.
- Are alert to improvement opportunities.
- Contribute "100%" to help their team meet its goals.
- Are genuinely interested in helping others.
- Know and attain (or exceed) their operation's quality and quantity standards.
- Are good communicators.
- Practice effective human relations skills.
- Respect all those with whom they work.
- Have imagination.
- Are creative.

- Follow high ethical and moral standards.
- Are self-confident.
- Admit mistakes and learn from them.
- Follow appropriate personal hygiene and dress standards.
- Have a sense of humor.

Professionals Please the Guests

Everyone in the operation must be concerned about pleasing guests. This is easy to understand if you are in a guest contact position such as food server or cashier. However, the need to please guests is also important for kitchen managers and their employees in positions with little or no guest contact.

Three points are especially important for kitchen managers to consider when thinking about guests:

- The concept of hospitality means being respectful and helpful to people. Assume you are inviting friends to your home, and you are going to prepare a meal for them. Would you want to prepare a nice meal? Would you want them to enjoy it? Would their enjoyment make you happy? These are the thoughts that professional kitchen managers have about those who visit their operation even if they do not know and cannot see them. There is a difference between "throwing ingredients together" and taking care and pride as foods are produced. Both kitchen managers and their guests can tell the difference.
- In today's food service operations, almost every staff member serves a guest or serves someone who serves a guest. Kitchen managers, for example, may not serve the guest directly, but they do prepare food that **service** personnel provide to guests. It is helpful to think about service personnel in the same way that they think about guests and, in so doing, team work is encouraged.

OVERHEARD IN THE KITCHEN

Service—The process of helping guests by meeting their wants and needs with respect and dignity in a timely manner.

- You know that your personal opinion of a food service operation relates to the quality of the food you receive and how you receive it (service). You may not see the person who produces the food, but your opinion about the operation is affected by the food's quality.

Kitchen managers are professionals who represent their food service operation to the guests being served.

As well, you will likely tell your family and friends about the good (or bad) food and the good (or bad) service, and your decision about returning to the food service operation depends on good impressions. Other people think the same way that you do so it is easy to see that kitchen managers and back-of-house staff must please the guests all the time.

Professionals Are Concerned About Quality

What is **quality** and how does it impact the kitchen manager? Quality is the consistent delivery of products and services according to expected standards. However, it is easier to talk about quality than it is to implement and maintain it in many food service operations.

Quality is not a **fad** that will soon go away. Instead, it is an attitude of excellence that focuses on the guests. There are six things that kitchen managers can do to best ensure that quality is emphasized in their operation:

Step 1:   Know who the guests are. Some neighborhood restaurants only serve those who live in a few blocks around the property. Others in hotels serve guests from around the world. It is always important to remember that most guests enjoy a nice experience, **value** for the money they spend, a safe and clean operation, and a service with a smile.

Step 2:   Determine what guests want beyond the basics. Hopefully, **supervisors**, **managers**, and their employees in dining areas know what guests like and dislike. This information should be shared with the kitchen manager. It is interesting that dishwashers often know more about the guests' food preferences than their boss because they see what food remains on the plates that are returned for cleaning.

Step 3:   Discover practical ways to make changes that better please the guests. Some kitchen managers **benchmark** by learning how kitchen managers in other operations please guests. This is relatively easy to do when, for example, they are members of local or state restaurant or other food service-related associations because they can share ideas during these meetings. Other kitchen managers use **cross-functional teams** such as employees from different departments to resolve problems. Perhaps, for example, there are guest complaints about food service being slow. Members of the kitchen and dining room staff can meet to discover reasons for the problem and work together to find solutions.

Step 4:   Train and **empower** employees to please the guests. If new work methods are needed, or if new tools or equipment can resolve problems, kitchen managers must train employees to work in different ways. They empower their staff when they allow employees to help make decisions. Assume, for example, that the kitchen manager is off duty, and a guest wants to substitute cottage cheese for a vegetable in a dinner plate. Can the kitchen employee make this decision?

OVERHEARD IN THE KITCHEN

Quality—The consistent delivery of products and services according to expected standards.

Fad—A short-lived interest in something like a food item.

Value—Guest views about what they pay for something in comparison to what they receive for the payment.

Supervisor—A staff member who directs the work of entry-level employees.

Manager—A staff member who directs the work of supervisors.

Benchmark—The search for the best ways to do things and then comparing these ways to how a food service operation does them in order to learn how well the operation is doing.

Cross-functional team—A group of employees from different departments who work together to resolve problems.

Empower—The act of giving authority (power) to employees to make decisions within their areas of responsibility.

Step 5:   Implement revised procedures. When changes must be made, perhaps this can be done over time rather than "all at once." Also, new methods may need to be evaluated to assure that these methods help guests better.

Step 6: Evaluate and change service delivery systems as needed. As guests' desires change over time, new menu items and service styles may be preferred. The process of planning and managing these changes is part of the kitchen manager's job, and it is surprising how his/her knowledge and skills can help resolve problems in the dining room.

▌NOW IT'S YOUR TURN

A PINCH OF THE INTERNET (1.2)

1. If you never thought about food production personnel being professionals, type "what is a professional?" in your favorite search engine. You can read many definitions and short explanations about what a professional is, and you'll see that kitchen managers fit right in.
2. Must kitchen managers and their staff members really be concerned about guest service? Type "what is guest service?" into your favorite search engine, and you'll see that comments made in this section of the chapter are "right on."

3. Concerns about quality are an important part of the hospitality industry. Type "hospitality industry and quality" in your favorite search engine to learn more about this topic.

COMPLETING THE PLATE QUESTIONS (1.2)

1. What are some specific things that kitchen managers can do to please the guests?
2. What should a kitchen manager do if a guest has a specific complaint about the production of a food item?
3. Which is more important: the quality of a food product or the quality of the procedures used to serve it?

Kitchen Challenge Du Jour Case Study (1.1)

"The food is not hot, the size of servings is small, and different ingredients are used in the main dishes every time we serve them! I tell you, that's what so many of my guests say, and it really hurts my tips." Joey is talking to the kitchen manager about the comments he heard from guests during the last several shifts.

"I know we've talked about this before, Joey, and if there is a problem we want to fix it. I've spoken to my food production team, and they think that a large part of the problem is caused by service staff who do not know or explain the menu to the guests. Then they make ordering mistakes and have timing problems and that makes the guests angry when their expectations are not met."

a) What would you do if you were the kitchen manager to take care of this problem?
b) How, if at all, could a cross-functional team help address the situation?

BASIC SANITATION PRACTICES

OBJECTIVE

3. Discuss basic sanitation practices that are important in the kitchen.
   - Sanitation is an important concern
   - Kitchen sanitation tour
   - Hazard analysis critical control points
   - Other sanitation issues

Kitchen managers have many responsibilities, but none is more important than their need to protect the health and well-being of their guests and employees who consume the items produced by the operation.

Sanitation Is an Important Concern

It is easy to say that kitchen managers must make sure that no one is harmed from eating their food. However, each year, tens of thousands of cases of **foodborne illness** are reported, and it is likely that hundreds of thousands (or more) of cases are not reported. Therefore, this is evidence that sanitation is a problem in many food service operations.

OVERHEARD IN THE KITCHEN

Foodborne illness—A sickness caused by eating food that has been contaminated by germs, chemicals, or physical hazards.

Kitchen managers also know that their operations' reputation will be affected if foodborne illness occurs. Large outbreaks will probably make headlines in the community newspaper, and local health departments often notify the public about results of their **inspections**. Also, **law suits** filed by people claiming to have become sick after eating at the property may be successful and, if they are, this can cause serious financial problems. Even if they are not, much time and a lot of money is typically needed for legal help.

OVERHEARD IN THE KITCHEN

Inspection (sanitation)—An on-site review of a food service operation that is made to help assure that sanitation regulations are being followed.

Law suit—A legal action by one person or organization against another person or organization.

Hopefully, we have explained the need to be concerned about sanitation. Now let's examine how kitchen managers practice basic sanitation principles.

Kitchen Sanitation Tour

Let's see how sanitation concerns impact the way kitchen managers run their operations.

PURCHASING PRACTICES

People knocking on the operation's back door wanting to sell foods from their trucks and employees offering to bring in home-processed canned goods have no place in the purchasing systems used by professional kitchen managers. Products must be purchased from reliable sources to help assure that they have been produced and handled under sanitary conditions.

Suppliers should use clean delivery vehicles. Refrigerated and frozen products must be maintained at the correct temperatures until they reach the operation. The reason is that germs need time to reproduce, and they do so more quickly when they are in the **temperature danger zone**. There is only a four-hour maximum time that foods can remain in this temperature range and that includes the time before the products reach the food service operation. As well, the suppliers' storage facilities must be clean, and products should be properly handled before they reach your operation's receiving area.

INFORMATION ON THE SIDE
Food Safety Means Temperature Control

Kitchen managers always maintain the proper temperatures when handling food products. Recommended temperatures for storing food products are:

- Refrigerated food storage: 41°F (5°C) or below
- Frozen food storage: 0°F (−18°C) or below
- Dry storage foods: 50°F–70°F (10°–21°C)

Germs that are harmful to foods grow best in the temperature range of 41°F–135°F (5°C–57°C). The time that foods are exposed to these temperatures, including receiving, storing, preparation, production, and holding, should be less than four hours. An important caution: The four hours include the time before products reach the operation's back door, and that is why it is important to purchase from professional suppliers.

OVERHEARD IN THE KITCHEN

Temperature danger zone—The temperature range between 41°F (5°C) and 135°F (57°C) in which many harmful germs multiply quickly.

RECEIVING PRACTICES

Employees who receive products must be trained to know when incoming foods may be troublesome. Fruits and vegetables should be inspected for decay, mold growth, and discoloring, and canned items must be checked for bulges and dents along side seams and rims. Note: Bulges are caused by gas that may have been formed by living germs in the cans. Dents along rims and seams can allow germs to enter the cans.

Foods that were frozen may have thawed because of improper handling and then refrozen before delivery. Large ice crystals on the surface of frozen foods and individually quick frozen (IQF) items such as peas or corn that are frozen in clumps instead of being in pieces are signs of product misuse. They should be rejected.

STORING PRACTICES

Products should be quickly moved from receiving to storage areas to minimize the time that foods are in the temperature danger zone. Food should be stored away from walls and at least six inches off the floors so air can circulate and the storage area can be cleaned. Raw food products should be stored under cooked and ready-to-eat foods. Items should not be stored under water or overhead sewer lines. Foods should never be stored near sanitizing, cleaning, or other chemicals. Hopefully, chemicals will be stored in different areas to reduce mistakes.

PRODUCTION PRACTICES

Frozen foods should not be thawed at room temperature or left in a sink full of water. Three good ways to thaw frozen foods are in the refrigerator, as part of the cooking process, and in a sink with cold running water.

Foods in production should be kept at room temperature for the shortest time possible. The common practice of removing all items to be produced at the beginning of a shift for production during the shift is not a good one. Utensils such as knifes and cutting boards and the work counters upon which they are used should be properly cleaned between food preparation tasks to prevent **cross-contamination**. Also, accurate thermometers must be used to monitor food temperatures.

OVERHEARD IN THE KITCHEN

Cross-contamination—The transfer of germs between food and/or nonfood items by direct contact or indirect contact such as with equipment or utensils.

Think about a large turkey being roasted in the oven. As it cooks, its temperature will be hotter on the outside than on its inside. Therefore, the interior temperature must be measured because it will be within the temperature danger zone for a longer time than the product's exterior.

Frequent hand washing is necessary during food preparation and all other times during the food handling and serving process.

AFTER-PRODUCTION FOOD HANDLING PRACTICES

Some items such as **preportioned** steaks are served right after production, and their time within the temperature danger zone after production is slight. However, items such as casserole dishes and sauces may be held for a long time before service. Then, kitchen managers must make sure that the product is held above 135°F (57°C) until it is served.

Some operations provide self-service salad or dessert bars or hot food counters so guests can help themselves to these items. Food held in public areas must also be kept at temperatures of 135°F (57°C) or higher or at 41°F (5°C) or below. These self-service areas must be kept clean, and **sneeze guards** are required by most health codes.

This area of the kitchen is kept clean because a detailed kitchen facility sanitation checklist is in daily use.

OVERHEARD IN THE KITCHEN

Preportion—Menu items that have been divided into the proper weight or size before being purchased by the food service operation.

Sneeze guards—A see-through barrier used to protect foods in self-service counters from other guests who might sneeze or cough on the food.

MANAGING LEFTOVERS

Accurate food production estimates reduce the amount of leftovers. However, leftover foods that will be re-served must be quickly brought to a temperature below 41°F (5°C). Kitchen managers do this by storing items in shallow containers, using ice baths, and frequently stirring products in containers so the warmer product in the center of the container is moved to its sides, bottom, and top to help remove heat. It is generally best to not freeze leftovers for later use because germs can reproduce during the cool-down period. These germs will not die after the product is frozen and will begin to grow and reproduce again when the product is thawed.

CLEAN-UP PRACTICES

Final steps to prevent foodborne illness include clean-up activities. First, let's define two terms: **cleaning** and **sanitizing**. Cleaning involves removing soil and pieces of food from items being cleaned. Sanitizing involves eliminating germs that remain after cleaning.

OVERHEARD IN THE KITCHEN

Cleaning—The removal of soil and pieces of food from the items being cleaned.

Sanitizing—The elimination of germs that remain after cleaning.

Tableware such as plates and knives and forks along with pots and pans should be cleaned with a detergent or other cleaner to loosen soil, food, and germs and mix them in wash water. They can then be sterilized in one of two ways:

- With heat (typically 180°F [82°C] in mechanical dish or pot/pan washer and 165°F [40°C] in manual wash sinks).
- With certain chemicals in certain concentrations.

Equipment used for food production and service must be cleaned by following the manufacturer's instructions. Basic tactics include using a clean cloth, brush, or scouring pad and warm soapy water. Clean from the top-to-bottom or from one side-to-another and then rinse with fresh water and wipe dry with a clean cloth. An approved chemical sanitizing solution can be spread or sprayed onto food-contact services, and areas should be air-dried before use.

Cleaning chemicals can be dangerous and must be handled carefully. Handwashing sinks must be conveniently located and kept supplied with liquid or powdered soap. Bar soap should not be used.

Plumbing systems should be designed according to building codes that eliminate water **backflow**.

OVERHEARD IN THE KITCHEN

Backflow—The backward flow of contaminated water into a drinking water supply that is caused by back pressure in a building's plumbing system.

Kitchen managers must contract with professional waste haulers to remove **refuse** and **garbage**. Areas around dumpsters and other garbage areas must be regularly cleaned and maintained. Some operations, especially those in hot weather areas, refrigerate garbage until pick-up.

OVERHEARD IN THE KITCHEN

Refuse—Solid waste such as cardboard and glass that is not removed through the sewage system.

Garbage—Food waste that cannot be recycled.

Hazard Analysis Critical Control Points

Kitchen managers and their staff are very concerned about the potential for foodborne illnesses and use numerous food-handling procedures to help prevent them. Many also implement an organized system called **Hazard Analysis Critical Control Points** (**HACCP**) to continually emphasize sanitation.

OVERHEARD IN THE KITCHEN

Hazard Analysis Critical Control Points (HACCP)—A practical system using proper food-handling procedures along with monitoring and record keeping to help ensure that food is safe for consumption.

Figure 1.5 show steps in the HACCP system. When you review these steps, you'll note that the HACCP emphasis is on anticipating and correcting potential food safety problems before they occur rather than on taking corrective action(s) after a problem arises. Kitchen managers and their staff identify **critical control points** (**CCPs**) to focus attention on the highest priority sanitation concerns. The sanitation emphasis is continuous, and safe food-handling procedures are incorporated into "the way things are done" at the food service operation.

OVERHEARD IN THE KITCHEN

Critical control point (CCP)—Something that can be done in the movement of food from the times of receiving to service to help prevent, eliminate, or reduce hazards to those who consume the food.

Let's look at each of the steps in the HACCP system:

Step 1: *Assess Hazards*—Kitchen managers should review their menu items and the ingredients used to prepare them and identify those that are most potentially hazardous. These foods include items which are high in protein content such as meats, poultry, eggs, dairy products, and other foods such as beans, pasta, and rice which are frequently contaminated by microorganisms. The HACCP program addresses these

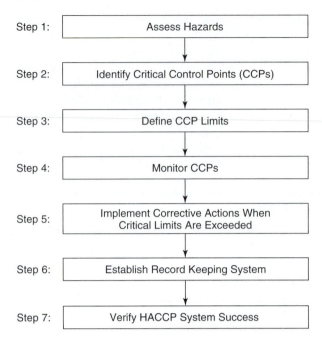

FIGURE 1.5 Steps in the HACCP System

biological **hazards** but, as well, also emphasizes chemical and/or physical objects which also can contaminate food.

OVERHEARD IN THE KITCHEN

Hazard (food contamination)—Microorganisms, chemicals, and physical objects which can contaminate food.

Step 2: *Identify Critical Control Points (CCPs)*—The second step in the HACCP system is to identify critical control points (CCPs) in food-handling. Examples of CCPs include cooking, cooling, reheating, and holding hot and cold products at the temperatures which recognize the importance of the danger zone (41 to 135°F; 5 to 57°C). Of these, cooking and reheating relate to efforts to destroy harmful microorganisms. The remaining three (cooling, hot food holding, and cold food holding) involve efforts to prevent or, at least, to slow bacterial growth.

A flowchart can be developed for each item which may create a potential hazard, and CCP analysis can be applied to each step in its processing. Let's look at an example in Figure 1.6.

In Figure 1.6, each step in the flow of food products through the restaurant is identified: purchasing, receiving, storing, preparing, holding, serving, and managing leftovers. Fresh seafood (an entrée) and frozen ground beef (an ingredient in an entrée) are traced through the product flow process. Purchasing is a critical control point for fresh seafood, and it must be purchased from a reputable supplier to best assure it is not contaminated. Special concern in supplier selection is a preventive measure. By contrast, frozen ground beef is available from several suppliers. Ground beef is inspected for wholesomeness as it moves though interstate commerce, and several reputable suppliers can provide it to the operation.

Numerous preventive measures are in place as seafood and frozen ground beef are received and stored. Personnel know and use proper receiving practices, and storage areas are monitored for proper temperatures and are kept clean.

Fresh seafood and frozen ground beef become special concerns during the preparing step. They are potentially hazardous foods and are treated carefully by production personnel trained to handle these products. Note: In the operation where this flowcharting

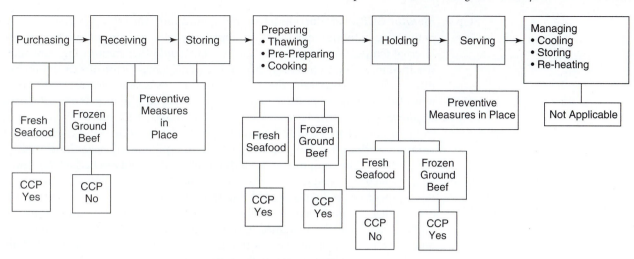

FIGURE 1.6   Example of Flowcharting and CCP Analysis

and CCP analysis is being done, frozen ground beef is thawed as part of the storage (refrigeration) process, and procedures are in place to assure that thawing is done properly.

Concerns about fresh seafood during the preparing step include minimizing the time that the product is at room temperature during cleaning and portioning. It is held in a refrigerated unit in the work station until it is prepared for immediate service.

Ground beef is removed from the refrigerator after thawing when it is added to the casserole dish. The casserole is baked and is held at a temperature above 135°F (57°C) until service. Any product that remains at the end of the meal period is discarded.

Why is fresh seafood not a critical control point? In this property, fresh seafood fillets are only used as an entrée, and they are prepared to order for immediate service. By contrast, frozen ground beef is an ingredient in a casserole dish made with a **batch-cooking** process after which proper holding temperatures are required until portions are served.

OVERHEARD IN THE KITCHEN

Batch-cooking—The preparation of food needed in large quantities in small volumes (batches) to maximize food quality by reducing holding times until service.

There is no concern about managing leftovers because they are not reused, and procedures for cooling, storing, and reheating these items are not applicable.

Step 3: *Define CCP Limits*—**Critical control point limits** establish the boundaries for control, and, when they are exceeded, hazards may exist or might develop. Each CCP should have a critical limit.

OVERHEARD IN THE KITCHEN

Critical control point limit (HACCP program)—Boundaries (maximum/minimum limits) which define the extent to which a critical control point must be controlled to minimize risks of foodborne illness.

Let's go back to Figure 1.6. A critical control point limit for fresh seafood at time of purchasing might be the requirement that it is supplied by a specific vendor to reduce the possibility of harvest from contaminated waters. Temperatures of fresh seafood and ground beef at time of receipt can be included in receiving procedures and specified in the recipes used to prepare them. As well, casserole dishes containing the ground beef will need to be held at a temperature above 135°F (57°C) until service and measured at frequent intervals by an accurate thermometer.

Kitchen managers should establish critical control point limits based upon food codes, safety experts (including health inspectors), and/or other sources. Critical control point limits should be easy to measure/observe.

Step 4:   *Monitor CCPs*—Production personnel should monitor critical control points. Some monitoring activities may be continuous (example: refrigeration units may maintain internal temperature records for later review), and other monitoring may be done as specified intervals: A cook may check the internal temperature of a casserole dish every fifteen minutes. The reason that CCP limits must be easy to measure and/or observe is now obvious. It is not possible to monitor control point limits that are not measurable.

Step 5:   *Implement Corrective Actions When Critical Limits Are Exceeded*—When critical control point limits are exceeded, a problem has been identified, and corrective action is required. Perhaps the holding temperature of a potentially hazardous food is below 135°F (57°C). The equipment used to hold the food should be checked. Meanwhile, the item should be reheated rapidly. If critical control points are monitored frequently (Step 4), the temperature reduction should be small because ongoing monitoring will have assured that the food was only in the temperature danger zone for a short time, and the product can be safely consumed. On the other hand, if monitoring (Step 4) is infrequent, the product should be discarded. (Kitchen managers do not worry about food costs when a food item is potentially contaminated.)

Step 6:   *Establish Record Keeping System*—A written HACCP plan should be developed and maintained to provide information about the hazards identified for each menu item/ingredient. The critical control points and their limits should be defined, and procedures and corrective actions, if any, taken to address CCPs and their limits should be noted.

HACCP records can be relatively simple to maintain while still assuring that information applicable to each step in the HACCP system is identified for applicable items/ingredients.

Step 7:   *Verify HACCP System Success*—Verification helps confirm that critical limits established for each CCP will prevent, eliminate, or reduce potential hazards. A second purpose is to confirm that the overall HACCP system is working effectively. This is done by reviewing HACCP plans and CCP records, conducting follow-up on corrective actions, if any, and using inspections (reviews) of procedures to address critical control points.

Other Sanitation Issues

Three other sanitation issues are of concern to kitchen managers: chemical, physical, and pest control hazards.

CHEMICAL HAZARDS

Some harmful chemicals occur naturally such as **toxins** (poisons) in shellfish, and others are man-made, including food additives and preservatives that cause illnesses in some persons. Examples include monosodium glutamate (MSG) and sulfites in food and wines.

Pesticides are applied to many fruits and vegetables to protect them before harvest. Some of these chemicals can remain on products when they reach the operation, so proper washing is necessary. Other chemicals, including those used for facility and equipment cleaning and sanitizing, may get into or onto foods and can cause illness and even death. Storing cleaning items away from food products and carefully labeling and using them can minimize risks from these items.

OVERHEARD IN THE KITCHEN

Toxin—A poisonous chemical produced by germs or other living things.

Pesticide—A chemical used to kill pests such as rodents or insects.

Pesticides and other chemicals are used to control insects, rodents, and other pests. Unless someone in the food service operation is trained, these chemicals should be applied by professionals to reduce the chance that residues remain in or on food storage and preparation areas. Chemical poisoning can also occur if foods are stored or processed in some containers such as those made from galvanized metals.

PHYSICAL HAZARDS

Foods can be contaminated with **physical hazards** that can cause illness, injury, or death.

OVERHEARD IN THE KITCHEN

Physical hazard (food)—Objects such as glassware and metal shavings in food that can cause illness and injury if they are eaten.

Examples of physical hazards include fragments from glassware broken around food and/or in food preparation areas, metal shavings from can openers, and wood splinters from toothpicks or skewers used in food production. Other examples include human hair, food container labels, and stones or rocks in bags of rice, beans, and other grains.

Food handlers must process foods safely, carefully inspect products being produced, and not wear unnecessary jewelry that can be lost in food while it is produced.

PEST CONTROL HAZARDS

Pests, including rats, mice, flies, and cockroaches, carry germs and can contaminate food as they move around preparation areas and onto food ingredients. Kitchen managers must use procedures to prevent their entry into the building. Then they must eliminate food, water, and places where these pests can hide if they do enter the building. Finally, they should use a pest control program to assure that their preventive actions are working. Food should be stored properly, and garbage should be kept covered until frequent removal. All areas of the operation should be regularly cleaned, and tight-fitting screens, doors, or air curtains can help prevent the entry of flying insects.

Proper housekeeping procedures can reduce problems caused by cockroaches, rats, and mice. Cracks, small holes, and other areas where these pests enter must be repaired. Foods and supplies entering the food service operation should be checked when received for signs of infestation as should the operation's own storage areas.

Chemical pest control tactics are needed only when the procedures discussed above are ineffective. Signs of rodent infestation include droppings (feces), burrows along walls and under rubbish, rub marks along wall baseboards, gnawing marks in wood, and tracks in dust.

Rodent control begins with keeping areas free of liter, waste, refuse, unused boxes, crates, and other materials. Traps can also be helpful. A **coordinated pest management program** is recommended and involves a five-step effort of:

- Inspection
- Identification
- Sanitation
- Use of pest management control procedures
- Evaluation of effectiveness

OVERHEARD IN THE KITCHEN

Coordinated Pest Management Program (CPMP)—A five-step program of inspection, identification, sanitation, application of pest management procedures, and evaluation to control and eliminate pests in food service operations.

NOW IT'S YOUR TURN

A PINCH OF THE INTERNET (1.3)

1. Want to see how the New York City Department of Health and Mental Hygiene make the results of its restaurant inspections available to the public? If so, go to www.ci.nyc.ny.us/html/doh/html/rii/index.html.

   Click on "inspection results" and you can then click on a borough button to select from a map to display a list of restaurants in that area. Click on a restaurant and check out results of the latest inspections.

   Does your community post restaurant inspections on its Web site? Find out and, if so, review the latest inspection results of your favorite restaurants.

2. Basic information about foodborne illness and how to prevent it is found at the following Web site: www.fightback.org.

   Much of the information in this site is for consumers. As you review it, think about how the information applies to restaurants and how kitchen managers can use the information to develop food safety programs for their staff.

3. Ecolab is one of the world's largest providers of commercial cleaning and sanitizing solutions. The company's Web site is: www.ecolab.com

   On this site, you'll learn lots of information about chemicals for facility and equipment cleaning and for kitchen and general food service use.

COMPLETING THE PLATE QUESTIONS (1.3)

1. What can you do as a kitchen manager in a busy work environment to develop and deliver high-quality sanitation training for your employees?
2. Kitchen managers always want to reduce operating cost. Many operations have policies that permit the reuse of hot entrée leftovers. At the same time, they are aware of potential sanitation issues which can arise. What factors would you consider as you make decisions about whether these leftovers should be reused?
3. What do you think should be the ideal relationship between your food service operation and the public health department's sanitation inspectors?

Kitchen Challenge Du Jour Case Study (1.2)

"Oh, not again," said Charlie, a cook at the Fair View Restaurant who was speaking with another cook. The kitchen manager had just returned from a training program and was now concerned about the operation's cleanliness standards.

"Every time the manager goes to a meeting, he comes back with ideas about how to change things. This time he's concerned about sanitation and must think that we work dirty."

Assume you are the kitchen manager and are concerned about food safety even though your operation's recent public health inspections have been "okay": There has never been a serious violation, but there have always been ways in which improvements can be made.

1. How would you emphasize to Charlie and the other cooks that the emphasis on sanitation cannot "go away."
2. How would you involve food production staff in the process to reestablish a sanitation priority?
3. How could you measure the success of your new sanitation efforts?

BASIC SAFETY PRACTICES

O B J E C T I V E

4. Describe basic safety practices.
   - Background
   - Kitchen safety tour
   - Managing emergencies

"**Safety**" means protecting a person's physical well-being and health, and it can include the emphasis on sanitation noted above. In fact, many people use the terms, "food safety" and "sanitation" to mean the same thing. Kitchen managers must keep persons safe from eating contaminated food (food safety or sanitation) and from other harm (safety).

OVERHEARD IN THE KITCHEN

Safety—The protection of a person's physical well-being and health.

Background

The reasons why safety is important include the same reasons why sanitation is a special concern:

- There are many reported and unreported cases of accidents that hurt employees and guests. Many could be prevented if basic safety principles were used.

- Kitchen managers do not want to harm anyone, and that is why they develop, implement, and manage safety practices.
- Government agencies develop safety laws that, if violated, can lead to warnings, fines, and even closing down the food service operation.
- The operation's reputation is affected by how it treats employees and guests. Injuries to one or a few employees or guests may (or may not) make the news, but, for example, fires can injure or kill many persons and forever change the restaurant's reputation.
- Lawsuits filed by those who say they've been injured will cost the food service operation much time and large fees for legal advice. At their worst, accidents can cost hundreds of thousands of dollars (or more), cause significant stress, and require uncounted hours of effort that could otherwise be used to manage daily operations.

Kitchen managers who use the best safety procedures may discover that not all accidents can be prevented. However, it is best to develop a program that emphasizes accident prevention rather than waiting until something happens and dealing with it then.

SAFETY IS EVERYONE'S CONCERN

The kitchen manager's concerns about safety begin during employee **orientation** when new employees learn there can be no short-cuts that violate safety concerns. It continues as new staff members receive basic training in the workplace. Also, kitchen managers "manage by walking around," and they can see if safety practices are in use or if there are safety concerns present.

OVERHEARD IN THE KITCHEN

Orientation—The act of providing basic information about the food service operation that must be known by all employees in all departments.

Kitchen managers know that "one accident is one too many!" Every accident, regardless of how small it is, should be studied, its cause should be learned, and something should be done so that, hopefully, it will never occur again.

Food service employees have a role to play in restaurant safety. They should:

- Use work practices that consider safety concerns and never take safety short-cuts.
- Be alert about and report safety concerns.
- Help protect teammates from safety problems.
- Avoid the "that's not my job" attitude when they see wet floors or notice chipped water glasses.
- Know about **Material Safety Data Sheets** that tell how to safely use chemicals.
- Maintain their own health in a way that does not threaten the safety of guests or fellow employees.

OVERHEARD IN THE KITCHEN

Material Safety Data Sheets—Written statements that provide information about a chemical substance, including hazards, and the best ways to handle them.

SAFETY BASICS

Food service employees receive several common types of injuries, including

- *Sprains and Strains* that occur from falls, improper lifting, slips and trips, and from bending, climbing, crawling, reaching, and twisting. These injuries mostly affect an employee's back, ankles, and knees.
- *Cuts and Lacerations.* Many production personnel work with knives and risk a cut injury. These wounds also are caused by food slicers, meat grinders, mixers, and blenders, and from broken dishes, cups, and glasses. Areas of the hand are most frequently affected.
- *Heat Burns and Scalds.* Food production personnel may work with hot equipment along with hot foods being produced on/in it that cause burns and scalds.

Kitchen Safety Tour

Let's take a kitchen safety tour and learn about safety problems along the way.

RECEIVING, STORING, AND ISSUING

Some food products are purchased in heavy containers that must be moved. When lifting, lift with your legs, not with your back because leg muscles are stronger than back muscles. Kneel down, grasp the item, keep your back straight, and stand up. Assure that the load is balanced before you lift it and get help when lifting heavy objects. Know exactly where you want to go with the heavy item and be sure that there is a place available for the heavy item when you get there. Figure 1.7 shows proper lifting techniques.

Carts or dollies can be used to transport heavy items. Move this equipment slowly and be careful going around corners (pull rather than push). Watch out for toes and feet.

INFORMATION ON THE SIDE
How to Reduce Slips, Trips, and Falls

Suggestions to reduce slips, trips, and falls include:

- Wear nonslip, water-proof shoes
- Clean-up spills immediately
- Eliminate cluttered work areas
- Do not run
- Use nonslip matting on floor surfaces
- Use no-skid waxes or surfaces coated with grit to create nonslip floor surfaces
- Use warning signs to alert persons to wet or damp floors

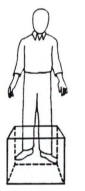

1. Get a firm footing   2. Bend your knees   3. Grasp the object with your hands and tighten your abdominal muscles

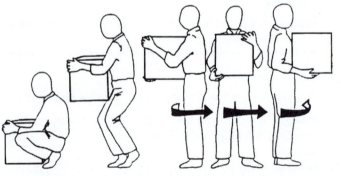

4. Pull the load close to your body   5. Lift with your legs   6. Keep your back straight

FIGURE 1.7 Proper Lifting Techniques

Heavy items can be stored close to the storeroom entrance to avoid moving them through the storeroom when they are received and issued. Store heavy items at the bottom (not the top) of shelving which must be sturdy and secure to hold the weight of products being stored. Use a stool or ladder to reach items on high shelves.

FOOD PREPARATION

Some food preparation equipment such as mixers, slicers, and grinders have moving parts that can crush fingers or hands or cause serious cuts. Machine guards should not be removed when the equipment is in operation, and instructions for cleaning and sanitizing the equipment should be followed. When working with any food preparation equipment:

- Use caution.
- Always turn off and unplug the equipment before cleaning it.
- Assure that the equipment is securely attached to benches or table tops, if applicable.
- Use pushers or tampers to move food; do not use your hands.
- Wear proper work clothing not loose clothing or jewelry that could catch in the equipment.
- Follow child labor laws about equipment operation by employees less than eighteen years old.

Before employees use equipment, they should receive training in its safe use, and the manufacturer's instructions for safe use and cleaning can be used to do so.

Figure 1.8 provides suggestions about the safe use of food preparation equipment:

Mixers, choppers, dicers, and slicers
- Tampers not your hands should be used to feed and remove products from the machines.
- Never bypass safety guards.
- Never put your hands into an operating machine.
- Turn off and unplug the equipment before disassembling and cleaning.

Food Processors and Mixers
- Do not open the lid of a processor while the equipment is operating.
- Assure that the equipment has been turned off before opening the lid.

Microwave Ovens
- Locate the oven at a proper work height to make it easy to place or remove hot foods in it.
- Cover food to avoid spattering.
- Be careful when opening a tightly covered container; remove it away from your face and body to allow the steam to escape.
- Use hot pads or other appropriate items to remove hot foods or hot containers.
- Do not use a microwave if it is not working properly. Door seals should be clean and in good condition, and doors should not be damaged.
- Do not place metals, foil, or whole eggs in microwave ovens.
- If sparking is noticed inside an oven, turn it off, unplug it, and do not use it until it is repaired.

Steamers
- Do not open the steamer door while the unit is on. Shut-off the steam and wait several minutes before releasing the pressure and opening the door.
- Clear the area around the steamer before opening the door.
- Open the steamer door by standing to its side and keep the door between you and the open steamer compartment.
- Use oven mitts to remove hot items.
- Place hot steamer trays on a cart for transport.
- Remove trays from the top compartment of a compartment steamer first and then from the lower compartment(s).

Pressure Cookers
- Turn off the steam supply and wait for the pressure to equalize before opening the lid.
- Stand to the side and open the pressure cooker away from your body; keep the open lid between you and the equipment.

Coffee Makers
- Do not place hot coffee makers close to the edge of counters.
- Be sure the coffee filter is in place before making coffee.
- Do not remove the coffee filter before the coffee has stopped dripping.
- When grinding coffee beans, do not put your fingers into the coffee grinder chamber.

FIGURE 1.8   Use Food Preparation Equipment Safely

INFORMATION ON THE SIDE

Use Knives Carefully and Correctly

- Be careful when working with sharp utensils; they are helpful tools, but they can be dangerous if not used correctly.
- Cut away from your body.
- Keep your fingers and thumbs from under knives; use protective gloves provided by the employer.
- Use the correct knife for the task. Examples: Use a paring knife to cut and a French knife to chop.
- Store knives in an assigned place and be sure the blade's cutting edge is not exposed.
- Don't try to catch a falling knife.
- Carry knives with their cutting edge angled slightly away from your body and be sure that the tip is pointed down.
- When handing a knife to someone, place it on a clean surface and let the other person pick it up.
- Don't put knives in sinks full of water.
- Do not talk to anyone when using a knife.
- Remember that dull knives are more dangerous than sharp knives because more force must be applied when using them.
- Keep knives sharp. Someone experienced in knife sharpening should sharpen them and inform others when knives are newly sharpened.

COOKING

Many dangers arise when cooking equipment is not used properly. For example, burns can occur from contact with a deep fryer or with hot splashing oil. Carbon monoxide poisoning is also possible from malfunctioning exhaust systems under which deep fryers and other cooking equipment are placed.

To remain safe when using a deep fryer:

- Use correct grease levels and proper cooking temperatures and extinguish hot oil/grease fires by quickly placing a lid over the container.
- Keep floor surfaces clean and dry to prevent slipping or falling. Wear slip-resistant shoes.
- Use a grease-cutting chemical to clean floors around the fryers.
- Do not spill water or ice in the oil.
- Do not overfill or pour excessive amounts of food products into the equipment at one time.

INFORMATION ON THE SIDE

How to Prevent Burns

- Wear long-sleeve shirts and pants and solid-toed leather work shoes to protect your arms, legs, and feet from burns and splashes.
- Oven mitts, hot pads, or other items should be used when handling hot containers.
- Tongs, oven mitts, or other equipment should be used to remove hot items from steamers and ovens.
- Do not reach above an oven or steamer. Hot air and steam rises and can burn you.
- Carefully place ingredients into boiling water, soups, or stocks to avoid splashing.
- Assume that all pots, pot handles, and utensils in pots are hot; use oven mitts to handle them.
- Adjust range burner flames to cover only the pan's bottom.
- Get help when moving a heavy pot of hot food.
- Don't let pot handles stick beyond the counter/stove fronts and keep them away from stove burners.
- Don't overfill pots and pans.
- Do not use a wet cloth to lift lids from hot pans.
- Do not lean over or extend your hand or arm over a pot of boiling liquid.
- Do not move hot oil containers; wait until the oil is cooled.
- Do not strain hot oil; wait until the oil is cooled.

INFORMATION ON THE SIDE

Heat Hazards in Food Production Areas

Food production employees typically work in very hot areas (100°F; 38°C or more) created by the heat from cooking equipment and the hot foods being produced. This can cause problems such as heat cramps and rashes, heat exhaustion, and heat stroke. Suggestions to reduce heat hazards include:

- Know the signs of heat illness, including dizziness, blurred vision, and nausea.
- If symptoms appear, stop working and inform a supervisor immediately.
- Take breaks from the hot environment and do not drink alcoholic beverages or those containing caffeine because they cause the body to lose water.
- Drink lots of water.
- Kitchen managers can best protect their staff members from heat-related illnesses by providing area cooling fans, evaporative cooling, air conditioning, general ventilation, and local exhaust ventilation at places with the greatest heat production.

CLEAN-UP

Employees may be exposed to electric shock or even **electrocution** hazards during clean-up if they contact faulty electrical appliances, worn electric cords, or damaged extension cords. Improperly wired/ungrounded outlets, damaged receptacles and connectors, and faulty equipment wiring can cause additional problems.

OVERHEARD IN THE KITCHEN

Electrocution—Being killed by an electric shock.

Strains and sprains can occur when washing dishes, mopping floors, and removing garbage. Work spaces should be arranged so cleaning supplies are easy to obtain and nonslip flooring should be available in dishwashing areas.

Wheeled carts to remove garbage and smaller trash bags may reduce weight if refuse must be manually removed. Also, the size of garbage containers can be limited to the weight of the load that employees must lift and dump.

Slips, trips, and falls can occur during clean-up as employees sweep and mop floors and clean parking lots. Special concerns are necessary to reduce burns and scalds as employees load and unload dishwashers and while washing dishes and pots/pans.

If conveyor-type dishwashers or glasswashers are used, the beginning and end of the machine should have protective curtains to prevent workers from being scalded by steam and hot water. Dishwashing equipment must be operated according to proper instructions. If the dish racks are used, they should be cooled on the clean-dish table before being removed. Dishwashing areas will be wet and slip-resistant flooring or mats are helpful.

Employees who manually wash dishes, pots, and pans should carefully test water temperature in sinks before placing their hands in the sinks.

Many hazards arise as employees work with chemicals used to clean equipment and the facility. For example:

- Soaps or detergents may cause skin allergies or irritations.
- Broken skin may allow infection or injury if it is exposed to chemical hazards.
- Some cleaning chemicals such as drain and oven cleaners can cause skin burns and eye and skin irritation.
- Ammonia (frequently used as a cleaning agent) and chlorine solutions (often use as dishwashing disinfectant) can cause skin, eye, and nose irritations. If chlorine and ammonia solutions are mixed, a deadly chlorine gas can result.
- Latex gloves worn to protect hands may cause skin irritations or allergic reactions in some employees.

- Kitchen managers can minimize risks to their employees from hazardous chemicals by:
  - Implementing a program that requires employees to learn about and have access to Material Safety Data Sheets.
  - Providing gloves, goggles, and splash aprons for employees handling hazardous chemicals.
  - Providing suitable facilities to drench and flush eyes and body parts exposed to corrosive materials.
  - Using nonhazardous cleaning chemicals.
  - Using automatic dispensing systems for cleaning chemicals.
  - Limiting employee contact with dishwashing detergents by providing automatic detergent and chemical dispensers.
  - Assuring that all cleaning containers are labeled. Don't remove products from an original container without labeling the new container.
  - Storing pesticides in the original labeled container.
  - Storing liquid chemicals on lower shelves rather than top shelves.

INFORMATION ON THE SIDE

Electrical Hazards

All food service employees should know how to reduce electrical hazards:

- Turn off the electric current when an emergency occurs.
- Pull the plug not the electrical cord.
- Keep power cords clear of equipment during use.
- Don't use faulty equipment or damaged wall receptacles or connectors.
- Don't plug in electrical equipment while touching a damp or wet surface.
- Don't use electrical cords that are worn or damaged or that feel warm during use.
- Report unsafe equipment or work practices immediately.

Managing Emergencies

Fires and terrorist attacks are two types of emergencies that concern kitchen managers.

FIRES

If procedures noted during the kitchen safety tour above are put in place, many fires can be prevented. However, small fires can become large and dangerous very quickly. How should a kitchen manager decide whether to try to put out a small fire or to evacuate? Small fires can often be extinguished quickly by a well-trained staff member using a portable fire extinguisher. However, evacuation plans that tell who should remain and fight fires and who should leave increase the complexity of an emergency plan and the training that must be incorporated within it.

INFORMATION ON THE SIDE

How to Reduce Fire Hazards

To reduce the possibility of fires:

- Extinguish oil/grease fires by (a) sliding a lid over the container's top, (b) pouring salt over the fire, or (c) using a carbon dioxide fire extinguisher (Class B or C).
- Do not carry or move oil containers when the oil is hot or on fire.
- Do not throw water on a grease fire.
- Empty grease traps frequently.
- Keep cooking surfaces clean and free from grease build-up that can cause a fire.
- Do not use defective electrical cords or equipment.
- Do not store flammable items near heat-producing equipment or open flames.

Assure that all employees know the operation's fire safety procedures, including how to call for help and what to do when there is a fire or other emergency.

Kitchen managers should consider three types of emergency action and fire prevention plans:

- *Option 1: Total Evacuation of Employees When an Alarm Sounds.* Fire extinguishers must still be inspected, tested and maintained.
- *Option 2: Selected Employees Should Use Fire Extinguishers; All Other Employees Must Evacuate When the Alarm Sounds.* General fire extinguisher requirements must be met, and the selected employees must be trained annually. Fire extinguishers must be inspected, tested, and maintained.
- *Option 3: All Employees are Authorized to Use Portable Fire Extinguishers.* All employees will need annual fire extinguisher training, and extinguishers must be inspected, tested, and maintained.

Figure 1.9 provides basic information about fire extinguishers. Portable fire extinguishers can control or extinguish small fires, and they can protect evacuation routes that a fire may block with smoke or burning materials.

TERRORIST ATTACKS

Imagine answering the operation's telephone and hearing a bomb threat. The response to this threat should be part of every kitchen manager's safety training program. Points to include in that training are:

- The employee taking the phone call should ask the caller if the manager can take the message. If the caller agrees, do so; if the caller does not agree, the employee should listen carefully and try to obtain the information shown in Figure 1.10.
- As soon as the caller hangs up, contact the local police and follow their advice.
- Any bomb search should be done by qualified local authorities; no food service staff, including the kitchen manager, should be involved unless requested by authorities.

KNOW YOUR FIRE EXTINGUISHERS

| | WATER TYPE | | | | FOAM | CARBON DIOXIDE | DRY CHEMICAL | | | |
| | | | | | | | SODIUM OR POTASSIUM BICARBONATE | | MULTI-PURPOSE ABC | |
saif State Accident Insurance Fund	STORED PRESSURE	CARTRIDGE OPERATED	WATER PUMP TANK	SODA ACID	FOAM	CO 2	CARTRIDGE OPERATED	STORED PRESSURE	STORED PRESSURE	CARTRIDGE OPERATED
CLASS A FIRES WOOD, PAPER, TRASH HAVING GLOWING EMBERS (ORDINARY COMBUSTIBLES)	YES	YES	YES	YES	YES	NO (BUT WILL CONTROL SMALL SURFACE FIRES)	NO (BUT WILL CONTROL SMALL SURFACE FIRES)	NO (BUT WILL CONTROL SMALL SURFACE FIRES)	YES	YES
CLASS B FIRES FLAMMABLE LIQUIDS, GASOLINE, OIL, PAINTS, GREASE, ETC. (FLAMMABLE LIQUIDS)	NO	NO	NO	NO	YES	YES	YES	YES	YES	YES
CLASS C FIRES ELECTRICAL EQUIPMENT (ELECTRICAL EQUIPMENT)	NO	NO	NO	NO	NO	YES	YES	YES	YES	YES
CLASS D FIRES COMBUSTIBLE METALS (COMBUSTIBLE METALS)	SPECIAL EXTINGUISHING AGENTS APPROVED BY RECOGNIZED TESTING LABORATORIES									
METHOD OF OPERATION	PULL PIN- SQUEEZE HANDLE	TURN UPSIDE DOWN AND BUMP	PUMP HANDLE	TURN UPSIDE DOWN	TURN UPSIDE DOWN	PULL PIN- SQUEEZE LEVER	RUPTURE CARTRIDGE- SQUEEZE LEVER	PULL PIN- SQUEEZE HANDLE	PULL PIN- SQUEEZE HANDLE	RUPTURE CARTRIDGE- SQUEEZE LEVER
RANGE	30'- 40'	30'- 40'	30'- 40'	30'- 40'	30'- 40'	3'- 8'	5'- 20'	5'- 20'	5'- 20'	5'- 20'
MAINTENANCE	CHECK AIR PRESSURE GAUGE MONTHLY	WEIGH GAS CARTRIDGE ADD WATER IF REQUIRED ANNUALLY	DISCHARGE AND FILL WITH WATER ANNUALLY	DISCHARGE ANNUALLY -RECHARGE	DISCHARGE ANNUALLY -RECHARGE	WEIGH SEMI- ANNUALLY	WEIGH GAS CARTRIDGE- CHECK CONDITION OF DRY CHEMICAL ANNUALLY	CHECK PRESSURE GAUGE AND CONDITION OF DRY CHEMICAL ANNUALLY	CHECK PRESSURE GAUGE AND CONDITION OF DRY CHEMICAL ANNUALLY	WEIGH GAS CARTRIDGE- CHECK CONDITION OF DRY CHEMICAL ANNUALLY

FIGURE 1.9 Basic Information About Fire Extinguishers

The need for fire safety training for this cook is obvious.

- Identity (male/female; adult/young person)
- Voice characteristics, including loud, fast, high/low pitch, raspy, nasal, slurred, soft, or deep
- Did the caller stutter, lisp, or appear intoxicated?
- Grasp of English language (excellent/poor)
- Language accent (foreign/none)
- Composure (calm, angry, irrational)
- Background noises, including street noises, airplanes, animals, "party" atmosphere, or quiet

FIGURE 1.10   Listening to a Telephone Bomb Threat

NOW IT'S YOUR TURN

A PINCH OF THE INTERNET (1.4)

1. Want to learn more about fire extinguishers and their proper use? If so, check out the following: www.osha.gov/SLTC/etools/evacuation/index.html.

   At this site, you'll learn about the decision to "flight or flee," basics of fire extinguishers and how they are used, and information about where fire extinguishers should be placed.

2. The Occupational Safety and Health Administration (OSHA) is a federal government agency concerned about workplace safety. To review numerous documents about restaurant safety, go to: www.osha.gov and type "restaurant safety" in the site's search box.

3. To review a wide variety of restaurant safety information, type "restaurant safety" into your favorite search engine.

COMPLETING THE PLATE QUESTIONS (1.4)

1. What are some simple steps that you as a kitchen manager could use to develop and implement an on-site safety inspection program for kitchen employees?

2. What steps could you as a kitchen manager take to be sure that all of your employees are informed about potentially hazardous chemicals with which they must work?

3. You are a kitchen manager who is the manager on-site while the restaurant manager is away. You receive a telephone call from a guest who alleges that she fell at your food service operation last night. What should you do?

Overheard in the Kitchen Glossary

Hospitality Industry
Profit
Commercial food service
    operations
Noncommercial food service
    operations
Self-operated (noncommer-
    cial food services)
Management company-
    operated (noncommercial
    food services)
Organization chart
Responsibility
Back-of-house
Steward
Front-of-house
Menu
Menu item

Ingredients
Purchasing
Receiving
Storing
Production
Issuing
Preparation
Cooking
Holding
Catering
Banquet
Job description
Professionals
Service
Quality
Fad
Value
Supervisors

Managers
Benchmark
Cross-functional team
Empower
Foodborne illness
Inspection (sanitation)
Law suit
Temperature danger zone
Cross-contamination
Preportion
Sneeze guard
Cleaning
Sanitizing
Backflow
Refuse
Garbage
Hazard Analysis Critical
    Control Points (HACCP)

Critical control point (CCP)
Hazard (food contamination)
Batch-cooking
Critical control point limit
    (HACCP program)
Toxin
Pesticides
Physical hazard (food)
Coordinated pest
    management program
    (CPMP)
Safety
Orientation
Material Safety Data Sheets
Electrocution

LESSON 1

If you are reading this textbook as part of a formal class, your Instructor may want you to apply and practice what you have learned in this chapter by completing Lesson 1 of the Pearson Education's Kitchen Management Simulation (KMS). If you are required to complete KMS Lesson 1; read **About Lesson 1** below, then go to: www.pearsonhighered.com/kms for instructions on how to access and complete it.

After you have successfully completed the lesson, think about the way you, as a professional kitchen manager, would answer the **For Your Consideration** questions that follow.

About Lesson 1

Serving food that is safe to eat is so important that the entire first lesson of the Kitchen Management Simulation (KMS) addresses this single topic. By reading the information presented in this text chapter you discovered how kitchen managers address food safety-related issues in their pre-production and production activities. The first KMS lesson you will complete was designed to reinforce the information presented in the chapter and let you practice applying what you have learned.

In this lesson you will see why ensuring food safety is so critical to kitchen managers. You will also show you understand the temperature range that makes up the *Temperature Danger Zone*.

Finally, you will prove you know, and can correctly apply, the concepts related to three very important food safety-related terms. These three concepts are:

1. Cleaning
2. Sanitizing
3. Cross-contamination

Lesson 1 has four important parts. When you have successfully completed all four activities you will have mastered the important food safety-related information that all professional kitchen managers must know.

For Your Consideration

1. Why are kitchen managers the ones ultimately held responsible for the safety of the food produced in their kitchens?
2. What do you think would happen to the business of a restaurant that was found to be responsible for a highly publicized outbreak of foodborne illness?
3. In addition to a restaurant's guests, who else do you think depends on kitchen managers to ensure all the food they serve is safe to eat?

Kitchen Managers Select and Train Production Employees

Learning Objectives

After studying this chapter, you will be able to:

1. Use effective procedures to recruit and select food production personnel.
2. Plan and implement effective orientation programs for food production employees.
3. Develop and deliver performance-based training programs for food production employees.

COMING RIGHT UP OVERVIEW

Kitchen managers have no more significant responsibility than to effectively facilitate the work of their food production employees. Food quality, labor costs, and a pleasant work environment are among the factors affected by the staff members who must work together as a team to achieve guest- and food service operations-related goals. The process of managing employees starts before they are hired, and that is where this chapter begins.

The first step in filling a vacant position is to have a current and accurate job description so that both you and the applicants know what those who will work in vacant positions are supposed to do. Then, the possible applicants must learn about the job opening, and there are traditional and exciting new "high-tech" ways to do so. A final step is to select the best person from among those who are recruited.

New employees must, first, learn about their new employer, and, second, they need to acquire the knowledge and learn the skills necessary to be successful on the job. A properly developed and implemented orientation program provides general information about which all employees must know. Then a well organized and performance-driven training program should be used to teach job knowledge and skills.

Effective orientation and training programs do not just "happen." A significant amount of creativity and effort is needed to assure that they are successful. You will learn about many principles that help make new staff members' beginning on-the-job experiences positive. Their consistent use will enable the food service operation to gain employees who will want to do their best to help the team succeed.

RECRUIT AND SELECT FOOD PRODUCTION EMPLOYEES

Oᴮᴊᴇᴄᴛɪᴠᴇ

1. Use effective procedures to recruit and select kitchen personnel:
   - Step 1: Develop job descriptions
   - Step 2: Recruit applicants
   - Step 3: Select the best employees

In this section, you'll learn a three-step method to recruit and select the best kitchen personnel.

Step 1: Develop Job Descriptions

Kitchen managers must develop job descriptions that describe what people working in the position must do. Also, persons applying for a position will want to know about their own job duties. For example, in some operations a dishwasher just washes dishes. In others, they may also bus tables and cut the grass and wash windows, among other tasks.

The job description is the tool that identifies tasks which are part of the job.

Figure 2.1 shows a shortened job description for a cook. Note that it tells (in Part I) the position to which the cook reports, indicates job tasks (Part II), and explains basic personal qualifications (Part III).

Job descriptions should be reviewed and updated when job tasks or other position changes occur so they explain what the job involves and describe the personal requirements that are important for job success.

Step 2: Recruit Applicants

Recruiting involves looking for persons who might be interested in vacant positions. Finding qualified and motivated staff members is never easy, but it is less difficult for food service operations that are considered **employers of choice** within their communities. These businesses enjoy a reputation for being a desirable place to work, and their recruiting efforts are easier because of their good name.

There are two general types of recruiting activities: **internal recruiting** and **external recruiting**.

OVERHEARD IN THE KITCHEN

Recruiting—The search for persons who may be interested in vacant positions.

Employer of choice—A business with a reputation for being a desirable place to work and whose recruiting efforts are easier because of its good name.

Recruiting (internal)—The use of existing employees to help fill position vacancies. Current employees may be promoted from within to fill positions with greater responsibility, or they may refer friends, neighbors, and others to the property.

Recruiting (external)—Activities used to inform persons who do not work for the food service operation that new staff members are needed.

Position Title:	Cook
Part I **Supervised by:**	Kitchen Manager

Part II: Position Tasks

Prepares and cooks hot foods
Carves and serves hot foods on buffet serving line for special events
Portions food on hot food serving line
Operates large-volume kitchen equipment
Maintains food production standards
Completes production sheets for quantities of food produced and left-over
Cleans and sanitizes work areas including equipment
Cleans food storage areas and maintains inventories within them

Part III: Job Specification (Personal Qualifications)

Must be able to lift 50 pounds, work constantly on feet, and carry hot pans of food in a hot kitchen for up to eight hours.

High school graduate or equivalent; ability to adjust standard recipes, and perform standard kitchen preparation measurements.

Date of last revision:	1/12/xx
Approved by:	J. Jones, Kitchen Manager

FIGURE 2.1 Sample Job Description

Kitchen managers can use many tactics to recruit employees. They can:[1]

- Identify and advertise the best features of the job.
- Use professional job titles ("steward" instead of "dishwasher.")
- Use a recruitment package that has a fact sheet, current job description, write-up of best job features, and an employee **compensation package** worksheet.
- Confirm that the compensation package is competitive.
- Assure that applicants are aware of the work environment that emphasizes the importance of all employees, that recognizes the need for a balance between their work and personal lives, and that provides opportunities for professional growth.
- Reward current employees for their referrals.
- Use positive statements from current employees in job ads.
- Recruit their guests. (Some persons who visit a restaurant may be looking for a position!)
- Add an employment section to the operation's Web site.
- Sponsor work-study programs and talk with career counselors at local schools.
- Invite students enrolled in high school, college, and university hospitality education programs to tour the operation.

OVERHEARD IN THE KITCHEN

Compensation package—The money and other valuable items (fringe benefits) provided in exchange for the work employees do.

INFORMATION ON THE SIDE

Use Twitter for Recruitment

Technology provides exciting new ways to recruit employees. For example, most young employees know about Twitter, a social networking service. Users send and read updates (tweets) from other users that are text-based posts of up to 160 characters long. Updates are shown on each the user's profile page and are delivered to those who have signed up to receive the short messages. This online messaging system allows kitchen managers to select their messages and communicate with new and old contacts.

Food service operations can use Twitter to give their company a "personality." They can provide information such as job opportunities to people who may not learn about them anywhere else, and the information and feedback are provided in real time. They can post job openings, provide recruitment updates ("We're still looking!"), and invite potential applicants to visit career expos, link to career content, and even research candidates who express an interest.

The best way to use Twitter is to target an audience and build a strong brand as you do so. Job advertisements ("job adverts") are displayed in the Twitter account with job title, brief summary, and a hyperlink for the actual advertisement (example: "Food preparation position in the most exciting new place in town. Join our team and grow with us").

Readers can apply for the job or e-mail a friend which increases the number of persons aware of the vacancy.

Twitter can be used for other purposes such as announcing a new menu item or daily special. Creative kitchen managers find ways to use Twitter and other social media to interact with guests and with others who should be guests in or employees of their operation.

Unfortunately, the employee turnover rates are so high in some food service operations that this "help wanted" sign must be continuously posted.

Step 3: Select the Best Employees

A formal **selection** process provides kitchen managers with accurate information from candidates who have been recruited. Sources of information about job applicants include:

- *Application form.* Figure 2.2 shows a sample **application form**. There are federal, state, and local laws and regulations about employment **discrimination** issues that must be considered when the application is developed. It is generally best to have drafts of an application form reviewed by an attorney before it is used. Essentially, application forms should only request information necessary to evaluate an applicant for a position.

OVERHEARD IN THE KITCHEN

Selection—The process to evaluate job applicants to assess their suitability for a position.

Application form—An early step in the employee selection process in which applicants provide job-related information that helps kitchen managers determine whether they are suitable for the position.

Discrimination—Treating persons unequally for reasons that do not relate to their legal rights or abilities, including race, nationality, creed, color, religion, age, sex, or sexual orientation.

- *Employment interview.* Two basic types of interview questions can be used to obtain information from job applicants. **Direct Interview questions** help kitchen managers learn specific information about job applicants. An example is: "How long have you worked in restaurants?" **Indirect interview questions** can be used to learn about applicants' opinions and attitudes: "What can food preparation staff do to please guests?" Most kitchen managers use both types of interview questions as they obtain basic information about job applicants.

Print or Type Clearly

Last Name First Middle	Position(s) Desired
Street Address	Wage/Salary Desired Date Available For Work
City State Zip	Social Security Number
Phone-Home Work	Are You Presently Employed? ☐ Yes ☐ No May We Contact Your Present Employer? ☐ Yes ☐ No
To verify previous employment, please indicate if you have worked under another name. ☐ Yes ☐ No If yes, other name used:	

EMPLOYMENT RECORD

List your previous experience beginning with your most recent position. (Include military experience as a job)

Employer 1 (Area Code) Phone Number	Employer 2 (Area Code) Phone Number
Address City, State, Zip Code	Address City, State, Zip Code
Starting Position Starting Salary	Starting Position Starting Salary
Last Position Final Salary	Last Position Final Salary
Dates Employed Immediate Supervisor	Dates Employed Immediate Supervisor
Duties	Duties
Reason For Leaving	Reason For Leaving

EDUCATION AND SKILLS

School	Location	Graduation Date	Major
High School			
College			
Additional Training			

FIGURE 2.2 Sample Application Form

Which languages do you speak fluently?	

Are there any hours, shifts, days of the week that you will not be able to work? Please specify.

I am able to work (check the following) F/T P/T On-Call Evenings Overnight Weekends Holidays Overtime

Do you have relatives or acquaintances working here? ☐ Yes ☐ No If yes, please indicate their name and relationship.	Have you ever been convicted of a felony within the last seven years? ☐ Yes ☐No If yes, please indicate dates and details. _____ _____ Do you have any felony charges pending against you? ☐ Yes ☐No _____ Conviction of a felony will not necessarily disqualify you from employment
Are you under age 18? ☐ Yes ☐ No	Are you authorized to work in the United States? ☐ Yes ☐ No

Can you perform the essential functions of the job for which you are applying with or without accommodation? Please explain. _____
_____
_____

PERSONAL REFERENCES (Not employers or relatives)

Name	Position & Company	Current Address	Telephone

Certification and Signature — Please Read Carefully

I declare that my answers to the questions on this application are true, and I give (company) the right to investigate all references and information given. I agree that any false statement or misrepresentation on this application will be cause for refusal to hire or immediate dismissal.

I agree that my employment will be considered "at will" and I may be terminated by this Company at any time without liability for wages or salary except for such as may have been earned at the date of such termination.

I understand that (company) is a drug free workplace and has a policy against drug and alcohol use and reserves the right to screen applicants and test for cause.

I acknowledge that if I need reasonable accommodation in either the application process or employment, I should bring the request to the attention of _____.

I authorize you to make such legal investigations and inquiries of my personal employment, criminal history, driving record and other job related matters as may be necessary in determining an employment decision. I hereby release employers, schools, or persons from all liability in responding to inquires in connection with my application.

I understand that an offer of employment and my continued employment are contingent upon satisfactory proof of my authorization to work in the United States of America.

Sign Here_____   Date _____
                    (applicant's signature)   month day year

FIGURE 2.2 (continued)

OVERHEARD IN THE KITCHEN

Interview questions (direct)—Specific questions typically organized in advance and followed to learn specific information about job applicants.

Interview questions (indirect)—Open-ended questions asked to learn about a job applicant's opinions and attitudes.

Kitchen managers who are in a hurry, distracted, or who answer the telephone during an employment interview are not making a good first impression. Review the applicant's application form before the interview to develop questions that will help you learn whether the applicant can do or learn required tasks.

Put the applicant at ease. Have an interview schedule and stick with it. Listen more than you talk and ask or follow-up only on questions that relate to the applicant's ability to do required work. For example, don't ask questions about the number or ages of children or religious holidays that the applicant observes. Examples of good questions relate to eligibility to work within the United States, whether one is eighteen years or older (to comply with labor laws), and about convictions (not arrests) for crimes.

- *Results of drug tests.* Wise kitchen managers recognize that employees who use drugs are more likely to have off- and on-job accidents and extended absences from work. While legal conditions allowing drug tests differ by state, voluntary testing is legal in every state.
- *Use applicable applicant tests.* Knowledge or skill tests can be used to determine an applicant's job eligibility. For example, someone stating previous experience as a cook might be asked questions about ingredients or preparation methods for a sauce.
- *Reference checks.* Applicants are typically asked for references, and these should be checked. Increasingly, however, the amount of information learned from reference checks is limited because past employers and others may fear negative legal consequences if they provide information that keeps an applicant from being hired. However, questions about employment dates, **wage** or **salary** levels and, perhaps, whether the job applicant would be rehired might be asked and answered.
- *Background checks.* Many resumes and applications include some false information. Concerned kitchen managers sometimes conduct **background checks** about education/training and criminal records. A consent form signed by job applicants to authorize the background check should be obtained if background checks are made.
- *Physical examination.* A physical examination that includes a tuberculosis test is always a good idea. State and local health laws vary, so you must know and follow all applicable local laws about employee testing. Also, you should not unfairly prevent workers with physical disabilities from gaining employment if their disability does not affect their job performance.
- *Other interviews.* If the new employee will be supervised by another person, the potential supervisor should also interview job candidates, and this second person's information about the applicant will be useful when the selection decision is made.

OVERHEARD IN THE KITCHEN

Wage (hourly)—Money paid to an employee for work performed during a one-hour time period.

Salary—Money paid to an employee for work performed that is calculated on a weekly, monthly, or annual basis.

Background check—A review of a job applicant's criminal history, credit, driving record, or other information that relates to an applicant's suitability for employment.

After the employee-selection decision is made, the **job offer** becomes important. It should be made in writing and contain the employment terms and conditions. If the applicant does not accept the job offer, it can then be made to the next most qualified person from the remaining applicants. If there are no other qualified applicants, the selection process must begin again. In fact, the selection process is on-going in many operations because of turnover which continually creates new position vacancies.

OVERHEARD IN THE KITCHEN

Job offer—An invitation, made by a kitchen manager to the most qualified job applicant, which outlines the terms and conditions under which employment will be offered.

NOW IT'S YOUR TURN

A PINCH OF THE INTERNET (2.1)

1. Many potential food service employees use the Internet to search for positions, and it is likely to be a useful tool for your own job search. Hospitality careers.com (www.hcareers.com) is a leading hospitality recruiting Internet site. Go to this Web site and see how you might use it when you are looking for a job as well as how you could use it if you were a kitchen manager seeking employees.

2. Experienced kitchen managers know that, unfortunately, some kitchen employees abuse drugs and alcohol. To learn more about substance abuse in the workforce, go to the federal government's substance abuse and mental health services administration's Web site: www.samsha.gov Enter "drugs in workplace" in the site's search box.

3. You've learned that job descriptions are an important tool in the recruitment and selection of kitchen personnel. To review job descriptions and to learn about the tasks they include, type "food service manager" or "food service production" and "job description" in your favorite search engine.

COMPLETING THE PLATE QUESTIONS (2.1)

1. What are the best ways to recruit young people for kitchen-related positions?

2. What, if any, role should selection tests play as hiring decisions are made? If they are important, what type of selection test would you use for "experienced" kitchen personnel?

3. How important is it to verify information on an employment application? How would you do so?

4. Assume you are the kitchen manager in a small food service operation in which the restaurant manager or owner made the final employee selection decision. What, if any, role would you like to play in assisting him/her with this decision?

Kitchen Challenge Du Jour Case Study (2.1)

"Finding good kitchen employees would be so easy if only we had a decent human resources department!" This statement was part of the conversation that Ann, the kitchen manager at Hilo Bay Hotel, just had with Ken, the dining room manager at the hotel's very large and very busy restaurant.

She continued: "Our employee turnover rate is so high, and a lot of the new employees they send us can't do the work and cannot be trained to do it. What's so hard about finding decent staff members, especially since a lot of people are out of work around here?

a) What employee recruitment tasks should be the responsibility of the human resources department? The kitchen manager?

b) What employee selection tasks should be the responsibility of the human resources department? The kitchen manager?

c) Assume you were Ann: What would you do to try to improve the relationship between your department and human resources personnel?

d) What are the best ways that the human resources department could help Ken in his kitchen personnel-related responsibilities?

ORIENTATION PROGRAMS FOR FOOD PRODUCTION EMPLOYEES

OBJECTIVE

2. Plan and implement effective orientation programs for food production employees.
   • Benefits of orientation
   • Basics of orientation

New staff members look for assurance that their decision to join the food service operation was a good one. You have probably heard the saying; "First impressions are lasting impressions." and this applies to the reactions of newly-employed persons as they begin their jobs. Effective orientation programs help new employees feel comfortable with their new position and with their new employer.

Benefits of Orientation

You've learned that orientation is the process of providing basic information about the food service operation that must be known by all staff members in every department. Implemented effectively, orientation provides initial on-job experiences that help new employees learn about the organization and its purposes, become comfortable with the work environment, and know where they "fit into" the organization. As well, discussions about basic policies and procedures help the trainees learn about matters of personal importance such as the employer's expectations and job-related benefits.

Goals of an orientation program include:

- *It provides an overview of the organization*—Newly-employed staff members will want to know about their employer's history, the products it produces and the services it provides, and, as importantly, the goals they and their new organization want to achieve. Hopefully, a **mission statement** that generally explains what the organization wants to accomplish and how it intends to do so is available. Hopefully as well, this mission statement serves as a guide for decision-making and is used everyday instead of just serving as an opening page in an employee handbook or a slogan on the back of the managers' business cards!
- *It reviews the new staff member's role in the organization*—If you were a new staff member would you like to see an organization chart that shows all positions, including yours? Would you like to learn where you "fit in," and about possible routes of promotion if you perform well? You probably would, and new staff members likely would as well.
- *It explains policies, rules, and other important information*—Staff want to know about general guidelines that affect them such as days and hours of work; uniform requirements, if any; break times; auto parking requirements; and other information to help them feel more comfortable in the workplace.
- *It outlines specific expectations*—Topics including responsibilities of the employer to the staff member and of the staff member to the employer should be addressed.
- *It provides details about employee benefits*—Staff members want to know about the nonsalary/nonwage compensation they will receive and the requirements for these benefits to be granted.
- *It motivates new staff members*—Enthusiasm and excitement shown by those who provide orientation experiences are important. The recognition that the new staff member is important helps to establish a solid foundation for the relationship between the organization, its managers and supervisors, and the new staff member.

OVERHEARD IN THE KITCHEN

Mission statement—A planning tool that generally explains what the organization wants to accomplish and how it intends to do so.

Taken together, the benefits of effective orientation programs can eliminate confusion, heighten a new employee's enthusiasm, create favorable attitudes and, in general, make a positive first impression.

Basics of Orientation

Properly conducted orientation sessions address the normal concerns of most new staff members. Those facilitating the orientation must encourage questions and recognize their important role when they provide an appropriate "welcome" to the organization.

INFORMATION ON THE SIDE

Effective Orientation Programs Address Staff Questions

Think about the types of questions and concerns that you would have if you began work in a new organization. Would you have questions such as:

- Where do I "fit in" the organization?
- Where and how can I contribute my time and talents?
- What are my duties?
- What are my rights?
- What are my limits?
- How can I advance (and to what positions) within the organization?

Effective orientation programs address the above and related questions. In the process, they help to establish a relationship between the employees and the food service operation that will have a significant impact upon their on-job success.

In a large food service operation, orientation may be a cooperative effort between human resources personnel and the kitchen manager. They both should review the organization chart and position description and preview the training program(s) in which the new staff member will participate. In smaller organizations, orientation may be the responsibility of the kitchen manager and one or more supervisors. Regardless, the basic concerns are the same because the basic needs and concerns of new staff members do not differ when they are employed by large or small organizations.

Careful planning of an orientation program is important. Figure 2.3 illustrates a checklist that identifies many concepts to include in an orientation program.

Many food service operations provide an **employee handbook** to new staff members during orientation. It provides detailed information about important policies and procedures that impact them. When it is provided during the orientation session(s), applicable sections can be referenced, and trainees can review this information as it is discussed. Note: Figure 2.4 provides an extensive list of topics that can be addressed in an employee handbook. While few food service operations include all of these topics, you can see the wide range of issues that are commonly addressed by employee policies.

OVERHEARD IN THE KITCHEN

Employee handbook—A manual given to employees that explains employment policies, including those relating to employment issues and compensation, including benefits, operating concerns, and legal requirements.

Organization Introduction
- ☐ Welcome new staff member(s)
- ☐ Present/explain mission statement
- ☐ Discuss history of organization
- ☐ Review clients served (if applicable)
- ☐ Note products and services provided
- ☐ Review organization chart

Staff Member—Related Policies
- ☐ **Appearance**
  - Hygiene
  - Uniform
  - Name tag
  - Jewelry

- ☐ **Conduct**
  - Attendance
  - Respectful behavior required
  - Drug-free workplace information
  - Harassment policy and discussion

- ☐ **Job Performance**
  - Review position description
  - Preview training program
  - Explain performance evaluation system
  - Work schedule
  - Breaks
  - Probationary period

FIGURE 2.3 Sample Orientation Checklist

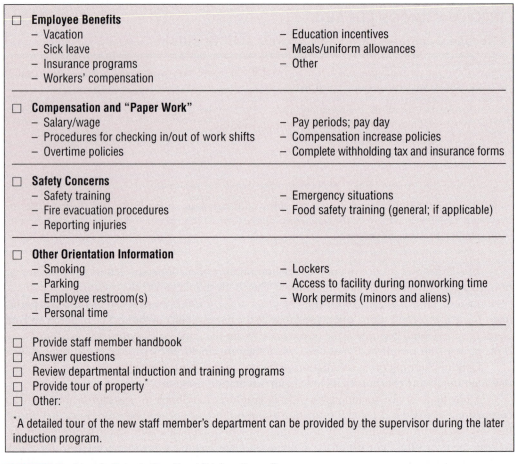

☐ **Employee Benefits**
- Vacation
- Sick leave
- Insurance programs
- Workers' compensation
- Education incentives
- Meals/uniform allowances
- Other

☐ **Compensation and "Paper Work"**
- Salary/wage
- Procedures for checking in/out of work shifts
- Overtime policies
- Pay periods; pay day
- Compensation increase policies
- Complete withholding tax and insurance forms

☐ **Safety Concerns**
- Safety training
- Fire evacuation procedures
- Reporting injuries
- Emergency situations
- Food safety training (general; if applicable)

☐ **Other Orientation Information**
- Smoking
- Parking
- Employee restroom(s)
- Personal time
- Lockers
- Access to facility during nonworking time
- Work permits (minors and aliens)

☐ Provide staff member handbook
☐ Answer questions
☐ Review departmental induction and training programs
☐ Provide tour of property*
☐ Other:

*A detailed tour of the new staff member's department can be provided by the supervisor during the later induction program.

FIGURE 2.3   Sample Orientation Checklist (*continued*)

- Absenteeism
- Accessibility for Disabled
- Accidents
- Accrual of Vacation
- Advancement
- Alcohol Testing
- Americans with Disabilities Act
- Announcements of Openings
- Appearance and Grooming
- Appraisal
- Attendance
- Awards
- Benefits Time
- Bereavement Leave
- Bids
- Breaks
- Call Back Pay
- Call Out Pay
- Changing Departments
- Child Care Leave
- Commercial Driver's License
- Compensation
- Competence
- Complaints
- Compliance
- Computer Use (Personal)
- Concerns
- Conferences
- Confidentiality
- Conflicts of Interest
- Consultants (Use of)
- Continuing Education
- Controlled Substances
- Conventional Standards of Workplace Behavior
- Corporate Compliance
- Counseling
- Criminal Convictions
- Customer Service
- Dental Insurance
- Department Transfer Questionnaire
- Differentials
- Disability Insurance
- Disciplinary Process
- Discrimination Claims
- Displacements
- Dress Code
- Drug Free Awareness Program
- Drug Free Workplace
- Drug Testing
- Drug Use
- Drugs
- Educational Assistance
- Educational Leave
- Emergency Plans/Preparedness

FIGURE 2.4   Possible Topics Addressed in Employee Handbook

- Employee Assistance Program
- Employee Badges
- Employee File
- Employee Identification Program
- Employee of the Month/Year
- Employee Performance Appraisal
- Employee-at-Will
- Equal Employment
- Ethics
- Evaluation
- Exit Interview
- Expenses, Noneducational
- Extended Sick Pay
- Family Medical Leave Act
- Fitness for Duty
- Funeral Leave
- Gifts/Gratuities
- Grant Employees
- Grants
- Grievance/Complaint Procedures
- Harassment
- Health Insurance
- Hiring
- Hiring of Family Members
- Holidays
- Hours of Work
- Identification
- Industrial Injury
- Integrity
- Investigation
- Job Evaluation
- Job Opportunities
- Job Postings
- Job Qualifications
- Job Rotation
- Job Vacancies
- Jury Duty
- Layoffs
- Leave of Absence
- Leaves
- Leaving Department
- Leaving Employment
- Lockers
- Lost Time Claims
- Meal Allowance/Periods
- Medical Claims
- Military Leave
- Multiple Employment
- New Jobs
- On Call Pay
- Orientation Period
- Overtime
- Overtime Pay
- Paid Holidays
- Parking
- Pay and Pay Periods
- Payroll Deductions
- Pension
- Personal Business
- Personal Code of Conduct
- Personal Holidays

- Personal Leave
- Personal Records
- Posting
- Probationary Employee/Periods
- Problems
- Professional Dues
- Professionalism
- Qualifications
- Qualifying Periods
- Recall
- Recording Time
- Recruiting
- Reference Checks
- Relationships (on-job)
- Resignation
- Retirement Programs
- Return to Work
- Safety/Security
- Salary
- Schedule Posting
- Scheduling Vacation
- Seniority
- Seniority Calculation
- Service Awards Recognition Program
- Severance Pay
- Sexual Harassment
- Sick Pay
- Sick Time Accumulation
- Sick Time Buy Back
- Smoking
- Staff Reductions
- Suggestion
- Tax Sheltered Annuity
- Telephone Calls (Personal)
- Termination?
- Time Clocks/Time Keeping
- Time Off Without Pay
- Training
- Transfers
- Transportation Allowance
- Transportation Work Program
- Travel
- Tuition
- Tuition Grant
- Tuition Reimbursement
- Uniforms
- Vacancies
- Vacation Accrual
- Vacation Banking
- Vacation Pay
- Vacation Scheduling
- Vacations
- Violence
- Voluntary Time Off
- Wages
- Weapons
- Weather (inclement)
- Work Rules
- Work Time
- Workers Compensation

FIGURE 2.4   (continued)

It is important to assemble all required materials before the orientation session begins. Examples include copies of the mission statement and employee handbooks, if applicable, and tax withholding, insurance application, and other forms.

Department **induction** is another responsibility of the kitchen manager. Technically, orientation and induction are two separate activities: Orientation relates to informing a new staff member about general information applicable to the organization, and induction refers to activities that provide general information about the specific department in which the new staff member will work. Examples of induction topics include descriptions of work flows and reviews of work stations, the location of equipment, and general safety practices.

OVERHEARD IN THE KITCHEN

Induction—Activities that provide general information about the specific department in which the new staff member will work.

INFORMATION ON THE SIDE

When Does Orientation End?

Typical orientation sessions require several (or fewer) hours or, perhaps, a half day (or longer). Too often, however, they conclude without follow-up sessions. Some food service operations do schedule additional orientation sessions several weeks or even longer after the initial session. By then, employees are familiar with the organization, department and position. Based on their on-job experiences, they can then ask additional questions, participate in discussions, and learn about service, teamwork, and other topics that can be better addressed and understood with personal knowledge of the operation's policies and procedures.

NOW IT'S YOUR TURN

A PINCH OF THE INTERNET (2.2)

1. Want to learn general information about employee orientation? If so, type "new employee orientation" into your favorite search engine. You'll be able to view articles on orientation tips, policies, program development ideas, and sample orientation programs among other related topics.

2. The Internet is a great source of information about orientation checklists, including sample forms. To see examples of checklists, type "orientation checklist" into your favorite search engine.

3. Employee handbooks are an important orientation tool. The Internet can provide much information about them along with sample contents and policies. Check out this topic by typing "employee handbook" into a search engine.

COMPLETING THE PLATE QUESTIONS (2.2)

1. Assume you are a kitchen manager who wants to develop an orientation program for new food production personnel:

- What persons in your food service operation could assist, and what type of information might they provide?
- Ideally, what orientation tasks would be your responsibility as kitchen manager?
- Who else would ideally participate in the orientation program and what would be their role?

2. Review the sample employee handbook policy topics shown in Figure 2.4:

- What are the ten most important topics that should be addressed in a handbook for an operation in which you would want to be the kitchen manager? Why are they the most important?
- What are the five least important policy topics? Why?

3. If you have or have had a job in any industry, what were the best and least liked features about how you were orientated to your position? What can you learn from this self-analysis that will be important when you plan and/or conduct orientation sessions?

TRAINING PROGRAMS FOR FOOD PRODUCTION EMPLOYEES

OBJECTIVE

3. Develop and deliver performance-based training programs for food production employees:
   - Benefits of training
   - Training principles
   - Traits of effective trainers
   - Defining training needs
   - Conduct Needs Assessment (Position Analysis)
   - Develop training objectives
   - Develop training plans and training lessons
   - Prepare trainees
   - Conduct on-job training
   - Evaluate Training, Trainees, and Trainers

Food service operations are **labor-intensive**, and kitchen managers must facilitate the work of numerous food production personnel. Recently employed employees who have completed orientation activities must acquire the knowledge and skills required to be successful in their jobs, and their more experienced peers must keep up with an ever-changing workplace. Effective **training** is critical to attain these goals.

OVERHEARD IN THE KITCHEN

Labor-intensive—A job situation in which technology cannot be used to replace employees.

Training—The process of developing one's knowledge and skills to improve job performance.

Training must be **cost-effective**. It must provide time and money benefits that outweigh its costs. To do so, it must be performance-based, and it should be planned and delivered in an organized way to help trainees learn how to perform the tasks that are essential for effective on-job performance.

OVERHEARD IN THE KITCHEN

Cost-effective—A situation in which time and money benefits gained are greater than the costs that are incurred.

The need for training to be performed-based can create a significant hurdle because, in order to do so:

- All **tasks** in a position must be identified.
- The specific knowledge and skills required to perform each task must be known.
- Training that addresses all of the knowledge and skills required for each task must be developed.
- **Competencies** (standards of knowledge, skills and abilities required for successful job performance) must be known in advance.
- An evaluation process is needed to discover if the training has been successful.

OVERHEARD IN THE KITCHEN

Task—A duty or responsibility that is part of a job position.

Competency—Standards of knowledge, skills, and abilities required for successful job performance.

Typically, performance-based training is best delivered at the job-site in one-on-one interactions between the trainer and trainee.

Benefits of Training

Benefits to effective training include:

- *Improved performance*—Trainees learn knowledge and skills to perform required tasks more effectively, and their on-job performance can be improved.

- *Reduced operating costs*—Improved job performance helps to reduce errors and re-work, and associated costs can be reduced.
- *More satisfied guests*—Training can yield production personnel who are guest service-oriented and who want to please them.
- *Reduced work stress*—Persons who can do required work will feel better about doing it. Stress created by interactions with supervisors upset about poor work performance or from frustrated guests about quality defects will be reduced.
- *Increased job advancement opportunities*—Who is more likely to be promoted to a more responsible and higher-paying position: a competent or an incompetent employee? Training increases worker competence.
- *Fewer operating problems*—Busy kitchen managers can focus on priority concerns and will not need to address routine problems caused by inappropriate training.
- *Higher levels of work quality*—Effective training identifies quality standards that define acceptable product and service outputs. Trained employees can operate equipment correctly, can properly prepare menu items, and know how to interact with service staff and guests.

INFORMATION ON THE SIDE

Training Myths

Myths (untruths) can create obstacles when training activities are planned and delivered. Examples include:

- *Training is easy*—In fact, when training only involves a trainee "tagging along" with a more experienced staff member, it is easy. However, the lack of planning and the increased possibility that basic training principles will be disregarded increase the likelihood that this training will be ineffective.
- *Training costs too much*—Food service operations with a history of inadequate training that has yielded unsatisfactory results are unlikely to invest the resources required to plan and deliver more effective training.
- *Only new staff need training*—New employees need training, but so do their more experienced peers when, for example, operating procedures are revised, when new items are added to the menu, or when new equipment is purchased.
- *There is no time for training*—Many priorities compete for the kitchen manager's limited time, and some managers believe training can be ignored to save time for other tasks. It cannot, and, in fact, proper training saves employees' time.

There are many opportunities for one-on-one training in almost every food service operation.

Training Principles

Experienced kitchen managers share an old saying: "A food service operation pays for training even if training isn't provided." They know that developing and delivering training takes time to do well, and costs are incurred to do so. However, they also know that, in the absence of training, wasted time and money occurs because of errors and rework.

If you accept the idea that kitchen managers will, one way or another, pay for training, it makes good business sense to implement effective training that returns benefits exceeding training costs. A first step is to recognize that several basic principles should be incorporated into the training process, and these include:

- Trainers must know how to train.
- Trainers must be taught to train. Those with training responsibilities must be taught how to train, just as they must learn how to schedule employees or operate a piece of equipment.
- Trainees must want to learn. The old expression, "You can lead a horse to water, but you can't make the horse drink," applies here. Trainees must want to learn and, for this to occur, they must recognize the worth of training.
- Training must focus on real problems. Frequently, problems (challenges) are encountered that must be resolved, and training is seen as a useful tactic to do so. Effective trainers must consider whether training should address "nice-to-know" or "need-to-know" issues. Since training time is normally limited, most or even all training should focus on topics required to improve job performance.
- Training must emphasize application. "Hands-on" training that teaches one employee at a time is typically the best way to teach most tasks to food production employees.
- Training should consider the trainees' experiences. Effective trainers establish a benchmark of what trainees already know and can do. Then they can maximize the worth of training by emphasizing the most important subject-matter with which the trainee is unfamiliar.
- Training should be informal. To the extent possible, training should be personalized, conducted in the workplace, and allow the trainer to interact with the trainee. It should be designed for delivery at the pace that is "best" for the trainee and should consider the trainee's specific questions and needs.
- Training should focus on trainees. Good trainers work hard to address trainees' needs. They do not try to impress them with their (the trainers') knowledge or skills, nor do they make training more difficult than it need be because everyone should "learn it the hard way." Using difficult language can create problems as can teaching advanced before basic skills.
- Trainees should be allowed to practice. Skills are typically learned by observing how something is done and then by practicing the activity in a step-by-step sequence. After the task is learned, time and repetition are often required to enable the trainee to perform the task at the appropriate speed.
- Trainers require time to train. Effective training takes time to develop, deliver, and evaluate. This time must be scheduled, and the resources required for it must be allocated.
- Trainees need encouragement and positive feedback. Do you want to know how your own boss feels about your work? The answer is probably "yes," and trainees also want to know how the trainer evaluates their performance during and, especially, after training.
- Teach the correct way to perform a task. Tasks should be taught using the correct work methods on a step-by-step basis with trainer presentation followed by trainee demonstration.
- Train one task at a time with a step-by-step plan. Tasks should be taught separately, and each should be broken into steps taught in proper sequence. Consider the task of following a standardized recipe. The trainer may begin by demonstrating the first required step. He/she can show the correct procedures, and then allow the trainee to perform the step. The trainer can identify where performance improvements could be helpful. After the trainee successfully demonstrates the step, this process is repeated until all recipe steps are presented and successfully demonstrated by the trainee.
- Consider the trainee's attention span and learning pace. Several short training sessions are generally better than one long session. Break down the total training requirement into manageable (short) parts to be facilitated in a single session. This paced learning allows the trainee to practice and improve upon basic skills in a focused way.

Traits of Effective Trainers

Who should provide the training? Whoever is available or wants to or has the time? These are important factors, but effective trainers share several characteristics:

- They want to train. Perhaps they want to help others or receive recognition for a job well-done.
- They have the proper attitude about their employer, peers, and training assignment. Food service operations that emphasize the importance of staff members and provide quality training opportunities to all employees will likely increase the morale of their trainers.
- They have the necessary knowledge and skills to do the job for which training is being provided.
- They use effective communication skills and speak in a language that is understandable to the trainee. They also use a questioning process to learn what a trainee has really learned.
- They know how to train.
- They have patience. Effective trainers have patience and understand that training steps must sometimes be repeated several times in several different ways.
- They show genuine respect for the trainees and treat them as professionals. This, in turn, will likely lead to mutual respect that allows training to be more effective.
- They celebrate the trainees' success. There is a saying that, "If a trainee hasn't learned, it is because the trainer hasn't trained." A successful trainer is one who has successfully trained.
- They use an effective training process. Training must be well-planned and organized, and many details must be considered. An overview of an organized training process is shown in Figure 2.5.

A discussion of the steps noted in Figure 2.5 will conclude this chapter.

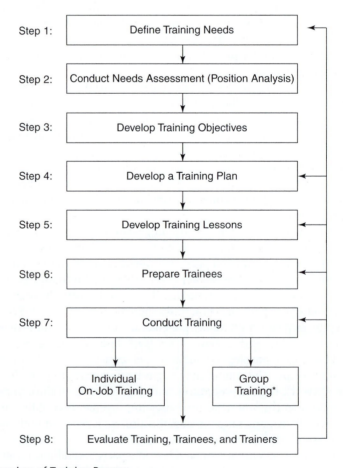

Step 1: Define Training Needs

Step 2: Conduct Needs Assessment (Position Analysis)

Step 3: Develop Training Objectives

Step 4: Develop a Training Plan

Step 5: Develop Training Lessons

Step 6: Prepare Trainees

Step 7: Conduct Training

Individual On-Job Training

Group Training*

Step 8: Evaluate Training, Trainees, and Trainers

FIGURE 2.5 Overview of Training Process

Note: Since kitchen managers primarily use individual on-job training procedures, it will be emphasized in this chapter.

Define Training Needs

Effective kitchen managers recognize that they are confronted by many challenges that can be addressed by training. If only the "squeaky wheel gets the grease," they will likely have little difficulty in discovering challenges that must be resolved. However, there are also "silent" problems that can create difficulties, and many of these can also be addressed with training.

Tactics that can identify training needs include:

- Observation of work performance—Kitchen managers who "manage by walking around" may notice work procedures that deviate from the standard operating procedures that should be used.
- Input from service staff and guests—Hopefully, kitchen managers have formal and informal ways to learn about how they can better help their food service team and those being served.
- Input from staff members—Suggestion boxes, open-door policies, and objective input from performance appraisal and coaching sessions can identify problems that affect food production staff.
- Inspections—Formal inspections such as those related to safety can identify problems. Informal inspections made by supervisors and others before, during, and after work shifts can also suggest revisions in work processes that lend themselves to training.
- Analysis of financial data—Differences between budget plans and actual operating data may suggest problems traceable to problems with training implications. Consider, for example, the many reasons that labor or food costs can be excessive. After these problems are identified, corrective actions that may include training can be implemented.
- **Exit interviews**—Formal or informal discussions with persons who have resigned may suggest training topics to help reduce turnover rates and to improve the department's operations.

OVERHEARD IN THE KITCHEN

Exit interview—A meeting held between a kitchen manager and an employee leaving the food service operation conducted to learn why the employee is leaving and what can be done to improve the organization.

Conduct Needs Assessment (Position Analysis)

Figure 2.5 indicates that a **position analysis** is useful after training needs are defined. It identifies how all tasks in a position should be performed and is helpful when operating procedure changes require employees to do things in new ways.

OVERHEARD IN THE KITCHEN

Position analysis—A process to identify each task in a position and how the task should be done.

There are four basic steps in the position analysis process, and these are shown in Figure 2.6.

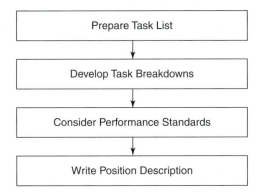

FIGURE 2.6 Four Steps in Position Analysis Process

PREPARE A TASK LIST

A **task list** indicates all tasks included within a position. It focuses on "how-to" activities that a successful employee in the position must be able to do. For example, a cook must know how to follow standard recipes, operate food production equipment, and clean the work station, among many other duties.

Procedures to develop a task list include:

- Asking supervisors of and experienced workers in the position being analyzed. Good questions are open-ended; for example, "Describe what you do in a normal work shift starting with when you begin work until you complete your shift."
- Reviewing available written information about a position. Examples include position descriptions, existing task lists, and training materials used to teach new staff about their jobs.
- Using a simple questionnaire that asks, "What do you and others in your position do as part of your job?"
- Observing staff members as they work in their positions. Compare what they actually do to the tasks they identified when questioned about their position responsibilities.

After analysis of information from the above sources, the kitchen manager can develop an extensive list of tasks in the position. Then similar tasks can be combined, other tasks can be clarified, and factors such as work shift or production volume can be identified that impact the tasks performed by those in the position.

Once developed, the scope of training requirements for a specific position is known. Then new employees must be taught how to correctly perform each task in their position.

OVERHEARD IN THE KITCHEN

Task list—A position analysis tool that indicates all tasks included within a position.

DEVELOP TASK BREAKDOWNS

A **task breakdown** indicates how each task identified in the task list should be done. For example, one task for a cook may be "to properly operate a compartment steamer." The task involves several steps that include safely loading, monitoring, and unloading the equipment.

OVERHEARD IN THE KITCHEN

Task breakdown—A position analysis tool that indicates how each task identified in the task list should be done.

Benefits of task breakdowns include:

- They indicate the correct way to perform a task to best assure that performance standards are attained.
- Trainees benefit from written instructions. A trainer can review a task breakdown with a trainee who can then demonstrate the task using the task breakdown as a guide. Another benefit: The trainee can practice each step and then compare procedures used with those noted in the task breakdown.

How are task breakdowns written? Experienced staff can be observed and interviewed, available information (example: existing task breakdowns and/or existing training documents) can be studied, and/or employees can be asked to write out, in sequence, the steps needed to perform a task.

Writing a task breakdown does not need to be complicated or time consuming. Consider a simple process such as when the kitchen manager:

- Watches an experienced staff member perform a task.
- Records each activity (step) in sequence.
- Asks the experienced staff member to review the information to confirm its accuracy.

- Shares the task analysis information with other experienced staff members and their supervisors.
- Makes modifications, if necessary, to yield an agreed-upon work method.
- Reviews the task work sheet with the staff member's supervisor and the employee.
- Validates the final, agreed-upon task breakdown by observing an experienced person who performs the task using the identified procedures.

CONSIDER PERFORMANCE STANDARDS

Performance standards specify required quality and quantity outputs for each task. Proper performance must be clearly defined so employees know what is expected of them and kitchen managers know when performance is acceptable. The goal of training must be to teach a trainee how to correctly perform a task, and the definition of "correct" refers to both the quality and quantity of work performed.

Performance standards for a task should be reasonable (challenging but achievable). Staff should be trained in procedures specified by task breakdowns, and they must be given the tools and equipment needed to work correctly.

Performance standards must be specific so that they can be measured. Which is better stated: "The cook will know how to prepare twice-baked potatoes" or, alternatively, "The cook will be able to prepare twice-baked potatoes according to the standard recipe and by following the task breakdown for the item." The second standard is best because it can be objectably measured.

WRITE A JOB DESCRIPTION

You've learned that a job description summarizes a position and lists the major tasks that comprise it. Some persons think job descriptions are used only for recruitment purposes because they provide applicants with an overview of a position. However, the role of job descriptions is much broader. First, they suggest training requirements. A new staff member must learn everything required to perform the job as summarized in the position description. Job descriptions also help with supervision because staff members should normally perform only those tasks noted in them. As well, they can be used for performance evaluation activities that consider the extent to which staff adequately perform the tasks in the position.

Develop Training Objectives

Training objectives are used for two purposes. They help the kitchen manager connect the purpose of the training program with its content. Specific reasons for training become clear when training needs are defined and when the content of the training-program is known after position analysis. Second, training objectives are used to evaluate training.

Training objectives specify what trainees should know and be able to do when they successfully complete the training. Those who plan training programs must know what the training is to accomplish, and training objectives help them with their planning activities. Effective training is performance-based and is organized to help trainees learn the tasks considered essential to correctly do their work.

Training objectives should describe the expected results of the training rather than the training process itself. Consider the difference between the following objectives:

As a result of satisfactory completion of the training session, the trainee will:

Objective One: Study the process to properly load a compartment steamer.

Objective Two: Properly load a compartment steamer.

The first objective is not performance-based because it emphasizes the training process ("study"). The performance expected if the training is successful is described in objective two ("properly load a compartment sterilizer"). The skills taught in training can be evaluated because the trainer can compare how the trainee loads a compartment steamer with the operating procedures taught during the training.

The knowledge and skills required for effective work performance drive training objectives which, in turn, dictate the content of the training program. The content of the training then impacts the training process that is implemented and the tactics used for training evaluation.

To be useful, objectives must be reasonable (attainable), and they must be measurable. Objectives are *not* reasonable when they are too difficult or too easy to attain. For example, the following objective for a supervisory training program to reduce employee turnover is not likely to be attained:

"As a result of successful training, there will be a zero turnover rate except for **attrition** beginning with staff members employed after 1/1/XX."

By contrast, an objective stating that, "The turnover rate for food production employees will be reduced by 20% within twelve months of training," may be a reasonable training objective.

OVERHEARD IN THE KITCHEN

Attrition—A reduction in the workforce caused by voluntary separation.

Training objectives typically use an action verb to tell what the trainee must demonstrate or be able to do after training. Examples include: "Operate," "Calculate," "Explain" and "Assemble." By contrast, verbs that are unacceptable because they cannot be measured include "Know," "Appreciate," "Believe" and "Understand."

Develop Training Plans and Training Lessons

Training plans should be developed after training objectives are written to organize training content and provide an overview of the structure and sequence of the training program. They show how individual **training lessons** should be sequenced to best allow trainees to use their skills and to learn the knowledge required for improved performance.

OVERHEARD IN THE KITCHEN

Training plan—An overview of the content and sequence of an entire training program.

Training lesson—The information and methods used to present one session in a training plan.

A well-organized training plan will:

- Provide an introduction that explains why the training is important and how it will benefit trainees.
- Include an overview of training content.
- Plan training lessons to progress from simple to complex, to help trainees feel at ease and comfortable with the learning situation.
- Build on the trainees' experiences and combine unfamiliar information with familiar content.
- Present basic information before more detailed concepts are discussed.
- Use a logical order. What must be known before other information is developed or as skills are attained?

Training plans allow kitchen managers to (a) plan the dates and times for each training lesson, (b) consider the topic (lesson subject), (c) consider the training locations, (d) decide who will be responsible for the training, and (e) indicate trainees for whom specific training lessons are applicable.

When a training plan is developed to teach all tasks to a new staff member, training dates and times must consider the availability of the trainer and the single employee. If the training addresses a special problem impacting several employees, other tactics may be necessary. For example, if a detailed safety program is being planned, each session might be scheduled for two (or more) alternate dates and times so that each employee who needs training can attend. The entire safety training program could be sequenced into three parts (example: 1. Introduction/overview/benefits, 2. Basic safety procedures, and 3. Managing special safety situations). The training location could be the same for every session (perhaps a small dining room), or it could involve training individuals in work stations. The trainees might include all food production personnel for Sessions 1 and 2 and only selected employees for Session 3.

Training activities for cooks must include procedures for interacting with serving personnel.

A training lesson tells the "why, what, and how" of a specific training session:

- Why—the training objectives
- What—the training lesson's content
- How—the training methods to be used

A training lesson may be used to teach new employees how to perform a single task such as operating a tilting braising pan, or it can be used to teach experienced staff new steps in a single task such as a revised process for taking inventory.

Figure 2.7 reviews procedures to develop training lessons.

Let's assume a training lesson about handling server complaints is being developed, and we'll follow the model shown in Figure 2.7:

- Step 1—Develop lesson objectives. A training objective is determined: "Cooks will be able to manage server complaints using a six-step service recovery process."
- Step 2—Determine how cooks can attain required knowledge/skills to meet objectives. The kitchen manager determines that a training video showing how to handle complaints will provide most of the necessary subject matter.
- Step 3—Consider topic sequence. The kitchen manager uses an organized topic sequence that begins with an introduction, continues with the video, and then plans a discussion to review the video's specific learning points.
- Step 4—Determine content for each topic. There is only one topic (managing complaints), and a review of off-the-shelf training resources reinforces the decision that the video will be effective.
- Step 5—Select training method(s) for each topic. A short (fifteen-minute) video followed by a ten-minute discussion will be used.
- Step 6—Consider time requirements for each topic. The kitchen manager knows that thirty minutes will be needed for the session: five minutes for the introduction, fifteen minutes for the video, and ten minutes for the follow-up discussion.
- Step 7—Identify (develop/purchase) required training resources. A training video will be required.
- Step 8—Consider other training tactics. The kitchen manager originally planned to facilitate a **role play** after the video but decided that a discussion would be more effective.

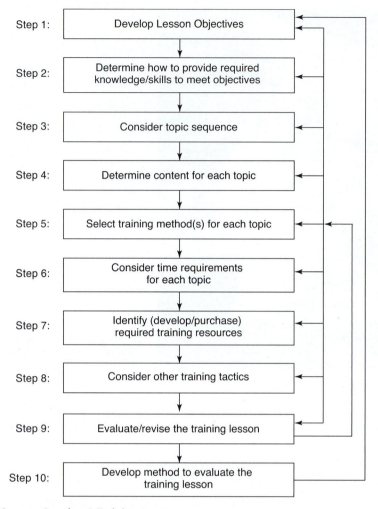

Step 1: Develop Lesson Objectives

Step 2: Determine how to provide required knowledge/skills to meet objectives

Step 3: Consider topic sequence

Step 4: Determine content for each topic

Step 5: Select training method(s) for each topic

Step 6: Consider time requirements for each topic

Step 7: Identify (develop/purchase) required training resources

Step 8: Consider other training tactics

Step 9: Evaluate/revise the training lesson

Step 10: Develop method to evaluate the training lesson

FIGURE 2.7   Steps to Develop A Training Lesson

- Step 9—Evaluate/revise the training lesson. The kitchen manager's experience with previous training sessions helps her plan an effective presentation.
- Step 10—Develop method to evaluate the success of the training session. The trainer will use a ten-question true/false test.

OVERHEARD IN THE KITCHEN

Role play—A group training activity in which trainees assume different roles (examples: cook and server) to apply information presented in the training session.

Figure 2.7 also indicates the cyclical nature of training lesson development: The evaluation/revision (Step 9) can lead to changes in any or all of the earlier steps in training-lesson development. The after-lesson evaluation (Step 10) helps the kitchen manager assess whether the lesson objectives (Step 1) were met.

Many resources can be used to develop training content, including

- Manufacturers' operating manuals for equipment
- Task breakdowns for positions.
- Applicable books and magazines, including e-editions.
- Training resources from professional associations
- Materials from suppliers.
- Ideas from other kitchen managers
- Notes taken from educational and training sessions
- The kitchen manager's own experience.

Prepare Trainees

A focus on the trainees is an obvious but sometimes overlooked concern when training is planned. Providing training materials and activities will not produce more knowledgeable and skilled staff members if they do not want to learn.

The implementation of training programs is easier when trainees have helped to develop them. This can occur, for example, when they provide suggestions about new ways of doing things and as task lists and task breakdowns are developed.

Other ways to motivate trainees for training include:

- Telling trainees what to expect. The "who, what, when, and where" of training should be provided, and their specific questions should be addressed.
- Explaining why the training is needed. State this in terms of "what's in it for the trainees" rather than how it will benefit the food service operation.
- Providing time for the training. Training cannot be rushed, and it cannot be done during times of peak business volume or "whenever time is available."
- Addressing trainees' concerns. Those with language or reading problems and others wanting to know about promotion opportunities after training have concerns that can be addressed before training begins.
- Explaining that training will directly relate to the trainee's work.
- Stressing that the training will be enjoyable and worthwhile. This tactic should be easy to implement when the trainees have had positive experiences with past training efforts.
- Telling the trainees how they will be evaluated. New staff will be looking for assurance that their employment decisions were good ones.
- Expressing confidence that they can master the training material.
- Recognizing that experienced employees will know about the "track record" of the kitchen manager relative to the importance of training and the benefits derived from it.

Conduct On-Job Training

On-job training is a commonly used training method in which the kitchen manager or other trainer teaches job skills and knowledge to one trainee, primarily at the work site (work station). It is an excellent training method because it uses many of the training principles discussed earlier in this chapter.

Advantages to on-job training include:

- It incorporates basic adult learning principles
- It provides maximum realism
- It provides immediate feedback
- It can be used to train new and experienced staff
- It is well-accepted by trainees

Done correctly, there are few, if any, disadvantages to on-job training. Practiced the way it is in some food service operations, however, persons who do not know how to train can make numerous errors if they conduct the training. As well, the training can be unorganized. This can occur when a new employee follows (shadows) his/her experienced peer and, instead, learns tasks in a haphazard sequence.

Think, for example, about a cook who must learn a standard recipe. The experienced employee (trainer) may perform one or two steps in the recipe and then be interrupted and need to do other things before resuming the preparation task. This is, at best, a disorganized way to teach someone how to prepare the recipe. At worst, it can suggest that neither the trainer nor the employer really cares about how or what the trainee learns.

Done incorrectly, on-job training can also ignore the correct way to perform a task. If task breakdowns are not used, the trainer is likely to teach the trainee how he or she does the work rather then the way it really should be done. This may be different from how the trainer learned the task from another trainer (who, in turn, performed the task differently from how he or she initially learned to do it!).

As noted in Figure 2.8 there are four phases in effective on-job training.

Let's look at each of these phases more carefully.

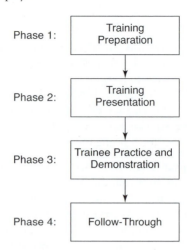

FIGURE 2.8   The On-Job Training Process

TRAINING PREPARATION

The basic principles useful when preparing for on-job training are straight forward, and they have been noted throughout our discussion of training:

- *State training objectives*—Hopefully, training objectives for the entire training program will be available in the training plan and for each segment of the training in the training lesson.
- *Use/revise applicable task breakdowns*—Trainers should review the applicable task breakdown because it indicates the training content. They can also duplicate a copy for each trainee's use during the training.
- *Consider the training schedule*—The training plan indicates the length of the training activity, and it should also indicate where in the overall training plan sequence the specific training topic should occur. The best time to schedule training is when there is time to adequately conduct it. This is likely to be when production volume is low, and when the trainer has adequate time to facilitate the training.
- *Select training location*—When practical training is needed, training should take place in the work station where the task will be performed.
- *Assemble training materials/equipment*—The training lesson will indicate what is needed.
- *Set up work station*—The trainer should assure that all necessary materials/equipment are available.
- *Prepare the trainee*—A new staff member should know that the training will provide the knowledge and skills necessary to perform all job tasks. Experienced staff should understand that the purpose of the training is to provide the knowledge/skills needed to perform a task differently or to learn a new task.
- *Determine what the trainee already knows*—If, for example, a piece of equipment must be operated as part of a task, the trainer may ask the trainee to demonstrate its proper operation. If the trainee can perform the required task, this part of the training is not necessary. If the trainee cannot operate the equipment, training should address equipment operation.

Figure 2.9 reviews important activities when preparing training programs.

TRAINING PRESENTATION

During this part of on-job training, the kitchen manager should be happy about the preparation activities already completed, because the work already done will make it easier to conduct the training. Each of the earlier steps in the training process build on each other, and the training lessons that result will be very useful to present the training.

In addition to using the training lesson, the trainer will likely find that the task breakdown, completed during the position analysis process, will be helpful as the training is presented.

To review appropriate training presentation procedures, let's consider how a kitchen manager might train an employee to conduct a physical inventory in the ideal location; the storeroom.

PREPARATION

The Trainer Should:

☐ 1. Develop a schedule that addresses when a specific training lesson should be offered, the amount of time to be allocated for it, and the sequence in which it should be taught.
☐ 2. Use a task breakdown to identify how a task should be done.
☐ 3. Have all necessary equipment, tools, and materials ready for the training session.
☐ 4. Select and properly arrange the appropriate training location.
☐ 5. Know *precisely* how to begin the training process.
☐ 6. Identify the tasks for the trainee to learn.
☐ 7. Put the trainee at ease.
☐ 8. Find out what the trainee already knows about the task.
☐ 9. Explain what the trainee should expect to learn in the session.
☐ 10. Set a good example for the trainee.
☐ 11. Explain "what's in it" for the trainee.

FIGURE 2.9   Checklist for On-Job Training: Preparation

The training session begins as the trainee receives a copy of the position description, which confirms that the inventory task is part of the trainee's position. The importance of the task can be explained: "A physical inventory count helps to confirm the accuracy of perpetual inventory records, and we do it monthly." The trainer can point out that the task overview in the job description indicates that, "To conduct a physical inventory count, one person physically counts the number of cases, cartons, or bags of each product in inventory. A second person verifies the inventory quantity and enters it onto a work sheet. This process is continued until all products are counted, and this usually takes about one hour."

After this brief explanation, applicable activities are demonstrated. The trainer shows the trainee how the storage area is organized and reviews how the inventory worksheet is completed. The counting process and tactics to assure that products are correctly shelved to promote product rotation are reviewed.

The trainer explains the first step in the task, answers questions posed by the trainee, and then allows the trainee to repeat, practice and/or demonstrate the step. If necessary, the sequence of steps can be repeated so the trainee can learn all steps in the task.

As the presentation process evolves, the kitchen manager follows several principles:

- He/she speaks in simple terms.
- Training in simple tasks is presented before more complex activities are discussed.
- Tasks are explained and demonstrated slowly and clearly.
- A questioning process is used to help assure trainee comprehension, and the trainer uses open-ended questions such as "Why do you think it is important to count full cases before counting opened cases?"
- The task breakdown is emphasized as the training evolves.
- Clear and well-thought-out instructions for each task are provided.
- Questions are asked to help assure that the trainee understands and to suggest when additional information, practice, or demonstration can be helpful.

Figure 2.10 reviews important training points when on-job training is presented.

TRAINEE PRACTICE AND DEMONSTRATION

Several principles are important during this phase in on-job training:

- The trainee should be asked to repeat or explain key points.
- The trainee should demonstrate and/or practice the task. If practical, the trainee should practice each step in the task enough times to learn the "basics" of the step before training continues to the next step. Typically, steps are taught by the trainer and practiced/demonstrated by the trainee in the sequence required to perform a task.
- When the task being trained is difficult, initial progress may be slow. Then the trainee will require more extensive repetition to build speed and to more consistently and correctly perform the task.

PRESENTATION

The Trainer Should:

- ☐ 1. Explain tasks and steps.
- ☐ 2. Demonstrate tasks and steps.
- ☐ 3. Make sure the trainee understands each task.
- ☐ 4. Encourage the trainee to ask questions.
- ☐ 5. Respond appropriately to questions, if asked.
- ☐ 6. Check for understanding by asking open-ended questions.
- ☐ 7. Provide information about and demonstrate only one task or step at a time.
- ☐ 8. Follow an orderly sequence using the training lesson as a guide.
- ☐ 9. Maintain a patient and appropriate pace throughout the training session.
- ☐ 10. Give only the amount of information or instruction that can be mastered during one session.
- ☐ 11. Make the training session interesting.
- ☐ 12. Make sure that all instructions are clear, concise, complete and accurate.
- ☐ 13. Provide an applicable task breakdown.

FIGURE 2.10   Checklist for On-Job Training: Presentation

- Some trainees learn faster than others. This principle is especially easy to incorporate into training when the on-job training approach is used. Training can be presented at the speed judged "best" for the individual trainee.
- Correct performance should be acknowledged before addressing performance problems.
- Trainees should be praised for their proper performance. Trainers should reward trainees for successful performance by noting the performance and by thanking the trainees for it.

Figure 2.11 reviews tactics helpful to implement the practice and demonstration step of on-job training.

FOLLOW-THROUGH

The final step in on-job training includes activities that allow the trainer to ensure that the training will be effective. Useful follow-through procedures include:

- At the end of the training session, the trainee should be asked to perform, in sequence, each step in the task.
- The trainer should encourage and ask questions.
- The trainer should provide ongoing reinforcement about a trainee's positive attitude as well as when the trainee improves his or her skills and knowledge as a result of successful training.
- Close supervision immediately after training and occasional supervision after a task has been mastered can help assure that the trainee consistently performs the task correctly.
- Trainers should request that the trainee always performs the task in the way that he or she has been taught.
- Trainees should be asked to keep copies of the training materials provided during the session for later use if needed.

PRACTICE AND DEMONSTRATION

The Trainer Should:

- ☐ 1. Request the trainee to perform the step after it has been presented.
- ☐ 2. Ask the trainee to explain the "hows and whys" of each task or step.
- ☐ 3. Correct all incorrect or substandard performance.
- ☐ 4. Assure that the trainee understands each step by asking open-ended questions.
- ☐ 5. Compliment the trainee when he/she correctly performs a task or step.
- ☐ 6. Point out errors made, if any, during practice and demonstration to help the trainee learn from mistakes.
- ☐ 7. Allow the trainee time to practice and build confidence and speed.

FIGURE 2.11   Checklist for On-Job Training: Practice and Demonstration

FOLLOW-THROUGH

The Trainer Should:

☐ 1. Encourage the trainee to seek assistance.
☐ 2. Tell the trainee who should be contacted if assistance is needed.
☐ 3. Check the trainee's performance frequently but unobtrusively.
☐ 4. Reinforce proper performance. Let the trainee know how he/she was doing.
☐ 5. Help the trainee to correct mistakes, if any.
☐ 6. Assure that mistakes, if any, are not repeated.
☐ 7. Ask the trainee about suggestions for better ways to do the task.
☐ 8. Encourage the trainee to improve upon previous standards.
☐ 9. Compliment the trainee for successful demonstration of the newly learned skill.

FIGURE 2.12   Checklist for On-Job Training: Follow-Through

Figure 2.12 reviews principles for effective follow-through activities in on-job training.

Evaluate Training, Trainees, and Trainers

Kitchen managers must determine whether the training has been beneficial. Other reasons to evaluate training include to:

- Assess the extent to which training achieved planned results—Training objectives identify competencies to be addressed in training and provide a benchmark against which training can be evaluated.
- Determine the success of individual trainees—Trainees who are successful and achieve planned results on the job will not require additional training. Other staff members may need additional training.
- Identify strengths and weaknesses of training—Some training lessons are better than others, some training activities are more useful than their counterparts, and some trainers are more effective at delivering training than their peers.
- Gather information to help justify future programs—When the success of a training activity is known, objective information can help determine whether future training efforts are justified.
- Some food service operations have formal or informal "fast-track" programs in which trainees who have successfully completed training are eligible for additional training. Assessing training results can help identify those workers who may qualify for additional training of this type.

WHEN TO EVALUATE TRAINING

Assume an employee attends a training session and missed only two questions of twenty on an after-training test. Most kitchen managers might assume the training was successful because the trainee answered 90% of the questions correctly (18 correct questions ÷ 20 questions = 90% correctly answered). However, the training could have been a waste of money and time if the trainee already knew, before the training began, the concepts addressed by the eighteen questions answered correctly.

A pretest-posttest process can address this concern. A kitchen manager can first identify key concepts to be addressed during training and then use a before-training test (pretest) to learn about existing knowledge or skills. This same test can be used at the end of the training (posttest) and the (hopefully) improved score represents a measure of training effectiveness.

It may also be helpful to assess training several months (or even longer) after the training is completed. Then the kitchen manager can learn the extent to which training content was retained and, more importantly, applied in the workplace.

TRAINING EVALUATION METHODS

Alternative training evaluation methods include:

- *Objective tests*—These can be written, oral, and/or skill-based. They should be written after training objectives and instructional materials are developed, and a separate test should be used for each objective in the training lesson.

- *Observation of after-training performance*—Managers, supervisors and trainers can manage by "walking around" and, in the process, note whether knowledge and skills taught are being applied.
- *Interviews with trainees and/or trainers*—The use of **open-ended questions** ("What do we do with the left-overs from our buffet?") may provide useful input about training effectiveness.
- *Exit interviews*—Formal and even informal conversations with staff members leaving the facility can provide input helpful for training evaluation.

OVERHEARD IN THE KITCHEN

Questions (open-ended)—A question that cannot be answered with a "yes" or "no." Open-ended questions require a thoughtfully considered response.

FOLLOW-UP DOCUMENTATION

Documentation is a final part of training evaluation. Training records should be maintained in the applicable staff member's personnel file and should include:

- Name of trainee
- Training dates
- Training topics
- Notes about successful completion
- Other information as applicable

Employees who have been carefully selected, oriented, and trained are prepared to do their jobs well. Kitchen managers must also do their part to ensure their workers are effectively managed. The specific ways in which professional kitchen managers do this will be presented in Chapter Three.

NOW IT'S YOUR TURN

A PINCH OF THE INTERNET (2.3)

1. Professional associations provide resources that busy kitchen managers can use for their training programs. To view some of these materials, check out:
   - Educational Institute of American Hotel & Lodging Association (www.ei-ahla.org)
   - National Restaurant Association Educational Foundation (www.nraef.org)
2. To review practical and hospitality industry-related articles about training, go to the Hotel-Online Web site: www.hotel-online.com. Then enter "training" in the "Search Hotel-Online" box.
3. To learn about the wide variety of videos available for hospitality training, enter "hospitality industry training videos" in your favorite search engine. Some of the Web sites you'll discover offer free video previews.

COMPLETING THE PLATE QUESTIONS (2.3)

1. The chapter notes benefits to effective training, including improved staff relationships. Can a kitchen manager measure whether staff relationships improve as a result of training? If not, does this mean an interest in improving staff relationships should not be considered as training benefits are analyzed? Why or why not?
2. What basic training principles were most frequently ignored or were applied inadequately in your past training experiences? Why do you think those who train sometimes fail to use these principles?
3. What would you as a kitchen manager say to a supervisor who indicates he or she is too busy to develop task lists or task breakdowns for the department?
4. How should a kitchen manager determine the amount of time that should be spent conducting a specific training lesson?
5. What are the most important reasons that specify why you would like to be trained with an on-job training method? That you would *not* like to be trained with the on-job training method?
6. What might you do if you were a kitchen manager and a new employee was not able to perform a relatively simple task after what should be a sufficient amount of time was allowed for practicing and demonstrating the task?
7. Do you agree with the following statement (why or why not)? "If a trainee hasn't learned, it is because the trainer hasn't taught."

Kitchen Challenge Du Jour Case Study (2.2)

"What's so hard about training," asked Paul, the kitchen manager, as he spoke to Phyllis, the head bartender after a management meeting of the Smith Brothers Restaurant. "We both started here in the same entry-level position about five years ago. We were smart enough to learn fast, we did what we were told, and we have been promoted several times. Why can't today's new employees understand that what worked for us will work for them?"

"You know, Paul, things have changed in just the last few years. Our new employees expect more, and they will work hard if we meet their expectations. However, we have difficulty in retaining them; think about our high turnover rate. Also, think about our competition for these staff members. Many of the employers who want the same workers we want are not even in the hospitality business. Think about another thing: We have lost some business because of service-related issues. I doubt that our revenues are as high as they can be, and I also think our expenses are greater than what they should be because we do not pay enough attention to training our staff."

"Well, I think on-job training is the best approach, and it certainly is easy, fast, and inexpensive," said Paul. "That's how we learned, and I'm not certain what you're saying."

"I don't think our training method is bad," said Phyllis, "Instead, I think that the way we do it is incorrect. There must be more to training than asking a busy employee to let a new staff member tag-along during a work shift."

"Well," said Paul, "We want to teach our staff members what's happening in the real world of our business. I think our approach does that."

"No," said Phyllis, "I don't think our training does what it should do. I think our experienced staff members teach new persons how to do the job the way they do it. Unfortunately, that might be significantly different from what we intend. In fact, do we even know what our definition of 'good' performance is?"

"We're pretty busy around here," Paul stated. "Maybe we'll have time to improve our training process when things slow down."

"You know," said Phyllis, "Things will never slow down because our problems stemming from inadequate performance are increasing. I am going to suggest that we reconsider why we train, how we do it, and what benefits can result from an increased priority on training."

Case Study Questions

1. Use of a more formalized on-job training process might help to resolve some of the issues addressed in the case study. What benefits might Phyllis cite? What should she do if she is asked about quantitative impacts of training?
2. What process should Phyllis suggest to plan, conduct, and evaluate on-job training in her organization? What assistance, including technical help and resources, might be available to Phyllis if she works in a small restaurant without a human resources department?
3. Assume that Phyllis has had negative experiences with on-job training when she began working with the organization. How can she use these experiences to improve the training provided to her staff?
4. How do you think a higher-than-necessary turnover rate might be related to inadequate training?

Overheard in the Kitchen Glossary

Recruit	Interview questions (direct)	Induction	Task list
Employer of Choice	Interview questions (indirect)	Labor-intensive	Task breakdown
Recruiting (internal)	Wage (hourly)	Training	Attrition
Recruiting (external)	Salary	Cost-effective	Training plan
Compensation package	Background check	Task	Training lesson
Selection	Job offer	Competency	Role play
Application form	Mission statement	Exit interview	Questions (open-ended)
Discrimination	Employee handbook	Position analysis	

LESSON 2

If you are reading this textbook as part of a formal class, your Instructor may want you to apply and practice what you have learned in this chapter by completing Lesson 2 of the Pearson Education's Hall Kitchen Management Simulation (KMS). If you are required to complete KMS Lesson 2; read **About Lesson 2** below, then go to: www.pearsonhighered.com/kms for instructions on how to access and complete it.

After you have successfully completed the lesson, think about the way you, as a professional kitchen manager, would answer the **For Your Consideration** questions that follow.

About Lesson 2

Much of this book and the KMS are about how kitchen managers plan menus, purchase and manage food products and control costs. Before that happens, however, kitchen managers must first recruit, select and train a team of kitchen workers who can help the managers reach the product quality and budgetary goals they have set for their kitchens.

In this lesson you will learn about how kitchen managers use job descriptions to identify the worker skills needed to assist in their kitchens. When kitchen managers carefully identify all of the skills their future workers must have, it is easier to choose employees who have those needed skills.

You learned in this chapter that after the best employees have been selected, they must then have the proper orientation and training. This lesson will show you know the importance of proper employee selection and training when developing your own professional kitchen.

Lesson 2 has three important parts. When you have successfully completed all three of them you will know how kitchen managers use effective job descriptions to choose skilled workers and then train those workers to be the very best they can be.

For Your Consideration

1. What personal characteristics do you think employees who work in professional kitchens must have to be successful?
2. What would be the effect on the quality of a restaurant's menu items if its kitchen workers were poorly trained?
3. Have you ever held a job in which your employer did not provide proper training? How did that make you feel about yourself? About your job? About your employer?

Endnote

1. The above list is adapted from: David Hayes and Jack Ninemeier. 50 One-Minute Tips for Recruiting Employees: Finding the Right People for Your Organization. Menlo Park, California. Crisp Learning Systems, Inc. 2001.

3

Kitchen Managers Lead Food Production Employees

Chapter Ingredients Outline

Learning Objectives

After studying this chapter, you will be able to:

1. Practice useful tactics to motivate and retain kitchen employees.
2. Utilize basic tools and skills to facilitate the work of food production employees.
3. Implement basic principles to manage labor costs.

COMING RIGHT UP OVERVIEW

Many food service operations enjoy low **employee turnover rates** that occur when professional kitchen managers know how to **motivate** and retain the employees they have selected, orientated, and trained. There are numerous "common sense" ways to create a work environment that allows employees to find pride and joy in what they do, and some of these methods will be explored in this chapter.

Much of a kitchen manager's time is spent facilitating the work of food production personnel. This chapter will review several common leadership styles that can be used and describe the situations when each may be most beneficial.

Basic principles for successful interaction with staff members should be consistently practiced. Some the most important of these will be discussed in the chapter. They relate to communication, team building, coaching, and conflict management. Workplace ethics is another issue that influences employee supervision, and this chapter also introduces this topic.

Finally, since labor costs are such a large expense, they must be effectively managed without lowering quality standards. One way to do so involves using the budget for planning labor standards, forecasting business volumes, planning the allowable number of labor hours, scheduling kitchen personnel, and evaluating performance. This five-step method will be discussed in the last section of this chapter.

OVERHEARD IN THE KITCHEN

Turnover rate (employee)—The number of employees who leave during a specific period of time divided by the number of employees working during that same period. The turnover rate is generally stated as a percentage. One calculation for annual turnover rate % is as follows:

Number of Employees Who Leave (÷) Total Number of Employees = Annual Turnover Rate %

Motivate—The act of providing an employee with a reason to do something. Employees are motivated when their supervisor offers them something they want (example: higher pay rate) in return for something the supervisor wants (example: work in a higher-level position).

MOTIVATE AND RETAIN KITCHEN EMPLOYEES

Oᴮᴊᴇᴄᴛɪᴠᴇ

1. Practice useful tactics to motivate and retain kitchen employees:
   • Follow sound management advice
   • Make a good first impression
   • Maintain a professional workforce
   • Supervise effectively
   • Help your employees be successful

The best way to reduce the need for ongoing employee recruitment and selection is to reduce turnover rates by keeping the employees that you have, and that is the topic of this section.

Follow Sound Management Advice

Kitchen managers make a large investment as they recruit and train entry-level personnel for food production, clean-up, and related duties. The money spent, along with the valuable knowledge, skills, and experience of these staff members, is lost when they leave. Also, low employee **morale** levels can be a challenge. However, the good news is that there are simple and practical ways for kitchen managers to improve **retention rates**.

OVERHEARD IN THE KITCHEN

Morale—The total of an employee's feelings about his/her employer, workplace, and other aspects of the food service operation.

Retention rate (employee)—The number of employees who remain during a specific period of time divided by the number of employees who worked in the kitchen during that same period. The retention rate is generally stated as a percentage. One calculation for annual retention rate % is:

Number of Employees Who Remain (÷) Total Number of Employees = Annual Retention Rate %

Some kitchen managers think that higher pay rates are the only tactic to avoid staff turnover and increase morale. However, "throwing money" at a problem is not likely to resolve it. While staff members must be paid a competitive wage, there are also many concerns that can be important to them.

Experienced kitchen managers use several tactics to help motivate and retain their employees. For example, they serve first and lead second.[1] A good kitchen manager facilitates the work of employees by training them properly, providing tools and equipment that are safe and well-maintained and by removing obstacles to success. They also help their employees resolve problems and provide them with continuing education opportunities to learn on the job.

The best kitchen managers eliminate employees who won't and can't do required work tasks. Employees who won't perform or don't meet work standards or who abuse attendance, vacation, and other policies affect the good employees who do most of the work. As well, poor performance by supervisors is likely to cause employee dissatisfaction and turnover. Ineffective managers cannot ask their employees to "go the extra mile" if the employees think that managers will not do the same for them. To improve your employees' morale, eliminate employees who won't work and managers who can't manage.

Make a Good First Impression

First, let's first think about the role of starting wages. Would a staff member (or you) change positions for 20¢ more each hour? How about for $20 more each week? Significant amounts of money do motivate entry-level personnel, but small amounts of additional pay may not. A competitive wage (and this does not mean the highest in the community) can build a foundation that will help to motivate employees. Then, the use of effective management practices will be useful to retain employees even if their job is not the very highest-paying one for which they might apply.

Kitchen managers should also make sure that their employees know that total compensation is more than just wages or salary. **Benefits** including meals, uniforms, educational assistance, healthcare, vacation, and sick leave cost a lot of money, and their value should be made known to the employees.

Four other tactics can also help to make a difference when new employees first begin work. You can:

- Explain the long-term benefits of staying. Examples include pay raises, extended vacation times, or other types of financial compensation and internal recognition. Review these benefits during orientation programs and then frequently during the new employees' first months on the job.
- Share your vision. Effective kitchen managers know what they want. Productivity standards and minimal **defects** are important. Employees should know how their position helps to attain their department's goals and what they and others must do meet or exceed them. Effective kitchen managers share their thoughts, ask staff members for ideas, and work together as a team to meet goals.
- Motivate entry-level employees. There are two types of entry-level staff members: those who have only been on the job a short while, and more experienced employees who have been in entry-level positions for a longer time. Tactics to retain entry-level staff members who meet work performance standards vary according to how long an employee has worked in the food service operation. For example, experienced employees may want to know how you can help them to advance, and new staff members may look to you to help them increase their comfort level and their sense of belonging to the team.
- Create a **career ladder**. This is a road map explaining how job advancement occurs. It shows employees how they can be promoted if they remain with your operation. The best kitchen managers analyze each entry-level position to think about how a talented staff member in that job might advance. Then they develop a career ladder that shows the title, rank, and pay level for each new job. Career ladders should be shared with staff members because it will motivate them. As well, they provide a plan for additional training and education as employees move forward in their career.

OVERHEARD IN THE KITCHEN

Benefits (employee)—Indirect financial compensation paid to attract and retain employees or to meet legal requirements. Some benefits are mandatory (example: social security taxes) while others are voluntary (example: vacation days).

Defect—Any output such as a food product that does not meet the standard set for it.

Career ladder—A plan that shows how one can advance to more responsible positions within a food service operation. Kitchen managers develop career ladders to plan and schedule training or other educational activities to help employees be promoted.

Maintain a Professional Workforce

Kitchen managers guard against liability from **harassment** charges, and they ensure a quality workplace for all staff members by requiring a **zero tolerance** for objectionable behavior. They include a harassment policy in their employee handbook and discuss it at employee orientation sessions and other staff meetings.

OVERHEARD IN THE KITCHEN

Harassment—Unwanted and annoying actions, including threats or demands, by one or more persons.
Zero tolerance—A policy that allows no amount or type of harassing behavior.

They also create a culturally diverse workplace that reflects the make-up of the community in which they work. One important benefit of **diversity** is that it often brings unique, important, and useful ideas to the workplace.

OVERHEARD IN THE KITCHEN

Diversity—The concept that people are unique with individual differences that result from variations in their race, ethnicity, gender, socio-economic status, age, and physical abilities, among others.

The best kitchen managers share appropriate financial information with their employees. Most staff members want to know what is happening that affects them. They like it when their boss respects and trusts them enough to share information that might not be available to others. Some kitchen managers provide monthly financial information to all employees. Note: This does not need to be an "all or nothing" tactic. If the total financial picture of the operation cannot be revealed, it might be possible to share other information such as food cost, number of meals served, guest comments, and other information. This is another way that the kitchen manager shows that the employees are a critical part of the team.

An effective kitchen manager can make even the most fast-paced work environment very safe, productive, and exciting.

Supervise Effectively

Effective kitchen managers supervise their employees the way they would like to be supervised. Examples to do this include:

- Administer policies fairly and consistently. Employees do not like it when some workers are favored over others, and they watch their supervisors' actions carefully to see if this occurs. For example, wise kitchen managers don't allow some employees to arrive at work later than they are scheduled without a word being said while others are punished when they do so. Policies should be fair and reasonable, and everyone should be treated the same way.
- Give employees a personal copy of their work schedule. There's nothing wrong with posting the employee work schedule on a bulletin board or circulating it through the operation's **intranet**. However, some staff members are more likely to follow a schedule if they receive a personal copy. Some managers text or e-mail workers the operation's schedule to make it easy for employees to know when they are to work.
- Know about employee assistance programs. Some employees who can work correctly still may need professional assistance because of problems such as alcohol or substance abuse and financial or personal difficulties. These challenges can affect their attendance, their ability to meet required work standards, and their personal interactions with other members of the work team. Kitchen managers can show concern by directing them to places where professional assistance is available.
- Invite "**fast-track**" employees to attend management meetings. Most employees like to know that they provide value to the food service operation. When they know their supervisor has important plans for them they are more likely to remain with the operation and be motivated as they do so.

OVERHEARD IN THE KITCHEN

Intranet—A network consisting of computers for a single food service organization that can be at the same or different locations.

Fast-track employees—Employees who meet the quantity and quality standards for all tasks in their existing position and who participate in a planned professional development program designed to quickly advance them within the food service operation.

- Conduct exit interviews. Why do staff members leave? Exit interviews with each departing staff member to learn reasons for leaving that can help you plan more effective retention strategies.
- Use employee recognition programs to publicly or privately praise good employees. For many staff members, verbal recognition for a job well-done is as effective a motivator as a cash award. Personal recognition letters, bulletin board announcements, plaques, and special recognition pins are ways that kitchen managers can show employees that their accomplishments are valued.
- Build a great team and praise it often. Members of winning teams want to be the best at what they do. To retain "star" players, assure that all new employees know they have joined a successful team and that they will be treated like the professionals they are.
- Reward employees who work on nonscheduled days. Recognition, rewards, and extra benefits are among the ways to say "thank you" for these efforts. Also, don't always ask the same employees to work extra shifts just because you know they will say "yes" while other employees always say "no."
- Make the workplace fun. Ask staff members what you can do to make the workplace more enjoyable. You may learn ideas that do not reduce productivity and will positively impact the employees' attitudes. The food service operation should not be boring and, if it is, you should change the situation.

Help Your Employees Be Successful

Satisfaction is a powerful motivator. Unfortunately, some food service work is routine, and it may be difficult to change the job to add more variety. Kitchen managers can, however, create a motivating work environment. All employees can probably demonstrate success in some area, and their strengths provide the key to recognizing employees for that success. If an employee has an excellent attendance record, make sure he or she knows you appreciate the dedication. If employees have been recognized in guest comment cards, the messages should be shared with them, and they should be thanked for their assistance.

Effective kitchen managers know they can be punishing their best employees by assigning extra work projects to them. For example, if you need someone to train a new employee or to work on a special project, would you ask your best or your worst employee to do this? Unfortunately, the best employees may think their contributions are being rewarded with extra work that is not required of others. Why, then, should someone want to be a superior employee if the only reward for their behavior is extra work? Recognition and rewards for special efforts are important and will benefit all kitchen managers and their food service operations.

▮ NOW IT'S YOUR TURN

A PINCH OF THE INTERNET (3.1)

1. A new employee's first impressions of the food service operation are very important, and an orientation program can be very helpful. To learn about the content for these programs, type "new employee orientation checklist" into your favorite search engine.

2. Busy kitchen managers do not have the time to develop all of the resources they need for their training programs. Check out the materials available from the Educational Institute of the American Hotel & Lodging Association: (www. ei-ahla.org) and the National Restaurant Association: (www.restaurant.org).

    How could you decide if any of these resources you review on the Web sites would be useful to your training efforts?

3. Motivated kitchen employees are likely to be "good" staff members who remain with the food service operation. To learn how to motivate kitchen employees, type "motivating food service employees" into your favorite search engine.

COMPLETING THE PLATE QUESTIONS (3.1)

1. This section of the chapter lists some no- and low-cost ways to retain kitchen employees. What are some additional tactics that you could add to these lists?

2. Do you think most kitchen employees want to receive additional training? If so, what are the reasons? If not, what can kitchen managers do to help employees recognize the benefits of additional training?

3. How would you describe the best boss you ever had? The worst boss? How can answering these questions help you to become a better boss?

Kitchen Challenge Du Jour Case Study (3.1)

"Our younger employees certainly think differently than our older employees, don't they?" Ester, a cook at a large chain restaurant was talking to her boss, the kitchen manager.

"Yes, I certainly agree," said Claudia, "In fact, it's hard to keep them motivated, satisfied, and on the job. Perhaps it's just a cost of doing business, but I wish we could keep the people we have so that we don't have to spend so much time recruiting and selecting new employees."

a) What are some ways that the views of older employees and newer employees could differ?

b) What are some ways that kitchen managers can motivate all employees regardless of their age?

c) Some young kitchen managers report that they have difficulty supervising kitchen employees who are older than they are. What are your suggestions about how young persons can manage and motivate older employees?

PRACTICE EFFECTIVE SUPERVISION

OBJECTIVE

2. Utilize basic tools and skills to facilitate the work of food production employees:
   • Leadership styles
   • Basic communication skills
   • Team building
   • Coaching
   • Conflict management
   • Workplace ethics

Kitchen managers must direct the work of food production employees, and we'll discuss some supervisory basics and useful tactics in this section.

Leadership Styles

Effective kitchen managers recognize the need to vary how they interact with people to meet specific needs of the individual and the situation itself. There are five basic leadership styles that reflect how leaders can interact with **subordinates**, and a brief description of each follows:

- **Autocratic** kitchen managers make decisions and resolve problems without input from affected staff members. They want to give instructions and expect them to be followed. They frequently develop a system of rewards and punishments to encourage compliance with orders, and they discipline employees when orders are not followed. They place results above concerns about staff morale and are generally unwilling to **delegate** assignments to employees.
- **Bureaucratic** leaders manage by the book. Those practicing this type of leadership place emphasis on the enforcement of policies, procedures, and rules. Problems that are not addressed by and cannot, therefore, be resolved by the rules are referred to higher levels of management.
- **Democratic** leaders involve staff members in the decision-making process. They keep employees informed about all matters that affect them, and they share decision-making and problem-solving responsibilities through empowerment. They also emphasize the employees' role in the organization and provide opportunities for employees to develop a high sense of job satisfaction.
- **Laissez-faire** leaders use a "hands off" approach and actually do as little directing as possible; instead, all or most **authority** is delegated to staff members. Employees are given as much freedom as possible, and they even develop goals, make decisions, and resolve problems.
- **Transformational** leaders interact with others in a way that permits both the leaders and their associates to raise one another to a higher level of motivation. They create a vision, constantly promote it to their staff members, and use it to determine the best courses of action.

OVERHEARD IN THE KITCHEN

Subordinate—A term referring to an employee (associate or staff member) in a lower organizational level.

Autocratic (leadership style)—A leadership approach in which decisions are typically made and problems are resolved without input from affected staff members.

Delegate—The process of assigning authority (power) to subordinates to allow them to do work that a higher level manager would otherwise need to do.

Bureaucratic (leadership style)—A leadership approach that involves "management by the book" and the enforcement of policies, procedures, and rules.

Democratic (leadership style)—A leadership approach in which staff members are encouraged to participate in the decision-making process.

Laissez-faire (leadership style)—A leadership approach that minimizes directing employees and, instead, maximizes the delegation of tasks to staff members.

Authority—Power; the ability to do something including to make decisions.

Transformational (leadership style)—A leadership approach in which leaders interact with employees in a way that permits both the leaders and their associates to raise one another to a higher level of motivation.

INFORMATION ON THE SIDE

Effective Leaders Vary Their Leadership Style

The most effective kitchen managers know when and how to adapt their leadership style to the event and situation at hand and when appropriate, to empower their staff. Adaptability is the key to leadership because it demonstrates that you have the capacity to get results and, at the same time, attract and retain desirable employees. Most persons want to work and will do their best when they feel appreciated, understood, and respected by their leaders.

It is easy to suggest that kitchen managers should vary their leadership styles based upon the individuals with whom they interact and the situation within which decisions must be made. It is, however, much more difficult to do this. They can, however, practice this basic leadership principle and, over time, can learn the tactics necessary to modify their approaches when interacting with associates.

Basic Communication Skills

Effective communicators understand and utilize three basic skills:

- *Skill 1.* Those sending messages consider those who will receive them and attempt to consider their viewpoints. If, for example, a kitchen manager anticipates reactions and thinks about what might make a person more receptive to a message, he/she can better plan the communication.
- *Skill 2.* They attempt to learn what others are thinking. For example, a kitchen manager may say something and then ask, "Do you understand?" This type of question may not be productive because simple "yes" or "no" responses may fail to indicate the extent of understanding. A better technique involves asking an open-ended question such as, "Why do you think this step must be performed before the next task can be done?"
- *Skill 3.* They make the message meaningful. For example, the way a kitchen manager gives instructions to new staff members and their experienced counterparts are likely to be different. Also, the way they talk to highly motivated employees and others with negative attitudes is not likely to be the same.

BARRIERS TO EFFECTIVE COMMUNICATION

Several barriers can hinder communication effectiveness and, if you are aware of them, you can develop strategies to help offset them. Here are examples:

- *Differing perceptions.* If one person is not interested in a message, the effectiveness of the communication will be lowered. If a kitchen manager suspects this, he/she can try to pose the message in a way that illustrates benefits to the person receiving the message.
- *Lack of knowledge.* Communication cannot be effective when one party does not understand the message.
- *Role of emotions.* Emotions that can be obvious or deeply-rooted can create communication barriers. While objective and rational communication is always best, it is difficult or impossible when someone's emotions are involved.
- *Personality problems.* People may reject communication from others they do not like. At other times, they might blindly accept communication from someone they do like.
- *Appearance.* The appearance of the person sending an oral message can, consciously or subconsciously, impact how the receiver of the message will interpret it.
- *Distractions.* Noise, people, uncomfortable temperature, and other factors in the busy kitchen may make communication difficult.
- *Language barriers.* In today's diverse workplace, employees may speak several different languages. In some food service operations, kitchen managers learn the basics of the language spoken by their employees. In others, the primary language of the majority is taught to employees. In still others, both supervisors and staff members are given language training to help ease communication challenges.

INFORMATION ON THE SIDE
Change and Communication

At times, it appears that the only thing that is constant is change, and workplace change can create fear and frustration in even the best employees. When kitchen managers communicate openly, they can help their entire workgroup accept change with less stress. Leaders and their staff members often have little control over changes that impact their work lives. When changes do occur, you should recognize their inevitability and make plans to implement the change in the best way possible.

MANAGING THE GRAPEVINE AND RUMORS

Each food service operation has an informal communication system that relies on word-of-mouth to transmit information. This system, commonly referred to as the "**grapevine**," can be a good way to transmit information if used in a positive manner. Then it can foster an environment that encourages the sharing of information and respect for each individual.

OVERHEARD IN THE KITCHEN

Grapevine—An informal channel of communication throughout an organization.

Conversely, informal communication systems can also cause numerous problems. Negative comments and the spread of gossip are two of the fastest ways to corrupt an informal communication system. If allowed to spread, negative communication can create a stressful work environment and destroy relationships between coworkers.

Sometimes, there is little that an employee can do about other employees' negative communication. However, all employees have control over their own communications. Gossip and negative comments will quickly die if they are not repeated. Kitchen managers must determine the type of work environment desired and then set the standard, monitor, and be prepared to follow-up if employee behaviors fail to meet the standard.

Rumors involve information circulated without a source, and they frequently circulate throughout the grapevine. Several techniques can be used to manage rumors:

- First, question whether the rumor may be true. Ask yourself questions such as "Why am I being told," "Would the person telling me gain something by saying something untrue?" Does the person have access to information?" and "Can the information be confirmed?"
- Recognize that, if the rumor appears to be gossip, several tactics are useful. Ask the person why you are being told, inform the subject of the rumor about it, and finally, do not repeat the information.

Kitchen managers should plug into the grapevine and obtain as much information as possible. That which can be confirmed as truthful can be useful input to problems being resolved and decisions being made. That which is not correct may be countered by use of the tactics noted above.

COMMUNICATING WITH NEW EMPLOYEES

New employees present a communication challenge to kitchen managers who must communicate work requirements effectively while creating an atmosphere that encourages questions. Respect and courtesy coupled with straight-forward instructions can create a good training environment.

New employees notice negative communications. Unprofessional behaviors demonstrated in front of them send a message that these behaviors are acceptable. Unfortunately, some behaviors that are tolerated in more experienced staff may not be tolerated from a new employee.

BODY LANGUAGE

Kitchen managers communicate when they speak, write, and listen. They can also communicate through **body language**; that is, their actions can communicate information to the receiver. Common examples of body language include a smile (which implies a friendly gesture), a frown (negative response), or a wink (that can be a friendly hello). Consider also a nod of the head; it can mean agreement if moved up and down or disagreement if moved from side-to-side.

OVERHEARD IN THE KITCHEN

Body language—Nonverbal communication, including gestures and eye movements, that send information about a person's intentions to another person.

The amount of personal space between two people is another element of body language. How do you feel if a person stands just a few inches in front of you when speaking? By contrast, how do you feel about a person who is seated on a raised platform and is looking down at you?

Body language and similar actions are often subconscious and subtle ways that a person communicates with someone. Effective kitchen manager leaders know how to read body language and use it to better understand messages being communicated.

INFORMATION ON THE SIDE

Mixed Messages: Verbal and NonVerbal Communication

Nonverbal communication can have a negative effect on workgroups. Consider someone who makes a face or rolls her eyes while speaking to someone on the telephone. This sends a negative message about the other person to anyone watching and listening to the person speaking on the phone.

Nonverbal communications sometimes yield different messages than verbal ones. For example, a work group may complain that it does not have time to accomplish its required tasks and then abuse break periods. The old saying "talk the talk *and* walk the walk" is an appropriate one for professional communications.

Team Building

Every food service operation involves a team of individuals acting together to achieve property-wide goals. This large team is divided into smaller teams such as food production and food service. Kitchen managers play a significant role in developing workgroups in their departments, and they serve as the coach and facilitator for their food production team.

One benefit of a team is the varied skills of its members, each of whom brings different skills, abilities, and ideas to the decision-making process. The goal is to develop teams that use the strengths of its members to create a high quality system.

TACTICS TO BUILD EFFECTIVE TEAMS

Successful teams do not happen by chance alone. Kitchen managers must establish and maintain an environment in which their employees work together effectively as teams. They must identify and use each member's strengths, and this requires coordination to make the best use of each member's skills.

Kitchen managers who are effective team leaders share several traits that include:

- They have great interpersonal (people) skills.
- They allow team members to make decisions and, when appropriate, share responsibilities with team members who have the knowledge, skills, and experience necessary for the tasks at hand.
- They ask team members about work improvement strategies, productivity, and other issues that affect goals.
- They practice the art and science of supervision to maximize morale levels, to minimize unnecessary turnover, and to best use limited available resources.
- They encourage active participation in problem-solving and decision-making, and they encourage creative alternatives that can be considered for implementation.

Successful kitchen managers are driven by their property's mission statement, and they share it with their team. Then they lead the development of a more specific departmental mission statement driven by the mission of the entire food service operation. This process allows food production team members to know how they and their team contribute to the success of the overall operation.

MORE TEAM-BUILDING TACTICS

Effective kitchen managers set expectations and monitor performance as work evolves. They also ask team members for ideas about how to achieve preestablished goals. By involving the team, tactics to address departmental challenges are better accepted by the team, and team members have a significant interest in their success. They also ensure their staff members are competent by providing access to training and professional development opportunities that help team members become successful.

The best kitchen managers empower their team members by giving them authority to make decisions within their areas of responsibility. This helps give the team a sense of ownership for the decisions they make in performing their jobs. They also know how to manage information to best serve their teams and provide the necessary information to help their teams plan and monitor progress toward goals. Good kitchen managers encourage team members to offer diverse opinions and ideas, and they encourage communication, networking, and feedback which, in turn, become input for additional team discussions. They also reward their teams when new methods are successfully implemented.

Kitchen managers who build successful teams encourage team members to be service-minded. First, they serve as role models by exhibiting attitudes, words, and actions that emphasize guest service. Second, they make service training available to all staff members. Third, they reward team members who provide the levels of service envisioned in the property's and department's mission statements by positive reinforcement on the job and favorable input during performance appraisals.

Coaching

Experienced kitchen managers understand that the training process discussed in Chapter Two never ends. If after-training assessment reveals that the training was successful, it is important to reinforce the desired on-job performance resulting from training. By contrast, if assessment suggests that training was not successful, additional training may then be required until on-job performance is acceptable, and then ongoing reinforcement of that performance is in order. This reinforcement is called **coaching**. As you've learned, coaching involves positive reinforcement used by a manager or supervisor that encourages staff members to follow proper work practices. It can also involve negative reinforcement: efforts that discourage staff from using improper work practices.

OVERHEARD IN THE KITCHEN

Coaching—Efforts made by kitchen managers to encourage proper job behavior

---

Coaching is not a formal activity. It typically involves informal conversations with staff members at the worksite. Positive reinforcement occurs when a kitchen manager "catches a staff member doing something right." For example: "Joe, I recognize that these new inventory reports can be difficult to accurately complete, and yet you never make a mistake! Thanks for your good work; we really appreciate it." Conversely, the coaching conversation with Joe could also go as follows: "Joe, it's pretty difficult to do these inventory reports, I know, and you're about 95% there in terms of fully knowing how to complete them. There's just one step that I'd like to talk to you about." After the step is discussed and/or demonstrated, the kitchen manager can conclude the coaching discussion with a "Thanks a lot, Joe; we appreciate your hard work. With a little effort, this one step shouldn't cause any future problems."

Coaching addresses a concern that we all have for wanting to know "how the boss views our work" on an ongoing and timely basis. Staff members really appreciate this input, and, since it costs no money and takes so little time, it should be a "must" tactic practiced by all kitchen managers.

Several principles can help assure that a coaching activity is effective:

- *Be tactful*—If corrective actions are required, focus on the employee's member's behavior—not on the staff member himself/herself. Which statement is best: "Joe, this is really an easy task; anybody can do it, and I don't know why you can't," and "Joe, sometimes its tough to do this one step correctly, but it's necessary, and I'd like to show you how to do it."
- *Emphasize positive actions*—Kitchen managers who interact with well-trained staff members will have many more opportunities to provide positive reinforcement than negative coaching conversations.

- *Demonstrate and review appropriate procedures*—More time should be spent in coaching activities showing the correct way to do something than in discussions complaining about incorrect performance.
- *Explain reasons for changes*—When possible, explain, defend and justify reasons for changes from the perspectives of the staff. For example: "Joe, we have simplified the way that this procedure is done. There should be fewer errors, and that should mean less stress and anxiety for you."
- *Maintain open communications with staff members*—An organizational culture that supports ongoing dialog, including coaching conversations, will reduce the possibility of concerns, such as "What does the boss want to talk to me about now?" that can otherwise occur.
- *Provide professional development opportunities*—Kitchen managers can reinforce desired on-job performance with a suggestion that continued acceptable performance can lead to additional training and professional development opportunities. These, in turn, can lead to promotional considerations and, therefore, very measurable awards for appropriate behavior.
- *Allow interested staff members to contribute to their work*—This occurs, for example, as staff member input is solicited when work procedures are evaluated, revised, and implemented and when they are asked about suggestions to address operating challenges.
- *Conduct negative corrective action interviews in private*—Praise staff members for proper performance in public and conduct conversations to improve performance in private.
- *Evaluate the work of individual staff by comparing their performance against requirements of the standards noted in task lists and task breakdowns*—The definition of performance should relate to how it compares to tasks identified in these position analysis tools rather than to how staff members work in comparison to others. Positive reinforcement should not be directed only to the "best" staff members; instead, it should address all staff members who correctly perform a task. Kitchen managers act as coaches when they focus on procedures taught during training and compare them to those used by trainees on the job.
- *Establish and agree upon time frames for corrective action*—If performance is not acceptable, the kitchen manager and staff member should agree upon what must be done to improve performance. A time schedule for acceptable performance or, at least, for an additional review of performance can then be determined.
- *Ask staff members how their work performance can be improved*—Providing them with task breakdowns and asking for improvement suggestions can be a useful tactic.

The philosophy noted in this coaching discussion is relevant here: Think about how you would like to be treated in your interactions with your own boss. As you do so, you'll likely identify tactics that your staff members would like you to use in interactions with them. Effective coaching is likely to be high on this list.

Conflict Management

Managing conflict is a challenge. Even the most enviable and quality-focused food service operation will likely experience conflict, and kitchen managers must know how to manage it. They recognize that their success is built on teamwork and effective problem-solving, and they know that the ability to rise above conflicts makes their department stronger.

Some conflicts such as differences in personal opinions may be small, while others may be significant and involve many people throughout the food service operation. In both cases, the use of conflict management skills can keep the staff focused and working toward common goals. Many conflicts can be avoided by improving communication or eliminating a specific obstacle, but there are times when conflict can be beneficial or necessary. For example, the budget process is purposefully competitive because department leaders make requests for the same limited funds. This competition is a form of conflict, but it ensures that the necessary resources are provided to the areas most in need, and this is in the property's best interests.

TYPES AND ORIGINS OF CONFLICT

There are several common types of conflict, including

- Conflict within a person that occurs when staff members experience conflicting feelings about their actions or goals.

Training never ends because the kitchen manager must coach employees to assure that quality standards are always attained.

- Conflict between employees that can result from personality conflicts or sincere differences in opinions about work methods or practices.
- Conflict between an individual and a group that can arise, for instance, when someone disagrees with policy changes recommended by a committee.
- Conflict between formal groups such as committees with different ideas about attaining goals or informal groups such as staff members disagreeing about how budgeted funds are being spent.

To manage conflict effectively, it is important to understand how they begin. Some conflicts can be caused by relationships between kitchen managers and **line-level employees**, others arise because of how to spend limited funds, and other conflicts involve differences of opinion about goals or how to attain them.

OVERHEARD IN THE KITCHEN

Line-level employees—Staff members whose jobs are considered entry-level or nonsupervisory and who are paid an hourly rate rather than a salary.

Food service operations have different **cultures** defined by team's unique goals and attitudes, and groups with different values have a potential for conflict.

OVERHEARD IN THE KITCHEN

Culture (food service operation)—The beliefs, values, and norms shared by persons in the food service operation that are considered valid and are passed on to new employees as they work within the operation.

CONFLICT MANAGEMENT TACTICS

Successful kitchen managers address conflicts in ways ranging from being cooperative to assertive. They can state their opinions clearly and positively without being aggressive and focus on cooperation to yield positive relationships and sustainable solutions. They can discuss honest feedback with those involved in a conflict, and they accept honest criticism and differing opinions without anger or reprisal. Those who manage conflict effectively maintain a degree of impartiality so that employees feel safe in voicing their feedback even when it involves the kitchen manager's style or decisions.

There are times when it may be best to increase, reduce, or resolve conflicts. Increasing conflict can encourage staff to use their creativity and critical thinking skills. For example, a team can be challenged to discuss ways to exceed an established quality performance measure. However, kitchen managers usually want to reduce conflict levels even if doing so does not always resolve its root cause.

Conflict can be reduced by redefining goals to increase agreements between two conflicting groups or individuals. Groups of persons can also be brought together by identifying a common external threat such as decreasing guest satisfaction levels. Conflict can also be resolved by compromise: Conflicting groups work together to identify an acceptable solution, or they appeal to a higher level of authority to resolve the matter.

Kitchen managers must remain objective and calm when they manage stressful situations. The goal of conflict management is to find the best possible resolution for the situation rather than to target or criticize individuals. Remain focused on the issue rather than on the employees involved and anticipate possible reactions to your own behavior. The reason: If someone feels directly attacked, threatened, or humiliated, the situation is likely to escalate.

LEADING DIFFICULT EMPLOYEES

There are several types of employees who may be difficult to manage:

- Some are openly abusive or hostile. When interacting with them, it is helpful to defend your position by remaining calm and restating your idea or position in a slightly different way. Remain friendly and avoid being aggressive. Maintain eye contact and, if appropriate, allow the employee a few minutes to calm down or sit together so the employee does not feel inferior.
- Some employees "know-it-all." They may be very competent but are overly self-assured and do not want to consider comments or alternatives suggested by team members. When speaking to an employee like this, do so firmly without engaging in a direct confrontation. Listen carefully to the employee's position, acknowledge what has been said, and be prepared with facts and supporting evidence, if needed.
- Other employees constantly complain and find fault with everything and everyone. Remain objective with them and do not discuss your personal feelings about other staff members. Listen carefully to specific concerns but try to limit these conversations to specific times, locations, and facts. Also, encourage these staff members to become actively engaged in the problem-solving process.
- Some employees are consistently negative. Do not be drawn in by negative attitudes when interacting with them. Instead, express constant and realistic optimism. Engage these staff members by analyzing the worst-case scenario and focus on using the information constructively: "How can we turn this into a positive outcome?"
- "Super-agreeable" employees do not express honest opinions. Remain nonthreatening when meeting with these employees, reassure them that you want honest feedback, and demonstrate approval of their performance. If they volunteer for a project or work task, assure that their commitments are realistic.
- Still other employees defer all major decisions. They are similar to their "super-agreeable" peers, but they are unable to make a decision because of a concern that they will disappoint others rather than because they cannot say no. Identify why these employees want to postpone a decision and help them to prioritize what needs to be done.

Workplace Ethics

Professional kitchen managers follow a code of behavior that includes ethical aspects of responsibility. **Ethics**, a concern relating to what is right and wrong, is an ever-present issue in the hospitality and all other industries today. There is a belief, for example, that it is no longer just a few "unethical" businesspersons who abuse the system, but, instead, there are many leaders who lack social responsibility and behave unethically.

OVERHEARD IN THE KITCHEN

Ethics—Concerns relating to what is right and wrong when dealing with others.

Ethical conduct is required of kitchen managers at all times. However, the difference between what is "right" and what is "wrong" can be viewed from different perspectives. Consider the following:

- A kitchen manager knows that a "favorite" employee regularly "beats the system" by arriving late and leaving early, or another employee spends lots of time in unproductive work while "on the clock." This situation represents a case where there is a loser (the food service operation) but the situations are ignored.
- Another kitchen manager consistently emphasizes the need for "quality, quality, and more quality." At the same time, many decisions place a higher priority on cost than on quality. There are inconsistent words and actions; in effect the kitchen manager is saying, "Do what I say—not what I do!" Are inconsistent words and actions of a role model (the kitchen manager) acceptable? Do they (or can they) impact the attitudes and behavior of the food production employees who do not know their boss's definition of "what is right?"

How does one decide if a proposed action is ethical? Answers to the following questions may be helpful:

- Is the proposed action legal?
- Does the proposed action hurt anyone?
- Is the proposed action fair?
- Am I being honest as I undertake the proposed action?
- Can I live with myself if I do what I am considering?
- Would I like to publicize my decision?
- What if everyone did it?

A **code of ethics** identifies how employees of a food service operation should interact with and relate to each other, and the groups with whom they interact. Today, being "ethical" might give some food service operations a competitive edge over counterparts whose actions are sometimes less than ethical. However, less-than-consistently ethical organizations will not survive. Therefore, Codes of Ethics and the conduct that they mandate in the future will be a prerequisite for success within the hospitality industry—not a factor that better assures it.

OVERHEARD IN THE KITCHEN

Code of ethics—A formal statement developed by a food service operation that defines how its employees should relate to each other and the persons and groups with whom they interact.

■ NOW IT'S YOUR TURN

A PINCH OF THE INTERNET (3.2)

1. To learn about a wide range of professional development resources that can be used to learn about supervision principles, check out the National Restaurant Association (www.restaurant.org). When you reach the site, type "supervision resources" into the search box
2. The internet is a great source of information about many of the concepts explored in this chapter relating to supervisory skills. For example, type the following phrases into your favorite search engine:
   - Motivating entry level employees
   - Building employee work teams
   - Coaching entry level employees
   - How to reduce workplace conflict
   - Ethics in the hospitality industry
3. Effective kitchen managers must be effective supervisors. Type "principles of effective employee supervision" into your favorite search engine to see (seemingly) innumerable sources of information about this topic.

COMPLETING THE PLATE QUESTIONS (3.2)

1. What type of leadership style do you think would be of ideal use when managing the work of a newly employed young person? An experienced older employee? Defend your responses.
2. What tactic might you as a kitchen manager use with an employee who does not want to be part of your food production team?
3. What factors would you consider when deciding whether a coaching or discipline tactic would be best to correct an inappropriate action of an employee?

4. What are some tactics you would use if you were a kitchen manager in a food service operation where food production personnel "never" got along with service employees?

5. What are two examples of things that a kitchen manager might do that you would consider to be unethical?

Kitchen Challenge Du Jour Case Study (3.2)

"I just returned from our local restaurant association meeting, and I attended a very interesting session that dealt with how to manage people," said Kamuela. He was talking to Elizabeth, the general manager of Vernon's Restaurant.

"As you know, I've been working in food service operations since I graduated from my culinary program about seven years ago, and I really enjoy my work as a kitchen manager since I was promoted a couple of years ago."

"I know that," interrupted Elizabeth, "and you're turning out to be a great manager for us."

"The session focused on an area that we've talked about before where I might do a better job," Kamuela continued. "It had to do with different leadership styles and how different approaches to managing people might be best for different employees."

"You know, Elizabeth, I was trained by a person who basically said, 'I'm the boss, there's only one way to do things around here, and that's my way.' I've certainly experienced that kind of leadership more than I have any other style. However, at the meeting, a panel of restaurant managers, kitchen managers, and an industry consultant made the point that other approaches could be useful. They also pointed out that, with just a little effort, managers who typically use one approach could vary their behavior during interactions with the wide range of kitchen employees that most food service operations employ."

"Well, Kamuela," said Elizabeth, "What you learned at the restaurant association meeting was good information, and I think some of your employees would like to see you use a different approach. What can I do to help?"

a) This chapter and this case study noted that different leadership styles should be used when facilitating the work of different employees. What do you think about this idea?

b) Assume that you thought you could modify your leadership approach based upon your employees. How would you decide the best leadership tactic to use with each staff member?

c) Some persons believe it is possible to use different leadership tactics at different times. However, they also think that, when there is a serious problem or one that involves emotions, the manager's "natural" leadership style may emerge, and this approach may be more emotional. What could Kamuela do to best assure that he will remain even-tempered and continue to use the "best" leadership style based upon the situation?

MANAGE LABOR COSTS

OBJECTIVE

3. Implement basic principles to manage labor costs:
   • Labor control and quality standards
   • Five-steps to controlling labor costs

Controlling labor costs is an important part of every kitchen manager's job. Some in-experienced managers may think that the best way to control labor costs is merely to create schedules with fewer labor hours. However, professional kitchen managers know that their guests are best served when the right number of well-trained employees is matched with the business volume measured by the number of guests served and/or the **revenue** collected.

OVERHEARD IN THE KITCHEN

Revenue—The amount of money generated from the sale of food and beverage products.

Labor Control and Quality Standards

Kitchen managers supervise staff members responsible for food storage, preparation, production, and clean-up, and they must always provide the proper quality of menu items to their guests. Successful kitchen managers recruit and retain an adequate number of well-trained staff members who must then be scheduled to meet the needs of the volume of business that is expected. When too few employees are available, the food service operation's quality standards will likely suffer. In contrast, too many employees scheduled to work at the same time will create unnecessary labor costs.

The best labor cost control systems ensure that guests are well-served and the operation's financial goals are met. The quality and number of staff required vary based on several factors.

THE MENU

Perhaps the most important factor in controlling labor costs is the menu. There can be just a few or many menu items that are simple or time-consuming to produce. Kitchen managers must provide their guests with the menu variety necessary to ensure the restaurant's popularity and success. At the same time, they must schedule employees who can adequately prepare and serve that menu variety while meeting quality standards.

FOOD PREPARATION METHODS

Few food service operations prepare all menu items from "**scratch**." Some **convenience foods** are commonly purchased in efforts to reduce labor costs more than the increased costs of the convenience food items. Kitchen managers must select convenience foods based on their quality and their labor-saving ability. The decision to "buy convenience" or "make from scratch" can only be properly made after considering two major factors: product quality and labor savings. A manager who buys inferior products to save labor costs will quickly learn that guests will not accept poor quality foods. Spending less for products that are not acceptable to guests does not make business sense nor does it save money.

OVERHEARD IN THE KITCHEN

"Scratch" (food products)—An industry term for foods made with raw ingredients on-site.
Convenience food—Food that has some labor built-in that otherwise would need to be added on-site. Examples include presliced meats, frozen vegetables, and baked desserts.

QUALITY OF TRAINING

Training improves the knowledge and skills of employees and, when done correctly, will result in increased productivity and lower labor costs. New employees must be well-trained to perform required job tasks. As they become more productive, they can work more cost-effectively. Training benefits the food service operation, its guests, and its employees. Food service operations that provide good training programs generally have lower labor costs than others that do not have effective training.

Five-Steps to Controlling Labor Costs

Kitchen managers should use a formal process to determine the number of labor hours needed during specific shifts to ensure proper food production for the expected business volume. This process has five basic steps and is shown in Figure 3.1.

Kitchen managers must know what their labor costs should be, and the approved **operating budget** tells them this (Step 1). Next, they forecast the number of guests and/or revenues for each day in the schedule period (Step 2) and plan the number of labor hours to be used (in Step 3). Employee schedules are then developed (Step 4) and, finally, budget information is used to evaluate the labor control results. You will learn about each of these five steps in the remaining part of this chapter.

OVERHEARD IN THE KITCHEN

Budget (Operating)—A plan that estimates revenues and expenses for a specific period of time.

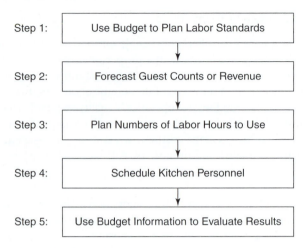

FIGURE 3.1 Five Steps to Controlling Labor Costs

STEP 1: USE BUDGET TO PLAN LABOR STANDARDS

Most kitchen managers use operating budgets for two purposes. First, budgets help them estimate their revenues and **expenses** for the next year. Second, they measure actual results against the budget **standards** to learn how well their plans worked out. Since labor cost is a large expense, kitchen managers pay very special attention to what it should be (estimated in the budget) and what it is as indicated in the **income statement**.

OVERHEARD IN THE KITCHEN

Expenses—Costs incurred by a food service operation to generate its revenues.

Standard—Something that can be used to compare one thing against another. For example: A labor cost standard indicates how many labor dollars or hours should be used. The actual number of labor dollars or hours spent can be compared to this standard to determine how well labor was controlled.

Income statement—A summary of how much profit, if any, the food service operation earned. It shows the revenues, expenses, and profits during a specific time period such as month or year; also called "profit and loss" ("P&L") statement.

Budgeted labor cost goals cannot be met unless they are used when employee schedules are developed. Therefore, the approved operating budget serves as a roadmap to help kitchen managers spend no more than the budget limits for labor costs.

Let's assume that Francine is the kitchen manager of Vernon's Restaurant. She has a monthly budget of $25,000.00 for waged employees (those paid by the hour) excluding benefits in February, 20xx. The food service operation is open only for dinner six days each week, and the employee schedule is planned on a weekly basis:

6	×	4	=	24
Days per week		Weeks in February		Days kitchen employees needed

The above calculation indicates that kitchen employees are needed 24 days in February. Francine can now determine how much can be spent on wages on an average day:

$25,000	÷	24	=	$1,042 (rounded)
Wage budget for February		work days in February		Average daily allowable wages

If the *average* hourly wage (not including benefits) is $16.00, Francine can schedule no more than 65 labor hours in the kitchen (food production and dishwashing employees) for an average day in February:

$1,042.00	÷	$16.00	=	65.00 (rounded)
Average daily wages		Average hourly rate		Average allowable waged labor hours per day

Her labor budget also suggests that no more than 390 waged hours can be worked in an average week:

65	$\times$	6	$=$	390
average allowable waged hours per day		days in week		average available waged hours per week

Note: the concept of "average" in the above calculations means more labor hours can be scheduled on high business volume days, and these will be off-set with fewer labor hours scheduled on lower business volume days to meet the average labor hours per day goal. Remember that Francine is only scheduling employees who receive wages (salaried employee labor costs are in a separate labor expense account). Also, employee benefits expenses are not included because they are also carried in other accounts.

We'll come back to Francine and Vernon's Restaurant later in this section to see her schedule and to learn if the labor standards in her budget were met.

STEP 2: FORECAST GUEST COUNTS OR REVENUE

Now that Francine knows how many labor hours can be used each day for waged kitchen employees, she can begin to work on the schedule. Her first task is to think about the **guest count** or how much guests will spend during the week. To do this, she must **forecast** that information for each day in the week.

OVERHEARD IN THE KITCHEN

Guest count—The number of guests to be served during a specific time period.

Forecast (labor cost control)—An estimate of the number of guests to be served or the amount of revenue to be generated for a specific meal period or day.

Learning to make accurate forecasts is an important management skill. Unfortunately, you cannot know exactly how many guests will be served each day next week and when they arrive. If you did, you could have the right number of employees available at the right times to produce meals meeting the operation's quality standards for your guests. You can, however, realistically predict the future. Forecasting is done by thinking about the past, present, and future.

What has happened in the past can be a good indicator of what is likely to happen in the future. The further back you track historical guest counts or revenues, the more information you will have to compare with your forecasted trends.

Modern **point-of-sale (POS)** systems make this easy and quick to do. Some kitchen managers use the following information to forecast guest counts and revenue levels:

- Yesterday's guest count and revenue
- Average guest count or revenue for the prior four *same* days (for example, last four Tuesdays)
- Last week's average daily guest count and revenue
- Last two weeks' average daily guest count and revenue
- Last month's average daily guest count and revenue

OVERHEARD IN THE KITCHEN

Point-of-Sale (POS)—An electronic system that collects information about revenues and guest counts, among numerous other data.

Historical information should always be considered in terms of recent events. Assume that a kitchen manager knows that revenues have normally increased 5% each month from the same period last year. However, during the last two months, there has been no revenue increase. This may mean that the trend in increased revenue has slowed or stopped, and the kitchen manager will consider this when the forecast is developed.

Evaluating future conditions also helps to estimate guest counts and revenue from future events. The opening of new restaurants, sporting events and concerts or holidays may cause changes in business volumes.

After all necessary information has been considered, Francine can estimate the guest counts and revenue for each day in the schedule period. Then she can plan the labor hours needed for her employee schedule.

STEP 3: PLAN NUMBER OF LABOR HOURS TO USE

Employee schedules can be developed by thinking about the number of labor hours that will be needed to produce meals for the estimated number of guests. However, a minimum number of labor hours are needed to operate the kitchen, and then additional hours are required as the guest count increases.

Francine's kitchen is open from 1:00 p.m. to do preparation work for the evening meal that begins at 5:00 p.m. Guests are served from 5:00 p.m.–10:30 p.m., and it takes until about midnight to clean-up after the kitchen closes. This means that *at least* 11 cook hours will be needed (1:00 p.m.–midnight), and a dishwasher will be needed for, perhaps, *at least* 6.5 hours (5:00 p.m.–11:30 p.m.). Persons in other back-of-house positions may also be needed to open the kitchen as well. It is only after a minimum number of guests are served that additional labor hours are needed and, hopefully, this is every evening!

Recall that Francine learned (Step 1 above) that she can, *on average*, schedule 65 hours for waged employees each day. Based on her experience, more hours will be scheduled for busy days, and fewer hours will be needed for low-volume days. However, only 390 hours (65 hours per day [x] 6 days per week) can be scheduled for the week to remain in line with the month's budgeted labor costs for waged kitchen employees.

INFORMATION ON THE SIDE

What If More Labor Hours Are Needed?

It is easy to do arithmetic and learn the number of labor hours that can be used to meet labor cost goals. It is another thing, however to have enough labor hours available when they are needed.

This concern is best considered when the budget is developed. For example, if kitchen managers forecast a large volume of guests or revenues, the budget goals for labor costs will be higher because they are driven by guest counts or revenue. Therefore, the challenge of how to produce the food with fewer labor hours than needed should be minimized when the forecast is accurate, and the budget is correctly developed.

What happens if the budget estimate is wrong? The answer should be that more labor hours will be needed, and labor costs will be higher than budget goals. Kitchen managers should remember that their operating plans are based on imperfect forecasts. If the estimates are not correct, quality standards should not be reduced to save labor hours or labor dollars. In these cases, kitchen managers and other budget planners must learn from their errors and try to develop more accurate budget estimates. They must also understand that, while labor dollars are higher because of greater production volume, the revenues will also be higher than expected. In for-profit operations, kitchen managers realize that the goal is not to maximize revenue or to minimize labor costs. Instead, the goal is to generate planned profits by consistently meeting quality standards.

STEP 4: SCHEDULE KITCHEN PERSONNEL

Kitchen managers know that their scheduling skills impact:

- the quality of products provided to guests
- the employees' level of job satisfaction
- the food service operation's profitability
- the view of the manager's own boss about the kitchen manager's ability to manage effectively.

Many kitchen managers use software tools to create employee schedules. They can pre-load employee data such as requested days off, pre-arranged vacations, maximum allowable hours to be worked, restrictions on when those hours can be worked (for minors), employee time preferences, and other factors. Effective employee schedules for waged staff members should clearly indicate:

- the dates covered by the schedule
- the day of the week covered by the schedule
- employee first and last names
- scheduled days to work

- scheduled days off
- scheduled start and stop times (indicate AM/ PM)
- total hours to be worked (excluding scheduled meal periods)
- requested vacation or personal days off
- date the schedule was prepared and who prepared it

Figure 3.2 shows a spreadsheet detailing the employee work schedule that Francine has created for the week of February 2–7. Note: All employees at her operation receive a one-half hour unpaid break that is built into their scheduled hours. Note also that Francine's own working times are not listed on the schedule because she is paid a salary rather than a wage, and her actual working hours depend upon when she is needed.

The employee schedule shown in Figure 3.2 shows the days that the employees will work and their shifts' start and end times. You'll see that column 9 indicates the total hours that each employee will work each week. Also, note that the total at the bottom of the column is 390 hours: the maximum number of hours that Francine can schedule. Column 10 will be used to report the number of hours each employee actually worked during the week, and that information will be discussed below.

INFORMATION ON THE SIDE
Scheduling Principles

Kitchen managers should use basic principles when they develop the employee schedule. These include:

- Develop a productivity target and schedule to meet it. In this chapter's example, Francine knows the maximum number of waged labor hours that can be scheduled for the week.
- Schedule for the needs of guests first and employees second. Many employees have strong feelings about when they want to work and for how long. Kitchen managers should ensure that employees are available when needed and not just when they prefer to work. .
- Don't schedule overtime whenever possible. **Overtime** pay is expensive, and it is a large portion of payroll costs in some operations. Some overtime may be unavoidable when scheduled employees are absent from work, and other staff on duty must work additional hours. Also, overtime pay may be reasonable when revenue volume levels unexpectedly increase. However, an employee schedule should not be developed with "built-in" overtime. If it does, the kitchen manager has failed to develop an effective staff with enough flexibility to address normal differences in business volumes.
- Use part-time employees for peak volume periods. In many operations, increases in business occur during traditional meal periods. For example, 6:00 a.m.–9:00 a.m. may be busy for a restaurant serving breakfast, and additional labor hours may be needed then to produce and serve the guests. Part-time employees can provide scheduling flexibility; however, remember that the total number of hours worked is important for employees who want to meet their personal financial goals.
- Minimize split-shifts. Some kitchen managers use **"split-shift"** employees to work a certain number of hours, leave the work site, and then return later the same day for a second shift. However, most employees do not like this arrangement and, in the long term, its negative impact on employee morale may offset any savings.
- Grant employee schedule requests whenever possible. Kitchen managers must balance the personal needs of employees with the operation's labor needs. Employees should be encouraged to request vacation time and preferred days off for personal time.
- Be fair when scheduling preferred time work periods. Many food service operations have work shifts which are less desirable than others. Kitchen managers should ensure that the most and least desirable work shifts are assigned in a fair and equitable manner.
- Comply with applicable laws and policies. For example, the Fair Labor Standards Act (FLSA) identifies restrictions on workers under the age of 18. All individuals under this age must obtain a work permit unless they have graduated from High School or have obtained a General Education Development (GED) diploma. Only one work permit may be issued at a time, and it can be denied or revoked if the minor does not remain in good standing at school. Minors are generally restricted in the number of hours they can work and when they can work. These and all other laws must always be followed.
- Complete and communicate scheduling decisions in a timely manner. Employees need time away from the job for many reasons, and they depend on their work schedules to provide this.

Vernon's Restaurant
From: 2-Feb through 7-Feb

Area/Employee	Monday 2/2	Tuesday 10/2	Wednesday 10/3	Thursday 10/4	Friday 10/5	Saturday 10/6	Sunday 10/7	Total Labor Hours Scheduled	Total Labor Hours Actual
(1)	(2)	(3)	(4)	(5)	(6)	(7)	(8)	(9)	(10)
Kitchen									
Kimo	1:00p–9:30p	OFF	1:00a–9:30p	1:00a–9:30p	1:00a–9:30p	1:00a–9:30p	OFF	40.0	
Janet F.	5:30p–12:00a	5:30p–12:00a	5:30p–12:00a	OFF	5:30p–12:00a	2:00p–8:00p	OFF	29.5	
Sarah H.	OFF	1:00p–7:30p	1:00p–7:30p	1:00p–7:30p	1:00p–7:30p	4:00p–11:00p	OFF	30.5	
Bill C.	5:30p–12:00a	OFF	5:30p–12:00a	5:30p–12:00a	5:30p–12:00a	5:30p–11:30p	OFF	29.5	
Mike C	4:00p–10:30p	4:00p–10:30p	OFF	3:00p–10:30p	3:00p–10:30p	4:00p–9:00p	OFF	30.5	
Talisha C	2:00p–9:30p	2:00p–9:30p	2:00p–9:30p	2:00p–9:30p	OFF	OFF	OFF	28	
Kylie M	OFF	1:00p–8:30p	1:00p–8:30p	1:00p–8:30p	1:00p–8:30p	1:00p–8:30p	OFF	35	
Morris	1:00p–9:30p	1:00p–9:30p	OFF	1:00p–9:30p	1:00p–9:30p	1:00p–9:30p	OFF	40.0	
Dishroom									
Lorenzo T	OFF	5:00a–11:00p	5:00a–11:00p	5:00a–11:00p	5:00a–11:00p	5:00a–11:00p	OFF	27.5	
Ron C	6:00p–12:00a	OFF	6:00p–12:00a	6:00p–12:00a	6:00p–12:00a	6:00p–12:00a	OFF	27.5	
Arthur A	4:00p–11:30p	4:00p–11:30p	4:00p–11:30p	OFF	4:00p–11:30p	4:00p–11:30p	OFF	35	
Shanna A	OFF	1:00p–5:00p	4:30p–9:00p	1:00p–11:00p	VACATION	VACATION	OFF	17	
Shane F	6:00p–11:30p	5:30p–11:30p	OFF	5:30p–11:00p	6:30p–11:30p	OFF	OFF	20	

Prepared: 1/26   **Approved by: JN Harrison 1/27**   **Total Hours: 390**

FIGURE 3.2 Sample Employee Schedule Worksheet

OVERHEARD IN THE KITCHEN

Overtime (legal)—The number of hours of work after which an employee must receive a premium pay rate (usually 1.5 times the basic hourly rate).

Split-shift—A work schedule in which an employee works a certain number of hours during a shift, leaves the work site, and then returns later in the same day for a second work shift.

Sometimes, as a result of unexpected business volume, unforeseen employee absences, and/or employee separations, schedule changes are needed. If so, affected employees should be quickly informed about the changes. In many operations, employees who begin work on schedule and who are sent home early or are not needed at all are paid a minimum amount regardless of the time actually worked. Know your company's policies before making schedule adjustments and communicate schedule adjustments and modifications appropriately.

In many operations, schedules are posted in one or more central areas, and they are sometimes included with paychecks. Increasingly, managers e-mail schedules or make them available on the restaurant's intranet system.

Kitchen managers should monitor schedules carefully and adjust them when there are:

- Significant changes in business volumes
- Unexpected employee **separations**
- Employee **call-ins** or **no-shows**
- Changes in operating hours or work assignments

OVERHEARD IN THE KITCHEN

Separation—The term for employees who leave the operation for voluntary or involuntary reasons.

Call-In—The term for employees who, when they are scheduled to work, notify managers that they will not work.

No-Show—The term for employees who, when they are scheduled to work, do not notify managers that they will not work and do not report for their assigned shift.

After kitchen managers have developed, distributed and implemented the employee schedule, they can evaluate the results. In this chapter, you are learning how labor costs for waged employees can be managed by using the labor cost standard estimated in the approved budget.

STEP 5: USE BUDGET INFORMATION TO EVALUATE RESULTS

When the labor cost goal is to meet budget requirements, the actual number of paid labor hours should be compared with the scheduled labor hours because they (the scheduled hours) are based on the budget. If the budget goal is not met, the amount by which actual performance differs from the goal is called a **variance**.

OVERHEARD IN THE KITCHEN

Variance (budget)—The difference between an amount of revenue or expense indicated in the budget and the actual amount of the revenue or expense.

Figure 3.3 shows Francine's employee schedule worksheet originally presented in Figure 3.2. It is the same as the earlier worksheet except that she completed column 10 after the week ended. It indicates the actual hours worked for each waged employee.

When you review Figure 3.3, notice that the scheduled (Column 9) and actual (Column 10) number of hours worked by each employee in the kitchen and dish room are recorded.

It also shows (bottom of Columns 9 and 10) that, while 390 labor hours were scheduled, 426.5 hours were actually worked. This created a variance of 36.5 hours (426.5 actual hours − 390 scheduled hours = 36.5 hours variance).

Is this variation significant? Let's do a quick calculation remembering that the average hourly wage for each staff member scheduled was $16.00 (without benefits).

Vernon's Restaurant
From: 2-Feb through 7-Feb

Area/Employee	Monday 2/2	Tuesday 10/2	Wednesday 10/3	Thursday 10/4	Friday 10/5	Saturday 10/6	Sunday 10/7	Total Labor Hours Scheduled	Actual
(1)	(2)	(3)	(4)	(5)	(6)	(7)	(8)	(9)	(10)
Kitchen									
Kimo	1:00p-9:30p	OFF	1:00a-9:30p	1:00a-9:30p	1:00a-9:30p	1:00a-9:30p	OFF	40.0	**42.0**
Janet F.	5:30p-12:00a	5:30p-12:00a	5:30p-12:00a	OFF	5:30p-12:00a	2:00p-8:00p	OFF	29.5	**29.5**
Sarah H.	OFF	1:00p-7:30p	1:00p-7:30p	1:00p-7:30p	1:00p-7:30p	4:00p-11:00p	OFF	30.5	**33.0**
Bill C.	5:30p-12:00a	OFF	5:30p-12:00a	5:30p-12:00a	5:30p-12:00a	5:30p-11:30p	OFF	29.5	**32.0**
Mike C	4:00p-10:30p	4:00p-10:30p	OFF	3:00p-10:30p	3:00p-10:30p	4:00p-9:00p	OFF	30.5	**30.5**
Talisha C	2:00p-9:30p	2:00p-9:30p	2:00p-9:30p	2:00p-9:30p	OFF	OFF	OFF	28	**28.0**
Kylie M	OFF	1:00p-8:30p	1:00p-8:30p	1:00p-8:30p	1:00p-8:30p	1:00p-8:30p	OFF	35	**37.0**
Morris	1:00p-9:30p	1:00p-9:30p	OFF	1:00p-9:30p	1:00p-9:30p	1:00p-9:30p	OFF	40.0	**43.0**
Dishroom									
Lorenzo T	OFF	5:00a-11:00p	5:00a-11:00p	5:00a-11:00p	5:00a-11:00p	5:00a-11:00p	OFF	27.5	**39.0**
Ron C	6:00p-12:00a	OFF	6:00p-12:00a	6:00p-12:00a	6:00p-12:00a	6:00p-12:00a	OFF	27.5	**34.5**
Arthur A	4:00p-11:30p	4:00p-11:30p	4:00p-11:30p	OFF	4:00p-11:30p	4:00p-11:30p	OFF	35	**39.0**
Shanna A	OFF	1:00p-5:00p	4:30p-9:00p	1:00p-11:00p	VACATION	VACATION	OFF	17	**19.0**
Shane F	6:00p-11:30p	5:30p-11:30p	OFF	5:30p-11:00p	6:30p-11:30p	OFF	OFF	20	**20.0**
								390	**426.5**

Prepared: 1/26   Approved by: JN Harrison 1/27   Total Hours: 390

FIGURE 3.3 Sample Employee Schedule Worksheet Showing Actual Hours Worked

Kitchen Managers Plan Their Menus

Chapter Ingredients Outline

Learning Objectives

After studying this chapter, you will be able to:

1. Explain why menus are important to the food service operation.
2. Indicate that different viewpoints must be considered when menus are planned.
3. Review basic menu planning strategies.
4. Describe important pricing concerns that should be considered when menus are planned.

COMING RIGHT UP OVERVIEW

Kitchen managers should serve on their food service operation's menu planning team, and this activity is one of their most important responsibilities. There's an old saying in the food service industry that is very true: "It all starts with the menu," and this chapter defends this idea and explains basic strategies to plan menus.

First, you'll learn why menus are important: They serve as links between the guests being served and what the kitchen manager and his/her production team must do to please them. The more the menu planning team knows about the guests, the better they can make their menu. Therefore, we'll discuss some of the guest-related factors that should be identified and considered as menus are planned.

Menus also impact financial success. Food service operations of all types have financial concerns that range from making a profit (commercial properties) to minimizing expenses (noncommercial operations), and financial control begins with the menu.

Finally, almost every aspect of the food service operation is impacted by the menu that is planned. Production personnel, equipment, layout and design, space, storage, and numerous other factors affect the kitchen manager's ability to implement the menu. Which comes first: the menu or operational planning? The answer is simple: The menu drives the operation.

A second major part of this chapter focuses on members of the menu planning team. While the kitchen manager is important, other viewpoints must also be considered. Large food service operations have specialized positions such as purchasing agent, dining room manager, and accountant, and they should serve on the team. While smaller operations may not have these positions, these viewpoints must still be addressed by someone as menus are planned.

There are numerous menu planning strategies that are helpful, and these are presented in detail. First, the planning team must consider its priorities: guests, quality, operational factors, and financial goals. Second, they must divide the menu items they will offer into categories such as entrées and desserts. Next, the specific menu items to be available in each category must be determined. Finally, quality standards must be considered. If the kitchen manager cannot produce an item at the required level of quality, it should not be offered.

A final section of this chapter provides an introduction to selling prices. Kitchen managers and others on the menu planning team should know what can happen if there is too wide of a range between the lowest- and highest-priced items in each menu category. They must also recognize disadvantages to the use of subjective pricing methods and about the advantages of objective menu pricing methods. You will know about all of these important concepts when you finish studying this chapter.

MENUS ARE IMPORTANT

OBJECTIVE

1. Explain why menus are important to the food service operation:
   - Marketing and the menu
   - Financial management and the menu
   - Daily operations and the menu

Why are menus so important? The answer is simple: They implement the food service operation's marketing plan, financial management plan, and daily operations plans. You'll learn about how menus influence the operation's success factors as we begin this chapter.

Marketing and the Menu

The food service operation's guests are an important first concern when the menu is planned. What do they want? Why do they visit the operation? How do they evaluate the food they receive and their experience at the property? Menu planners who can answer these and related questions begin to understand their **market**, and then they can plan a menu that their guests will enjoy.

OVERHEARD IN THE KITCHEN

Market—All of the people with the desire and ability to purchase the products and services offered by a food service operation.

Figure 4.1 summarizes the role of guests in a successful food service operation.

Let's look at Figure 4.1 more closely. First, it suggests that a successful food service operation is one that is enjoyed by its guests, and their acceptance is influenced by the menu that is available. Potential repeat guests will not want to return to the operation if they do not like the menu. However, when they do return, will they want the same type of food served in the same environment so they will always receive an enjoyable experience? Probably so, and that is why menu planners must focus on guest-related concerns to discover what the guests want.

One of the most important things to be discovered relates to why guests visit the operation. Do they want a fast meal in a quick-service property or an elegant dinner to celebrate a special

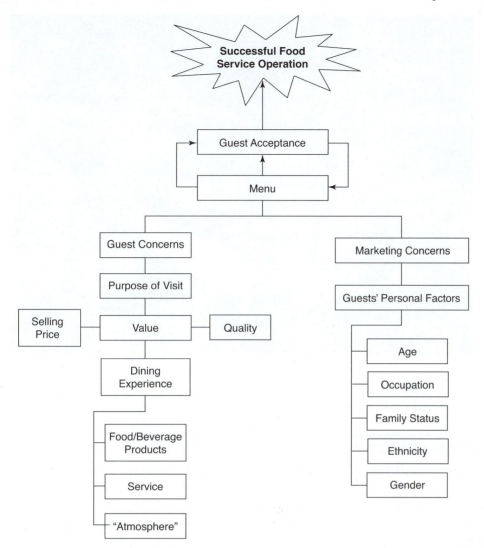

FIGURE 4.1 Menu Planners Consider the Guests

occasion? Regardless of the reason for their visit, they will be concerned about value (the relationship between selling price and quality) when they consider their dining-out alternatives. Also, they will think about the experience they are likely to have, and this relates to the food and beverage products they will receive along with the service and atmosphere (environment) of the alternatives they are considering.

Kitchen managers and their production teams cannot offer menus that will appeal to everyone all of the time. They must be aware of the concerns just discussed. However, they must also understand that potential guests are influenced by personal factors, including their age, occupation, family status, ethnicity (race and culture), and gender. In other words, it is important to know a lot about the concerns and backgrounds of the specific group of guests that the food service operation wants to attract.

Kitchen managers who know details about the wants and needs of their guests and who incorporate this knowledge into the menu when they plan it have taken an important step on the journey to restaurant success.

Financial Management and the Menu

Kitchen managers in commercial food service operations must generate a profit from the sale of food and beverage products to stay in business. Their peers (equals) who work in noncommercial facilities must control their costs. However, doing just enough to "keep the doors open" is not likely to satisfy those responsible for the operation. Profits enjoyed by restaurants, dining outlets

A carefully planned menu is the most important marketing tool for every food service operation.

in lodging properties, and other for-profit operations must meet the long-term **return on investment (ROI)** goals of the owners.

OVERHEARD IN THE KITCHEN

Return on Investment (ROI)—An accounting calculation that relates profit with the investment made to generate the profit.

The formula for ROI is: Annual Profit ÷ Investment = ROI

Example: if an owner invests $500,000 in a restaurant that has a $40,000 profit in one year, its ROI is 8% ($40,000 ÷ $500,000 = 8.0%).

A menu that offers products targeted to those most likely to visit the property and which is priced at a level that provides value to the guests is critical for financial success. Procedures to plan this type of menu are the topic of this chapter.

Daily Operations and the Menu

The menu directly impacts the **resources** that the kitchen manager can use to meet marketing and financial goals. These resources include:

- Labor (managers and other employees)
- Food and beverage products
- Equipment for product storage, production, service, and clean-up
- Operating expenses that are included in the approved budget
- Time (perhaps the most limited and impossible-to-replace resource of all!)
- Utilities and related costs
- Space available for storing, production, service, and clean-up
- Standard operating procedures (methods)

OVERHEARD IN THE KITCHEN

Resources—What the kitchen manager has available to attain goals. Examples include people, food products, time, and money.

Let's see how each of these resources is impacted by the menu by considering one common and simple item—french-fried potatoes—that the kitchen manager plans to offer. At first thought, little labor (the first resource noted above) is needed. After all, doesn't a cook just open up a bag of frozen French fries and put them in the deep fryer? Perhaps, but it is also possible that the property's guests believe that "fresh is best." Then they may want to serve a product made from whole potatoes processed on-site. If so, production personnel with adequate skills will need time (another resource in the above list) to prepare the potatoes.

Continuing with our example, frozen French fries or fresh whole potatoes must be purchased. If a frozen product is required, freezer space (storage equipment) will be needed. If a fresh whole potato is to be used, a different type of storage (refrigerated or dry) will be needed. Regardless of the product's **market form**, a deep fryer will be necessary. This, in turn, requires space that must be well-ventilated with access to a **fire suppression system**. The expense (money) to purchase the equipment and to provide a venting and fire-suppression system of adequate size can be significant. This is especially so if an existing kitchen without a deep fryer and proper suppression equipment must be modified to accommodate the new French fry item.

OVERHEARD IN THE KITCHEN

Market form—Different ways that food products can be purchased. For example, frozen bread dough or baked sliced bread can be used, fresh hamburger (ground beef) is available in bulk or preportioned patties, and hamburger can also be purchased frozen in bulk or preportioned patties. Each of these alternatives is a market form.

Fire suppression system—A ventilation system containing chemicals that are sprayed on equipment below if a fire begins beneath it.

To complete our example, the appropriate utilities (energy) are required for the storage and deep-frying equipment. As well, operating procedures including a standard recipe are needed to help assure consistency each time the product is produced.

From this brief example you can see that menu planning is an important management task. A menu planner's idea to "just add French fries" can have a serious impact on almost every aspect of the food service operation.

INFORMATION ON THE SIDE
"It All Starts with the Menu!"

The introduction to this chapter included an old saying that "It all starts with the menu." Experienced kitchen managers know that almost every aspect of daily operations is affected by the menu items to be served. For example, menu ingredients must be available so they can be purchased, and the cost of purchases is always a concern. They know that there is a maximum quantity of any food product that can be produced without sacrificing the food service operation's quality standards. What happens if the item becomes very popular, and this peak capacity is reached?

New menu items can also affected by sanitation concerns. For example, is the proper amount of storage space available for each ingredient required to produce the item? If products are produced in large quantities and held for service over a several-hour period, can this be done without subjecting the product to improper temperatures in the danger zone?

Layout and equipment concerns are also important. Kitchen managers want their staff members to be productive, but this is not possible if they must waste steps including back-tracking when they prepare menu items. As well, the proper equipment must be available to produce and serve all items required by the menu.

As you've learned, the kitchen manager knows a great deal about these and related daily operating concerns so he or she should always be a member of the menu planning team.

NOW IT'S YOUR TURN

A PINCH OF THE INTERNET (4.1)

1. A simple definition of marketing is "the business from the viewpoints of the guests." To learn more about restaurant marketing, type that term into your favorite search engine. Another suggestion: type "Restaurant Branding" into your search box to learn more useful information.
2. To learn about financial management and the menu, type "Restaurant Profitability" in your favorite search engine.
3. If you are interested in noncommercial food service operations, check out articles on menu planning, financial management and related topics on the Web sites of these magazines:
   - Restaurants and Institutions: www.rimag.com
   - Food Management Magazine: www.food-management.com

   Just type the topic in which you are interested in each Web site's search box.

COMPLETING THE PLATE QUESTIONS (4.1)

1. The chapter indicates that kitchen managers and other members of the menu planning team should learn as much as possible about the concerns and personal factors of those in their market (see Figure 4.1). What are some practical ways to do this?
2. What are some ways that the financial management concerns of for-profit food service operations and others that do not have a profit goal are the same? How are they different?
3. Assume you are the kitchen manager in a restaurant, and the owner has suggested that you begin an on-site bread baking program. How would a baking program impact each of the resources available to kitchen managers that are noted in this section of the chapter?

THE MENU PLANNING TEAM

O B J E C T I V E

2. Indicate that different viewpoints must be considered when menus are planned.

In some operations, the kitchen manager plans the menu without much help from others. One reason often stated to defend this tactic is that, since they must prepare the foods, they should determine what products to offer. In fact, the kitchen manager's ideas are invaluable. Who probably best knows if the items to be offered can be produced with the kitchen's existing personnel, equipment, space, design, and other limiting factors? However, the ideas of others who represent special nonfood preparation concerns are also important, and the menu is likely to be much better when their ideas are considered when it is planned.

Figure 4.2 indicates the positions of those who might be part of the menu planning team, and it indicates the concerns that persons in these positions may have about the menu being planned.

POSITION	MENU PLANNING CONCERNS
Owner/manager	Will the menu help to meet **profit maximization** or **cost minimization** goals?
Kitchen manager	Will guests enjoy these items, and can they consistently be produced to the necessary quality and quantity standards?
Dining room manager	Will the menu please the guests and help build **repeat business**?
Purchasing agent	Will the ingredients needed to produce menu items be available at a reasonable price when they are needed?
Controller (accountant)	Will financial goals be met? Note: Controllers in some food service operations are also involved in determining **serving costs** and selling prices.

FIGURE 4.2 The Menu Planning Team

OVERHEARD IN THE KITCHEN

Profit maximization—A financial goal of commercial food service operations that exist to make a profit; abbreviated "profit max."

Cost minimization—A financial goal of non-commercial food service operations that exist for reasons other than making a profit but that want to keep expenses low; abbreviated "cost min."

Repeat business—Guests who return to the food service operation because they enjoyed a positive experience during earlier visits.

Controller—The person who records, classifies, and summarizes a food service operation's business transactions. This person develops financial statements and provides suggestions about what they mean to the property owner/managers; also called accountant or bookkeeper.

Serving costs—The cost to produce one serving of a menu item when it is prepared according to the standard recipe.

When you look at Figure 4.2, notice that the owner/manager heads the list. One or multiple persons may employ a manager to be responsible for the on-site operation. The owner/manager is concerned about the financial success of the operation and understands the critical importance of the menu in that success. The owner of a commercial operation has likely invested a lot of money. He or she will first be concerned about not losing it and, second, about making a financial return that considers the risk of losing the **investment**.

OVERHEARD IN THE KITCHEN

Investment—The amount of money that an owner has used to start and operate the business.

As you've learned, the kitchen manager must be able to produce all of the items required by the menu, and he/she is probably best aware of how to do so with equipment, employees, and other resources that are available.

The dining room manager will know what the guests do and don't like about the existing menu. He or she should have ideas about other items that would be popular. Can these products be produced at the desired quality, quantity, level and cost levels? Others on the menu planning team can make this decision, but they will want to consider guest preferences as the menu is planned. Also, if banquets are offered, the manager with that responsibility should be part of the team that plans these menus to assure banquet guests' viewpoints are understood by the menu planning team.

The purchasing agent should have specialized knowledge about product availability, supplier sources, and price trends, and these views should be considered when planning the menu. As well, the controller (accountant) has suggestions about important financial concerns.

It is likely that only high-volume food service operations will require all of the positions shown in 4.2. However, someone in every operation must be responsible for all of the concerns that are noted. Therefore, even if there are fewer persons on the menu planning team, each of these concerns must be thought about and implemented into the menu when it is planned.

This food service operation employs a bakery chef, and the wide variety of items he can prepare must be represented in the menu that is planned.

INFORMATION ON THE SIDE
History of Menus

You might be surprised to learn that the first menus were used by the chefs and cooks who prepared the meals—not by the guests who consume them. The earliest menus were really "shopping lists" used by chefs to help remember the items that they had to purchase.

The earliest chefs were employed by royalty and wealthy persons, not by restaurants or other food service operations open to the public. They needed shopping lists because they often prepared banquets of many items (sometimes over a hundred!) that were typically divided up into thirteen or more different courses without counting beverages.

Traditionally, there had been no reason to provide menus to guests in public restaurants and taverns because complete meals were served at a set price and there was little, if any, choice or selection.

À la carte (individually priced) menus for individual guests came into common use in restaurants in Paris, France, during the 1880s. Sometimes these were posters placed at the entrance to a restaurant so guests could decide if they wanted to dine at the property before they entered. (This practice is still popular in many properties today.)

The first guests who received table-side menus probably read information handwritten on a small card. It has only been recently that the almost endless variety of menus creatively designed to attract the attention of guests and interest them in selected items has become popular.

As you can see, then, the concept of a menu has evolved from a list of items available for production purposes to a list of items available for sale to guests.

NOW IT'S YOUR TURN

A PINCH OF THE INTERNET (4.2)

1. Noncommercial food service operations often use a team approach to menu planning. To learn more about this concept and menu planning in noncommercial facilities, type "team approach to menu planning" in your favorite search engine.
2. Want to learn more about the job of a food service accountant? If so, type the term "food service accountant" into your favorite search engine.

COMPLETING THE PLATE QUESTIONS (4.2)

1. Many food service operations have different menus for each meal period such as breakfast, lunch, and dinner. Do you think the roles of the menu planning team members change when they are planning menus for different meal periods? Why or why not?
2. If you were the kitchen manager, how would you obtain suggestions from your kitchen staff about new menu ideas when menus were revised?
3. You've learned that the dining room manager must represent the guests when menu planning decisions are made. If you were the dining room manager, how could you learn about guest preferences so you could bring these ideas to the attention of the menu planning team?

Kitchen Challenge Du Jour Case Study (4.1)

"I know we have to consider the needs of our guests when we plan our menus," said Shari-Ann, the kitchen manager at the Big City Restaurant." Her operation was very popular with senior citizens who visited the property in large numbers everyday to take advantage of the senior-citizen specials.

One of the most-liked menu items was a chicken salad sandwich plate in the summer and a chicken a la king casserole dish during the cooler months. For many years, Big City Restaurant kitchen personnel had been producing both of these items by cooking fresh whole chickens, removing and chopping the meat, and including it with the other recipe ingredients.

"I also know the kitchen salad and chicken a la king items taste great, but they require so much labor to prepare," she continued as she spoke with Ralph, the Big City Restaurant's purchasing manager.

"I agree," said Ralph. "We could purchase frozen chicken breasts and thighs, and you could quickly cook and remove the meat and save a lot of labor. I could also look into buying frozen chicken off the bone, and then you could really reduce labor costs."

"Wait a minute," said Betty, the dining room manager who was also enjoying a cup of coffee during their break. "Is our objective to save money or to please the guests?" "Everybody knows that the way the menu items are produced now really makes them taste the best. I don't think we should make changes that can affect so many of our very loyal guests."

Note: This case study shows how different the viewpoints of Big City Restaurant employees can help a menu planning team to focus on specific concerns while the menu is being planned.

a) Do you think the conversation about the chicken items is helpful? Why or why not?

b) What are some ways to evaluate the suggestions about using frozen chicken parts or even boneless chicken as menu item ingredients?

c) Who should make the final decision about these two menu items? Why?

MENU PLANNING STRATEGIES

O BJECTIVE

3. Review basic menu planning strategies:
    • Remember menu planning priorities
    • Consider menu categories
    • Select menu items for each category
    • Steps in make or buy analysis
    • Establish quality standards for menu items

Menus inform guests about the food and beverage items that are available. They can be revised very often, almost never, or sometime in between these extremes. For example, a chef-owned restaurant may feature daily offerings and market-fresh items that require changing a large part of the menu everyday. At the other extreme, a family-owned property with an ethnic theme may feature items prepared with traditional family recipes, and these menus may change almost never, if at all. In between these extremes are, probably, most other restaurants that revise menus one or more times every year (perhaps each season of the year) to keep up with the changing preferences of the guests they serve.

Figure 4.3 notes strategies that can be used to plan a menu. It provides a "recipe" for the menu planning process that will be discussed in this section.

Note: Procedures for writing menu descriptions and designing the menu are presented in Chapter 5.

The best menu planning teams use the strategies shown in Figure 4.3 to assure that the menu will be well accepted by the guests while, at the same time, it meets the food service operation's financial goals. These strategies are discussed in detail in this section of the chapter.

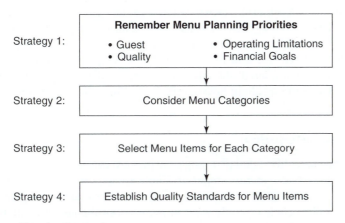

FIGURE 4.3 Menu Planning Strategies

Remember Menu Planning Priorities

Strategy 1 reminds the menu planning team to never forget its priorities: the food service operation's guests, quality, operating limitations, and the property's financial goals.

GUESTS

You've learned that the guests' expectations about their dining experience and their reasons for dining out are important, and the menu should reflect these concerns. As well, personal factors about the guests including their age, occupation, family status, ethnicity, and gender are other important factors to consider when menus are planned.

QUALITY

All menu items must meet the food service operation's quality requirements. They should reflect what the guests want and are willing to pay for. Quality factors include each menu item's flavor, consistency, texture, form, shape, nutritional content, visual and aromatic (sense of smell) appeal, and temperature.

The use of convenience foods is an important concern (will the guests like them?) and their role, if any, in implementing the menu must be considered. Note: This topic is addressed later in this section.

Experienced kitchen managers know that their guests' ideas about quality can change as can their interests in the products that meet their quality standards. For these reasons among others, the task of menu planning and revision is usually ongoing. Quality concerns are built into **standard recipes**. When they are consistently used, food and beverage items produced by the property's team should meet the food service operation's standards. Note: Standard recipes are discussed in Chapter 6.

OVERHEARD IN THE KITCHEN

Standard recipe—Instructions to produce a food or beverage item that, if followed, will help assure that the food service operation's quality and quantity standards for the product are met. Standard recipe information should include the type and amount of ingredients, preparation procedures including equipment and tools, yield (number of servings and serving size), garnishes, and any other information needed to properly produce and serve the item.

OPERATING LIMITATIONS

Factors that limit a kitchen manager's ability to produce menu items include the knowledge and skill levels of production staff, the availability of ingredients, and volume production requirements including equipment capacities. Other operating concerns include layout and equipment limitations, sanitation issues, and operating costs that impact both product selling prices and the guests' perceptions of value.

FINANCIAL OBJECTIVES

A basic attitude of many food service professionals is to "take care of guests, and the finances will take care of themselves." Wise kitchen managers use this idea, but they also consider their operating budget when their menu is developed. Knowing prices that guests in their market consider "reasonable" helps to determine how much can be spent for product costs. These costs must be known and can then be considered when the menu is planned and when selling prices are determined. Note: You'll learn more about how to establish selling prices later in this chapter and also in Chapter 6.

Consider Menu Categories

Figure 4.3 indicates that, after menu planning priorities are considered, the second basic strategy requires planners to consider **menu categories**. These are logical ways to divide all of the items that will be available on the menu into similar groups of items that will, hopefully, be of interest to guests. For example, people typically want to know about the **entrées** that are available, and these would not be placed in the same menu category or list as desserts or beverages.

OVERHEARD IN THE KITCHEN

Menu category—A group or list of alternative menu items such as entrées, salads, and desserts.

Entrée—A food item served as the primary (main) course in a meal; sometimes call main course.

Menu items are typically organized into logical categories such as:

- *Entrées (main course).* Most menu planners plan items for their entrées first, and then they consider categories of food items on their menu. Popular entrées include meat items such as beef, pork, poultry, and lamb. Seafood alternatives are also popular as are entrée salads and **vegetarian** items. Many guests think entrées are items served hot, and typically they are. However, others (for example, a chef's salad) may be served cold. Some entrées may be hot and cold (example: a cold salad served with hot grilled chicken). **Casseroles** are entrées that can include combinations of meat or seafood with pasta such as lasagna or spaghetti or cheese and pasta such as baked macaroni and cheese.

OVERHEARD IN THE KITCHEN

Vegetarian (menu item)—Food items that do not contain meat or animal products.

Casserole—An entrée that can include combinations of meat or seafood and pasta such as lasagna or spaghetti or cheese and pasta such as baked macaroni and cheese.

- *Specialties of the house.* Food service operations that specialize in items such as barbequed ribs, steaks, or chops may feature these items in a separate menu category. Then they can highlight these items to be sure the guests know about them.
- *Appetizers (starters).* **Appetizers** are served before the meal and are often bite-sized. They may be hot (stuffed mushrooms) or cold (shrimp cocktail). Some restaurants offer fruit or vegetable juices in this menu category.

OVERHEARD IN THE KITCHEN

Appetizer—A food item served as the first course in a meal to stimulate one's appetite; sometimes called starter course.

- *Soups.* Some restaurants consider soups as a separate category; others include them with appetizers or with salads. Most soups are served hot. They can be clear (made of a **consommé** or **broth**) and produced with or without vegetables or meats. They can also be thick (a chowder or cream soup) and served with meats, seafood, poultry, and fruits or vegetables. Some soups are served cold. For example, Vichyssoise is a cold soup made from potatos, onions, and leeks.

OVERHEARD IN THE KITCHEN

Consomme—A clear soup made by combining a flavored stock or broth with other ingredients to produce a soup that has no fat.

Broth—A clear liquid soup made by simmering meaty cuts in water until the desired flavor, body, and color are developed.

- *Salads.* Some restaurants offer entrée salads and accompaniment (side) salads. Many are made from lettuce and other leafy greens and from other vegetables (example: potato salad). Popular salads can also be made of fruits including oranges, melons, and apples.
- *Sandwiches and wraps.* Common sandwiches include hamburger, bacon, lettuce, and tomato, and others made with deli items such as ham, turkey, and cheese. Sandwich wraps

such as spring rolls, tacos, and burritos with numerous types of fillings are also popular with guests of many food service operations.

- *Vegetables and accompaniments (side dishes).* Potatoes, asparagus, broccoli, peas, carrots, onions, and other vegetables of many types and preparation styles are available on many menus. Other vegetable and accompaniment dishes include seasoned or white rice, corn, and beans made using numerous preparation methods, and pastas, dumplings, and noodles. Accompaniments are often suggested by the operation's **cuisine** such as beans and rice in Southwestern and Mexican cooking and pasta items in a property with an Italian theme. Fresh vegetables are an important part of many menus, and they frequently change according to availability, quality, and costs.

OVERHEARD IN THE KITCHEN

Cuisine—A style or manner of preparing food.

- *Desserts.* After-dinner items are often included on menus. However, a separate dessert menu is sometimes used or, perhaps, a dessert cart or tray is brought tableside to tempt guests with available desserts. A wide variety of high quality ready-prepared dessert items allows menu planners to offer more items with fewer preparation challenges.
- *Beverages.* An increasingly large variety of beverages are available to guests that desire them. Traditional items such as coffees, teas, and soft drinks may be listed on the menu. Sometimes separate coffee menus are used. Some menus suggest traditional cocktails, and many operations feature (often with separate menus) alcoholic beverages including specialty drinks and domestic and imported beers along with beverages from "**boutique breweries**." Many properties have wine lists and, when wines are wisely selected and wine lists are creatively developed, the wine lists can be very useful sales tools. Bottled waters are often available, and some restaurants even feature water menus.

OVERHEARD IN THE KITCHEN

Boutique (brewery)—A small-volume business that produces very high quality beer that is typically distributed within a small area.

Some properties offer a **signature item**. Examples include a one-pound pork chop or a "mile-high" pie that is unique and, over time, becomes a very popular menu item that people think about when they consider visiting the food service operation.

OVERHEARD IN THE KITCHEN

Signature item—A food or beverage item that guests associate with a specific food service operation. Examples may include a "one-pound pork chop" and an "oyster boat" (a loaf of French bread hollowed and filled with deep-fried oysters).

How many menu categories are needed? The answer to this question involves considering issues such as:

- How many categories are needed for the variety of menu items our guests will want?
- Is a category needed to list unique items and, therefore, to provide a **competitive edge** to the food service operation?

OVERHEARD IN THE KITCHEN

Competitive edge—Something desired by guests that is not offered by competitors. Examples may include an ocean view, special entertainment, or a food item requiring specialized skill in its preparation or equipment for its production.

- Are the needs of our guest market carefully defined? If so, this may reduce the number of menu categories and items needed.
- What are the most frequent reasons for guest visits? Table-service restaurants with a high-volume lunch business must serve guests quickly, and menu items must be selected with this concern in mind. Therefore, a four-course menu is not a good choice for the mid-day meal. However, a slow-paced meal with several courses may be preferred for dinner guests who visit the operation later in the day.
- How many categories will make the menu easy-to-read? Too few categories create long lists of food items within each category. This can, in turn, increase the time it takes for guests to order, and **table turns** are important in many food service operations. Note: The reverse is also true; it is not typically wise to offer a menu category with just one or two items unless they are in a specialty category like that discussed above.

OVERHEARD IN THE KITCHEN

Table turn—An industry term relating to the number of times a dining room table is used during a dining period.

Select Menu Items for Each Category

Strategy 3 in Figure 4.3 indicates that after, menu categories are determined, items should be selected for each category.

The best way to plan a menu is use the approach judged best by the menu planning team. One popular technique is to plan items for basic menu categories in the following order:

- Entrées
- Appetizers
- Potatoes, rice, and related items
- Soups
- Salads
- Desserts
- Breads
- Beverages

Why are entrées selected before items in other categories? One important reason is that guest decisions about where to go are most often based on entrée selections. ("I'm hungry for a steak. Who offers a good one?") Also, food service operations with dining themes need specific types of entrées to help "deliver" their cuisines to the guests as part of their dining experience. Consider, for example, steaks featured in properties with an "Old West" theme and pizza and pasta items offered in an Italian restaurant. By contrast, many restaurants offer a wide range of entrées in the hope they will have "something for everyone."

All menu categories and items within each category are important to menu planners; if they were not, they would not be on the menu!

One basic tactic to select specific items for a menu category is to consider many items and to then use an elimination process to select the items that will be offered. When this approach is used in an existing food service operation that already has a menu:

- Undesirable items within a category are first deleted. Note: This is most typically done because they are unpopular, unprofitable, ingredients are difficult to purchase, and/or because production difficulties are encountered.
- A list of possible items to add to the menu category is suggested by menu planners. Perhaps a **brainstorming** session is used, and each member of the menu planning team promotes one or more items. For example, the kitchen manager may suggest items that are part of a **trend**, and the dining room manager can remind the team about what the guests are requesting. The purchasing agent can tell about the costs of ingredients based on what he or she is learning from the suppliers, and the owner may mention items that were enjoyed at a similar type of property on a visit to another city.

OVERHEARD IN THE KITCHEN

Brainstorming—A method to gain ideas from group members in which each person makes suggestions without comment by other members of the group.

Trend—A gradual change in guests' food preferences that is likely to continue for a long time in the future.

- The list is reduced to proper size by considering factors that are discussed later in this section.

When a new food service operation is planning its first menu, the same basic elimination process can be used. A relatively long list of possible menu items for each category is developed. Then those that do not meet the property's specific selection concerns (see below) are eliminated.

USE MENU PLANNING TOOLS

Some special menu planning tools can be helpful to the menu planning team, and these include:

- *Copies of old and existing menus.* These can help planners think about items that have (and have not) been popular, profitable, and/or efficient to produce and serve.
- *Copies of competitors' menus.* Knowledge of the competitors' product offerings may suggest items that should be added.
- *Menu evaluation information.* Objective information such as that derived from menu engineering (discussed in Chapter 10) can help determine the most popular and/or profitable menu items.
- *Standard recipes.* Standard recipes for proposed menu additions are an absolute "must" to assure that the items which are suggested can be produced according to the food service operation's standards. If they can (and this may be a decision made by the kitchen manager), the menu items can be considered. If they cannot be produced in a way that will meet or exceed the guests' expectations, the items cannot be considered for the revised menu.
- *Product inventory and ingredient availability.* The availability of products and ingredients at the right quality and acceptable cost during the time for which the menu will be available is an important concern. This is information that the purchasing agent on the menu planning team can provide, perhaps after discussions with the operation's suppliers. As well, the ability to maintain the ingredients for proposed menu items in on-site storage without loss of quality is important unless the operation is willing to accept frequent deliveries of the ingredients.
- *Input from managers, employees, and guests (if applicable).* These sources can provide helpful suggestions about current and proposed menu items. Be sure to talk with servers who have significant guest contact and dishwashers who know what items guests return uneaten.

MENU ITEM SELECTION FACTORS

How exactly should menu planners determine which items should be included in each of their menu categories? Several factors are important, and among them are:

- *Variety.* A range of serving temperatures, preparation methods, textures, shapes, and colors should typically be available in the items available within each menu category. Menu planners can simplify production and still provide guests with a wide variety of items when they use **menu rationalization**. This tactic involves using one ingredient such as shrimp in several different items (for example, in one or more appetizers, soups, entrées, and accompaniments) in different menu categories.

OVERHEARD IN THE KITCHEN

Menu rationalization—The menu planning tactic that involves using the same main ingredient in several different menu items.

Kitchen managers know that too little variety within a menu category is generally not good because, for example, even persons in a closely defined market like different items. Consider, for example a group of several persons making a dining-out decision. Since each may have different preferences, the menu must anticipate and provide popular choices for the guests. An exception: Food service operations that feature very popular signature items will likely attract many guests who want to order these items, and a wide variety of other selections may not be needed.

Menu planners also know that, when there is large variety, guests may become confused, servers may need to spend more time taking orders, and then order times will increase. As well, all of the ingredients for a large variety of foods will have to be purchased, stored, and produced, and these are activities that increase labor hours and costs.

INFORMATION ON THE SIDE
The "3Ps" of Product Variation

One way to consider the proper amount of variety in menu items offered in each category is to think about the "3 Ps":

- **Product (menu item) variation**—You've learned that a reasonable variety of items is needed within each menu category. Entrées cannot generally feature only items made from beef, side dishes must offer more than just potatoes, and desserts may include one or more fruit pies but should offer other items as well.
- **Preparation variation**—This factor relates to market form (cut), preparation/cooking style, and serving size/quantity.
  - **Market form (cut).** Earlier in this chapter, you learned that the term, "market form," relates to different ways that food can be purchased. If a hamburger sandwich will be offered on the menu, the main ingredient (beef) can be purchased fresh or frozen in bulk or in preportioned patties. In this example, the market form of ground beef does not directly increase the variety of menu items. Regardless of how the beef is purchased, only one item—hamburger sandwich—will be available. However, if it is purchased in a convenience form (patty rather than bulk), preparation labor can be saved that can then be used to produce additional items that will provide greater menu variety. Note: It is also possible for a product's market form to directly impact variety. Consider a chicken breast baked for service as an entrée and chopped for use as an ingredient in chicken salad.
  - **Preparation/cooking style.** The preparation method and cooking style can also help to add variety to the menu. For example, the same portion of seafood can be steamed, blackened, broiled, or pan-seared with little difficulty, and this tactic will yield four different entrée alternatives to the guests. If several types of seafood (salmon, white fish, and mahi mahi, for example) were also available, a large number of different seafood entrées becomes available without excessive production labor required to prepare them.

    Meats can be cooked with **moist heat** (steaming, boiling, or poaching) or **dry heat** (roasting, baking, broiling, grilling, sautéing, or pan frying). Preparation methods using moist and dry heat (braising and stewing) are also possible. Vegetables can be boiled, baked, braised, fried, or sautéed. Some items including chicken might be prepared to order (deep- or pan-fried, grilled, or baked). Desserts can be served fresh, chilled, cooked, or baked.
  - **Serving size/quantity.** Serving size and quantity variations are also easy to implement. Consider, for example, one-half and full servings of a seafood dish. Think also about different serving sizes (number of ounces or thickness of cut) of steaks or prime beef, as well as sandwiches of different sizes made of the same ingredients. Also, almost everyone knows about small, medium, and large pizzas and soft drink servings.
- **Price variation.** Within a carefully calculated range, price variations for different menu items can also add variety. Items for guests on a budget and for others with higher spending limits can be offered as long as quality compared with the selling price represents a value to the guests. Note: The final section of this chapter discusses selling price concerns in greater detail.

OVERHEARD IN THE KITCHEN

Moist heat—A cooking method in which food is cooked by extended exposure to steam or hot liquids. Examples: stewing and braising.

Dry heat—A cooking method in which the food to be cooked is exposed directly to heat or flame. Examples: broiling and frying.

- *Temperature.* Guests typically expect some items to be served hot (mashed potatoes) and other items to be served chilled (tossed salads). Hot and cold items can be offered within the same menu item category. You've learned that temperature is a very important sanitation (food safety) concern. The kitchen manager is likely to be the member of the menu planning team who will best know if required temperatures can be consistently maintained. These concerns are especially important for items that are produced in quantity and then held for later service when ordered by the guests. If there are ever any doubts about food safety issues, affected items should not be placed on the menu.

INFORMATION ON THE SIDE

Add Variety with a Nutrition Focus

Many guests are increasingly concerned about nutrition, and some make dining out decisions based upon the availability of items that meet their nutrition concerns. Does this mean that the typical food operation must have an entire menu category devoted to nutritious items, or that specific menu items must be added because they will appeal to nutrition-conscious guests? The simple answers to both questions are that it depends upon the specific food service operation and the extent to which the menu planning team believe nutrition concerns are important for their guests.

Good news! It is likely that some items planned for the menu can be made more appealing to health conscious consumers with just minor and practical changes. For example, the deep-fried chicken now listed on the current menu might be offered baked without the skin to reduce the entrée's fat content for guests desiring this option.

As a second example, perhaps the chicken entrée now available with a rich sauce can be broiled and offered without a sauce or with sauce "on the side." Then the guest who is served this item may decide to use the sauce to supplement the taste but on a much more sparing basis than would be true if a kitchen staff member ladled it on the entrée.

As a third example, perhaps a smaller serving of some existing menu items can be offered. As these and related tactics are used, existing menu items will appeal to guests with few, if any, production challenges for kitchen personnel.

Each of the above examples shows how the preparation method can be varied to yield a product more suitable for specific guests. These preparation and service variations can be presented in the menu descriptions when the menu is designed. Note: This topic is addressed in more detail in Chapter 5.

- *Texture.* **Texture** relates to how a food feels, and it is an important factor in food quality. Menu items can be soft or hard, firm or crunchy, liquid or solid, or wet or dry. It is important that menu items have the proper texture so they will be well accepted when they are selected by guests. For example, would you like scrambled eggs that were more liquid than solid because they were under-cooked? Today, many guests like cooked vegetables such as carrots and celery to be "crisp tender" rather than soft; therefore, these menu items should not be over-cooked. These examples stress an important point: The kitchen manager and his or her staff must be able to consistently "deliver" the quality of items offered on the menu that the guests desire.
- *Shape and sizes.* Menu items can be round, square, or long, and they can be served in a flat or tall portion. Sometimes an item's **garnish** can even impact a guest's viewpoint of an item's height. Consider how slivers of very thin and tall fried vegetable strips may be used to make menu items attractive in **fusion cuisines**.
- *Flavor.* When menu planners think about **flavor**, they often think about taste. Common taste sensations are sweet, sour, salty, and bitter. Some consider another taste, **umami**, that refers to savory, brothy, or meaty. Guests also use terms such as hot (buffalo wings), spicy (Thai dishes), and smoked (barbecue meats) when they describe taste, and these terms may be useful in menu descriptions. The concept of "flavor" is complex and involves more than taste. Professional chefs know that flavor really refers to the total experience that one has with food as it is consumed. In fact, all of our senses (sight, taste, touch, smell, and even sound: just think of a sizzling steak served on a very hot platter!) are involved in a food's flavor. Flavor sensations vary between guests, and they are a very important factor in the guests' acceptance of a menu item.

OVERHEARD IN THE KITCHEN

Texture—A description of how a food feels that is an important factor in food quality.

Garnish—An edible decoration used to make a menu item attractive.

Fusion (cuisine)—Foods that blend the traditions of more than one cuisine. Example: Many Hawaiian menu items include ingredients and use cooking methods popular in the culture of numerous ethic or regional traditions.

Flavor—A food quality factor that affects how it tastes and smells.

Umami (taste)—A term that describes a savory, brothy, or meaty taste.

- *Color.* Color is part of a menu item's appeal. Multiple colors are preferred. It would generally be considered poor presentation, for example, to serve fried chicken, a baked potato, and baked beans on the same plate because all of these items are brown. The preparation method may affect color (example: The coating of fried chicken is typically darker than the surface of an oven-baked chicken), and color also relates to the specific food item. Guests expect broccoli to be a shiny, medium-dark green, and they want green beans to be a duller (olive) green. Plate garnishes can help assure that the color of a plate presented to a guest is appealing. Note: Garnishes are important because they impact the guests' first impressions of the plate. They should be colorful, creative, edible, and fresh.
- *Composition and balance.* Menu planners are concerned about the impact of menu items that are served to guests. Sometimes, one has no control over the relation of food items to each other. (Consider guests in a buffet serving line who help themselves to what they want.) By contrast, when items are plated for service, menu planners do have control over these factors. Then, the composition of the "overall" plate is important. The **center of the plate** concept is often used to create a pleasing "picture" of the food items that are presented on the plate.

OVERHEARD IN THE KITCHEN

Center of the plate—The concept that the entrée should be positioned on a plate by placing the entrée in the center of the plate. Then other menu items should be slightly overlapped moving toward the plate's rim so there is no center area of the plate that is not covered with food.

MAKE OR BUY DECISIONS AND ITEM SELECTION

You have been learning about procedures to select items for each menu category. As you may be thinking, this topic is easier to read about than it is to actually do. On the one hand, for example, you have learned about limitations imposed by employee skills, equipment, space, and other factors. At the same time, you learned that factors such as guest preference, variety, and preparation method are also very important. You can see, then, that menu item selection involves using facts, thinking about the guests, and using some common sense.

Kitchen managers want to assure that all of the menu items that are offered meet the required quality standards, and you have learned that this is the most important factor that influences the selection of menu items. Sometimes they have all of the resources needed to produce all desired items selected by menu planners except one: labor (time). Then they have two basic choices: Do not offer an item or, depending upon the specific situation, use a convenience food alternative for it. You've learned that convenience items may reduce labor hours and kitchen equipment needs because some of the labor that would be needed for on-site production is "built-in" to the product before it is purchased. If one or more of these market forms of food can be used, planners can decide to offer a wider variety of items for entrée, soup, appetizer, dessert, and other menu categories.

Should convenience foods be used in a professional kitchen? The answer is not a simple "yes" or "no," and it is also not "all or nothing" decision. Example: Chicken Cordon Bleu, a frozen chicken breast stuffed with ham and cheese could be purchased and served with a tasty honey mustard sauce that has been prepared on-site. Instead, a **make-buy analysis** is needed to assure two things. First, are the food service operation's quality requirements met by the products prepared on-site and purchased as a convenience food? If quality is acceptable, then it is important to learn about the costs of the convenience item alternative so it can be compared with the costs that will be incurred if the item is produced on-site. Not surprisingly, make or buy analysis decisions have significant marketing, financial, human resources, and other implications.

OVERHEARD IN THE KITCHEN

Make or buy analysis—The process of deciding whether a menu item should be prepared on-site or purchased as a convenience food.

In large food service operations, make or buy analyses are often performed by purchasing personnel. Concerns that prompt the analyses may involve an interest in menu revision. However, there can also be production challenges with existing menu items that might be resolved if a convenience food alternative could be used. In small properties, the decisions may be made by the kitchen manager or others in the **chain of command**.

OVERHEARD IN THE KITCHEN

Chain of command—The path by which authority (power) flows from one management level to the next lower level within the food service operation.

Several issues should be considered as make or buy decisions are made. Figure 4.4 identifies some questions that might prompt an interest in a make or buy analysis when products are currently being produced by the kitchen manager's production team.

Two very important concerns must be part of every make or buy decision:

- Which alternative (making the item on-site or purchasing it partially or completely prepared) consistently yields the product that is the right quality from the guest's point of view?
- Assuming equivalent and acceptable quality, which product (from scratch or convenience food) is least expensive to produce?

The make or buy analysis process discussed in this section addresses these two questions. Experienced kitchen managers know that thoughtful study is needed, and the more the decision impacts guest value and property costs, the more carefully the decisions must be made.

OVERHEARD IN THE KITCHEN

Chain recipe—A recipe that produces an ingredient used in another recipe.

- Are changes in production volumes causing difficulties?
- Are prices for necessary products or ingredients increasing?
- Is there an interest in increasing the variety of menu items without increasing labor costs?
- Is new or expensive equipment needed to continue on-site production?
- Is it difficult to maintain a consistent source of supplies?
- Is there a limited number of suppliers available?
- Are alternative products in the marketplace?
- Is a menu item made from a **chain recipe**? Example: Does a menu item require a sauce that is also an ingredient in other menu items?
- Is equipment and/or space available to store products purchased in other market forms?
- Will the future costs of on-site product production change? If so, why and by how much?

FIGURE 4.4 Questions That Prompt Make or Buy Analysis: Products Produced On-Site

INFORMATION ON THE SIDE
What Is Best?

Which type of automobile is "better:" a Ford or a Chevrolet? Fans of both brands of cars will be able to defend their answers to this question, and it is unlikely that anything can be said or done to change their opinions.

Which is better: beef stew "made from scratch" at a restaurant or a frozen market form of the product? Responses are often based upon the same factors used to determine auto preferences including experience and subjective judgment. However, the best answer to both of the questions just posed may be "the facts must speak for themselves." Many factors must be addressed to answer the make or buy question for a specific food service operation. The purpose of the analysis is not to "confirm" what those conducting the study already think or know. Instead, it is to assess the best option for the food service operation by considering the factors that its menu planning team judge to be the most important.

Steps in Make or Buy Analysis

Several steps are involved in the make or buy analysis process for a new menu item, and they are introduced in Figure 4.5.

While the steps noted in Figure 4.5 may, at first, appear complicated, they really are not. Notice, for example, that the first five steps in the figure relate to quality concerns and only two steps (6 and 7) relate to costs. This emphasizes a point made earlier: Make or buy analysis is not a decision about cost alone. Instead, it is a decision about quality and costs. It does little good to determine the cost of product alternatives if the product cannot be used because its quality is unacceptable.

Let's review Figure 4.5:

- **Step 1: Determine Quality Requirements**—How is the quality of the product being considered for the menu actually defined? What type, quality, and amount of ingredients are used? What is the serving size? This step is critical because, when it is completed, menu planners should have a description that provides a standard against which to evaluate

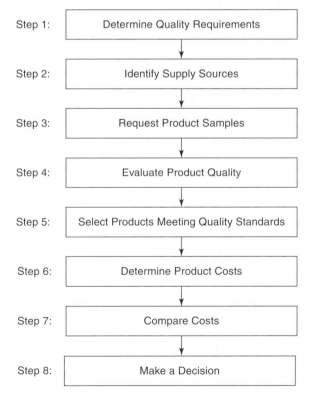

Step 1:	Determine Quality Requirements
Step 2:	Identify Supply Sources
Step 3:	Request Product Samples
Step 4:	Evaluate Product Quality
Step 5:	Select Products Meeting Quality Standards
Step 6:	Determine Product Costs
Step 7:	Compare Costs
Step 8:	Make a Decision

FIGURE 4.5 Steps in Make or Buy Analysis for New Menu Item

alternative products. If an acceptable product cannot be produced, it will either have to be purchased, or it cannot be added to the menu.

- *Step 2: Identify Supply Sources*—The kitchen manager and the person responsible for purchasing (if that is not the kitchen manager) may know about multiple suppliers of the convenience food alternative. Numerous electronic buying guides are also available to identify potential sources of supply.

- *Step 3: Request Product Samples*—Potential suppliers should be alerted about the food service operation's interest in the convenience food product. The kitchen manager or other purchaser should know the operation's policy about product samples. If a sample is being requested for a new item on the menu, samples of alternative products that meet general quality requirements will need to be requested.

- *Step 4: Evaluate Product Quality*—Product samples that are received should be evaluated using the product currently produced on-site as a **benchmark (standard)**. If the samples will be used to assess an interest in a new product, the menu planning team may ask several employees and guests to participate in a **taste test**. This process can range from being very simple ("What do you think?") to very formal with specific factors identified and rating scales used for each factor.

OVERHEARD IN THE KITCHEN

Benchmark (standard)—A standard against which to compare and improve one's products or services.

Taste Test—A process to learn the opinions of managers, employees, and guests about the food items being considered for the menu.

This step cannot be implemented without a standard recipe that yields a product that can serve as the benchmark. This will be the recipe already in use if the convenience food will replace an item already on the menu. Otherwise, it will be the recipe that the kitchen manager has selected for use if the item will be produced on-site. Then those helping with the taste test can compare the benchmark (currently used product or item produced with the approved standard recipe) against samples of the alternative products.

- *Step 5: Select Products Meeting Quality Standards*—The evaluation of product alternatives (Step 4) will identify those that meet the property's quality requirements (Step 1). It then becomes necessary to determine the costs of acceptable products and to compare them with the cost of producing the item. Note: As you've learned, if no convenience food is judged acceptable, the menu item will need to be prepared by the kitchen manager's team or not offered at all. There is no place on any menu for an item that merely "sounds good," that is added because a competitor offers it, and/or that is added because it is a favorite of someone on the menu planning team. All items must meet quality requirements without exception.

- *Step 6: Determine Product Costs*—All significant costs incurred as the product is produced should be identified. What is "significant?" Consider a kitchen manager evaluating the costs of baking bread on premise versus purchasing bread that is already baked. The utility costs incurred by the oven used to bake the bread may be difficult to determine, and they may be considered "insignificant." By contrast, the labor costs (number of labor hours) used to prepare the bread are likely to be significant and, fortunately, will be relatively easy to determine. A good rule-of-thumb is to determine the estimated amounts for all expenses required to produce a product if it is considered practical (cost-effective and reasonable) to do so.

- *Step 7: Compare Costs*—The costs for purchasing and preparing a required product should be compared. If the steps in Figure 4.5 are followed, it will be an "apples-to-apples" comparison based on products of equal quality rather than an "apples-to-oranges" comparison in which products of different quality are compared.

- *Step 8: Make a Decision*—At this point, the menu planning team will know the quality and cost differences of products being considered for the item that can be prepared on-site and purchased as a convenience food. While these are the most important factors, others may also need to be considered. For example, it is unwise to select a product of acceptable quality and at a very favorable price from an undependable supplier (hopefully, they were eliminated in Step 2 above.) However, supplier service as well as quality and price concerns are among those that should be thought about as the make or buy decision is made. Another concern relates to the issue of whether it would matter if the guest knew a convenience food was served. For example, a pre-baked apple pie selling for $2.00 a slice at a diner will probably be acceptable if the guests knew it was not prepared at the diner. However, a gourmet French restaurant charging premium prices and serving frozen Chicken Cordon Blue may find its customers to be less forgiving.

Purchase conversations with the selected supplier will be necessary if a "buy" decision is made. Alternatively, if the decision is made to add the item to the new menu and to prepare it on-site, it will be necessary to begin the purchase any new ingredients and to train production staff about standard recipe procedures.

Establish Quality Standards for Menu Items

Strategy 4 in Figure 4.3 indicates that quality standards must be developed after the specific menu items within each category are identified. Experienced kitchen managers use two tools to develop quality standards. First, standard recipes are needed. They have briefly been discussed in this section, and they will be fully explained in Chapter 6. The second quality tool, purchase specifications, will be explained in Chapter 8.

Standard recipes specify the ingredients, amounts of ingredients, and preparation methods, among other details that must be used when each menu item is produced. By contrast, purchase specifications define the quality requirements that must be met by the ingredients specified in the recipes that must be purchased. Working together, then, these two quality tools help kitchen managers to provide consistency and assure that the guest and property expectations are met.

NOW IT'S YOUR TURN

A PINCH OF THE INTERNET (4.3)

1. Menu labeling is a current topic in the many cities and states that are considering legislation that requires nutrition information to be included on a food service operation's menu. To learn more about this topic, type "menu labeling" in your favorite search engine. In what ways might these laws impact menu planning?

2. You learned that standard recipes are helpful menu planning tools. To view innumerable recipes, type "restaurant recipes" into your favorite search engine.

3. If you want to learn more about the menu categories used by restaurants, just type "restaurant menus" into your favorite search engine. While you are reviewing the menu categories, you can also look at the menu items. Is the property using menu rationalization? Does it appear to be using simple and practical ways to add variety without creating difficult preparation challenges?

4. To view an example of an electronic buying guide, go to: www.business.com. Then enter an item such as frozen beef stew or fresh cheesecake into the site's search box.

COMPLETING THE PLATE QUESTIONS (4.3)

1. What are some menu items that you enjoy when you visit your favorite restaurants? How important are the menu items in your decision to visit these operations? Do you think the menus do a good job of telling you about the items that are available?

2. What are some ways that you as a menu planner could consider your food service operation's financial objectives as you plan the menu?

3. What types of food service operations typically have the largest number of menu item categories? Of menu items within each category? The smallest number of menu categories and items within each category? Why do you think more and fewer categories and number of menu items are required in these different types of operations?

4. What do you think is the most important concern when a make or buy analysis is done: quality or cost? Why?

Kitchen Challenge Du Jour Case Study (4.2)

"Hey, Chef Dante, I'm glad to see you because I want to share something with you," said Bill." Bill, a long-term food server at the Small Town Restaurant was leaving at the end of his shift at the same time that Dante, the kitchen manager at the property, was also ending work.

"What's going on?" asked Dante. "I haven't been able to talk to you for a while during work because we've been so busy lately. I know you're glad about that, and so am I."

"Yes, Dante, you're right," said Bill. "I wanted to tell you that at least two or three people every week tell me that they wish we had more seafood choices. At the same time, I almost never get an order for pork chops or that casserole dish that was added to the menu when it was last revised. I know you are working on menu revisions right now, and this might be something for you and the other managers to think about."

"Well, you're right about that; it is something to think about," replied Dante. "However, there are about a million other things to consider as well. This is good information to know, and I will mention it when our team meets later in the week. Thanks for letting me know, Bill; I really appreciate your interest in making our guests happy."

a) Assume that Chef Dante shares this information with the menu planning team. How should they consider whether to add more seafood items to the entrée category and/or to eliminate the pork chop and casserole items?

b) What are some practical things that the menu planners at the Small Town Restaurant can do to include more seafood variety on the menu?

c) Assume that a business person who brings clients to the restaurant several times a month almost always orders the pork chop entrée. Does this make a difference in the decision to keep pork chops on the menu? Why or why not?

MENU ITEMS AND SELLING PRICE

OBJECTIVE

4. Describe important pricing concerns that should be considered when menus are planned:
   • Menu item selling price spreads
   • Subjective menu pricing methods
   • Objective menu pricing methods

Menu planners must think about the selling price of items when they plan their menus not just when they design them. The price that is set must meet the operation's financial goals while providing value to the guests. While there are several important pricing concerns, two will be discussed in this section: menu item selling price spreads and menu pricing methods.

Menu Item Selling Price Spreads

You know that price is an important concern when you decide where to go for a meal, and it is also an important factor for most people. However, the price people are willing to pay for a meal depends, in part, upon, the purpose of the visit. For example, if they want to celebrate a special occasion such as a wedding anniversary or birthday, they may choose a fine dining restaurant with a high **check average**. The next time they eat out may be with some friends at a casual dining (mid-check average) operation. Their children may prefer quick-service (low check average) meals, and that may be where they go with their families.

OVERHEARD IN THE KITCHEN

Check average—The average amount spent by a guest at a food service operation.

The formula for check average is: Revenue/Number of Guests Served = Check Average.

For example, if 100 guests are served during the evening meal period, and revenues of $1500.00 are received, the check average is $15.00 ($1500.00 revenue ÷ 100 guests = $15.00 check average).

Kitchen managers know, then, that guests in their market go to different types of restaurants based upon the reason they are dining out. That is why "purpose of visit" was included as an important concern in this chapter's earlier discussion about marketing and the menu. However, regardless of the occasion, they want to receive value for the money they spend.

When the prices for menu items are determined, the planning team should be concerned about **excessive price spread**. This is the concept that the range in menu item selling prices cannot be too large because it may encourage guests to select lower-priced items.

OVERHEARD IN THE KITCHEN

Excessive price spread—The concept that, as the range in menu item selling price increases, there is a decrease in check average.

Let's think about Jeff and Lisa. They are celebrating their engagement and decide to go to a "nice" restaurant. The menu indicates that they can select a steak dinner for about $25.00 each or a chicken dinner for about $12.00 each. Jeff and Lisa realize that they can enjoy the same atmosphere, entertainment, cleanliness, service, and other aspects of their dining out experience for $12.00 each or for $25.00 each. They can also tell all of their friends about the fancy place where they went to celebrate. The only difference in what happens will be that they will have a chicken entrée instead of a steak entrée. In fact, the salads, potato, and other vegetable choices, breads, and beverages will also be the same. Is the steak a better choice than the chicken in this situation?

The menu planners will have to hope that Jeff and Lisa think so! Kitchen managers should know, then, that the range between the lowest-priced and highest-priced items cannot be too large. Note: This same concept applies to other menu categories. For example, do you think Jeff and Lisa will select a $15.00 appetizer or a $6.00 appetizer?

Let's assume that the kitchen manager decides that the highest-priced entrée with other dinner accompaniments should be $14.00 and the price spread for other entrée dinners should not go below 75% of this highest-priced item. With this information, the kitchen manager can determine the lowest price for an entrée:

All the kitchen manager must do is determine the selling price that equals 75% of $14.00:

$$\text{Lowest Price Entrée} = \$14.00 \times (1.00 - .25) = \underline{\$10.50}$$

The selling price range would then be from $14.00 (highest price) to $10.50 (lowest price).

The kitchen manager can also determine the selling price range if he/she knew that $12.00 was the lowest price that should be charged and the highest-price item should not, for example, be more than 30% higher than the lowest priced item:

$$\text{Highest Price Entrée} = \$12.00 \times (1.00 + .30) = \underline{\$15.60}$$

The selling price range would then be from $12.00 (lowest price) to $15.60 (highest price).

Subjective Menu Pricing Methods

In addition to providing value for their guests, kitchen managers and their menu planning team must establish selling prices for menu items that meet their operation's financial goals.

Historically, many food service operations have used subjective menu pricing systems (those not based on facts). Today, however, they are increasingly using more objective systems (those that are based upon facts) to "win" in an increasingly competitive marketplace.

Although pricing is critical, the subjective methods don't consider financial or guest-related concerns. Here are some common pricing methods and notice that each is based simply on beliefs that may (or may not) be correct:

- *The Reasonable-Price Method.* A price is set that is judged to represent a value to the guest. The manager may ask, "If I were a guest, what price would I pay for the item being served?" The manager's best guess about this question then becomes the product's selling price.
- *The Highest-Price Method.* The menu item selling price is based on the highest price the owner or manager thinks the guests will pay. The manager's belief about the guests' viewpoint of value may be stretched to the maximum and then be "backed off" to provide a margin of error.
- *The Loss-Leader Method.* An unusually low selling price may be set for a menu item. The manager assumes guests will be attracted to the food service operation by the low price. Then, once there, the manager believes the guests will select other items during their visit to off-set the low price charged for the loss-leader item.
- *The Competitive Method.* In this system, the manager learns what everyone else in the area is charging for a similar menu item and then establishes menu prices that are consistent with these other businesses.
- *The "Wild Guess" Method.* When this selling price method is used, the manager makes little more than a wild guess about the selling price. Closely related to this approach is trial-and-error pricing: If one price doesn't seem to "work," another is tried.

The above and related pricing methods are based on assumptions, hunches, and guesses. They are generally ineffective because they do not consider the operation's profit requirements nor the product costs necessary to put the item on the table. A better approach: Use objective menu pricing methods to establish base selling prices and then make adjustments, if necessary, by evaluating whether they promote value to the guests.

Objective Menu Pricing Methods

Kitchen managers should use objective pricing methods that consider the food service operation's financial goals when selling price decisions are made. If selling price affects profitability (which it does!) and, if selling price is of concern to the guests (which it is!), then attention to how prices are established is important. Several methods are available that use information from the operation's approved budget, and these better address financial and guest-related issues than do the subjective methods reviewed above. For example, a common approach uses the food cost percentage in the approved operating budget.

Assume, for example, that the kitchen manager's operating budget indicates that the food cost should not exceed 37% of revenue. In other words, of all revenue generated from food sales, no more than 37% should be spent for food.

Knowing this, the kitchen manager, perhaps working with the owner/manager and/or accountant can make some basic menu pricing decisions. For example, he/she can calculate a mark-up that can be multiplied by the standard food cost for each menu item to establish a base selling price:

100% of budgeted revenue/37% of revenue allocated for food costs = 2.7 (mark-up)

Assume, for example, that the total food cost incurred to produce a menu item is $5.22.* The kitchen manager can multiply the cost of the food required to produce the menu item by the mark-up to determine a base selling price for the item:

$5.22 (Menu Item Food Cost) × 2.7 (Mark-Up) = $14.10 Base Selling Price (rounded)

If the base selling price just determined seems reasonable, the menu item can be sold for about $14.00 – $14.25. If, in the management team's judgment, the actual selling price should be adjusted upward or downward this can be done. However, making a tentative pricing decision based upon budget estimates such as in this example is better than arriving at a selling price based solely upon the subjective menu pricing tactics discussed above.

These guests are enjoying their meals because they have been priced at a selling price that is of value to the guests.

Objective menu planning decisions consider the food cost of the items being priced. When the items are prepared according to standard recipes, this does not create a problem because the amount of each ingredient used will be known. Then a method called **costing** can be used to determine the cost of each ingredient that should have been used to produce the item.

OVERHEARD IN THE KITCHEN

Costing (recipe)—The process of determining the cost to produce all (or one) serving of a recipe by considering the recipe's ingredients, current ingredient costs, and the number of servings which the recipe yields.

Chapter 6 will discuss standard recipes in detail, and you'll learn about procedures to pre-cost standard recipes in Chapter 7.

NOW IT'S YOUR TURN

A PINCH OF THE INTERNET (4.4)

1. What is the relationship between a restaurant's regular menu item pricing and that for menu pricing for specials? To get an idea, enter the term, "menu specials," in your favorite search engine. Then select some of your favorite restaurant chains and other local food service operations to see how their pricing for specials relates to other items.

2. To learn common menu pricing methods, type the term, "menu pricing methods," into your favorite search engine. You'll then be able to read numerous articles about the topic.

3. This section suggested that there should be some relationship between the food cost of a menu item and its selling price. To learn more about this topic, type

"food cost and menu pricing" into your favorite search engine.

COMPLETING THE PLATE QUESTIONS (4.4)

1. Why do you think kitchen managers and other members of the menu planning team often use subjective menu pricing methods like those noted in this section?

2. What would you do if you were Jeff or Lisa and you visited the restaurant that offered a $25.00 steak dinner and a $12.00 chicken dinner? Why? What does this teach you about the pricing of specific menu items within a menu category?

3. What would a restaurant have to be like for you to pay $10.00 for a hamburger and French fry plate? By contrast, what would you expect in a restaurant that sold the same menu item for $4.50?

Overheard in the Kitchen Glossary

Market	Standard recipe	Competitive edge	Umami (taste)
Return on investment (ROI)	Menu category	Table turn	Center of plate
Resources	Entrée	Brainstorming	Make or buy analysis
Market form	Vegetarian (menu item)	Trend	Chain of command
Fire suppression system	Casserole	Menu rationalization	Chain recipe
Profit maximization	Appetizer	Moist heat	Benchmark (standard)
Cost minimization	Consommé	Dry heat	Taste test
Repeat business	Broth	Texture	Check average
Controller	Cuisine	Garnish	Excessive price spread
Serving costs	Boutique brewery	Fusion (cuisine)	Costing (recipe)
Investment	Signature item	Flavor	

LESSON 4

If you are reading this textbook as part of a formal class, your Instructor may want you to apply and practice what you have learned in this chapter by completing Lesson 4 of the Pearson Education's Kitchen Management Simulation (KMS). If you are required to complete KMS Lesson 4; read **About Lesson 4** below, then go to: www.pearsonhighered.com/kms for instructions on how to access and complete it.

After you have successfully completed the lesson, think about the way you, as a professional kitchen manager, would answer the **For Your Consideration** questions that follow.

About Lesson 4

By mastering the information in this chapter you have learned how kitchen managers plan their menus. This KMS lesson was designed to let you practice what you have learned. In it you will first see why kitchen managers create menu categories that are designed to help their guests make informed menu choices more easily.

You will also practice choosing menus that exhibit the product variation you learned about in this chapter. Menu variation is very important to guests. In this lesson you will practice choosing menu items that add market form, preparation method, and portion size variation to your menus. This KMS lesson also lets you practice using the pricing formulas you learned about by asking you to apply them to the kinds of real-world decisions kitchen managers make when they plan their menus.

Kitchen managers know that "It all starts with the menu." Lesson 4 of the KMS allows you to practice the tasks kitchen managers use to plan menus that appeal to a wide range of guests by emphasizing variety in menu items offered, item presentation, and menu item prices.

For Your Consideration

1. Do you think all menus should be planned in ways that make them appealing to a wide range of diners?
2. What are some specific ways kitchen managers could find out if their current guests thought their menus would be better if they offered more variety?
3. Do you think that planning a menu with a large number of items is the same as planning a menu with a wide variety of items? Why?

Kitchen Managers Design Their Menu

Learning Objectives

After studying this chapter, you will be able to:

1. Review basic ways to classify menus.
2. Explain how to design menus to sell.
3. Discuss basic menu design concerns.
4. Review procedures to design wine lists and pair (match) foods with wines.

COMING RIGHT UP OVERVIEW

In Chapter 4, you learned about some of the challenges kitchen managers face as they serve as members of the menu planning team for their food service operations. In this chapter, you'll see how menu-related concerns continue when menus are designed.

First, you'll learn about the basic types of menus. For example, they can be classified by how the items are sold, how the menus are designed, and whether they have a traditional (hardcopy) or nontraditional format including all types of creative alternatives.

The best menus don't just indicate the items available and their selling prices. Instead, they also help to promote the sale of the items that the kitchen manager and other members of the property's team want to sell. There are several basic menu design procedures to do this, and you'll learn about them in this chapter.

There are numerous other concerns that the menu design team must consider. These include issues about menu descriptions, menu pricing, menu accuracy, menu appearance, and issues about special menu items. By the time you've finished this section of the chapter, you'll understand that much thinking and creativity is required to plan a menu that really reflects the best of the food service operation, what it wants to be, and how it wants to present itself to guests.

The final section of this chapter discusses wine menus. Do all kitchen managers develop wine lists? No, they do not, but some do make suggestions. They know about the long-standing tradition that wine is a natural companion to food, and they have ideas about the types of wine that best go with the food items they produce. They also know that a properly developed wine list represents the food service operation in the same ways as its counterpart, the properly designed food menu. Many kitchen managers have a great deal of experience with wine selection, and their help with promoting the sale of wine in their food service operation is very beneficial.

BASIC TYPES OF MENUS

Oᴮᴶᴱᴄᴛɪᴠᴇ

1. Review basic ways to classify menus:
   - Menus classified by items sold
   - Menus classified by design
   - Traditional and nontraditional menus

In the last chapter, you learned that the term, "menu," is French, and that it means "detailed list." You also learned about commonly-used tactics that are utilized to plan the list of menu items to be offered by the food service operation. In this chapter, you'll discover how food items to be offered to guests will be placed on the menu they will receive. We'll begin our study of **menu design** by reviewing the basic types of menus that food service operations can use. This will provide background information to help you focus on the specific menu design factors that will be discussed throughout the rest of the chapter.

OVERHEARD IN THE KITCHEN

Menu design—The process by which the planning team develops a format for the menu that will be presented to guests to inform them about the items available.

Menus Classified by Items Sold

There are several common types of menus:

- **À la carte menu**. The phrase, *à la carte*, means individually priced; an à la carte menu lists food items that are separately priced. The guest charge is then based on the prices of the items that the guest orders.
- **Table d'hôte menu**. This term basically means *all at one price*. In other words, the guest charge does not vary based on what the guests select. For example, a restaurant may seat guests at 6:00 pm and 8:30 pm and serve all guests the same meal at both seating times. This would be similar to a banquet except the guests rather than a banquet host or hostess pay for the meals. Another alternative: The meal may be divided into courses, and the guests may select one menu item from a list of several for each course with no price difference regardless of the items that are ordered. Many properties also offer a weekend or holiday **buffet** for a specified (fixed) price. The items offered on this buffet are priced table d'hôte

The menu informs the guests about the food items that are available and is a critical marketing and communication tool.

because the guest is charged a fixed price that is unrelated to which or how much of the specific buffet items are selected.

- **Cyclical (cycle) menu.** The word *cyclical* refers to a cycle in which the menu is planned for a specified time period and then repeated. The food service operation may, for example, offer a twenty-eight-day menu which is repeated every four weeks (twenty-eight days). When these menus are used, it is common to make substitutions during days of special events and holidays. Cycle menus are most typically offered by noncommercial food services such as those in schools, colleges, retirement centers and military bases, but they may also be used for commercial buffet operations.
- **Du jour menu.** The phrase, *du jour*, means *of the day.* Many food service operations offer daily specials (du jour items) in addition to their regular menu items.

OVERHEARD IN THE KITCHEN

À la carte menu—A menu in which each food item served during the meal is sold at a separate price, and the total guest charge depends upon the items selected.

Table d'hôte menu—A menu in which food items comprising a meal are sold at a fixed price, and the total guest charge does not depend upon the items selected.

Buffet—A style of food service in which menu items are generally selected and portioned by guests as they pass along one or more serving counters. Some buffets use food production personnel to carve roast beef or ham and to make omelets or other items to order.

Cyclical (cycle) menu—A menu in which the food items rotate according to a planned schedule such as every twenty-eight days.

Du jour menu—A menu in which some or all food items are changed daily.

Menus Classified by Design

In most table-service restaurants, guests receive a physical, printed menu when they are seated. These menus come in several different shapes and sizes. Figure 5.1 illustrates some of the most common types:

- *A—Single-sheet menus.* These menus feature information including item descriptions on one or both sides of a single sheet.

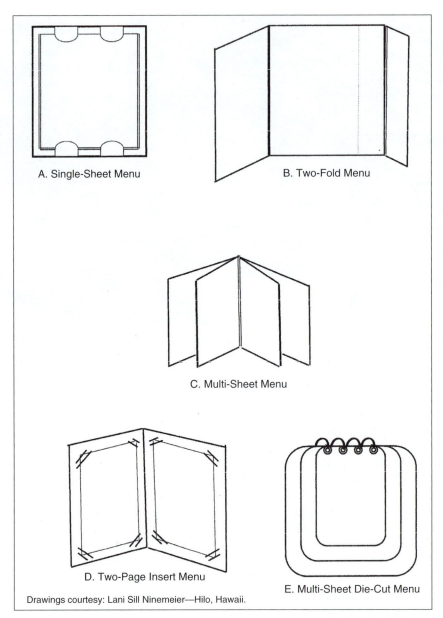

A. Single-Sheet Menu

B. Two-Fold Menu

C. Multi-Sheet Menu

D. Two-Page Insert Menu

E. Multi-Sheet Die-Cut Menu

Drawings courtesy: Lani Sill Ninemeier—Hilo, Hawaii.

FIGURE 5.1   Common Types of Menus

- *B—Two-fold menus.* These open like a book. They may show the restaurant's name on the cover and then include menu items on the remaining pages. Note: The example shown in Figure 5.1 features an opening that is to the right of the menu's center.
- *C—Multi-sheet menus.* These are like the two page insert menus, as shown in Figure 5.1 (D), except that they have additional inside sheets.
- *D—Two-page insert menus.* These menus have two sheets that are placed into a relatively sturdy and often colorful cover. These inserts can be changed daily or as frequently as desired.
- *E—Multi-sheet,* die-cut *menus.* These allow the menu planners to present eye-catching menus that are often part of a restaurant's theme.

OVERHEARD IN THE KITCHEN

Die-cut (menu)—A menu that has been punched or cut into a special shape with a metal tool called a die.

INFORMATION ON THE SIDE

Many Food Service Terms Are French Words

The role of French chefs and culinarians is well-known in the history of early quantity food production, and French terms are still widely used in modern food service operations. Two examples—chef and menus—are used extensively in this book. Other terms such as brigade (how a kitchen and dining room are organized), toque (chef's hat), sous chef (the first assistant to the chef), bouillon (a clear, delicately seasoned soup, usually made from lean beef stock) and haute cuisine (high or fine food preparation) are among numerous common examples.

Professional kitchen managers know and properly use the language of their profession. They also teach these terms to those whom they supervise.

Traditional and Nontraditional Menus

To this point, we have been discussing traditional hardcopy and hand-held menus. These types of menus are very popular because they can be:

- Presented to guests when they are seated.
- Sent to potential guests as advertising.
- Attached or posted on a sign outside the food service operation to attract persons walking by.
- Left on tables for guests to read after they are seated.

However, if you recall our definition of menu (a detailed list), there are other ways that guests can learn about the food items that are available.

Food service operations in hotels have used door-knob menus for many years. These allow guests to note their preferences for room service breakfasts and then place the menu on the knob or handle of their outside the guestroom door. Today, guests in many lodging properties can order meals using room service menus available on guest room televisions. Note: Some health-care facilities also allow their patients to place electronic food orders.

Perhaps the most common hardcopy alternative is one that almost everyone recognizes: The menu board at a **quick-service** restaurant. Most of these operations have menu boards at drive-through lanes and also at the dine-in order counter. Word and/or picture descriptions can be provided on simple (even handwritten) models or on modern electronic menu boards where changes to items, descriptions, graphics and selling prices can be inputted in much the same way as you would enter words or other information into a word processor.

OVERHEARD IN THE KITCHEN

Quick-service (restaurant)—A food service operation that provides a limited menu and limited service (generally self-serve at counters or through vehicle drive-through windows) at low prices; also called a QSR, or "fast-food" restaurant.

A restaurant's theme may suggest how the menu is presented. Think about a restaurant with a high-tech theme with its menu on a video screen, a steak house with a menu etched into a wooden cutting board, and a "rock-and-roll"-themed property with a menu presented on old vinyl (plastic) records. In some operations, service persons recite or sing menu items and, in many buffet operations, the menu involves small signs placed near each food item on the serving line. There are, indeed, many traditional and very creative ways that food service operations inform their guests about available items.

NOW IT'S YOUR TURN

A PINCH OF THE INTERNET (5.1)

1. Do you want to learn more about modern electronic menu boards? If so, type "restaurant menu boards" into your favorite search engine.
2. Many persons collect old menus, and many food service professionals are interested in learning about the history of menus. If you would like to learn more about and see numerous examples of old menus, type "vintage menus" into your favorite search engine.
3. Menu design consultants are available to help kitchen managers and others on their planning team to design creative menus. To learn about their services, type "restaurant menu design consultants" into your favorite search engine.

COMPLETING THE PLATE QUESTIONS (5.1)

1. What are examples of nontraditional menus that you have seen in restaurant operations you have visited?
2. This section of the chapter mentioned mailing menus to potential guests as an advertising technique. What are other ways that menus can be used to advertise a food service operation?
3. Pretend you are a guest at a restaurant that you have never before visited. What are things you might learn about the restaurant besides the actual items that it serves when you look through the operation's menu?
4. How might a kitchen manager contribute to conversations about menu design being conducted by other members of the property's menu planning and design team?

DESIGN MENUS TO SELL

O B J E C T I V E

2. Explain how to design menus to sell:
   • How long should menus be?
   • How can menu items be promoted?
   • Where should menu items be located?

Modern menus have come a long way since they were initially used to inform potential guests about the items available when they were standing at the front door of the food service operation and deciding whether they should enter. In contrast, today's menus are a critical menu **merchandising** tool.

OVERHEARD IN THE KITCHEN

Merchandising—The act of promoting certain menu items in efforts to encourage guests to select them.

In this section, we'll answer some questions about menu development so you will be better able to design menus that do an effective job selling your menu items.

How Long Should Menus Be?

There is no definite answer to this question. However, when menus contain more pages, it takes guests longer to review the items that are available, and they may have more questions as they read about the items. This, in turn, slows the ordering process and reduces the table turn rate. While guests should be allowed the time they wish to dine, menus designed to sell recognize that faster table turns yield more opportunities for additional guests to be seated and served and for additional revenues to be generated.

Menus offering many pages of menu items may offer "something for everyone," and, sometimes, restaurants offering extensive menus can have a competitive edge over their counterparts.

Very short menus such as those consisting of just a single sheet or page may also create problems because the lessened variety of menu items may not provide enough variety to appeal to large numbers of guests. Food service operations with short menus are often highly specialized and, in effect, may offer only a signature food category and just a few other items. Note: Signature foods were discussed in Chapter 4.

Menu planners know that the number of pages in their menu is partially determined when the menu is planned, not designed, because the menu must inform guests about all of the items the menu planners want to make available. This again reemphasizes the critical need for menu planners to consider their target market of guests and what these guests want. Then the menu being designed will be attractive to the guests for whom it is planned.

How Can Menu Items Be Promoted?

Menus should be designed to promote the sale of items that the food service operation wants to sell: Those that are the most profitable and/or the most popular **Menu engineering** is a widely-used process that helps to determine the best items to promote, and the process will be discussed at length in Chapter 10. For the purposes of this chapter, let's assume that Vernon's Restaurant has determined that its Starry Nights Linguine entrée is an item it wants to promote. Figure 5.2 shows several ways that menu designers can help assure that guests are aware of this item.

Tactic 1: Use a Box

★ **Starry Nights Shrimp Linguine** ★

Tender shrimp sautéed in a special garlic and scallions butter sauce with a touch of heavy cream and special seasonings served over our fresh-made Linguine pasta.

(A lighter portion is available)

★ **Starry Nights Shrimp Linguine** ★

Tender shrimp sautéed in a special garlic and scallions butter sauce with a touch of heavy cream and special seasonings served over our fresh-made Linguine pasta.

(A lighter portion is available)

Tactic 2: Use Shading

★ **Starry Nights Shrimp Linguine** ★

Tender shrimp sautéed in a special garlic and scallions butter sauce with a touch of heavy cream and special seasonings served over our fresh-made Linguine pasta.

(A lighter portion is available)

★ **Starry Nights Shrimp Linguine** ★

Tender shrimp sautéed in a special garlic and scallions butter sauce with a touch of heavy cream and special seasonings served over our fresh-made Linguine pasta.

(A lighter portion is available)

Tactic 3: Use a Different Type Style

★ **Starry Nights Shrimp Linguine** ★

Tender shrimp sautéed in a special garlic and scallions butter sauce with a touch of heavy cream and special seasonings served over our fresh-made Linguine pasta.

(A lighter portion is available)

★ **Starry Nights Shrimp Linguine** ★

Tender shrimp sautéed in a special garlic and scallions butter sauce with a touch of heavy cream and special seasonings served over our fresh-made Linguine pasta.

(A lighter portion is available)

FIGURE 5.2 Tactics To Promote Selected Menu Items
Courtesy of Lani Sill Ninemeier, Hilo, Hawaii

OVERHEARD IN THE KITCHEN

Menu engineering—A method of menu evaluation that focuses on the goal of selling as many as possible of the menu items that are the most popular for guests and the most profitable for the food service operation.

When reviewing Figure 5.2, notice that there are some simple ways to help a menu item that you want to promote stand out from other items. Which item does the kitchen manager want guests to notice? It is easy to tell in the three examples shown in 5.2. A simple or "fancy" box (Tactic 1) can be placed around the desired item. Alternatively, shading (Tactic 2), or a larger or different type font (letter style) can be used (Tactic 3).

Note: Colored print is another possibility, but this creates an additional menu printing expense. Some food service operations also use color photos of selected menu items or color/black and white illustrations of concepts in line with the property's theme.

INFORMATION ON THE SIDE

Common Menu Design Problems

- Menu type is too small so it is hard to read.
- The menu appears cluttered; there is too much to read.
- Words are printed on top of graphics (or vice versa).
- There is decorative script and/or typefaces that are difficult to read.
- The menu cannot be easily read in dimly lighted dining areas.
- The menu is not designed to sell items that the property wants to sell (i.e. those items that are popular and/or profitable).
- Foreign or unusual culinary words are used without sufficient explanation.
- The poor design fails to help the guests' eyes follow from category-to-category and from item-to-item.
- Graphics do not contribute to the menu's **aesthetic** appeal nor do they help to sell items.
- Selling prices are placed so that the guests focus on them rather than on the menu item itself.
- Printing is expensive, and this makes it more difficult to justify frequent menu replacements.
- The menus are physically too large to handle or read.
- The menus are physically too small to handle or read.
- The menus are printed on too lightweight a paper stock and, therefore, lack durability and cannot be easily cleaned.
- The menus do not accurately represent the actual items that will be served to the guests.

OVERHEARD IN THE KITCHEN

Aesthetic—Relating to one's sense of beauty.

There are numerous other menu design tactics that are important, and these include:

- Be sure the menu is attractive and presents a good first impression. Ask yourself the question, "Am I proud of this menu?" "Does it represent the food service operation to our guests in the most favorable way?"
- Be sure the type can be easily read.
- The menu should not be cluttered; as a rule of thumb, approximately one-half of the space on a menu page should be blank.
- Assure that all words are correctly spelled, and that there are no hard-to-read or hard-to-understand foreign terms.
- Be sure that the menu descriptions rather than the selling price are the focus of the guests' attention. Note: This topic is discussed later in this chapter.
- Consider the menu's size; it should be neither too big nor too little to comfortably read and handle at the table.
- Menus are durable and easy-to-clean unless they are disposable (single-use).

Menus that promote specific items use available space wisely. For example, it is not usually necessary to spend a significant amount of space to describe a common product such as a tossed salad or apple pie. In contrast, less common items, including those unique to the restaurant, will likely need more space and description. Caution: Be careful when naming an item like "Chef Priscilla's Garden Soup" unless you also describe the item in detail. This is because no one other than frequent guests will know about the item's ingredients and preparation methods, and servers will require additional time to explain the soup to the guests.

Where Should Menu Items Be Located?

Menu layout relates to where items are placed on the menu. Normally, an operation's menu categories drive or influence the layout. If appetizer, soup and salad, and entrée categories have been identified, the layout must include space for them. Some menu designers place categories on the menu in the sequence of service. In these cases, appetizers are listed before soups and salads which are listed before entrées. However, kitchen managers must recognize that menus have **prime real estate** areas where the most popular and highly profitable items should be placed.

OVERHEARD IN THE KITCHEN

Menu layout—A term relating to the placement of menu item categories on the menu.
Prime real estate (menu design)—The areas on a menu most frequently viewed by guests and which, therefore, should contain the items that menu planners most want to sell.

A menu item's location on the menu can influence the frequency of its sale because guests typically look at certain areas of the menu more than other areas.

Figure 5.3 shows the prime locations on three common types of menus.

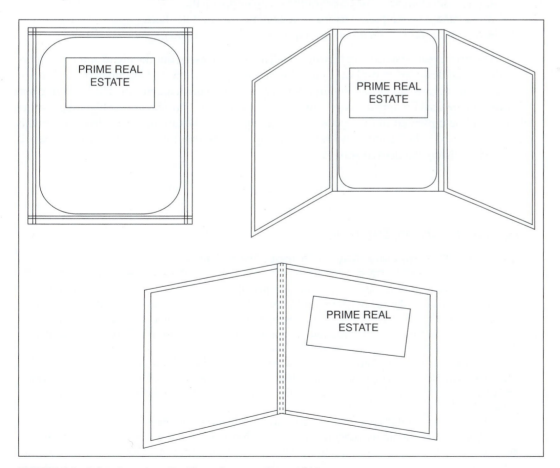

FIGURE 5.3 Prime Locations On Three Common Types of Menus
Courtesy of Lani Sill Ninemeier, Hilo, Hawaii.

This menu is carefully planned and designed and will help sell the items that are the most profitable and popular at the food service operation.

When you review Figure 5.3, note the critical space on:

- *A single-sheet menu*—the center of the menu's upper half.
- *A two-folded (three-panel) menu*—the center of the middle sheet.
- *A two-sheet (folded) menu*—the top center of the right-hand page.

The prime real estate concept creates challenges when laying out the menu and it is important that menu designers know how to use this limited space wisely. For example, you've learned that many menus are laid out in sequence for each course. What happens, then, if the prime real estate would be used for appetizers or soups/salads when specific entrées are the highest priorities that should be presented in this space? Menu designers should carefully consider whether this space is best used to build additional sales from appetizers or other items or whether the space is best used for listing the desired entrées.

INFORMATION ON THE SIDE
Menus Are Not the Only Way to Promote Menu Items

You've learned that effectively designed menus can help the food service operation to sell the items it wishes to sell. However, the menu should only be one tool in the restaurant's sales tool box to achieve this goal. For example, food servers can be encouraged to make recommendations, table tents can encourage guests to order selected items, and media advertising and on-site promotional activities can all reinforce the emphasis on the menu items the operation wants to sell.

Kitchen managers and their food preparation teams also can do a lot to encourage the sales of specific items. Consider, for example, the sizzling steak on a platter that is noticed by guests getting ready to order their own entrée, or the flaming dessert that is lighted in the kitchen before servers walk past the guests' tables.

How about beautifully prepared and garnished food items in serving pans in commercial cafeterias and the attractive pastry or other menu items on display in breakfast-oriented retail outlets in a hotel's lobby? While the menu can help to sell items, it cannot replace the need for kitchen managers to consistently deliver the quality of items represented on the menu and to make the desired items attractive to the guests.

■ NOW IT'S YOUR TURN

A PINCH OF THE INTERNET (5.2)

1. Want to see some free menu layout graphics? If so, go to: www.specialweb.com/original

2. Want to learn about menu design software? If so, type this term into your favorite search engine.

3. One of the very best ways to learn about menu design is to review existing menus. As you do so, you'll learn lots of "do's and don'ts" that can be considered as you plan menus. Just type "restaurant menus" into your favorite search engine, and you will find, literally, millions of menus for your review.

COMPLETING THE PLATE QUESTIONS (5.2)

1. What are some things that you personally like and dislike about menu design that you notice when you read a printed menu or look at a menu board?

2. Many states and/or communities are considering nutrition labeling laws that require certain nutritional information to be included on menus along with the items. Do you favor or oppose this type of legislation? Why?

3. How would you determine the physical size of a menu that will be used in your operation?

Kitchen Challenge Du Jour Case Study (5.1)

"I don't get it!" said Robert, a cook at Vernon's Restaurant. "It seems like all they want to do is make work harder for us."

Robert was talking to another cook after they had both learned that a very labor-intensive menu item ("Vernon's Home-Baked Pot Pie") was going to be featured on the new menu. "We have to make the pastry, do lots of vegetable and meat chopping, and prepare the sauce for our pot-pie recipe."

"Yes, it does taste good, but so are other items on the menu. In fact, if all of the items on our menu weren't good, why would they even be there?" replied Jacelyn, the second cook. "The way it's been, the pot pie was on the menu, and we had to prepare a few servings each shift. However, now I understand it's going to take up a large part of one page on our menu, be highlighted in big type, and the servers are being trained to 'push' the item. Why are they doing that to us?" Jacelyn continued.

1. Assume you were Robert's and Jacelyn's kitchen manager, and they approached you and asked, "Why do you want to emphasize the pot pie when it takes so much work for us to prepare it?" How would you respond to them?

2. What are some things that the kitchen manager might do to make it easier (more practical) to prepare the greater quantities of Vernon's Home-Baked Pot Pie that will (hopefully!) be sold?

MENU DESIGN CONCERNS

OBJECTIVE

3. Discuss basic menu design concerns:
   - Menu item descriptions
   - Menu pricing
   - Menu accuracy
   - Menu appearance
   - Special menu items

In this section, you'll learn about several other issues that must be considered as menus are designed.

Menu Item Descriptions

Effective menus tell what items are available, and they help to influence the guest's choices. Item descriptions answer potential questions that menu readers may have. Consider two menu items: "Seafood Fettuccine" and "Bouillabaisse."

Many guests may know that fettuccine is a pasta. However the menu should tell guests about the type of seafood and the sauce used for this item. If it does not, guests will likely be annoyed because they will have to ask their server who, then, will have less time to provide the quality of service that other guests deserve.

Unless guests are from southern areas of the United States, many guests may not be familiar with bouillabaisse. Many food items in the Cajun and Creole cuisines have evolved from a unique blend of worldwide food traditions and ingredients. There is no **standard of identity** to define what must be included in this (usually) spicy seafood soup or stew. Therefore, the menu must inform guests about this product in general (it is a spicy stew) and, more specifically, about the ingredients used by the kitchen manager to prepare it at the specific food service operation.

OVERHEARD IN THE KITCHEN

Standard of identity—A detailed description of ingredients to be included in a specific food product. For example, "fruit cocktail" must have a specified percentage of maraschino cherries and other fruits. If it does not, the product must be called "mixed fruit."

What kinds of questions might a guest have about an item called "Walnut-Crusted Salmon?" Is it a fillet? Is it fresh or was it frozen? What is its approximate **as-purchased** weight, and how is it prepared? Is there a sauce? Our list of possible questions can continue. However, a basic guideline menu designers must address relates to what readers need to know to make an informed purchase decision. Then this information must be provided in the menu description.

OVERHEARD IN THE KITCHEN

As-purchased (weight)—The weight of a product before it is prepared or cooked; also called "AP weight."

The kitchen manager and other members of the menu design team must consider several other things as menu descriptions are written. For example:

- They must write plainly. Avoid technical culinary terms and foreign words unless the average guest is likely to know these words. For example, write "dumplings" instead of "quenelles," "shredded vegetable" garnish instead of "chiffonade," and "sautéed tomato" instead of "pince."
- Define menu items carefully and correctly. For example, New England clam chowder (white) is not the same as Manhattan clam chowder (red).
- Be sure to spell all words correctly and that means carefully checking every word in early drafts of the menu. Menu writers should know how to spell Portobello (mushrooms), vinaigrette (dressing), and au jus (with juice) and many other commonly used words that will present spelling challenges.
- Write carefully and use the correct pronunciation and use correct punctuations. Some descriptions are, at the same time, inaccurate and sometimes funny. For example, only the last description is accurate in the following list:
  - A seafood fillet served with a baked potato ladled with our special sauce.
  - A seafood fillet ladled with our special sauce and baked potato.
  - A seafood fillet ladled with our special sauce and served with a baked potato.
- Rewrite and reedit. Several persons on the menu design team should carefully review all menu descriptions. As well, someone with a solid command of writing and editing skills should also be retained for this purpose.

The food on this plate looks beautiful but it must also adhere to its description on the menu.

INFORMATION ON THE SIDE
Nutrition and the Menu

Kitchen managers offering nutritional food alternatives have several options when they design the menu. They can:

- Place these items in a separate section of the menu. Some operations use, for example, sections labeled "Heart-Healthy," "Lite Selections," or a similar heading. Note: The term "Heart-Healthy" is copyrighted by the American Heart Association, and it has established restrictions for its use.
- Include the nutritional items with other items in the same category and mark them with a symbol that suggests a special nutritional feature.
- Make a general statement on the menu such as: "We recognize the nutritional concerns of many of our guests, and we can prepare some of our items to meet your nutrition concerns. Please discuss your preferences with your server." Note: Nutrition content and healthy claims on the menu must be truthful. The health and well-being of guests concerned about nutrition are too important to take lightly, and it is not appropriate (and may be unlawful) to misstate dietary claims in menu descriptions. Sometimes, for example, menus indicate the number of grams of fat and/or the milligrams of cholesterol and sodium in selected menu items. These amounts may be very accurate when the item is prepared in a controlled situation with a detailed standard recipe, and when precision portion tools and exacting measurements are used. However, this extreme accuracy becomes difficult (impossible?) to attain in a quantity food kitchen when many meals must be prepared quickly by production personnel with, perhaps, good intentions but with pressures for fast output. A better approach: Omit this detailed information or say, "about" or "approximately" before the detailed information (example: "contains approximately 400 calories").
- Terms such as "free" (such as in "fat-free"), "low" (such as in "low-fat"), and "lean" (such as in "lean beef") have a specific meaning for persons who are knowledgeable and concerned about the nutritional content of meals they consume. A better approach: Specify, for example, that an item is made with margarine (instead of butter) and that low-fat cottage cheese is used on a salad plate. Nutrition labeling regulations required for the margarine and cottage cheese will help managers and production personnel know what they are serving to guests who order special items based upon health-conscious concerns.

Menu Pricing

Guests reading the menu descriptions will want to know the selling price of each menu item. Does it make any difference how selling prices are indicated on the menu? Many experienced menu designers believe that it does, and this section reviews some of their thoughts.

First, some menu writers like to use odd-cents pricing. They reason that the human mind can sometimes distort reality and influence price perceptions. For example, do you think you receive a better value when a menu item is priced at $7.99 instead of $8.00 even though there is only a one-cent difference in the selling prices? Also, after a quick read could you think for a moment that the difference between $3.69 and $3.79 is less than between $3.99 and $4.09 even though there is only a 10 cent range in both example?

The number of digits (numbers) in the selling price may also influence guests' perceptions. Consider, for example, the 26 cents difference between $7.99 and $8.25 and the 50 cents increase from $18.25 to $18.75. The first increase (26 cents) may initially seem to be larger than the second (50 cents) increase to some persons.

Wise menu designers know that guests have an overall impression of the food service operation's selling prices before they receive a menu. They will know that a casual dining restaurant will have a lower check average than a fine dining, high-check average property, and that is an important concern for many guests when they make a dining-out decision. Therefore, while some of the pricing tactics just noted may influence how guests make purchase decisions, this can only happen after they have decided to visit the food service operation and then receive the menu or look at the menu board.

INFORMATION ON THE SIDE
Where Should the Selling Price Be Placed?

Menu designers recognize that the emphasis of a menu item description should focus on the item available for sale rather than its cost. How, then, can this idea be addressed in menu item descriptions? One way is to carefully think about where the menu item's selling price should be placed.

Do you think the placement of selling price in the following list will make any difference about what is emphasized: the menu item or the selling price?

- Stuffed green pepper served with choice of vegetables..........$6.95
- Stuffed green pepper served with choice of vegetables $6.95
- Stuffed green pepper served with choice of vegetables 6.95
- Stuffed green pepper served with choice of vegetables..........($6.95)
- Stuffed green pepper served with choice of vegetables ($6.95)
- Stuffed green pepper served with choice of vegetables (6.95)

Menu Accuracy

Kitchen managers and others writing menu descriptions must truthfully describe the items being served, and they must know about **truth-in-menu** issues.[1]

OVERHEARD IN THE KITCHEN

Truth-in-menu—The requirements (and laws in some locations) that menu descriptions honestly tell the quantity, quality, point of origin, and other information so that readers will understand the items being described; for example, "fresh gulf shrimp" cannot be frozen shrimp from the Indian Ocean.

Problems with menu accuracy include the following:

- *Quantity.* A two-egg omelet should contain two eggs; an eight-ounce steak should weigh approximately eight ounces (AP).
- *Quality.* The term "prime" used to describe a steak refers to a specific U.S. Department of Agriculture (USDA) grading standard. U.S. Grade A or U.S. Fancy (for vegetables) and

Grade AA (for eggs and butter) also indicate specific quality grades. Only the quality of products actually used should be indicated on the menu.

- *Price.* If there are extra charges (for example, for **call brand** or **premium brand** liquors), these prices should be identified. If **service charges** will be added when the number of guests at a table equal or exceed a certain size, these should be indicated.
- *Brand names.* If a specific product brand (example: Coca Cola) is noted on the menu, this brand should be served.
- *Product identification.* Maple syrup and maple-flavored syrup are not the same nor are orange juice and orange drink.
- *Points of origin.* "Pacific" shrimp, for example, cannot be from the Indian Ocean; Idaho potatoes cannot be from Wisconsin.
- *Merchandising terms.* Guests recognize that **trade puffing** is different from purposeful misrepresentation.
- *Preservation.* Frozen apple juice or canned green beans should not be called "fresh."
- *Food preparation.* "Made on-site" does not apply to a convenience food product produced elsewhere.
- *Verbal and visual presentation.* A menu photograph depicting eight shrimp on a shrimp platter means that eight shrimp should be served when the item is ordered.
- *Dietary and nutritional claims.* If the menu indicates "egg substitutes are available," they should be, and they must be used when this product is requested.
- *Preparation style.* If the preparation method is listed on the menu, this technique should be used to prepare the item. For example, if an item is listed on the menu as grilled, the item cannot just have mechanically-produced grill marks and then be steamed before service. Also, if an item is called "home made," it should be prepared on-site.
- *Nutritional benefits.* There are very strict guidelines about what menus can—and cannot say about nutritional claims.[2]

OVERHEARD IN THE KITCHEN

Call brand (liquor)—A specific brand of liquor requested by a guest. Typically, these brands are more expensive and of a higher quality than the brands that would be served if no specific brand was requested.
Premium brand (liquor)—The most expensive brands of quality liquor available at a food service operation.
Service charge—A labor-related fee added by the management of a food service operation that must be paid by the guests. Service charges are typically computed as a percentage of a guest's food and beverage expenditures.
Trade puffing—The tactic of boasting about a product when advertising. A "Mile-High Pie" is obviously not one mile tall, and the "best hamburger in the world" is probably more of a merchandising statement than it is a provable fact.

When applicable, caution statements should be added to menus that alert guests about potential problems such as small bones in fish, sulfates in wine, and eating under-cooked meats. Also, statements on some menus request that guests should alert servers to any food allergies when ordering menu items.

Menu Appearance

Several factors contribute to how a menu looks including:

- *Cover.* The menu cover provides guests with an early visual impression of the restaurant and the dining experience they should expect. How the front cover should look depends on the type of restaurant. Its design must fit with the restaurant's décor and theme. At the least, it should include the restaurant's name. Padded menu covers and backs made from imitation (or genuine!) leather, velvet, or other materials are available. Inexpensive paper covers that change daily are used in some food service operations that use **desktop publishing systems**. Menu covers containing see-through "pockets" with the cover on one side and a menu page on the cover's back are common. Paper menus can be laminated (coated) with a plastic film that makes them easily cleaned, and these are popular in family service properties.

OVERHEARD IN THE KITCHEN

Desktop publishing systems—A personal computer and specific software used to create high-quality page layouts and documents that otherwise would need to be developed by a professional printer.

- *Overall size.* The menu can be small (8.5 inches by 11 inches or smaller) or large (15 inches by 20 inches or larger). The number of menu items and other factors such as the number of pages, spacing, graphics, and type styles affect a menu's size. If a menu panel is too small, the print is typically small, and then it may be hard to read; a large menu may be inconvenient for guests to handle.
- *Materials.* A menu's construction material affects its durability and cleanability. If a menu cannot be cleaned, it must be discarded regardless of cost. The cost and ease of cleaning menus must be considered when the menu is developed.
- *Menu shape.* An unusual menu shape may help project a particular image. Paper can easily (but not inexpensively!) be cut into shapes other than the typical rectangle. Consider a breakfast menu in the shape of a doughnut or coffee cup or a luncheon menu shaped like a hamburger.
- *Type style.* An otherwise attractive menu is made less so when the menu's type style is hard to read. The primary concern in choosing a typeface for a menu is its readability. Type that is too small or too closely-spaced can create confusion. Then, instead of the ordering process being a pleasurable introduction to a fine meal, it becomes a less-than-hospitable experience that can affect repeat business. The actual lighting level in the dining area affects the menu's readability. Wise menu designers look at their menus in the dining room at its lighting level rather than just in a well-lighted office.
- *Letter case.* Menu copy set primarily in lowercase type is easier to read than type set with all uppercase letters that should normally be used only for headings such as menu categories. Variations in type such as italics for emphasis are effective if done sparingly.

Subheadings are sometimes used within menu item categories, for example, to separately feature several seafood, beef, chicken, and pork entrées. An example is shown in 5.4. With the appropriate descriptions for these items and with a carefully thought-out location, menu planners are more likely to have a successful menu.

Space is needed for menu categories, but it is also required for other purposes such as:

- *Supplemental descriptions.* What accompaniments go with the entrées? What is available on the self-serve salad bar?
- *Cross-selling opportunities.* Information on a dinner menu that promotes a weekend brunch and a description of banquet capabilities or a lunch menu can be useful advertising tactics.

ENTRÉE SELECTIONS

Seafood Choices
    Seafood Enchiladas
    Tequila-Glazed Scallops
    Dungeness Crab Cakes

Chicken Choices
    Monterey Chicken
    Margarita-Glazed Chicken
    Grilled Chicken Pasta

Beef Choices
    Sirloin Steak (Choice-Cut)
    Flame-Grilled Rib-Eye
    Special Marinated Strip Steak

FIGURE 5.4 Entrée Selections

OVERHEARD IN THE KITCHEN

Cross-selling (menu)—Tactics used to advertise other products and services offered by the hospitality operation in addition to those noted on a specific menu.

- *Property information.* Name, address, telephone and fax numbers, e-mail addresses, and hours of operation should be included on take-home menus. Other guests may want to make note of this menu information for future reference so it must be written on the menu.
- *Special information.* Examples may include a discussion of service charges for groups of a specified size and the food service operation's history and mission.
- *Mechanics.* The use of color, decorative design details, and **clip-ons** are important considerations. Clip-ons can be very effective when they do not cover existing menu copy. A better approach is to design the menu to leave a space where the clip-on will be placed. Note: This space need not be left blank. An illustration, a picture or information about the restaurant can be included. Then, when the clip-on is not utilized, the menu will still look complete and well-designed.

OVERHEARD IN THE KITCHEN

Clip-on (menu)—A menu insert or attachment that advertises daily specials or emphasizes other menu items.

Lighter menu colors suggest a warm atmosphere; darker colors on a light background can help emphasize selected items. Decorative details such as pictures, drawings, and designs can add appeal. A menu's graphic design can "bring it all together" and help assure that the menu is attractive and well-spaced.

INFORMATION ON THE SIDE

Menu Printing

Printing concerns are of importance as the menu is designed. Today very professional menus can be printed in-house with desktop publishing technology. The price of quality color printers is low, and quality menus can easily and "neatly" be produced in-house.

The ability to print the menu in-house has advantages: simple selling-price changes can be made rapidly, and menu items can quickly be inserted or deleted.

How many menus should be printed? This question can be best answered by considering:

- *Use of inserts.* If they are used and, if they are printed in-house, relatively expensive menu covers can be purchased, and inserts can be printed daily.
- *Size of restaurant and discard rate.* If inserts are not utilized, the number of menus needed must be based upon the number of seats in the property and the "life expectancy" of the menu. As the number of seats and discard rate increases, more menus must be purchased. Note: Printers typically establish order points and charge a lower per-menu printing cost as the number of printed copies increases.
- *Other factors.* If there are many "regulars" who do not utilize a menu and/or if prices remain constant, this reduces the number of menus that will be needed.

Each operation must determine its own printing needs regardless of whether the menu is professionally produced or printed in-house. However, servers should never be put in a position where they must use a menu that does not meet cleanliness or condition standards just because no paper menu is available.

Special Menu Items

The menu design team must be aware about several additional menu concerns, and they are discussed in this section.

VEGETARIAN MEALS

Some potential guests are **vegetarians** who want to avoid foods that require animal death or discomfort and/or because of dietary reasons. Other guests like to select vegetarian meals on some occasions because of taste preferences and/or dietary concerns.

OVERHEARD IN THE KITCHEN

Vegetarian—A person who eats no meat or fish and, often, no other animal products. Their diets are chiefly comprised of fruits, grains, and nuts.

While all vegetarians avoid meat, there are several categories based on what a person eats in addition to vegetables, fruits, grains, and soy-based foods, legumes (example: peas), and nuts. Diet classifications include:

- *Vegans*—Vegetarians who eat no foods of animal origin, including milk, cheese, and honey.
- *Lacto-vegetarians*—Those who do consume dairy products in addition to their vegetarian diets.
- *Ovo-vegetarians*—Those who add eggs to their vegetarian diets.
- *Lacto-ovo-vegetarians*—Those who add both dairy products and eggs to their vegetarian diets.

It is important that kitchen managers understand the basic types of vegetarian diets. Then, when a server says, "One of our guests is a lacto-vegetarian; what can we serve them?" the kitchen manager will have an accurate answer.

ORGANIC FOODS

The production and sale of **organic foods** is increasing and many guests are looking for organic food items on menus.

OVERHEARD IN THE KITCHEN

Organic foods—Foods that are produced, processed, and packaged without using chemicals such as antibiotics or growth hormones in animals and without pesticides, fertilizers or radiation, among other polluting chemicals and practices, while growing fruits and vegetables.

According to the U.S. Department of Agriculture (USDA),[3] it is unclear whether organically-grown foods contain more or better nutrients than food products grown conventionally. In fact, the U.S. standards for organic foods do not consider food quality. Instead, they only relate to the methods of food production and handling. However, organic produce does carry much fewer pesticide residues than conventional produce. Note: The USDA indicates that the amounts of residue on both types of products, organic and nonorganic, are safe for human consumption.

In addition to perceived safety issues, guests desiring organic foods are often concerned about the environment and are willing to pay higher prices for organically-grown foods. While some food service operations plan their entire menu around the use of organic foods, many of which are locally grown, other properties provide organic food alternatives to appeal to guests with this concern and to demonstrate an interest in the environment.

KOSHER FOOD

Some food service operations offer complete **Kosher** meals and many others offer Kosher food alternatives for guests desiring them.

OVERHEARD IN THE KITCHEN

Kosher (food)—Food that is prepared according to Jewish dietary laws.

Ingredients including pork, rabbit, catfish, and any shellfish cannot be included in a Kosher meal. Further, meat and dairy products cannot be paired or consumed together, and any Kosher

INFORMATION ON THE SIDE
What Does "Organic" Really Mean?

Organic farming practices emphasize soil and water conservation and the reduction of pollution. Those who grow these products don't use additional chemicals to fertilize, control weeds, or prevent livestock disease. Instead, for example, they use natural fertilizers such as manure to feed soil and plants. They also use organic feeds for animals, and they allow them access to the outdoors rather than giving them antibiotics and confining their movements.

The U.S. Department of Agriculture (USDA) offers an organic certification program that requires all organic foods to meet specific standards that regulate how the foods are grown, handled, and processed. Only foods that meet these standards can be certified by the USDA.

As is true with any other food item, just because a supplier makes a claim it doesn't mean the claim is accurate. Organic foods meeting federal government standards have a "USDA Organic" seal to confirm that the requirements have been met. A copy of the seal follows:

food that is processed or cooked together with a non-Kosher food or anything made from a non-Kosher food is also not allowed.

The above and related details make it clear that a thorough understanding of Kosher food laws can be very challenging. Today, Kosher certification labels are printed on the packages of Kosher food. However, unless they are served alone, kitchen managers should understand that problems can still arise. Therefore, those managing food service operations with Kosher foods on the menu should consult with an expert to assure that the menu items meet requirements.

HALAL FOODS

The word, "**Halal**," is Arabic, and it means lawful or permitted. While most foods are considered Halal, there are exceptions that include:

- Swine/pork and its by-products.
- Animals improperly slaughtered or dead before slaughtering.
- Alcoholic drinks and intoxicants.
- Carnivores (meat-eating animals), birds of prey, and certain other animals.
- Foods contaminated with any of the above products.
- Some foods including those containing gelatin, enzymes, emulsifiers, and flavoring ingredients are questionable in the Halal diet because their origin is not known.

OVERHEARD IN THE KITCHEN

Halal (food)—Foods that meet Muslim dietary laws.

Food service operations with menus offering Halal foods must offer accurate descriptions and assure that Halal foods do, in fact, meet specific requirements. It is always best to be conservative and to discuss these requirements and food items with the appropriate supplier sources to assure that the requirements for producing and serving Halal foods are consistently met.

FOOD ALLERGIES

Kitchen managers should recognize that any menu item can create special problems for some guests who consume them. **Allergies** to food are common and can be very serious.

OVERHEARD IN THE KITCHEN

Allergy (food)—An unusual response to a food triggered by the body's immune system. Allergic reactions to food can cause serious illness and even death.

The following foods cause about 90% of all allergic reactions:

- Milk
- Eggs
- Peanuts
- Tree nuts such as almonds, walnuts, and pecans
- Soy beans
- Wheat
- Fish
- Shellfish such as crab, lobster, and shrimp

Unfortunately, the above items are common ingredients in many menu items. Therefore, kitchen managers and their staff must be aware that these ingredients can cause allergic reactions. As well, food servers must be trained to recognize that allergic reactions can be very harmful, even deadly, and they should know how to react when guests ask questions. The kitchen manager may be part of the team that trains servers about allergies, and he or she must know what to do when servers and/or guests ask questions about items on the menu.

INFORMATION ON THE SIDE

What Are Symptoms of Allergic Reactions to Food?

Depending upon the specific person, allergic reactions can occur as soon as the food is eaten or several hours later. Common reactions include some or all of the following:

- Itching in and around the mouth, face, or scalp
- Tightening in the throat
- Wheezing or shortness of breath
- Hives
- Swelling of the face, eyes, hands, or feet
- Stomach cramps, vomiting, or diarrhea
- Loss of consciousness
- Death

Kitchen managers should be sure that, when a guest asks, "I'm allergic to peanuts; are there any nuts in anything I have ordered?" the question must be taken seriously. Depending upon the policy of the food service operation, the server should probably notify the on-duty manager and/or the kitchen manager for an accurate follow-up response to the question.

It may seem easy for a kitchen manager to know what ingredients are in a menu item, since standard recipes listing all ingredients are used to prepare each menu item. However, the challenge becomes difficult because the food service operation may use some pre-prepared foods. For example, eggs are used in some salad dressings that are purchased already prepared, and the kitchen manager must check that product's ingredient label to know exactly what preparation ingredients were used.

INFORMATION ON THE SIDE

Signature Items

In Chapter 4 you learned that a signature item is a food or beverage product that guests associate with a specific food service operation. Like other items that are popular and which the food service operation wants to sell, special menu highlighting, perhaps a more extensive menu description, and the use of **table tents** are all tactics that should be used to manage signature items.

Signature items are very important for many properties because the regular guests enjoy them, and potential guests hear about them and may visit the property to sample them. These items can, then, provide an on-going and steady source of revenue for the property. In addition to a well-designed menu and table tents, **suggestive selling** by servers can help assure that all guests know about these items. Hopefully, kitchen managers conduct **line-up training** sessions with servers on a regular basis, and they can emphasize these items and request that servers alert guests about them during the training.

often a consideration since, unlike menu items that must be pre-costed, the bottle cost is easily known from purchase information. Note: Most guests are also aware of the price of a bottle of wine sold at a retail store, and they may question the selling price at a food service operation, especially when it is several times higher in price on the wine list than at a retail store.

Regardless of the strategy used, wine list designers should recognize the need for their prices to encourage sales while generating a profit, and it is within this observation that the selling price must be determined.

With these points in mind, suggestions for pricing wines include the following:

- Keep selling prices in line with the overall pricing structure of the restaurant. Typically, less expensive restaurants will not sell high-choice wines, and higher-priced restaurants will lose revenues if they offer only inexpensive wines.
- Some inexpensive wines should be offered so cost-conscious guests can enjoy a special occasion with the opportunity to include wine with their meal.
- Think about the guests when pricing wines. Those desiring an alcoholic beverage typically have choices including beer and other alcoholic drinks besides wine when they make selection decisions. How does the selling price of a glass or bottle of wine relate to that of the other alcoholic beverages that are available? Some guests will consider the value of each alternative and make selection decisions after doing so. Note: It is more profitable to sell beer or liquor instead of wine in many operations because the mark-up (selling price − ingredient cost) is often much higher. This is yet another consideration creating a challenge for wine list designers.
- Consider **contribution margin** rather than the **cost percentage** represented by the selling price. Note: The contribution margin is the wine's selling price minus its product cost, and the cost percentage is the product cost ÷ by the selling price. The contribution margin is more important than the product cost percentage because it represents the money left after the purchase price has been considered. It represents the amount of money that remains to pay for other expenses and to contribute to the property's profit. Therefore, it should be the priority concern.

OVERHEARD IN THE KITCHEN

Contribution margin—Product selling price (−) product cost. For example, assume a bottle of wine is purchased for $9.50 and sells for $16.99:

Contribution margin = $7.49 ($16.99 selling price − $9.50 cost)

Cost percentage—Product cost ÷ by selling price. For example, assume a bottle of wine is purchased for $9.50 and sells for $16.99:

Cost percentage = 55.9% ($9.50 ÷ $16.99)

INFORMATION ON THE SIDE
Mark-Up Factors By Wine Type

If wine list design team desires to use a **mark-up factor** to price its wines, suggestions to do so follow:

Type of Wine	Mark-Up Factor
Bulk wines (box or house wines, for example)	4–5 times
Inexpensive bottled wines	3 times
Moderately expensive bottled wines	2 times
Highest-price bottled wines	Less than 2 times

OVERHEARD IN THE KITCHEN

Mark-up factor (pricing)—The number of times by which a product's cost is multiplied to arrive at a selling price.

These two glasses of wine may have never been ordered if the wine list had not been planned to meet the preferences of the guests being served.

NOW IT'S YOUR TURN

A PINCH OF THE INTERNET (5.4)

1. If you want to review sample wine lists from around the world, just type "wine list" into your favorite search engine.
2. To keep up with wine selection and merchandising in restaurants, check out "Restaurants and Institutions Magazine." Type "www.rimag.com" into your favorite search engine. Then type "wine" or "wine trends" into the site's search box.
3. If you want to learn what merchants charge for specific types of wine in your area, type "www.wine-searcher.com" into your favorite search engine and follow the directions at the site.
4. Check out the Web site for "All about wine" (www.allaboutwine.com) to review a wide range of information about this topic.

COMPLETING THE PLATE QUESTIONS (5.4)

1. If you as a kitchen manager were asked to provide information to service staff about wine, what topics would you discuss?
2. Assume a bottle of wine cost a food service operation $7.50. How would you determine its selling price on the wine list?
3. Which do you think is more important when pricing a bottle of wine: its contribution margin or its cost percentage? Why?
4. What are your thoughts about the traditional notion that, for example, red wines should be served with red meats and white wines should be served with seafood or chicken dishes?

Kitchen Challenge Du Jour Case Study (5.2)

"Normally I agree with you, Joe, but this time I really don't!" Claudia, the kitchen manager at the Duke's Restaurant, was meeting with Joe, the property's dining room manager.

"Well," said Joe, "I really think we should recommend a specific wine for each entrée on our menu. We would, of course, train the service staff so they know how to suggest other wines and to agree that, whatever wine the guest wants, is the wine the guest should have. What's wrong with that approach, Claudia?"

"There are lots of good wines to go with every entrée," replied Claudia, "So how do you or I select the one that's the very best to be recommended? Also, I get kind of turned off about all these adjectives like "oaky," "a hint of fruit nectar," and "earthy." I think that, while maybe an expert can explain these things, most people could not. I think these descriptions and suggestions take away something from our great menu. That's why I suggest we have, for example, a list of our wines and then indicate the types of foods that many people enjoy them with rather than to recommend a specific wine for a specific item?"

a) What is your opinion about the two approaches to selling wines at Duke's Restaurant?

b) Assume you were the property's general manager and had to make a decision about which approach should be used. What would you decide? Why?

Overheard in the Kitchen Glossary

Menu design	Menu layout	Clip-on (menu)	Half-bottle (wine bottle)
À la carte menu	Prime real estate (menu design)	Vegetarian	Pairing (food and wine)
Table d'hôte menu	Standard of identity	Organic foods	Haute cuisine
Buffet menu	As-purchased (weight)	Kosher (food)	Wine list
Cyclical (cycle) menu	Truth-in-menu	Halal (food)	Bin number (wine)
De jour menu	Call brand (liquor)	Allergy (food)	Aficionado (wine)
Die-cut (menu)	Premium brand (liquor)	Table tent	Vintage (wine)
Quick-service (restaurant)	Service charge	Suggestive selling	Viticultural
Merchandising	Trade puffing	Line-up (training)	Contribution margin
Menu engineering	Desktop publishing systems	Carafe	Cost percentage
Aesthetic	Cross-selling (menu)	Split (wine bottle)	Mark-up factor (pricing)

LESSON 5

If you are reading this textbook as part of a formal class, your Instructor may want you to apply and practice what you have learned in this chapter by completing Lesson 5 of the Pearson Education's Kitchen Management Simulation (KMS). If you are required to complete KMS Lesson 5; read the **About Lesson 5** below, then go to www.pearsonhighered.com/kms for instructions on how to access and complete it.

After you have successfully completed the lesson, think about the way you, as a professional kitchen manager, would answer the **For Your Consideration questions** that follow.

About Lesson 5

This lesson is all about the importance of a well-written and accurate menu. There are a variety of ways to design and layout a menu. This KMS lesson allows you to practice some of the important techniques kitchen managers and owners use to do just that. This KMS lesson uses a variety of methods designed to teach you how to direct a guest's attention to certain "specialty" items (for example, items that yield a high contribution margin or may be the restaurant's signature dishes).

As you have learned in the KMS and in this chapter, a menu is a way to communicate and sell your products and services to your guests. If a

menu is poorly written, then it may make a less than desirable impression about your restaurant and its service. A well-written menu allows your guests to easily navigate through the items to make their selections. It also identifies potential allergens found in menu choices. It must also accurately describe the items you will serve. You will practice doing that in this lesson.

Wine lists are a special type of menu. Kitchen managers use wine lists to describe the wines they are selling and in some cases to suggest wines that would go well with a particular menu item. Practicing wine list making is a crucial part of this lesson.

As a kitchen manager, you should remember that you will plan your best menus if you always keep your guests and their preferences in mind.

For Your Consideration

1. Why do you think it is important to your guests that you develop a well-written and accurate menu?

2. Why do easy to read wine lists help restaurants improve their wine sales?

3. What are some implications to a restaurant of a poorly written menu that causes a guest to become ill because that guest unknowingly consumed a menu item that contained an ingredient to which he or she was allergic?

Endnotes

1. In 1977, the National Restaurant Association developed a position paper ("Accuracy in Menu") upon which some of this discussion is based.

2. See: A Diner's Guide to Health and Nutrition Claims on Restaurant Menus. Center for Science in the Public Interest. www.cspinet.org.reports/dinersgu.html.

3. U.S. Department of Agriculture. National Agricultural Library. Alternative Farming Systems Information Center. AFFSIC Research Guide. October, 2008.

6

Kitchen Managers Require Standard Recipes

Chapter Ingredients Outline

Learning Objectives

After studying this chapter, you will be able to:

1. Explain why standard recipes are important to kitchen managers and their food preparation staff.
2. Describe procedures to develop standard recipes.
3. Review procedures to convert standard recipes for larger or smaller yields.
4. Review how standard recipes should be used and evaluated.

COMING RIGHT UP OVERVIEW

In the last two chapters you learned that the menu drives many of the guest-related and operational planning concerns of the food service operation. Standard recipes, the topic of this chapter, are the tools used to implement the menu.

    In this chapter, you'll learn that the availability and consistent use of standard recipes is absolutely critical to provide menu items that consistently meet the operation's quality and quantity goals. This is necessary to assure that the menu items produced do not disappoint guests and, at the same time, allow the property to operate within its established food cost plan or limitations. The first sentence in the opening section of this chapter provides an excellent summary of the importance of standard recipes: "All food service operations in every industry segment serving every type of guest needs standard recipes."

Kitchen managers working with their food preparation team must develop the standard recipes that will be used. Fortunately, there is an easy eight-step method that can help with this purpose, and it is explained in this chapter. The process can be used to develop recipes for those menu items currently being produced, but for which no standard recipe has been created. As well, the process can be modified slightly and then used to develop recipes that are selected for new items that will be added to the menu.

An excellent standard recipe using all the correct ingredients and preparation techniques may have a yield (number of servings and/or serving sizes) that is different from that desired by the kitchen manager. In this chapter, you'll learn how to convert recipes to increase or decrease the number of servings, change the serving size, or change both the number of servings and serving size. You'll also learn basic information about the need to be accurate when weighing or measuring ingredients required by standard recipes.

A final section of the chapter addresses the need to consistently use the standard recipes that have been selected and developed and to evaluate them. You'll learn that it is much easier to say, "Use a standard recipe," than it is to actually do so. In fact, a significant amount of knowledge and skill is required. Examples of these attributes are reviewed in the final section of the chapter as are techniques to evaluate standard recipes as kitchen managers make important decisions about whether recipe revisions are necessary.

STANDARD RECIPES ARE IMPORTANT

Oᴮᴶᴇᴄᴛɪᴠᴇ

1. Explain why standard recipes are important to kitchen managers and their food preparation staff.
   - Every operation requires standard recipes.
   - Benefits of standard recipes.

All food service operations in every industry segment serving every type of guest need standard recipes. It is very seldom that such a broad generalization can be made in a study of the diverse and complex world of food service operations but, in this instance, it is possible to do so. In Chapter 4 you learned that standard recipes contain the instructions necessary for kitchen managers and their employees to produce a food item in a way that helps to assure that the operation's quality and quantity standards will be met.

Information in a well-developed standard recipe includes the type and amount of necessary ingredients, preparation procedures including equipment and tools, **yield** (the number of servings and serving size produced by the recipe), garnishes, and any other information needed to properly produce and serve the item. When this information is used to prepare menu items, the resulting products will meet cost and guest expectations: two of the most important keys to the success of all food service operations.

OVERHEARD IN THE KITCHEN

Yield (recipe)—The number of servings and the size of each serving that are produced when a standard recipe is followed. For example, a standard recipe may yield fifty 3 oz. servings of a specified food item every time it is correctly used.

Every Operation Requires Standard Recipes

You've learned that kitchen managers and other menu planners work hard to identify the menu items that their guests will enjoy. They consider many factors that lead to the decision about adding items to or removing them from the menu. After the menu is planned, it becomes important to ensure that the items available are prepared the way they should be. In other words, they must be consistently produced and served according to quality/quantity standards planned by kitchen managers and their teams. To do so requires a standard recipe.

In some chef-owned restaurants, the chef/owner closely supervises food production personnel. Recipes that yield products meeting the chef's quality requirements may be less formally developed (some may not even be written down!). However, these chefs and their assistants still follow a specific set of procedures to assure that product quality standards are consistently attained. Those working in other types of high-volume food service operations may also follow standard recipe procedures with or without referring to an actual copy of the standard recipe. Therefore, in this chapter, the concept of standard recipes will refer to the usually written (but sometimes unwritten) set of standard procedures that detail how menu items should consistently be prepared.

Benefits of Standard Recipes

A standard recipe helps assure consistency, and this benefits the guests and the restaurant. Let's first think about the guests. Each time a guest orders the same item, it will taste, look, and even smell the same. As well, the serving size will be the same, and it will contain the same appropriate amount of all ingredients. The guests will like this because they receive consistent value: They will pay the same amount each time they order an item, and they will receive the same quality and quantity of the item each time it is served.

Think about a guest who visits a restaurant and enjoys a seafood platter. The guest tells friends about the great meal and organizes a group to visit the property to enjoy a meal that includes the seafood platter. If that menu item is served during the second visit in exactly the same way as the item was served during the first visit, the guest will enjoy it again. As well, the new guests may also like (or, at the least, will not hear the host expressing disappointment about it), and the restaurant has taken a step toward attracting additional "**regulars**."

OVERHEARD IN THE KITCHEN

Regular (guest)—An industry term referring to a guest who frequently visits a food service operation.

However, if the entrée is prepared and served differently (for example, with fewer or different seafood items included in the platter), the guests may be disappointed. Then the opportunity for continued repeat business from these guests may be lost.

How does a standard recipe help to assure consistency for the food service operation? Typically, the selling price of a menu item is based, at least in part, on the cost of its ingredients. Therefore, use of a standard recipe helps to assure that the same type and quantity of ingredients are used each time the product is prepared so the food cost can be more accurately measured. Also, the yield will be the same and, when the cost of ingredients and the yield are the same, food costs will be predictable, and the food service operation can best meet its financial goals. In other words, food cost control can only be assured when standard recipes are used.

The use of standard recipes also helps the kitchen manager's team to prepare the menu items. Properly developed, a standard recipe indicates:

- The necessary ingredients including the quantity (weight or volume) that must be on hand to produce the item. This helps kitchen managers with their purchasing activities.
- The required small utensils (measuring tools and pots and pans, for example) that must be used to produce the recipe.
- Large equipment such as a slicer, range or oven with requirements including cooking and baking times along with the temperature settings that should be used.
- Procedures for pre-preparation, preparation, cooking (if applicable), holding, and serving.
- Yield (number of servings and serving size).

You can see, then, that the use of standard recipes also assists with labor cost control. Since the same preparation activities will be used, it will take approximately the same amount of time to prepare the item regardless of which food preparation employee makes it. This consistency will help the kitchen manager with employee scheduling tasks.

Standard recipes result in operational consistency and this uniformity benefits the guests and the operation. Standard recipes assure that product-related quality standards will be attained because food production will be standardized.

Interestingly, some kitchen managers seem to recognize the importance of standard recipes but still do not use them. The typical reasons (excuses) given for not utilizing standard recipes may vary but usually include one or more of the following:

- "My production staff members are all professionals so they don't need to look at recipes to make high quality products."
- "Using standard recipes will slow us down; we are too busy to take the time to read recipes."
- "Our recipes are a secret. If we write them down someone might steal them."
- "The recipes are too hard to keep up-dated."
- "My staff can't read our language well enough to understand the recipes."

Of these excuses, only an inability to read recipes has any validity. Even in that case, kitchen managers can have recipes produced in the language of the kitchen staff member(s) responsible for making the item.

In addition to the many operational advantages for users of standard recipes, there are even more reasons today's kitchen managers should insist on their use. Three of the most important relate to:

- Guest health and safety
- Accuracy in menus
- Advanced technology

GUEST HEALTH AND SAFETY

The dietary and health concerns of some guests, especially the very young, the very old, and those who are ill require that kitchen managers know the exact ingredients and their amounts used in recipes. Then the proper and accurate nutrient calculations can be made. For example, guests who are on diets that severely restrict their sodium (salt) intakes trust kitchen managers to ensure menu items are produced in such a way that their sodium contents are known and consistent. Standard recipes help to do just that.

ACCURACY IN MENUS

Increasingly, guests are concerned about the way the foods they buy are produced and the ingredients that are in the items they purchase. The result has been an increase in legislation requiring food service operators to indicate exactly what items are used to produce the products they are serving. For example, many communities have banned the use of **trans fats** in cooking. Standard recipes help ensure that kitchen managers are in compliance with local laws and ordinances such as these when the recipes are carefully developed and consistently followed.

OVERHEARD IN THE KITCHEN

Trans fats—A form of fat that has been shown to raise blood cholesterol levels.

ADVANCED TECHNOLOGY

Increasingly, kitchen managers use computers and advanced software programs to calculate costs, estimate purchases, and even schedule employees. If standard recipes are not used, these tasks cannot be performed properly because accurate recipe costing, purchasing, menu pricing, and scheduling depend upon consistency of data, and that is not possible without standardized recipes. As a result, modernization and the ability to utilize advanced technology tools are severely reduced for those kitchen managers not using standard recipes.

This cook is chopping the quantity of onions required for a standard recipe.

INFORMATION ON THE SIDE

What Is a Recipe Yield?

The yield of a standard recipe relates to the amount of a menu item that is produced each time the recipe is consistently followed.

Recipe yields can be expressed in three basic ways:

- *By volume*—a standard recipe may yield 2 gallons of beef stew.
- *By weight*—a recipe may yield 8 pounds (as purchased) of meat loaf.
- *By number of servings*—a recipe may yield 25 servings of Caesar salad.

In addition to knowing the number of servings in the recipe's yield, kitchen managers must also know the serving size. For example, the desired size of a serving of beef stew may be one cup, the required serving of meat loaf may be 4 ounces (**edible portion**), and the serving size for a Caesar salad may be the amount required to put a "rounded" at-the-top serving in a salad bowl of a specified size.

You can see that kitchen managers and their staff must control both the amount of specified ingredients that go into a standard recipe and the serving size of the recipe's yield to meet the property's quality and quantity standards. Careful measuring, weighing, and counting are necessary when the recipes are prepared and when their yield is portioned into individual servings. Tools for both of these purposes must be are available and should be consistently used to meet the operation's standards. For example, if a recipe requires one cup of milk and six ounces of flour, the required measuring tool for the milk and a scale for the flour must be available so the recipe can be carefully followed.

OVERHEARD IN THE KITCHEN

Edible portion—The amount of a food item that can be served to guests after the product is cooked. For example, a hamburger patty that weighs four ounces when placed on the grill may only weigh 3.6 ounces after it is cooked; often abbreviated "EP."

NOW IT'S YOUR TURN

A PINCH OF THE INTERNET (6.1)

1. Increasingly, quantity recipes are available from Internet sources. Some suppliers to the food service industry feature a wide variety of recipes with large quantity yields as a service to the food service industry. For example, check out those on Sysco Corporation's Web site: www.sysco.com/recipes/recipes.html

   Select the type of recipes for which you are searching (for example, appetizers or breakfast entrées), and you will discover numerous recipes with yields useful to many food service operations.

2. The Internet features an (almost) uncountable number of quantity food recipes of every type you can imagine. Type "Restaurant Recipes" into your favorite search engine. Then you can see different recipe formats and, perhaps even more importantly, you can discover some recipes that you would like to prepare.

3. Did you know that recipes used in healthcare facilities are very tasty, nutritious, and might even be well-suited for adoption by commercial food service operations? Just type "hospital recipes" into a search engine. You'll probably like what you see.

COMPLETING THE PLATE QUESTIONS (6.1)

1. Assume you are the owner of a small restaurant, and only you and some of your close family members prepared the food. Do you think standard recipes would be necessary for your operation? Why or why not?

2. Have you ever visited a restaurant several times, ordered the same menu item, and discovered that the items served did not look or taste the same or have the same serving size on different visits? If so, what did you think? What can a kitchen manager do to better assure that there is consistency in the menu items served?

3. How do you think the use of standard recipes can help with food purchasing? With food production? With food evaluation?

PROCEDURES TO DEVELOP STANDARD RECIPES

O BJECTIVE

2. Describe procedures to develop standard recipes.
   - Recipes for current menu items
   - Recipes for new menu items

Now that you understand the critical importance of standard recipes, let's discuss how they are developed. Kitchen managers that are not using standard recipes can usually develop them by observing and recording the procedures currently used to produce food products. When new menu items are desired, recipes available from external sources can be modified as necessary for use in the kitchen manager's food service operation. You'll learn about both of these tactics in this section.

Recipes for Current Menu Items

Let's assume the kitchen manager wants to implement a standard recipe system for a property in which some or most menu items are now produced without the use of receipes. An important "first step" is to explain and justify the need for them to the food production personnel. The advantages to their use cited in the previous section can be an important part of this discussion. As well, requesting their assistance in development and evaluation activities will be helpful in gaining their cooperation because then the recipes to be used will be those developed by the food production team and not just by the kitchen manager.

Some kitchen managers or food production personnel may resist the use of written standard recipes because they want to defend the status quo (how things have always been done): "We have never used them before; why should we start now?" These concerns can be addressed as the kitchen manager considers and explains the numerous advantages to their use.

Some persons may also even have a concern for their job: "Once recipes are written down, anyone can use them, and I may no longer be needed." This concern can be reduced by remembering that the menu items must be produced for work shifts when the kitchen manager and some preparation employees enjoy time off. Also, the property's need for the entire food

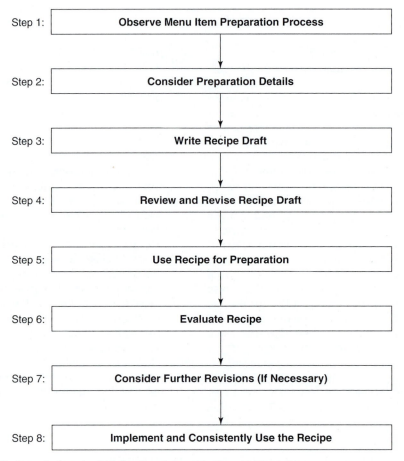

Step 1:	Observe Menu Item Preparation Process
Step 2:	Consider Preparation Details
Step 3:	Write Recipe Draft
Step 4:	Review and Revise Recipe Draft
Step 5:	Use Recipe for Preparation
Step 6:	Evaluate Recipe
Step 7:	Consider Further Revisions (If Necessary)
Step 8:	Implement and Consistently Use the Recipe

FIGURE 6.1 Steps in Standard Recipe Development: Current Menu Items

production team extends far beyond preparing specific food items on the menu. For example, their talents are required when menus are planned, special food preparation techniques are needed, and when daily specials and banquet function menu items are prepared. Kitchen managers who enjoy a professional relationship of respect and mutual confidence and cooperation with their own boss will have little problem in reaching agreement about the importance of standard recipes. Those with a more troubled professional relationship will likely have difficulties that extend much further than just a discussion about recipes.

The steps required for developing a standard recipe for a menu item currently being used in a food service operation are illustrated in Figure 6.1.

Let's look at the recipe development steps suggested in Figure 6.1. Note: The discussion that follows applies to the development of a standard recipe for a food item. However, the kitchen manager can also share the process with the bar manager. Why should this be done? One important reason is because the process is useful to develop the standard recipes needed for beverage production. It should be no surprise that the same benefits to the use of standard food recipes also accrue from the use of standard beverage recipes.

Step 1: *Observe Menu Item Preparation.* The kitchen manager can personally prepare the item or observe preparation employees as they prepare the menu item. What ingredients are used and in what quantities? How and when are the ingredients weighed and measured? What kitchen **smallwares** and large equipment are needed, for what purpose, and when? What ingredient measuring tools are used and, if applicable, how is the item portioned after preparation? Note: If different preparation personnel produce the same item, it may be beneficial to observe the production techniques used by each staff member who prepares it.

Step 2: *Consider Preparation Details.* Can some preparation tasks be combined? For example, if smallwares are needed for several preparation steps and, if they are all stored in the same general area, a preparation procedure stating, "*Obtain the following items required for preparation*" can be included as an early step in the recipe. This can help to increase

productivity by saving the time required for extra trips to utensil storage areas when they are gathered for use.

When employee productivity is increased without affecting product quality, the time saved can be used for other purposes, and this can help, in some small way, to reduce labor costs. Note: The suggestion of obtaining all necessary ingredients that are stored together on the same trip to the refrigerated, frozen, or dry storage areas can also be a helpful early standard recipe procedure.

Sanitation concerns can also be addressed when preparation details are considered. For example, assume an item such as left-over beef stew will be re-served. A recipe notation that the item should be quickly refrigerated at the end of the serving period and the need to quickly refrigerate it in small batches with occasional mixing to hasten the cooling process can be emphasized. A second example: If hollandaise sauce is used, the recipe can emphasize the need to check its temperature during the serving period and to discard it at the end of service.

Step 3: *Write Recipe Draft.* A first draft of the recipe that incorporates observations (Step 1) and details (Step 2) now becomes important. A standardized format (see the example in Figure 6.7) should be used.

Step 4: *Review and Revise Recipe Draft.* The recipe draft (Step 3) should be carefully reviewed by the kitchen manager and other production personnel who regularly prepare the item. Revisions, if necessary, should then be made.

Step 5: *Use Recipe for Preparation.* The recipe should be used to prepare the menu item. It should be carefully followed unless obvious production problems are noticed which should be corrected before production continues.

Step 6: *Evaluate Recipe.* The recipe used for preparation (Step 5) and the food product it yields should be carefully evaluated. Does the item produced by the recipe meet the operation's quality standards?

Step 7: *Consider Further Revisions (If Necessary).* If the "answer" to the question, "*Does the item produced by the recipe meet the operation's quality standards,*" posed in Step 6 is "no," this will indicate that further revisions to the recipe are necessary.

Step 8: *Implement and consistently use the recipe.* After the recipe is developed and everyone agrees that the resulting product is of the desired quality, the recipe should be used each time the product is prepared.

OVERHEARD IN THE KITCHEN

Smallwares—Pots, pans, measuring and portioning devices, and other utensils used for food production and service.

Productivity—The quality and quantity of output compared to the amount of input such as labor hours needed to generate the output. For example, if it takes 1.25 hours to prepare a recipe, and changes are made to reduce the preparation time to 1.0 hour, productivity has increased. This 15 minutes (.25 hours) can then be used for other tasks.

Recipes for New Menu Items

The process described in Figure 6.1 above can be used to develop a standard recipe for an item in current production. Let's assume, however, that the menu planning team has revised the menu, and now a new item will be added. Where does the kitchen manager locate the recipe for this new item? Perhaps he or she has already identified one or more possible recipes for the item when it was discussed prior to the final decision to add it to the menu. These sample recipes provide a starting point for the one that will be developed or modified for the operation.

Frequently, the kitchen manager can work with his or her preparation staff to develop the recipe for the new item. If so, a process similar to that described in Figure 6.1 can be helpful. Alternatively, recipes from external sources may be utilized.

Standard recipes with yields of twenty-five, fifty, and even one hundred (or more) servings are readily available in (seemingly) innumerable cookbooks and on the World Wide Web. Many kitchen managers, like other professionals, know other food service professsionals who are also excellent sources of potential recipes. Those belonging to local restaurant or chefs' associations will likely know many persons who can be asked about recipe needs.

Dining room managers know much about their guests' dining preferences and it is wise to consult them as standard recipes are being developed for menu items.

When external recipes are initially identified, they should be reviewed for potential use. The trained and experienced eye of the kitchen manager can frequently determine whether a potential recipe should be considered. Note: We will consider more formal aspects of recipe evaluation later in this chapter.

Recipes from external sources should be thoroughly tested before they are fully implemented. If the yield is relatively small, the menu item can be prepared by strictly following all procedures in the recipe. Careful evaluation, changes, if necessary, and further testing may be in order. Note: The kitchen manager can follow Steps 5–8 in Figure 6.1 to test recipes for their use in the operation.

NOW IT'S YOUR TURN

A PINCH OF THE INTERNET (6.2)

1. One Web site (www.allrecipes.com) boasts about having more than 40,000 recipes available on the Web site. While they typically yield a small (family-sized) number of servings, these recipes can still provide creative kitchen managers with a starting point for developing recipes for use in quantity food operations. There are too-many-to-count other sources for recipe ideas available on the Internet. Just type "recipes" into your favorite search engine.

2. Did you know that menus can tell you a lot about the recipes used to produce the items that are available? For example, type "restaurant menus" into a search engine, select several menus, and ask yourself the following questions as you review them:
   • Are some of the items on the menus probably prepared to order? Are some items perhaps made in batches that must be held until service?
   • What serving sizes are indicated for the available items? What utensils are required to serving these items?

   • Do you think it might be difficult to consistently purchase the proper quality of the menu items' probable ingredients?
   • Would it be difficult to develop standard recipes for some of the items? (Search the internet for applicable standard recipes.)

COMPLETING THE PLATE QUESTIONS (6.2)

1. What are some common reasons why you think some kitchen managers may not want to use standard recipes? If you were his/her boss, how would you counter this reason?

2. Assume you were a kitchen manager who used standard recipes, and you were having a problem such as inconsistent food quality even when the recipe was carefully followed. What are some possible reasons for this problem? What steps would you use to correct this problem?

3. What steps might you as a kitchen manager use to develop a large quantity recipe from a family-sized recipe that you located on the Internet?

Kitchen Challenge Du Jour Case Study (6.1)

"What is Louis trying to do now?" asked Randy as he spoke with another food preparation assistant during a coffee break at Vernon's Restaurant.

"I have been working here for five years, and there has never been a single complaint about the taste or quality of the food I have prepared," Randy continued. "And now Louis has come in as the new kitchen manager with this idea about developing a recipe that everyone has to use all the time without exception. If we're not having any problems, why change things now? I get the feeling that either Louis doesn't trust us, or he wants to get our preparation ideas and then hire somebody with a lot less skill who will work for a lot less money!" Assume you were Louis, the kitchen manager, and you overheard part of this conversation.

a) What points would you make to Randy and his co-worker about the need for using standard recipes in this operation when they have never been used previously?

b) What role would you request that Randy and the other food preparation personnel play in developing and implementing the new standard recipes?

CALCULATING RECIPE CONVERSION FACTORS

OBJECTIVE

3. Review procedures to convert standard recipes for larger or smaller yields.
   • Converting the number of servings
   • Converting the serving size
   • Converting the number of servings and serving size
   • Other recipe conversion issues

You've learned that production staff must always use standard recipes to prepare the food items required by the menu. Sometimes recipes with desired yields are readily available. Frequently, however, recipes must be converted (adjusted) to meet the operation's specific needs. There are three basic types of recipe conversions that may be needed:

   • Those that revise (increase or decrease) the number of servings.
   • Those that revise (increase or decrease) the serving sizes.
   • Those that revise (increase or decrease) the number of servings and the serving sizes.

Let's review procedures to make these three kinds of standard recipe conversions.

Converting the Number of Servings

Sometimes, a recipe has the serving size (for example, 3 ounces or 3/4 of a cup) that is desired, but it yields more or fewer servings than the kitchen manager wants to produce. What should be done? Let's look at Figure 6.2.

When reviewing Figure 6.2, remember that the serving size (3.0 ounces) is the same as the serving size needed for the new recipe. However, the number of servings needed must be increased from 40 to 70. In the first step, the kitchen manager calculates the **recipe conversion factor (RCF)**.

OVERHEARD IN THE KITCHEN

Recipe conversion factor (RFC)—A factor (number) that is used to adjust ingredients in a standard recipe when the number of servings and/or serving size of a current recipe must be changed because they differ from those in a desired recipe. The calculation required to determine this factor is:

$$\frac{\text{Desired Recipe Yield}}{\text{Current Recipe Yield}} = \text{Recipe Conversion Factor (RCF)}$$

Assume the current standard recipe yields 40 servings (3 ounces each), and the kitchen manager desires 70 servings (3 ounces each). What quantity of each recipe ingredient is needed for the converted recipe?

Step 1:   Calculate the recipe conversion factor:

$$\frac{\text{Number of Desired Servings (3 ounces)}}{\text{Number of Current Servings (3 ounces)}} = \frac{70}{40} = 1.75 \text{ (RCF)}$$

Step 2:   Multiply the quantity of each ingredient in the current recipe by the recipe conversion factor.

Example: assume 6 ounces of flour are specified in the current recipe. The amount of flour needed in the revised recipe is 10.5 ounces:

6 ounces of flour (current recipe)	×	1.75 (recipe conversion factor)	=	10.5 ounces of flour (new recipe)

FIGURE 6.2   Converting the Number of Servings

The kitchen manager's judgment is always needed when determining the quantity of herbs needed for an adjusted recipe.

The RCF is calculated by dividing the desired number of servings (70) by the current number of servings (40).

In the second step, the quantity of each ingredient in the current recipe is multiplied by the RCF to determine the quantity of each ingredient needed for the new recipe. Note: If the serving size does not change in the desired and original recipe, the RCF will always be *less than 1.0* if *fewer* servings are desired in the newly converted recipe and *greater than 1.0* if *more* servings are needed.

Converting the Serving Size

Sometimes kitchen managers select a standard recipe that yields the required number of servings, but they want to serve different serving sizes. For example, an existing recipe may yield seventy 3-ounce servings of tuna salad but seventy 4-ounce servings may be desired by the kitchen manager. Figure 6.3 shows how to make this conversion.

When reviewing Figure 6.3, remember that the number of servings (70) is the same, but the serving size must be increased from 3 ounces to 4 ounces. Note that a two-step process similar to that used in Figure 6.2 can be used.

In Step 1 the desired yield for seventy 4-ounce servings is calculated (70 servings × 4 ounces each = 280 ounces). That number is then divided by the current yield (70 servings × 3 ounces each = 210 ounces) to determine the RCF.

Then, in Step 2, the RCF (1.33) is multiplied by the quantity of each ingredient in the current recipe to yield the amount needed for production. Note: if the number of servings does not change in the desired and current recipe, the RCF will always be *less than 1.0* if a *smaller* serving size is desired and *greater than 1.0* if a *larger* serving size is needed.

Converting the Number of Servings and Serving Size

Sometimes kitchen managers like a standard recipe but want to change both the number of servings and the serving sizes in a new recipe. The process to do this is illustrated in Figure 6.4.

The process to convert a recipe when a different number of servings and a different serving size are desired is similar to the process illustrated in Figure 6.3. First, the total quantity (yield) of both recipes is determined, and then desired yield is divided by the current yield. The RCF factor that results is multiplied by the quantity of each ingredient in the current recipe.

The basic arithmetic procedures used in the recipe conversion process are simple, and these procedures do not require much time to perform. However, experienced kitchen managers understand that, when they are busy in a hectic work environment, mistakes are easy to make. These mistakes can create wasted time and unuseable ingredients, can cause production stress,

Assume the current recipe yields 70 servings (3 ounces each), and the kitchen manager desires 70 servings (4 ounces each).

Step 1:   Calculate the recipe conversion factor:

$$\frac{\text{Number of Desired Servings} (\times) \text{ Serving Size (4 ounces)}}{\text{Number of Current Servings} (\times) \text{ Serving Size (3 ounces)}}$$

$$= \frac{70 \, (\times) \, 4 \text{ oz.}}{70 \, (\times) \, 3 \text{ oz.}} = \frac{280 \text{ oz.}}{210 \text{ oz.}} = 1.33 \text{ (RCF)}$$

Step 2:   Multiply the quantity of each ingredient in the current recipe by the RCF.

Example: assume 12 ounces of chopped onion are specified in the current recipe. The amount of chopped onion needed in the revised recipe is 16 ounces (1 pound):

12 ounces of onion (current amount)	$\times$	1.33 (recipe conversion factor)	$=$	15.96 ounces of onion (1 pound *) (new recipe)

*Note: There are 16 ounces in one pound, so the kitchen manager would round up 15.96 ounces to one pound of chopped onion.

FIGURE 6.3   Converting the Serving Size

Assume the current recipe yields 50 servings (1/4 cup each), and the kitchen manager desires 70 servings (3/4 cup each).

Step 1:   Calculate the conversion factor:

$$\frac{\text{Number of Desired Servings} (70) \times \text{ Serving Size}}{\text{Number of Current Servings} (50) \times \text{ Serving Size}}$$

$$= \frac{70 \, (\times) \, \frac{3}{4} \text{ cup}}{50 \, (\times) \, \frac{1}{4} \text{ cup}}$$

$$= \frac{52.50 \text{ cups}}{12.50 \text{ cups}}$$

$$= 4.20 \text{ (RCF rounded)}$$

Step 2:   Multiply the quantity of each ingredient in the current recipe by the RCF.

Example: Assume that 3 ounces of flour is specified in the current recipe. The amount of flour needed in the revised recipe is:

3 ounces (current amount)	$\times$	4.2 (recipe conversion factor)	$=$	12.5 ounces (rounded) (new recipe)

FIGURE 6.4   Converting the Number of Servings and Serving Sizes

and may disappoint guests, so it is always important to double-check calculations. Kitchen managers should also review recipe conversions made by their food preparation assistants before the recipe is used, if these tasks have been delegated.

INFORMATION ON THE SIDE

What About Herbs and Spices?

Assume a current recipe yields 25 servings and 150 servings (same serving size) are required. What should be done about the quantity of **herbs**, **spices** and other seasonings needed? These ingredients should be gradually adjusted. Many kitchen managers use a "rule of thumb": The amount of an herb or a spice needed should be determined initially by multiplying the current quantity needed by the recipe's conversion factor used for all ingredients. That quantity should, then, be reduced by one-half. Additional amounts of herbs and spices can then be added on a "to taste" basis until the kitchen manager is satisfied with the menu item's taste.

Let's review the process:

Step 1:   Multiply the quantity of herb or spice in the current recipe by the recipe conversion factor used for other ingredients.

Step 2:   Reduce the result in Step 1 by one-half. (Divide by two).

Step 3:   Modify the quantity in Step 2 by "to taste" amounts as necessary.

Example: Assume the current recipe calls for one teaspoon of pepper and is being increased six times (the recipe conversion factor is 6).

Step 1:   Multiply the current quantity by the recipe conversion factor:

$$1 \text{ teaspoon } (\times) \ 6 = 6 \text{ teaspoons}$$

Step 2:   Reduce (divide) the result in Step 1 by one-half.

$$(6 \text{ teaspoons} \div 2 = 3 \text{ teaspoons; same as 1 tablespoon})$$

Step 3:   The adjusted amount in Step 2 (1 tablespoon) is added to the recipe which is then modified (the amount of pepper is increased) on a "to taste" basis.

OVERHEARD IN THE KITCHEN

Herb—A leaf of an aromatic (fragrant) plant used to add flavor to foods being cooked.

Spice—A seasoning obtained from the seeds, fruit, roots, bark, or other nonleaf part of a plant.

Other Recipe Conversion Issues

There are three other issues relating to the conversion of standard recipes with which kitchen managers should be aware. These relate to measurements, use of family-sized recipes, and computer-generated recipes with adjustments made daily.

MEASUREMENTS

Recipe ingredients must always be carefully weighed, counted, and measured, as appropriate. Knowledge of basic measurements and their equivalents are needed to do this. It is especially important to express the amounts required for a standard recipe in the way that is easiest for preparation personnel to weigh or measure the ingredients. Figure 6.5 contains information about the U.S. measurement and weight systems that will help you when you convert and use standard recipes.

INFORMATION ON THE SIDE
Metric Lengths, Weights, and Measures and the Celsius Temperature Scale

Almost every country in the world except the United States uses the metric system of measurement. It uses three basic units:

- *Meter*—To measure length; about 3.2 feet (U.S. system)
- *Gram*—To measure weight; about the weight of a paper clip
- *Liter*—To measure volume; about 1.05 quarts (U.S. system)

Units that are very large and very small are expressed in multiples of ten of the base unit.

Greater than Base Unit	Base Unit	Less than Base Unit
Kilo 1,000 times	Meter (m) – length	Deci – 1 times
Hecto 100 times	Gram (g) – weight	Centi – 0.01 times
Deka 10 times	Liter (l) volume	Milli – 0.001 times

There are two different temperature scales in common use: U.S. (Fahrenheit; °F) and Celsius (Centigrade; °C)

The Fahrenheit temperature scale is based on 32°F for the freezing point of water and 212°F for its boiling point. The Celsius temperature scale is based on 0°C for the freezing point of water and 100°C for its boiling point.

The Internet is a good place to look for tools to convert U.S. measurements and temperature scales to the metric system and centigrade scales or to do the reverse. For example, check out: worldwidemetric.com/metcal.htm

Part I: Volume Measure – Gallon to Teaspoons

1 gallon	=	4 quarts	=	128 fluid ounces
1 quart	=	2 pints	=	32 fluid ounces
1 pint	=	2 cups	=	16 fluid ounces
1 cup	=	16 tablespoons	=	8 fluid ounces
1 tablespoon	=	3 teaspoons	=	½ fluid ounces

Part II: Volume Measures – Cup to 1/2 Tablespoon

1 cup	=	16 tablespoons
¾ cup	=	12 tablespoons
⅔ cup	=	10 tablespoons + 2 teaspoons
½ cup	=	8 tablespoons
⅓ cup	=	5 tablespoons + 1 teaspoon
¼ cup	=	4 tablespoons
⅛ cup	=	2 tablespoons
1 tablespoon	=	3 teaspoons
½ tablespoon	=	1½ teaspoons

Part III: Weight-Pounds to Ounces

1 pound	=	16 ounces
¾ pound	=	12 ounces
½ pound	=	8 ounces
¼ pound	=	4 ounces
1 ounce	=	½ fluid ounce

FIGURE 6.5   Common U.S. Measurements and Weights

Figure 6.6 provides some information about the metric system. Part II shows the progression from centiliter to kiloliter for volume measurements and from centigram to kilogram for weight measures. Part III shows the U.S. measurement and metric equivalents for some common volume and weight measurements.

FAMILY-SIZED RECIPES

Recipes used in family situations yield a relatively small number of servings and require special attention before they can be used in a quantity food production operation. Enlarging a small-quantity recipe involves several steps.[1]

Step 1: The product should be prepared in the amount of the original recipe, and this recipe should be followed exactly.

Step 2: The product that is prepared should be carefully evaluated to assure that it is acceptable for the food service operation's use.

Step 3: The recipe's yield should be doubled, or it should be expanded to the appropriate amount for the pan size that will be used. For example, perhaps the total quantity needed would be the amount required for three 12″ × 20″ × 2″ pans. After the original recipe has been successfully prepared (Step 1), the next conversion could increase the recipe size to yield one pan. The product should again be prepared, observations should be made about changes from the original recipe, and the final product should be evaluated.

Step 4: If results are satisfactory, the recipe yield can be doubled once again for further evaluation and revisions, if necessary.

Step 5: If the product is still satisfactory, the recipe can then be increased by increments of 25 servings (or complete serving pans) until the required number of servings is successfully produced.

COMPUTER-GENERATED RECIPES

A final issue relating to recipe adjustment involves the increasingly common use of an automated system to convert recipes on a daily basis to consider the specific number of servings to be pre-

Part 1: Volume Measurements

Volume Measure

10 milliliters (ml)	=	1 centiliter (cl)	
10 centiliters	=	1 deciliter (dl)	= 100 milliliters
10 deciliters	=	1 liter (1)	= 1,000 milliliters
10 liters	=	1 dekaliter (dal)	
10 dekaliters	=	1 hectoliter (hl)	= 100 liters
10 hectoliters	=	1 kiloliter (kl)	= 1,000 liters

Part II: Weight Measurements[2]

Weight

10 milligrams (mg)	=	1 centigram (cg)	
10 centigrams	=	1 decigram (dg)	= 100 milligrams
10 decigrams	=	1 gram (g)	= 1,000 milligrams
10 grams	=	1 dekagram (dag)	
10 dekagrams	=	1 hectogram (hg)	= 100 grams
10 hectograms	=	1 kilogram (kg)	= 1,000 grams

Part III: U.S. Measurements and Metric Equivalents

Volume

U.S.	Metric
Gallon	3.79 liters
Quart	.95 liters
Pint	473.2 milliliters
Cups	236.6 milliliters
Tablespoon	14.8 milliliters
Teaspoon	4.9 milliliters

Weight

Pound	480 grams*
¾ pound (12 oz.)	360 grams*
½ pound (8 oz.)	240 grams*
¼ pound (4 oz.)	120 grams*
1 ounce	30 grams*

* = rounded measurement

FIGURE 6.6 Volume and Weight Measurement in the Metric System

pared on that day. Consider, for example, Vernon's Restaurant that is known for, among other things, "homemade" meatloaf. At the end of each day, the kitchen manager does two things. First, he or she determines the quantity of meatloaf remaining because it can be re-served the next day. Second, the manager also estimates the number of servings to be sold the next day and makes a simple calculation:

$$\text{No. of Servings Needed Next Day} - \text{No. of Servings Available End of Shift Today} = \text{No. of Servings Required for Next Day}$$

The kitchen manager's recipe system is computerized so it is only necessary to enter the number of servings required for production the next day into the system. Then a recipe will be generated that indicates the quantity of each ingredient needed for the number of servings required for the next day's service. Each morning when production employees report to work, they will have a clipboard on a work station counter that holds the recipes adjusted to yield the number of servings each menu item that they must produce that day. This system allows kitchen managers to minimize food costs and maximize food quality as they move toward "fine tuning" the system used to estimate sales (production quantities) and minimize left-overs.

■ NOW IT'S YOUR TURN

A PINCH OF THE INTERNET (6.3)

1. The Internet makes it easy to convert liquid to dry measures or to do the reverse. For example, check out:southernfood. about.com/library/info/blconv.htm
    Also, type "recipe conversion factors" into your favorite search engine to see other conversion tools.
2. To learn more about U.S. weights and measurements and their conversions, type "U.S. weights and measurements" into your favorite search engine.
3. To learn more about the metric system of weights and measurements, type "Metric system" into a search engine.

COMPLETING THE PLATE QUESTIONS (6.3)

1. Assume you are the kitchen manager in a large food service operation with numerous food production assistants. What role would you personally want to play in the conversion of standard recipes to determine the quantity of ingredients necessary when recipes of different yields are needed? What responsibility, if any, would you delegate to the preparation personnel who prepare the recipes?
2. What are examples of the types of weighing and measuring tools that must be available in food service operations to accurately weigh and measure the ingredients required for common standard recipes?
3. If you were a kitchen manager searching for a recipe for a new menu item, would you first look to recipes with quantity yields or smaller, family-sized recipes? Defend your answer.

STANDARD RECIPES MUST BE USED AND EVALUATED

OBJECTIVE

4. Review how standard recipes should be used and evaluated.
    • Always use standard recipes
    • Knowledge and skill are needed
    • How to evaluate standard recipes

Now that you've learned how to develop and convert standard recipes, let's discuss how to use and evaluate them.

Always Use Standard Recipes

We have emphasized the need for consistent use of standard recipes; they should be followed every time a food item is prepared. However, there are many food service operations that have standard recipes available in the kitchen manager's office and/or even in food preparation areas that are not used except, perhaps, as a very general guide to preparation of the item. This is unfortunate because, at the least, the creative effort and time expended on their development has been wasted. At the most, the recipes are not able to help deliver the consistent quality products that guests demand and the consistent cost standards that the restaurant itself desires.

Figure 6.7 illustrates one format for a standard recipe. When followed, it will help assure that the guests will be pleased (the correct quality and quantity of the item will be produced), and the food service operation will enjoy cost and operating efficiency benefits.

Note that the recipe illustrated in Figure 6.7 meets all the requirements for a standard recipe noted earlier in the chapter. It indicates all necessary ingredients and the quantities of each, preparation procedures, and necessary utensils and other equipment. It also provides other information, including baking time and any special instructions which the chef might desire. As importantly, it tells:

• The yield in number of servings (96) and in serving size (1/24 of a 12″ × 2″ steam table pan)
• The serving size that results when each pan is cut into five even pieces lengthwise and four even pieces widthwise.

These chefs are closely following a standard recipe even though it is not out in the workstation because they have prepared the menu item many times before.

UTENSILS NEEDED: Stock pot, cutting board, French knife, wire whip, mixing bowl, gallon/quart/ cup measures, measuring spoons, plastic gloves, clean foodservice cloths, 2 − 12″ × 20″ × 2″ steam table pans	YIELD: 48 servings OVEN TEMP: 350°F (176.6°C) BAKING TIME: 30 minutes SERVING SIZE: 1/24 pan SERVING TOOL: Spatula/spoon	Chicken (Turkey) Tetrazzini Recipe 1098

Ingredients	Quantity/Volume	Procedure
Spaghetti	6 lb.	1. Cook spaghetti in slated water. Rinse and drain. <u>Do not overlook</u>.
Margarine	2 lb.	2. Cook onions and celery in margarine until transparent.
Celery, cut fine	2 qt.	3. Make roux by adding flour, salt and pepper to above. Cook 5 minutes.
Onions, cut fine	2 qt.	4. Add chicken stock and cook until thick, stirring as necessary.
Flour, pastry	1 lb. 4 oz.	5. Add cubed chicken (or turkey) and mushrooms; mix.
Salt	1/4 c	6. Add spaghetti; mix well.
Pepper, black	1 tsp	7. Add green peppers just before panning.
Chicken (turkey) stock	2 gal. 2c	8. Scale 12 lb. into each of 4 (12″ × 20″ × 2″) pans.
Chicken (turkey) cooked & cubed	12 lb. 8 oz	9. Mix topping. Top pan with 1 qt. Topping
Mushrooms, fresh/chooped	2 c	10. Bake at 350ºF (176.6ºC) for 30 minutes.
Green Pepper, chooped	3 c	11. Serving: Divide into servings by cutting pan contents 6 (length) 3 4
Total Weight	48 lb.	(width).
Topping		*Example:*
Bread Crumbs, fine	2 qt.	
Sharp Cheddal Cheese, grated	2 qt.	
		Holding: Hold prepared product at 140ºF until service.

SPECIAL INSTRUCTIONS:

Do not over cook spaghetti. See recipe for chicken stock if none is available.

FIGURE 6.7   Sample Standard Recipe: Chicken (Turkey) Tetrazzini[3]

While food preparation personnel have the responsibility to carefully follow standard recipes, kitchen managers and other managers and supervisors have the responsibility to assure that the ingredients and tools their staff need to follow the recipes are always available. For example, all required ingredients meeting quality standards must always be on-hand in necessary quantities. If they are not, challenges will arise when desired items cannot be produced. Production problems will occur ("What can we prepare as an alternative item?"), and the guests may be disappointed ("I came here just for that item"). As well, cost concerns arise if the kitchen manager and/or preparation personnel substitute more expensive ingredients in efforts to please the guests.

Smallwares specified by standard recipes must also be available. Why specify a six-ounce serving of a meat entrée if an accurately **calibrated** scale is unavailable to weigh the entrée? Why indicate that a number-8 scoop (producing eight level servings per quart) or a six-ounce ladle should be used for serving if these tools are broken or unavailable? Many problems concerning the use of standard recipes relate to the kitchen manager's failure to provide production staff with the utensils required to follow the recipe.

OVERHEARD IN THE KITCHEN

Calibrate—To check or verify. For example, the thermostat of an oven should be calibrated (verified) on a routine basis to confirm that the internal temperature is that for which the thermostat has set.

Some food service operations use a one gallon measure (4 quarts) because this tool provides lines or ridges to indicate each quart amount. Perhaps more commonly, however, kitchen managers provide tools for different volume measurements including gallon, quart, pint (2 cups), cup (16 tablespoons), and tablespoon, teaspoon, and even for fractions of a teaspoon.

It is important to always remember the role of standard recipes in cost control. Food costs impact the food service operation's ability to attain its financial goals. Kitchen managers must consider these goals as well as those relating to guests because the consistent use of standard recipes will control product costs. This is not possible when standard recipes are not used.

Sometimes two standard recipes are used to produce one menu item. These are called **chained recipes** because one recipe contains an ingredient that must be prepared by following another standard recipe. For example, the kitchen manager's staff may prepare a seasoned Italian tomato sauce which is used as an ingredient in several items including meatloaf, stuffed green peppers, baked spaghetti, and lasagna. In this example, the sauce may be prepared in sufficient volume for the day's estimated production requirements for all necessary menu items early in the work shift. Then it would be refrigerated and added to the other recipes either cold or pre-heated as specified by the recipe for each item.

OVERHEARD IN THE KITCHEN

Recipe (chained)—A recipe that yields an ingredient used in another recipe.

INFORMATION ON THE SIDE

What Does "Use" a Standard Recipe Mean?

You have learned that standard recipes must be used each time a food item is produced. What does "use" mean? Sometimes the word means just what it says. For example, when a new menu item is being prepared and when a new food production employee is being trained, the recipe must be followed with each step studied and carefully completed.

Sometimes, "use" may mean "followed." For example, after cooks prepare a food item several times, they will learn required procedures and can use (follow) them without the need for the applicable recipe to be physically available in the work station. The ability to "use" standard recipes based upon memory can become very important, for example, during busy times at the food service operation.

Knowledge and Skill Are Needed

Professional food preparation personnel understand that there is much more to using a standard recipe than to "just do what it says to do." When a new recipe is introduced, the kitchen manager should go over it in detail with those staff members who will use it. They should read through the recipe together, assure that everyone understands what each procedure means, and agree on the weighing and measuring tools that should be used.

Accuracy is very important to assure that correct amount of ingredients is used, that the items produced consistently taste the same, and that cost to produce one serving and the total number of servings (yield) from the recipe are the same. You've learned that standard recipes are absolutely critical because they are important control tools. However, they cannot be used for control purposes unless care is always taken when using them.

INFORMATION ON THE SIDE

How Are Chefs and Cooks Like Bartenders?

Food production personnel must have, and always follow, standard recipes for the food products they produce. In the same way, bartenders must have and follow standard recipes for the beverages they prepare. Sometimes bartenders like to **free pour** instead of using a shot glass, jigger, or other measuring tool. In this case, they merely pour the alcoholic beverage out of the bottle and directly into the glass. The reason often given: "I'm an experienced bartender, and I've done this so many times, I just know the quantity that is needed. Besides, I'm too busy, and I don't have time to use a measuring tool."

Hopefully, food production personnel don't have this attitude. Kitchen managers must provide and food preparation personnel must use weighing and measuring tools for the ingredients required by the standard recipe. Kitchen managers should never allow their employees, regardless of the length of their experience, to do otherwise. The comment, "I'm an experienced cook, and I know how much 3 pounds of rice weighs, and I can tell when I have poured 2 quarts of milk into a bowl," doesn't sound like it would come from a professional food preparation employee who knows about the need for careful and accurate weighing and measuring.

Consistency, a primary advantage of standard recipes, is only possible when all ingredients are accurately weighed or measured, when preparation procedures are carefully followed, and when cooking equipment has been carefully calibrated to assure accuracy.

OVERHEARD IN THE KITCHEN

Free pour (alcoholic beverages)—A manual system of making cocktails and other alcoholic drinks which relies on the bartender to control the quantity of alcohol in the drink without use of a portioning tool such as a jigger or shot glass.

There are three basic ways that standard recipes indicate the quantity of ingredients that are necessary:

- *By count*—A standard recipe for a shrimp cocktail appetizer may specify six shrimp. Note: There should be a **purchase specification** for the shrimp that indicates, for example, the desired size of the shrimp (measured in the number of shrimp per pound).
- *By volume*—You've learned that volume measurements in common use in the United States relate to teaspoons, tablespoons, ounces, cups, pints, quarts, and gallons. In most parts of the world, metric volume measurements such as milliliter and liter are used.
- *By weight*—In the United States, weights are expressed in pounds and ounces (there are 16 ounces to one pound). When the metric system is in use, measurements such as milligrams and kilograms are used.

OVERHEARD IN THE KITCHEN

Purchase specification—A description of the quality requirements that must be met by the products purchased by the food service operation.

Most scales show measurements in both U.S. and metric weights, so that they can be used to measure items on either weight system. Many food service operations have at least three scales: a receiving scale that may weigh up to 100 pounds or more, a larger quantity production scale that weighs quantities up to 25 pounds or more, and a scale weighing in ounces and fractions of an ounce up to, for example, 32 ounces which is 2 pounds.

Professional kitchen managers recognize the importance of calibrating scales for accurate weight just as they calibrate cooking equipment for accurate temperature. This can easily be done, for example, by placing a container of known weight on a scale. For example, a five pound bag of sugar should obviously weigh five pounds. If it does not register this weight, calibration is required.

Many scales have a **tare allowance** feature that production staff find very useful for planning items to be weighed directly into the container in which food preparation will be done. With a tare allowance feature, a pot or pan is placed directly on to the scale, and its dial is rotated to zero. Then, for example, if three pounds of flour are required, all that must be done is for the food preparation employee to scoop flour into the pot or pan until the scale reads three pounds. By contrast, without this tare allowance feature, the pot must be placed on the scale, and its weight must be observed. Then three pounds of flour must be added to that weight. For example, assume the pot weighs 1 pound 2 ounces, and 3 pounds flour are required. Flour must be added to the pot until the scale reads 4 pounds 2 ounces (1 pound and 2 ounces for the pot (+) 3 pounds for the flour). In a busy, noisy, and hectic kitchen, simple features such as a tare allowance scale makes it much easier to accurately follow standard recipes.

OVERHEARD IN THE KITCHEN

Tare allowance—An adjustment feature on a scale that excludes the weight of a pot or pan placed on the scale to hold food ingredients being measured.

INFORMATION ON THE SIDE

Is a Pint Always a Pound?

There is an old saying that "A pint is a pound the world around." It would be easy to convert measures to weights if this statement was always true. Unfortunately, it is not, and that is the reason that kitchen tools such as scales and measuring utensils are needed.

It is true that a pint measure (2 cups) holds 1 pound (16 ounces) of water. However, the same pint measure may only hold 8 ounces of flour. The actual weight depends upon, among other things, whether the flour has been sifted or packed into the pint measure.

Fortunately, there are tables of measurements and yields that can help to determine the quantities required as standard recipes are developed. Then it is the responsibility of food production personnel to use these tools and carefully and accurately use the amounts required by the recipe.

Note: One reference for weight and measure equivalents in common use is: www.onlineconversion.com/cooking.htm

It is interesting to note that weighing is always more accurate than measuring. For example, even though most people might measure water, many professional bakers weigh the water required for their recipes. For example, instead of a recipe specifying 2 cups of water, it will require 16 ounces of water (the weight of 2 cups of water), and the ingredient will be weighed instead of measured in the bake shop.

There are numerous other tactics that should be used to help assure that the quality and quantity standards desired by those who develop standard recipes will be attained. Entire books and training and education courses are devoted to the topic. However, this brief discussion highlights just a few concerns that are important when weighing and measuring ingredients. It should help you to understand that it is much easier to say, "Always follow the recipe," than it is to actually do so. Professional food preparation personnel recognize the importance of standard recipes, and they have the knowledge, skills, and experience needed to use the techniques required to follow them.

How to Evaluate Standard Recipes

As you learned earlier, it is relatively easy to locate external standard recipes when it becomes necessary to do so for new menu items, for "daily specials" and for special banquets (among other purposes). It is also not a difficult task to evaluate standard recipes, and this should be an ongoing activity. A formal system of **recipe evaluation** helps to ensure that the recipes are the very best that they can be. Figure 6.8 shows a standard recipe evaluation form.

When you review Figure 6.8, you'll see that several specific evaluation factors are listed, and raters can consider them on a four-point scale ranging from "poor" to "excellent." As well, the form allows the evaluators to provide specific and general comments about the recipe.

OVERHEARD IN THE KITCHEN

Recipe Evaluation—A formal process in which evaluators determine the extent to which a standard recipe is acceptable by considering the product it yields according to several predetermined factors.

Standard Recipe Name: _____					Recipe Category:_____

Evaluation Date(s):_____   Recipe No.:_____

Instructions: Check the box that best represents your analysis of each factor.

Evaluation Factor	Your Analysis Poor				Excellent	Comments
Portion Size	❏	❏	❏	❏	❏	
Color	❏	❏	❏	❏	❏	
Texture	❏	❏	❏	❏	❏	
Taste	❏	❏	❏	❏	❏	
Aroma	❏	❏	❏	❏	❏	
General Appearance	❏	❏	❏	❏	❏	
Ingredients	❏	❏	❏	❏	❏	
Compatibility	❏	❏	❏	❏	❏	
Garnish	❏	❏	❏	❏	❏	
Other: _____	❏	❏	❏	❏	❏	
Other: _____	❏	❏	❏	❏	❏	

Should we use this recipe?   ❏ Yes   ❏ No
Comments:

Name of Evaluator: _____

FIGURE 6.8 Standard Recipe Evaluation Form

Who can help evaluate standard recipes? Hopefully, as many persons as possible including the restaurant manager, the kitchen manager and his/her assistants, food and beverage servers, other staff members, and even selected guests including the operation's "regulars."

The recipe evaluation process is helpful when new items are added to the menu and also to analyze existing recipes. Perhaps, for example, an item on a "help yourself" salad bar is less popular than it used to be. Maybe preparation "short-cuts" are being taken. Also, many of the items used on the salad bar may have been offered for a very long time. During that interval, guest preferences may have changed. Hopefully, the kitchen manager tracks the consumption of items consumed on the salad bar. Then, when there is an increasing amount of left-overs for some items, consumption records and standard recipes can be evaluated to determine whether some items should be replaced.

Consider also the availability of new ingredients: Would turkey or ostrich products be useful in a stew or casserole? **Blind tasting** can provide information about preferences for alternative recipes. When this process is used, persons sample items produced from alternative standard recipes without knowledge of ingredients, preparation methods, or other aspects of the recipes. This procedure helps eliminate biases (pre-conceived attitudes) that can arise when reviewers know they are sampling items made from their favorite (or nonfavorite) recipes.

OVERHEARD IN THE KITCHEN

Blind tasting – The process of evaluating food items in a way that raters are not aware of the recipe's ingredients, preparation methods, or other information when they sample the food items.

Kitchen managers and their staff should carefully and regularly review the results of the recipe evaluation forms because the information gathered can help the operation to improve. Also, these evaluation forms will be useful when menu planning and revision activities are undertaken.

NOW IT'S YOUR TURN

A PINCH OF THE INTERNET (6.4)

1. Kitchen managers increasingly incorporate "green" food preparation techniques into their standard recipes and general food production processes. To review information about sustainable food service operations, go to: www.dinegreen.com. Also, check out: www.greenrestaurants.org and enter "green restaurants" into your favorite search engine.

2. The Internet is a good source of information about recipe usage procedures. Just type "using standard recipes" into your favorite search engine.

3. Numerous types of kitchen utensils are required for food preparation, and they should be referenced in standard recipes whenever possible. To learn about and view pictures of common kitchen utensils, type "common cooking utensils" into a search engine.

COMPLETING THE PLATE QUESTIONS (6.4)

1. Do you think it is a good idea to put special warnings about sanitation or other concerns in the instructions for standard recipes? Why or why not?

2. Do you agree that a food preparation employee who prepares the same menu item everyday does not necessarily need to have the standard recipe available in the food preparation area? Why or why not?

3. What are the advantages to the use of chained recipes?

4. What are some times when you as a kitchen manager would want to formally evaluate one of more of the standard recipes that you are currently using? What procedures would you use to undertake the evaluation?

Kitchen Challenge Du Jour Case Study (6.2)

Kimo, the newly appointed kitchen manager at Vernon's Restaurant has a problem: The operation is always busy, the guests really enjoy the food, but the business is losing lots of money! A fast walk through the kitchen pick-up area where food is transferred to the servers and through the dining area itself reveals something that is a big part of the problem. The portions are gigantic (many guests ask for take-home containers), and the selling prices do not reflect the large serving sizes that are served.

Kimo had seen a three-ring binder full of recipes in his office, and he knew there was a similar booklet in the kitchen. The serving sizes being served were not even close to those specified in the recipes.

After the lunch rush period slowed down, Kimo approached Lovi-Ann, a cook who had been with the property "forever." Lovi-Ann," said Kimo, "I know we have recipes that indicate portion sizes, but the servings we serve seem to be much different and much larger."

"Yes, I know," Lovi-Ann replied. "We used to follow the recipes very closely, and you know what? We had complaints about small servings and high prices. We were losing a lot of business including some regular guests. The last kitchen manager became concerned and increased the serving sizes. Our restaurant manager at the time didn't say a thing and, in fact, once she told me that it was nice to see the dining room full of guests again. She said that larger servings did cost us a little more, but we made up for that small loss with the larger volume of business."

a) Kimo thinks that the current restaurant manager knows about the larger serving sizes. What should Kimo say to him or her about standard recipes and serving sizes?

b) What, if anything, should Kimo do to put things back in order in the kitchen?

c) What should be done about the regular guests who will know about the return to smaller serving sizes?

Overheard in the Kitchen Glossary

Yield (recipe)	Productivity	Calibrate	Tare allowance
Regular (guest)	Recipe conversion factor	Recipe (chained)	Recipe evaluation
Trans fats	(RCF)	Free pour (alcoholic	Blind tasting
Edible serving (EP)	Herb	beverages)	
Smallwares	Spice	Purchase specification	

LESSON 6

If you are reading this textbook as part of a formal class, your Instructor may want you to apply and practice what you have learned in this chapter by completing Lesson 6 of the Pearson Education's Kitchen Management Simulation (KMS). If you are required to complete KMS Lesson 6, read the **About Lesson 6** section below, then go to www.pearsonhighered.com/kms for instructions on how to access and complete it.

After you have successfully completed the lesson, think about the way you, as a professional kitchen manager, would answer the **For Your Consideration** questions that follow.

About Lesson 6

By reading the information in this chapter, you have learned the importance of measurement equivalencies and standardizing recipes as well as how to use recipe conversion factors to expand or reduce recipes to meet your restaurant's needs. The KMS is created to let you take what you have learned in this chapter and bring it to life by practicing with realistic and interactive activities.

Knowing how to use standardized recipes is important because it helps ensure a consistent experience for your guests each and every time. Kitchen managers know that if customers visit them on two separate occasions and order the exact same item each time, those customers expect it to taste the same each time. If it does not, dissatisfaction is the inevitable result. This is avoided when kitchen managers enforce the use of standardized recipes.

Standardized recipes produce a known yield. To change that yield to meet your own needs, you must first learn measurement equivalents. For example, after a recipe is converted it may call for 6 teaspoons of salt. By understanding measurement conversions you recognize that 6 teaspoons is the same 2 tablespoons. Understanding this equivalency makes standardized recipes easier to work with. You must also master the calculation of recipe conversion factors (RCFs). When you do, you can better control the production of food and beverage products—thus improving the uniformity and quality of the items you serve.

In this KMS lesson you will practice all of the important steps required for working with standardized recipes.

For Your Consideration

1. Why is it critical to your guests that your kitchen team consistently use standardized recipes? Why will it be critical to the operation's service staff?

2. Without the use of standardized recipes, items on the menu will vary in taste and portion size based on the skill level of the production staff member preparing the item. What steps should kitchen managers take to assist those team members with poor math skills when the team members must calculate RCFs to aid in their recipe expansion or reduction efforts?

3. Do you think it is more important that kitchen managers know how to standardize a recipe or that they know how to modify (expand or reduce) one? Explain your answer.

Endnotes

1. These steps were suggested in: Mary Molt. Food for Fifty. Eleventh Edition. Upper Saddle River, New Jersey. Prentice-Hall, Inc. 2001.
2. National Institute of Standards and Technology (http://ts.nist.gov)
3. Recipe courtesy of: Chef Robert Nelson, CEC, CCE, CFBE, AAC. The Dr. Lewis J. and Mrs. Ruth E. Minor School of Hospitality Chef de Cuisine. Michigan State University. East Lansing, Michigan. 2004.

Kitchen Managers Cost Recipes and Assist Food Servers

Learning Objectives

After studying this chapter, you will be able to:

1. Describe the need for and use of basic recipe costing procedures.
2. Explain how kitchen managers and their food preparation personnel assist front-of-house team members with food serving tasks.

COMING RIGHT UP OVERVIEW

You're learning that kitchen managers have many responsibilities before food production begins. For example, in Chapter 1, you learned about basic sanitation practices and kitchen safety standards. Scheduling to control labor costs was discussed in Chapter 2 and, then, procedures to plan and design menus were presented in Chapters 4 and 5.

Chapter 6 discusses the importance of and procedures to develop and convert standard recipes. In this chapter you'll learn how to cost these recipes and, as well, about ways that food preparation personnel assist those on the food service team who actually serve high-quality products to guests.

In Chapter 6, you learned that standard recipe costing involves determining the cost to produce all (or one) serving of a recipe by considering the recipe's ingredients and their current costs and the number of servings the recipe yields.

At first, the task sounds fairly easy. If 1 pound (16 ounces) of ground beef cost $3.20, it will cost the kitchen manager 80¢ ($3.20 ÷ 4 servings) to prepare a one-quarter pound hamburger (as purchased weight). However, what if celery costs $2.75 a pound, and the recipe calls for 6 cups of chopped celery? Some of the celery's weight will be lost when it is cleaned and its resulting weight must be converted to volume (cups). Then the amount in recipe-ready cups of celery per pound must be known to determine the cost of the celery in the recipe. This chapter will tell you how to accurately make these calculations.

In the first part of this chapter you'll learn how to determine the cost of individual recipe ingredients and how to calculate the cost of all of the ingredients in a standard recipe. You'll also discover how to cost the individual food servings that comprise an entire meal and how to calculate food costs for "help yourself" buffets and salad bars.

Three additional concerns, computerized costing, how to use cost information to establish base selling prices, and procedures to control buffet and salad food costs will also be addressed.

The second major part of this chapter focuses on how food production personnel assist service personnel to help the guests. You'll learn there is an importance difference between **food serving** and **food service**. Food serving involves moving the food items that have been prepared by production staff to service personnel, and service involves the process of transferring food products from service staff to the guests. This process must be completed in a way that ensures guests receive menu items of the highest possible quality. You'll review the roles played by production personnel in four different types of food delivery systems: à la carte dining, banquet operations, room service, and hotel **lobby food services**.

Hopefully, you're discovering that food service operations of all types comprise interrerlated subsystems. For example, kitchen managers must purchase, receive, store, and issue food products. They must plan, design, and implement menus, and they must work closely with those members of food service operations team who are in greatest guest contact. Kitchen managers and their staff must be knowledgeable and skilled in a diverse set of competencies, and those examined in this chapter are among the most important.

OVERHEARD IN THE KITCHEN

Serving (food)—The process of moving prepared food items from production staff to service personnel.

Service (food)—The process of transferring food and beverage products from service staff to the guests.

Lobby food services (hotel)—Food services typically offered by limited-service hotels; those lodging operations that offer few, if any, food and beverage services.

THE FOOD COSTING PROCESS

OBJECTIVE

1. Describe the need for and use of basic costing procedures:
   - Purposes and benefits
   - Costing recipe ingredients
   - Costing standard recipes
   - Calculating plate cost
   - Calculating buffet and salad bar costs
   - Three additional concerns

In the previous chapter, you learned that two important goals are met when standard recipes are used. First, the consistent quality of products desired by guests is best assured. The same ingredients and the amounts of each should be used every time the recipe is followed even when basic factors such as the number of servings and/or serving sizes change. Guests can enjoy the same menu items every time they order them without any surprises in ingredients or serving sizes.

Second, when standard recipes are used, the menu items will always cost the food service operation a known amount because there will be no variation between the amount of ingredients required by the recipe and the amount actually used. It then becomes possible to calculate the menu item's food cost.

Kitchen managers cost recipe ingredients, standard recipes, plate costs (entire meals), and "help yourself" buffets and salad bars, and procedures to do so are presented in this section.

Purposes and Benefits

Suppose you were shopping for a new desk at a furniture store, and you found one you liked that cost $150.00. How do you think that selling price was determined? First, you understand that it is probably being sold for more than it actually cost the store's owner because he/she wants to make a profit. The owner's cost becomes the base used to help determine the desk's actual selling price. You are also probably aware that the selling price you will pay includes enough to compensate the owner for the cost of rent, utilities, salespersons, and other expenses incurred in making the desk available for sale. As well, the owner's personal income is likely based on selling furniture at a profit. As a result, the total price you will pay includes the owner's costs of acquiring and selling the desk as well as providing for a profit on its sale.

In addition to these factors, the amount you will pay for the desk (your cost) probably includes the owner's thoughts about the influence of **supply and demand** on the pricing decision. For example, if the desk is popular and hard to find, the selling price might be set higher than otherwise. Conversely, if the desk is a "slow mover" and has been in the showroom for a long time, the selling price might be reduced. However, the owner will always want to know the amount of his/her investment in the product when determining its price.

OVERHEARD IN THE KITCHEN

Supply and demand (law of)—A belief about the supply (availability) of an item and its price compared to its demand. Often, as the price of an item increases, demand for that product decreases; the reverse is also true.

Owners of food service operations share some basic cost concerns with owners of furniture stores and, probably, of every other business. One difference between the furniture store owner and the owner of a food service operation is that the furniture is already produced when it is purchased. The owner buys a desk for a specific price rather than pieces of lumber at different prices that are used to manufacture the desk. However, kitchen managers must buy individual ingredients such as meat, vegetables, fruit, and dinner rolls and butter. They know what the individual prices for these ingredients are because they received an **invoice** when they paid for each ingredient. However, the ingredients must be measured, counted, or weighed and combined with other ingredients to yield the product (menu item) that will be sold. The way the ingredients are combined is specified in the standard recipe, and the way their cost is determined is by recipe costing: the topic of this section.

OVERHEARD IN THE KITCHEN

Invoice—A statement (bill) from a supplier that indicates the products, quantities, and resulting charges that must be paid by the food service operation that receives them.

Accurate recipe costing helps kitchen managers in several ways:

- If costs to produce menu items are considered when menus are planned, they can consider whether the items can be produced at the desired quality level and still yield the desired contribution margin (selling price minus product cost).
- They can evaluate the items being offered on "help yourself" buffets and salad bars. If product costs are excessive, they will know this, and they can make decisions about replacing some items and/or increasing selling prices for the buffet/salad bar.
- They can establish selling prices for the menu items being sold. Note: Every objective method of establishing menu selling prices is based, at least in part, on the cost of the food items being sold, and this topic will be discussed later in this chapter.

INFORMATION ON THE SIDE
Standard Recipe Costing Is Not Difficult

Hopefully, you've learned that recipe costing is very important. Fortunately, it is not a difficult process because kitchen managers need only know about ingredient yields and use some basic arithmetic to do it. Increasingly, computerized methods are used to minimize the time and increase the accuracy of costing. Note: Computerized costing will be discussed later in this chapter.

The food costing task can be very simple. Consider a breakfast comprising two scrambled eggs, three strips of bacon, two pieces of toast, and one individual portion pack of jelly:

- Eggs are purchased by the dozen (12 eggs), and if they cost $2.79 per dozen, the cost of one egg is $0.23 cents ($2.79/12 eggs = $0.23 per egg). There are two eggs in the breakfast so their total cost is $0.46 ($0.23 per egg × 2 eggs = $0.46).
- Bacon is purchased by the pound for $3.89 per pound, and the specification calls for 32 strips (½ ounce) per pound. As a result, bacon costs 12 cents per strip ($3.89 lb/ 32 strip = $0.12 per strip). A breakfast containing three strips of bacon would, then, cost 36 cents ($0.12 per strip × 3 strips = $ 0.36).
- Bread costs $1.89/ loaf of 22 slices, so the two slices of bread in the breakfast cost $0.17 ($1.89 per loaf/22 slices = $08.6 per slice × 2 slices = $0.17).
- Portion controlled jellies cost $8.00 for a carton of 100 packets. Therefore, one packet used in the breakfast costs $0.08 cents ($8.00/100 = $.08)

The total cost of all ingredients in the breakfast is $1.07 (.46 + .36 + .17 + .08 = $1.07), and this cost can be determined without difficulty.

Costing becomes a greater challenge when each menu item contains several ingredients. Consider, for example, a meal comprised of a trip to a "help yourself" salad bar, a serving of beef stew served with freshly-made biscuits, and a slice of fresh-baked apple pie.

Consider also a **steamship round** that is carved and served on the buffet line. It may weigh 22 pounds when it is purchased but, even after it is properly roasted, there may be only 16½ pounds (edible portion) that can be carved and served.

In each of these and related examples, food yields must be determined before ingredients can be costed. Fortunately, there are yield guides that make this task simple and allow kitchen managers to cost recipes for all menu items offered by using the basic procedures described in this chapter.

OVERHEARD IN THE KITCHEN

Steamship round (beef)—A large beef roast that consists of the whole round with rump and heel.

Costing Recipe Ingredients

The task of costing recipe ingredients requires kitchen managers to know the cost of each ingredient and how much of each ingredient is used in the recipe. This is easy when the **purchase unit (PU)** is the same for the item when it is purchased and when it is used. For example, consider fluid whole milk:

Purchase Unit	Cost per Purchase Unit	Quantity in recipe	Ingredient (milk) cost
Gallon	$4.75	2 gallons	$9.50

Costing is more difficult when an ingredient is purchased in one purchase unit and used in the recipe in a variation of that purchase unit. For example, consider fluid whole milk in this example:

Purchase Unit	Cost per Purchase Unit	Quantity in recipe	Ingredient (milk) cost
Gallon	$4.75	2 quarts	$2.38*

*To determine the cost of milk in this recipe, one must know there are 4 quarts in one gallon. Then the ingredient cost can be determined: 4 quarts (one gallon) cost $4.75 so one quart costs $1.19 ($4.75/gallon ÷ 4 quarts = $1.19). Two quarts are needed in the recipe so the cost of milk is $2.38 ($1.19 per quart × 2 quarts = $2.38).

The ingredient costing process becomes more challenging when an ingredient is purchased in one purchase unit and used in an entirely different purchase unit as in the following example:

EXAMPLE

Celery costs $1.69 per pound, and one cup of chopped celery is needed in the recipe. To cost this ingredient the kitchen manager must know two things:

- How to convert pounds (weight) to cups (volume)
- How much celery is lost in cleaning and removing celery leaves and ends. For example, one pound (16 ounces) of celery as purchased may yield only 14 ounces of celery that can be chopped for the recipe.

Fortunately, guides to **edible food yields** are available to help with those decisions. These guides eliminate the time that would otherwise be needed to, for example, conduct yield tests to determine the quantity (weight and number of cups) of cleaned, chopped celery that can be expected for every one pound of celery that is purchased.

OVERHEARD IN THE KITCHEN

Purchase unit—The unit weight, volume, or container size in which a product can be purchased. For example, salad oil can be purchased in pint, quart, or gallon-sized containers.

Edible food yield—The useable amount of a food ingredient that can be prepared from a given purchase unit of that ingredient. Example: One pound (16 ounces) of fresh mushrooms yields 6 cups of cleaned sliced mushrooms or 5 cups of cleaned chopped mushrooms.

INFORMATION ON THE SIDE

Edible Food Yields

To see numerous charts and tables that provide volume and weight conversions for commonly used ingredients, just type "edible food yields" into your favorite search engine.

Figure 7.1 uses the information just discussed to cost the recipe originally shown in Figure 6.7 in Chapter Six. The ingredients used in that recipe have been costed, and the explanation about how this was done is provided.

Recipe: <u>Chicken Tetrazzini</u>

Yield: <u>48 servings</u>   Serving Size: <u>1/24 (12" × 20" × 2" pan)</u>

Ingredient (1)	Amount (2)	Purchase Unit (3)	Cost Per Purchase Unit (4)	No. of Purchase Units (5)	Ingredient Cost (6)
(A) Spaghetti	6 lb.	(lb)	$1.03	6	$ 6.18
(B) Margarine	2 lb.	(lb)	.89	2	1.78
(C) Celery	2 qt.	Bunch	.99	1.5	1.49
(D) Onions	2 qt.	(lb)	1.69	2.2	3.72
(E) Flour	1 lb., 4 oz.	(lb)	2.10	1.25	2.63
(F) Salt	2.5 oz.	(lb)	.88	.16	.14
(G) Pepper	1 tsp	(lb)	—	—	—
(H) Chicken Stock	2 gal., 2 c	—	—	—	—
(I) Chicken	12 lb., 8 oz.	(lb)	2.35	26	61.10
(J) Mushrooms	2 c	(lb)	4.95	.33	1.64
(K) Green Pepper	3 c	(lb)	3.05	1.2	3.66
(L) Bread Crumbs	2 qt.	(lb)	1.90	1.75	3.33
(M) Sharp Cheese, shredded	2 qt.	(lb)	5.25	2.0	10.50
				Total Cost:	**$96.17**

Abbreviations used: lb – pound; qt = quart; oz = ounce; c = cup; gal = gallon; tsp = teaspoon

FIGURE 7.1   Recipe Costing Worksheet

Let's look at each ingredient in the recipe in more detail. Recall that the purpose of the costing process is to determine the cost of each ingredient used in the standard recipe. Recall also that a table of edible food yields will need to be reviewed to cost some ingredients.

- *Item A: Spaghetti.* 6 pounds are needed (column 2), the purchase unit is pound (column 3), and the cost per purchase unit is $1.03 (column 4).

$$
\begin{array}{ccc}
6 \text{ pound} & \times & \$1.03 & = & \$6.18 \\
(\text{col. 2}) & & (\text{col. 4}) & & (\text{col. 6})
\end{array}
$$

- *Item B: Margarine.* 2 pounds are needed (column 2), the purchase unit is pound (column 3), and the cost per purchase unit is .89 (column 4).

$$
\begin{array}{ccc}
2 \text{ pound} & \times & \$.89 & = & \$1.78 \\
(\text{col. 2}) & & (\text{col. 4}) & & (\text{col. 6})
\end{array}
$$

- *Item C: Celery.* 2 quarts are needed (column 2), the purchase unit is bunch (column 3), and the cost per purchase unit is .99 (column 4). To cost this item, the purchase unit (bunch in column 3) must be converted to the amount needed (quart in column 2). One bunch of celery weighs about 2 pounds (32 ounces; as purchased (AP) weight) and yields 22 ounces after cleaning and trimming. One cup of cleaned/trimmed celery weighs 4 ounces. Therefore, there are 5.5 cleaned/trimmed cups per bunch of celery:

$$
\begin{array}{ccc}
22 \text{ oz.} & \div & 4.0 \text{ oz.} & = & 5.5 \text{ cups} \\
(\text{bunch of cleaned/} & & (\text{cup of cleaned/} & & (\text{cleaned/trimmed} \\
\text{trimmed celery}) & & \text{trimmed celery}) & & \text{celery/bunch})
\end{array}
$$

The recipe requires 2 qts (col. 2) which is eight cups:

$$2 \text{ qts.} \times 4 \text{ cups/quart} = 8 \text{ cups}$$

Therefore, the kitchen manager will use 1.8 bunches (as purchased) in the recipe

$$
\begin{array}{ccc}
8 \text{ cups needed} & \div & 5.5 \text{ cups} & = & 1.5 \text{ bunches} \\
(2 \text{ quartsin col. 2}) & & (\text{cups in celery/bunch}) & & (\text{cleaned/trimmed rounded})
\end{array}
$$

$$
\begin{array}{ccc}
1.5 \text{ bunches needed} & \times & .99 & = & \$1.49 \\
(\text{amount of celery} & & (\text{cost/purchase} & & (\text{celery cost in} \\
\text{needed}) & & \text{unit in col. 4}) & & \text{recipe [col. 6])}
\end{array}
$$

- *Item D: Onions.* 2 quarts are needed (column 2), the purchase unit is pound (column 3), and the cost per purchase unit is $1.69 (column 4).

The onions provide another example of the need to convert the purchase unit (pound in column 3) to the amount needed (quart in column 2). One cup of trimmed/cleaned onions weighs 4 ounces. One pound (16 ounces) of onions weighs 14.5 ounces after they are cleaned and trimmed. Therefore, one pound of onions (AP) yields 3.6 cups of trimmed/cleaned (EP) onions:

$$
\begin{array}{ccc}
14.5 \text{ oz.} & \div & 4 \text{ oz.} & = & 3.6 \text{ cups} \\
(\text{trimmed/deaned} & & (\text{cup of trimmed/} & & (\text{trimmed/deaned} \\
\text{onions/pound}) & & \text{clean onions}) & & \text{onions/pound})
\end{array}
$$

The kitchen manager requires 2.2 pounds (as purchased) of onions:

$$
\begin{array}{ccc}
8 \text{ cups needed} & \div & 3.6 \text{ cups} & = & 2.2 \text{ pounds} \\
(2 \text{ quarts in col. 2}) & & (\text{trimmed/deaned}) & & \\
& & \text{onions/pound} & &
\end{array}
$$

$$
\begin{array}{ccc}
2.2 \text{ pounds} & \times & \$1.69 & = & \$3.72 \\
(\text{amount of onions} & & (\text{cost/purchase} & & (\text{onion cost} \\
\text{needed}) & & \text{unit in col. 4}) & & \text{in recipe})
\end{array}
$$

- *Item E: Flour.* One pound, 4 ounces are needed (column 2). Therefore, 1.25 pounds of flour are required: 1 pound + .25 pound = 1.25 pounds

The total cost of flour required for the recipe is $2.63:

1.25 pounds	$\times$	$2.10	$=$	$2.63
(amount of flour needed)		(cost of flour per pound [col. 4])		(cost of flour in recipe [col. 6])

- *Item F: Salt.* 2.5 ounces of salt are needed (column 2); the purchase unit is pound (column 3), and the cost per purchase unit is .88 (column 4).

.88	$\div$	16. oz.	$=$	$0.055
(cost per pound)		(ounces in pound)		(cost per ounces)

$0.055	$\times$	2.5 oz.	$=$	$0.14
(cost per ounce		(amount of salt needed [col. 2])		(cost of salt in recipe [col. 6])

INFORMATION ON THE SIDE

Do a Few Cents Really Make a Difference?

Does the 14¢ cost for salt in a recipe yielding 48 servings really make a difference in the recipe cost? Kitchen managers must answer that question for themselves when they cost recipes.

Some will say "Yes; it only takes a few seconds to determine these small costs, and a lot of small costs will add up to a large cost." Others will say "No; the time saved can be used to control larger costs in other areas of the operation." Many of these kitchen managers do not include small costs (they must decide what "small" means) and, instead, add an amount such as a few dollars to the total of the more expensive ingredients that they have included in the recipe costing process.

What would you do?

- *Item G: Pepper.* The amount of pepper (1 teaspoon in column 2) is judged to be insignificant; no cost is calculated for this ingredient (column 6).
- *Item H: Chicken stock.* While a large amount of chicken stock is needed for the recipe (2 gallons + 2 cups in column 2), there is no direct cost for this ingredient because it is made in-house from chicken bones and other items remaining from vegetable trimmings.
- *Item I: Chicken.* 12 pounds + 8 ounces are needed (column 2), the purchase unit is pound (column 3), and the cost per purchase unit is $2.35 (column 4).

    To cost this ingredient, the kitchen manager must convert the as purchased (AP) yield of one pound of raw chicken to its edible portion (EP) weight to determine the cost for the chicken required by the recipe.

    A table of edible food yields indicates that one pound of chicken (whole bird, large fryer) has a 48% yield: For every pound that is purchased, only 48% will be left after cooking and bone and fat removal. The recipe requires 200 ounces of edible chicken: 12 pounds $\times$ 16 ounces/pound + 8 oz. = 200 oz.

    Therefore, 26 pounds of chicken must be purchased to yield 200 oz. for the recipe:

$$\frac{200 \text{ (edible oz/needed)}}{.48 \text{ (percent yield)}} = \frac{417 \text{ oz.}}{\text{(ounces to purchase)}}$$

$$\frac{417 \text{ (edible oz/needed)}}{16 \text{ (ounces/pound)}} = 26 \text{ pounds}$$

26 pounds	$\times$	$2.35	$=$	$61.10
(amount of chicken to purchase)		(cost/pound)		(chicken in recipe [col. 6])

- *Item J: Mushrooms.* 2 cups are needed (col. 2), the purchase unit is pound (column 3), and the cost per purchase unit is $4.95 (column 4). To cost the mushrooms, the kitchen manager must use the same approach as for the celery and onions which are also purchased by weight but used in a volume measurement in the recipe. A table of edible food yields indicates that 1 pound of mushrooms yields 6.0 cleaned cups. Therefore, the recipe requires .33 pound.

$$\underset{\text{(cups per pound)}}{6.0} \qquad \div \qquad \underset{\text{(cups needed)}}{2} \qquad = \qquad 3$$

Now the number of pounds can be calculated:

$$\frac{1.0 \text{ pound}}{3} \quad = \quad .33 \text{ pound needed}$$

$$\underset{\substack{\text{(cost per pound)}}}{\$4.95} \qquad \times \qquad \underset{\substack{\text{(amound needed)}}}{.33} \qquad = \qquad \underset{\substack{\text{(mushroom cost} \\ \text{in recipe [col. 6])}}}{\$1.64}$$

- *Item K: Green pepper.* As with the other vegetables in this recipe, an edible food yield table is required to determine the cost of green peppers:

One pound (16 oz. as purchased) yields 81.3% (13 oz. edible portion)

$$16 \text{ oz.} \times 81.3\% = 13 \text{ oz.}$$

One cup of cleaned green pepper weighs 5.2 oz. so 1 pound (AP) of green peppers yields 2.5 cups:

$$13 \text{ oz.} \div 5.2 \text{ oz.} = 2.5 \text{ cups}$$

Therefore, the kitchen manager will require 1.2 pounds of green pepper (AP) in the recipe:

$$\underset{\substack{\text{(amount needed)}}}{3.0 \text{ cups}} \qquad \div \qquad \underset{\substack{\text{(amount/pound)}}}{2.5 \text{ cups}} \qquad = \qquad \underset{\substack{\text{(amount to purchase)}}}{1.2 \text{ pounds}}$$

$$\underset{\substack{\text{(amount of pepper)} \\ \text{to purchase)}}}{1.2 \text{ pound}} \qquad \times \qquad \underset{\substack{\text{(cost per pound)}}}{\$3.05} \qquad = \qquad \underset{\substack{\text{(green pepper cost} \\ \text{in recipe [col. 6])}}}{\$3.66}$$

- *Item L: Bread crumbs.* 2 quarts are needed (column 2), the purchase unit is pound (column 3), and the cost per purchase unit is $1.90 (column 4). A table of edible food yields indicates that there are 4.6 cups of bread crumbs per pound. The recipe requires 8 cups (2 quarts × 4 cups/quart), so 1.75 pounds are needed:

$$\underset{\substack{\text{(amount needed)}}}{8 \text{ cups}} \qquad \div \qquad \underset{\substack{\text{(cups/pound)}}}{4.6 \text{ cups}} \qquad = \qquad \underset{\substack{\text{(rounded)}}}{1.75 \text{ pounds}}$$

$$\underset{\substack{\text{(amount needed)}}}{1.75 \text{ pounds}} \qquad \times \qquad \underset{\substack{\text{(cost per pound)}}}{\$1.90} \qquad = \qquad \underset{\substack{\text{(bread crumb cost} \\ \text{in recipe [col. 6])}}}{\$3.33}$$

- *Item M: Sharp cheese.* 2 quarts are needed (column 2), the purchase unit is pound (column 3), and the cost is $5.25 per pound (column 4).

A table of edible food yields indicates that there are 4.0 cups of shredded (grated) cheddar cheese per pound. The recipe requires 8 cups (2 quarts × 4 cups/quart), so 2 pounds of cheese are required.

$$\underset{\substack{\text{(amount needed)}}}{8 \text{ cups}} \qquad \div \qquad \underset{\substack{\text{(amount of cheese/pound)}}}{4 \text{ cups}} \qquad = \qquad 2 \text{ pounds}$$

$$\underset{\substack{\text{(amount needed)}}}{2 \text{ pound}} \qquad \times \qquad \underset{\substack{\text{(cost per pound)}}}{\$5.25} \qquad = \qquad \underset{\substack{\text{(cheese cost in} \\ \text{recipe [col. 6])}}}{\$10.50}$$

Each ingredient in the standard recipe has now been calculated.

While some time is required to calculate the recipe's cost, the benefits, including knowledge of product costs for menu item pricing decisions, are worth the effort. Knowledgeable and experienced kitchen managers can perform the calculations very quickly. Also, as you'll learn in a later section, computerized costing is increasingly being used to quicken the process and better assure that the resulting calculations are accurate.

Costing Standard Recipes

Now that all of the ingredient costs in the standard recipe shown in Figure 7.1 are known, the kitchen manager knows the total food cost to produce the recipe. As you'll note in that figure (bottom of column 6), the total food cost is $96.17.

INFORMATION ON THE SIDE

Nothing Happens By "Magic"

Wise kitchen managers remember that the advantages to costing standard recipes cannot be enjoyed just because the costing process is completed. Instead, they know that three important requirements must be in place for food cost advantages to be helpful to their food service operation:

- First, the standard recipe must be used to produce the menu item. Note: In the last chapter you learned that some operations have but do not consistently use or follow standard recipes.
- Second, every ingredient must always be accurately weighed, measured, or counted to assure that the proper quantity of each recipe ingredient is used.
- Third, the standard recipe must be costed using the current purchase costs for each ingredient. Unfortunately, the costs for the recipe that were determined in the previous section will likely change over time, and then the costing process will need to be repeated. When a manual costing system is used, every recipe containing mushrooms, for example, will need revision to reflect a different mushroom cost. By contrast, when a computerized system is used, all recipes containing mushrooms will be automatically revised when the change is entered into the recipe management system.

In addition to knowing the total ingredient cost to prepare the standard recipe ($96.17), the kitchen manager can also calculate the food cost to produce one serving of the recipe:

97.17	÷	48	=	$2.00
(total recipe cost)		(recipe yield − no. of servings)		(per serving cost)

In the example above, the per-serving food cost for one serving of chicken tetrazzini is $2.00. Recall, however, that the actual serving cost will only be this amount if standard recipes are available and carefully followed, if ingredients are carefully weighed, measured, and counted, and if the standard recipe has been costed with current market costs.

Calculating Plate Cost

Some restaurants use an à la carte pricing system. For example, entrées, sandwiches, soups and salads, and other items on the menu are priced individually, and guests "build" a meal to establish the meal's total selling price when they place orders or select their items from a cafeteria counter. When this pricing plan is used, the food cost for each menu item that has been determined as a result of recipe costing can be used for menu pricing decisions. Note: It can also be used for menu engineering purposes; see Chapter 10 for a detailed discussion of the menu engineering process.

More frequently, however, several food items prepared with different recipes are offered to the guest as a complete meal. For example, a food service operation may offer entrée items at different prices with **accompaniments** such as salad, potato, and vegetable included in the selling price. Just as often, guests are offered a choice of some or all of these accompaniments; example: a choice of three different types of potato.

In these instances, the cost to produce one serving of a specific food item must be combined with the costs of other food items to determine the total food cost for the guest's meal.

OVERHEARD IN THE KITCHEN

Accompaniment (menu)—An item such as a salad, potato, and/or other choices that are offered with and included within the price charged for an entrée.

Entrée:	Fresh White Fish Dinner	
Costing Date:	8/03/20xx	
Item	**Menu Item**	**Cost Per Serving**
Entrée	Fresh White Fish	$ 4.23
Potato	Three Choices Daily	0.37
Vegetable	Four Choices Daily	0.42
Salad	Tossed Green, Caesar, Spinach	1.12
Dressing	5 Choices Daily	0.37
Garnish	Lemon Wheels	0.02
Bread Loaf		0.27
Butter	Butter/Margarine	0.06
Condiment(s)		0.03
	Total Entrée and Accompaniments Cost	$ 6.89

FIGURE 7.2   Menu Item Costing

When meals comprised of several menu items rather than individual products are sold, **costing** again becomes necessary to determine the food cost of all items which comprise the "meal."

OVERHEARD IN THE KITCHEN

Costing (menu)—The process of determining the food cost required to produce all menu items that make up a meal (plate cost) offered at a set selling price when standard recipes for all menu items are utilized.

Figure 7.2 illustrates the process used to determine the total of all per-serving costs for menu items in a specific meal. If all meal components are prepared, portioned, and served according to their respective standard recipes and, if each recipe has been costed with current ingredient costs, the total food cost for the Fresh White Fish Dinner will be $6.89.

Figure 7.2 indicates that guests selecting the Fresh White Fish Dinner are offered a choice of three potatoes and four vegetables, and they may also choose between tossed green, Caesar, and spinach salads. Those selecting the tossed green salad have a choice of five dressings. As well, there is a lemon wheels garnish, and guests also receive a small loaf of bread, butter, and condiments as desired.

How did the kitchen manager who did the costing calculate the costs of potato, vegetable, salad, and dressing choices since each of these items likely has a different food cost, and guests will likely order different items to accompany their white fish entrée? How can these alternatives be costed? One approach (and the most conservative one) is to use the highest-cost choice in each category.

Assume that a serving of twice-baked potatoes has a higher cost than other potato choices. Its cost could be used for costing all potato choices and, in Figure 7.2, that cost is shown to be $0.37. The same tactic could be used to determine the cost of the vegetable, salad, and salad dressing choices in the Fresh White Fish dinner.

You've learned that costing does little good in predicting or managing costs unless all assumptions made by the kitchen manager have been implemented. For example:

- Standard recipes, including serving sizes, *must* be followed.
- Standard recipes *must* be costed with current ingredient costs.
- The per-serving costs of all food component alternatives *cannot* be exceeded.

What happens when, for example, the purchase cost of a vegetable choice such as broccoli or sautéed mushrooms increases? There are several alternatives that include:

- Replacing the vegetable choice with another that is within the food cost limits for the vegetable choice.

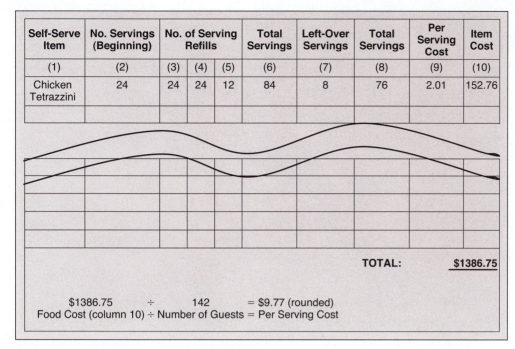

Self-Serve Item	No. Servings (Beginning)	No. of Serving Refills			Total Servings	Left-Over Servings	Total Servings	Per Serving Cost	Item Cost
(1)	(2)	(3)	(4)	(5)	(6)	(7)	(8)	(9)	(10)
Chicken Tetrazzini	24	24	24	12	84	8	76	2.01	152.76

TOTAL: $1386.75

$1386.75   ÷   142   = $9.77 (rounded)
Food Cost (column 10) ÷ Number of Guests = Per Serving Cost

FIGURE 7.3   Costing Sheet for Self-Service Items

- Retaining the vegetable choice on the menu but pricing it on an à la carte basis and supplement it with another vegetable choice that is within cost limitations.
- Serving a smaller serving size of the vegetable.
- Raising the food cost limit allowed for the vegetable choice on the menu.

Calculating Buffet and Salad Bar Costs

When guests serve themselves to a "help yourself" buffet or self-service salad bar, how can the cost of food used be determined so the menu selling price for the buffet or salad bar visit is determined? Figure 7.3 illustrates a worksheet that can be used for this purpose.

Note that the chicken tetrazzini prepared according to the standard recipe illustrated in Figure 7.2 is available on the buffet (column 1). A pan containing 24 servings is issued to the buffet at the beginning of the service (column 2). During the meal period, 60 additional servings are brought to the buffet line (see columns 3 to 5). Therefore, 84 servings were available during the meal period (column 6). When buffet service ends, 8 servings of chicken tetrazzini remain (column 7). Therefore, 76 servings were selected by the guests (84 servings − 8 servings). Since each serving costs $2.01 (column 9), the total food cost for all servings of chicken tetrazzini is $152.76 (76 servings × $2.01). The process just described is repeated for all other items available on the buffet.

The total item food cost (column 10) for all items served on the buffet is calculated and is divided by the number of buffet guests to calculate the average per-serving cost. In Figure 7.3, you'll note that the total item food cost is $1386.75, and the total number of buffet guests is 142. Therefore, the per-serving food cost for the buffet was $9.77 ($1386.75 ÷ 142). Note: If different items were on a salad bar offered as a menu item choice, the total per-serving cost for the salad bar visit would be the cost determined by a costing sheet similar to that in Figure 7.3.

The process of determining per-serving costs on buffet or salad bars does not need to be ongoing. For example, the worksheet in Figure 7.3 could be used for several meal periods, and the results could be averaged to calculate the average per serving costs. As product costs change over time and/or as the variety of self-service items change, the costing process should be repeated to determine current costs.

Kitchen managers cost the foods consumed in this "help yourself" buffet to help them determine the selling price for the buffet.

Three Additional Concerns

This section of the chapter concludes with a discussion of three issues related to costing: computerized costing, menu pricing, and control of buffet and salad bar costs.

COMPUTERIZED COSTING

Each of the steps and types of calculations required for costing are the same regardless of whether the kitchen manager does costing manually or with the assistance of a computerized system. Technology is increasingly impacting many aspects of food production operations, and this includes activities relating to planning for food costs before they are incurred. Common **recipe management software** frequently maintains three **files** that help to control food costs: **ingredient file**, **standard recipe file**, and **menu item file**.

OVERHEARD IN THE KITCHEN

Recipe management software—Written programs, procedures, instructions, or rules relating to the operation of a computer system that involves or impacts standard recipes.

File (computer)—A block of information containing a program, document, or collection of data.

Ingredient file—A computerized record that contains information about each ingredient purchased, including purchase unit size and cost, issue unit size and cost, and recipe unit size and cost. Interestingly, each of these units can differ. For example, prepared applesauce may be purchased in a case of six #10 cans (purchase unit size), issued one can at a time (issue unit = #10 can) and used in recipe by the cup (recipe unit = cup).

Standard recipe file—A computerized record that contains the recipes for the menu items produced. Data includes each recipe's ingredients, preparation method, yield (number of serving and serving size), and ingredient costs along with each item's selling price and food cost percentage (food cost ÷ selling price).

Menu item file—A computerized record about information relating to menu items tracked with the operation's point-of-sale (POS) system.

Let's look at each of these files more closely:

- *Ingredient file*—The time required to initially develop and maintain an ongoing ingredient file for each ingredient purchased by the food service operation can be lengthy. With some computerized systems, the ingredient file is available through the inventory software that maintains information about the quantity and cost of items in current inventory and those that have been issued. The ingredient file must maintain current and accurate information because its data drives the standard recipe files and menu item files.

- *Standard recipe file*—Electronic systems are available to determine recipe yields based upon estimated yields and then print a recipe converted for the desired amount. Recipe conversion software can convert recipe ingredients from weight-to-volume measurements or vise-versa and then calculate the ingredient cost for preparing the recipe.
- *Menu item file*—This record contains information tracked by the food service operation's point-of-sales system, and it includes the menu item's selling price, ingredient quantities, and unit sales totals.

As suggested above, some time must be spent in the ongoing task of updating ingredient files as, for example, purchase prices change. However, a kitchen manager will spend significantly less time maintaining current ingredient costs in standard recipes using an electronic system rather than performing these calculations manually. For example, assume that there are five recipes using canned tomato sauce, and the cost of this ingredient increases. The kitchen manager needs only to change the price once in the ingredient file, and the new purchase cost will carry over to and adjust each affected standard recipe accordingly. Many observers believe that the use of automated software to control food costs will increase, and recipe management software is probably among the elements that will be more commonly used.

MENU PRICING

You have learned that objective tactics to determine menu item selling prices require knowledge about the estimated food cost for the menu items being sold. You have also learned that this information is generated by costing standard recipes for each menu item.

Let's review how the kitchen manager at Vernon's Restaurant uses recipe costing information to establish selling prices. Assume a pork chop entrée at the restaurant consists of the following menu items and that the estimated portion cost for each item is as shown:

Pork chop entrée	$3.75
Salad/Dressing	.47
Potato Choice	.38
Vegetable Choice	.25
Dinner Roll/Butter	.14
Total estimated food cost for pork chop dinner	**$4.99**

The **base selling price** of the pork chop dinner can be calculated if a 37% (.37) food cost is desired based upon the agreed-upon operating budget for Vernon's Restaurant:

Step 1: Determine the **selling price multiplier** by dividing the budgeted food cost percentage into 100% ($1.00):

$$\frac{1}{\text{Budgeted food cost percentage}} = \frac{1.00}{.37} = 2.70 \text{ selling price multiplier}$$

Step 2: Determine the menu item's base selling price by multiplying the estimated food cost by the selling price multiplier:

$4.99	×	2.70	=	$13.47
(food cost for pork chop dinner)		(selling price multiplier)		(base selling price)

OVERHEARD IN THE KITCHEN

Base selling price (menu item)—The benchmark selling price of a menu item calculated by the use of an objective pricing method. After its calculation, kitchen managers may modify the actual selling price based upon marketing issues, competitive pricing structures, and the "psychology" of pricing.

Multiplier (selling price)—The mark-up by which the plate cost of a menu item must be multiplied to determine the item's base selling price; see plate cost.

In the example above, the kitchen manager at Vernon's Restaurant has learned that the pork chop dinner should be priced at about $13.47 if the budget goal of a 37% food cost is to be achieved for this item. However, recall that several control procedures must be used to best ensure that the base selling price ($13.47) will meet the budgeted food cost percentage goal:

- Standard recipes must be used to prepare each menu item in the pork chop dinner.
- Standard recipe costs must be based on current purchase costs.
- Each item must be correctly portioned.

With the proper control procedures in place, the kitchen manager and other members of the menu planning team can evaluate proposed menu changes in terms of selling price ranges that have been established for the operation. Then they can determine the actual selling price that will be stated on the menu.

INFORMATION ON THE SIDE

What's This About Base Selling Price?

You learned that the pork chop dinner at Vernon's Restaurant will require a base selling price of $13.47 to achieve the desired (budgeted) food-cost goal.

The base selling price results from the use of a pricing formula, and it is not necessarily the final selling price for the menu item. Instead, it is benchmark or target number used by the kitchen manager and other members of the menu design team to establish the actual price. Factors to consider when adjusting the base selling price include value (price relative to quality from the guests' perspective), supply and demand, production volume concerns, and prices charged by competitors for similar items.

CONTROL OF BUFFET AND SALAD BAR COSTS

Experienced kitchen managers understand that it does little good to cost "help yourself" items offered on buffets and salad bars unless efforts are made to control the actual food costs that are incurred. At the same time, they realize the importance of providing value to the guests who self-select items from the buffets and salad bars. Is there any way to control food cost when portioning is done by the guests rather than the kitchen manager's staff? The answer is "yes," and practical tactics to do so are numerous.

First, kitchen managers recognize that food waste benefits neither the guests nor the food service operation. Food that is produced, transferred to the serving area, returned at the end of service, and discarded does not benefit anyone. As well, food selected by guest that is not consumed that is then scrapped into the garbage disposer yields the same result.

"Managing by walking around" and looking at plate waste on tables being cleared for re-use, in garbage cans, and at the soiled dish counter often provide a first-step in food cost control: being aware that a food waste problem exists. As well, an analysis of food production and leftover records can be helpful to reevaluate production quantities.

It is just as important to consistently use standard recipes for "help yourself" items as for those portioned by food production personnel and served by members of the food service operation's service team.

The use of basic portion control techniques in self-service areas can be very helpful. For example, consider these ideas:

- Preportion items onto small plates or into small bowls.
- Cut items such as chicken into quarters rather than halves.
- Separate items such as meatloaf slices so items do not stick together.
- Serve "small" cookies at dessert bars rather than larger-sized servings.
- Replenish self-service stations with less food more frequently.
- Use the correct-sized serving utensils. For example, if a large ladle is used for salad dressing, it is possible that guests will pour more dressing than desired over the salad. The result: higher-than-necessary food costs and a potentially disappointed guest.
- If applicable, signage can be used to remind guests that they may return to the self-service unit for additional servings. This may encourage them to take smaller servings initially rather than larger-than-desired servings if they are not aware that they can return to the service area.

NOW IT'S YOUR TURN

A PINCH OF THE INTERNET (7.1)

1. There are several Internet sites that provide information about volume to weight equivalents and trim and cooking yields. One popular source used in large quantity food production operations is found at: www.chefdesk.com Note: This site describes the information, shows sample screens, and has free food service calculations.

2. Other online sources of food yield information can be found by entering "edible food yields" in your favorite search engine.

3. Check out the following Web sites to learn more about recipe management software:

   CALCMENU
   www.calcmenu.com

   foodsoftware.com
   www.foodsoftware.com

   Comus Restaurant Systems
   www.comus.com

   FOOD-TRAK Software
   www.foodtrak.com

   CostGuard Foodservice Software
   www.costguard.com

   MenuLink Computer Solutions
   www.menulinkinc.com

   Culinary Software Services
   www.culinarysoftware.com

   Radiant Systems Inc.
   www.radiantsystems.com

   Eatec Corporation
   www.eatec.com

Note: Some of these sites have demonstration modules that allow you to work through sample costing activities.

COMPLETING THE PLATE QUESTIONS (7.1)

1. Do you think it is important to cost ingredients required in very small quantities such as one or two teaspoons or ounces in a recipe yielding fifty or more servings? Why or why not? If you do not think it is practical, what would be your cut-off point beyond which ingredients should be costed? How did you arrive at this cut-off number?

2. If you were the kitchen manager in a food service operation that costed recipes, would you convert ingredient quantities in standard recipes to purchase unit sizes when possible? For example, if you purchased onions by the pound, would you convert the quantity needed to ounces or pounds rather than cups or quarts?

3. What are the advantages and disadvantages to computerized costing of standard recipes? Would you use an electronic system in your food service operation? Why or why not?

Kitchen Challenge Du Jour Case Study (7.1)

"Hey, Pauli, I learned something yesterday I would like to talk to you about," said Shari-Ann, the general manager of Vernon's Restaurant. "I attended a state restaurant association educational meeting yesterday, and the speaker talked about how to control food costs in salad bars. I especially wanted to attend this session because, as you know, we have a great salad bar (or at least, it has a large number of items on it), and I am always anxious to learn ways to better control costs without reducing quality."

Shari-Ann was talking to Pauli, the kitchen manager at the restaurant who replied: "Well, Shari, I agree that we should find ways to reduce costs, and there are likely some things we can do better here. For example, I'd start analyzing how things are done over in the bar with all of the drinks they sell. However, I believe in the old saying that if it ain't broke, don't try to fix it. I haven't heard a guest complain about the salad bar, and I haven't heard you talk about it until now. Aren't things going okay?"

"I don't know," replied Shari-Ann, "and that is part of the problem. What should our salad bar cost us on a per person basis, and what does it actually cost us? How did we arrive at a selling price of $8.95 for the guest who only wants to visit the salad bar? How is the cost of the food consumed by a guest considered when he or she selects the salad bar instead of a tossed Caesar salad as part of a full meal? The speaker at yesterday's session did a good job of explaining the need to check these things out."

"I don't think it is necessary," replied Pauli, "and we're really busy around here. I'll do whatever you suggest, but I think we should talk about it when we have more time. I'll bet I can convince you that we don't have a problem, and I really think the first thing to do to control costs is to see how bartenders are portioning drinks at the bar."

    a) Is Shari-Ann correct to be concerned about the salad bar costs?

    b) Why do you think Pauli is reluctant to investigate them? What should Shari-Ann do now?

FOOD SERVING RESPONSIBILITIES

OBJECTIVE

2. Explain how kitchen managers and their preparation personnel assist their front-of-house team members with food serving tasks:
   - À la carte dining
   - Banquet operations
   - Room service
   - Lobby food service

The responsibilities of kitchen managers and their preparation staff do not end when the food is produced. Instead, they may undertake tasks that relate to food serving, an activity defined earlier to include moving food products from the production personnel to serving employees. They may do this in a food pick-up area in the kitchen as is common in many à la carte dining operations. Alternatively, they may transport food to buffet serving lines in guest service areas. Also, they typically **pre-plate** foods that will be served in banquet operations and in hotel room service operations. Another example: many **limited-service hotels** provide breakfast service with offerings ranging from a simple **continental breakfast** to much more extensive breakfast menus featuring a variety of hot foods. We will conclude this chapter with a discussion of the role of food production personnel in food serving procedures needed to help ensure guests receive the highest possible quality products.

OVERHEARD IN THE KITCHEN

Pre-plate (banquet)—The portioning of menu items onto plates that will be served to banquet guests. These plates are frequently covered to keep hot foods hot or placed in heated transport equipment to move the food to banquet service areas.

Limited-service hotel—A lodging property that offers very limited food service or none at all; sometimes a complementary breakfast is served, but there is not a table-service restaurant.

Continental breakfast—A breakfast that typically includes a bread item such as a roll or pastry, fruit juice, and coffee or tea but no hot food items.

À la carte Dining

Kitchen managers and their employees may undertake three basic types of food preparation in à la carte dining operations:

- They prepare items such as stews, baked dishes, sauces, and many desserts in relatively large quantities because they cannot be quickly produced.
- They cook other items on a by-the-order basis such as grilled steaks, broiled seafood, and deep-fried chicken.
- They preportion items such as salads and chilled fruits for quick service when ordered.

    Orders for each type of menu item must be filled promptly, and careful interaction with service staff is required for this goal to be achieved.

    Increasingly, servers place food orders electronically using **order printers** that transmit guest orders to the kitchen, often to the **workstations** where specific items are produced.

OVERHEARD IN THE KITCHEN

Order printer—Equipment that transmits food service orders from point-of-sale equipment to the order pick-up area and prints or electronically displays orders in that area; also called kitchen printers or remote printers.

Workstation—An area with necessary equipment in which closely-related work activities are performed by persons working in similar positions. For example, food preparation personnel may work in a cooks' line that houses several items of food equipment used to hold or produce food items that have been ordered by service staff.

Figure 7.4 shows part of the layout for an à la carte restaurant that also has a banquet dining area.

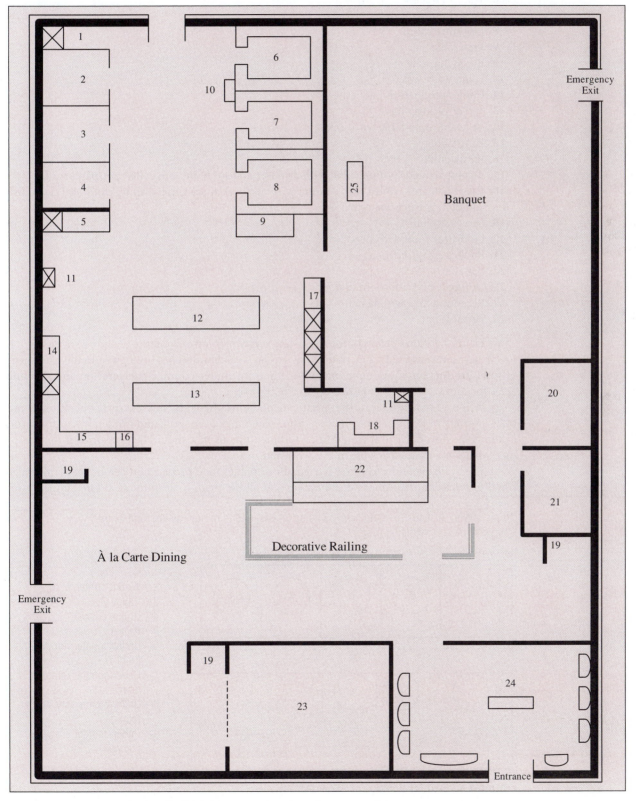

FIGURE 7.4 Functional Areas for À la carte Restaurant (not drawn to scale)

As you review Figure 7.4, the numbers relate to the following areas and equipment:

1. Can/cart wash
2. Employee locker room (men)
3. Employee locker room (women)
4. Manager's office (with windows)
5. Entrée prep table with sink
6. Walk-in freezer
7. Walk-in refrigerator
8. Dry store room
9. Prep table
10. Receiving scale
11. Hand wash sink
12. Cook's production line
13. Server pick-up line
14. Vegetable prep table with sink
15. Pantry area
16. Ice machine
17. 3-compartment pot/pan sink with disposer and spray rinse in soiled pot/pan counter
18. Dish wash area (soiled dish counter with disposer/spray rinse, dish machine and clean dish counter (booster heater below)
19. Server station
20. Public restroom (women)
21. Public restroom (men)
22. Bar area
23. Dining area (with room divider for semi-privacy)
24. Reception area with benches
25. Portable bar

Figure 7.5 shows details of the cooks' line/server pick-up area (items 12 and 13) in Figure 7.4.

As you review Figure 7.5, notice that special consideration has been given to the placement of food production equipment (items 1–5) and for under-counter refrigeration and shelving areas for cooks and for under-shelving for food servers.

While we may not know the specific menu items offered by this à la carte operation, it can offer a variety of items because it has a deep fryer, range oven, grill, and broiler. By contrast, you can imagine how difficult it would be to add menu items that should be deep-fried if the equipment to do so was not available in this workstation area.

The available under-counter refrigeration enables food preparation personnel to minimize travel to refrigerators in more distant areas and allows them to keep foods at safe temperatures

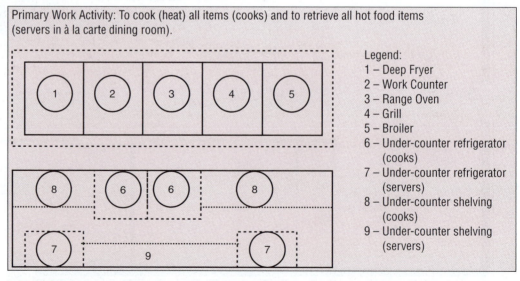

FIGURE 7.5 Kitchen: Cooks' Line/Server Pick-up Area

Note: All production equipment must be under a ventilation/fire-suspension system.

for long time periods in what is often a very warm environment. This again emphasizes the need for careful consideration of **work simplification** principles to enable production personnel to be very productive during busy guest serving periods.

OVERHEARD IN THE KITCHEN

Work simplification—The design of a work process such as producing food on a cooks' line in a way that requires a minimal number of steps or motions that will yield products meeting the property's quality requirements.

Some food service operations use an **expediter** to coordinate the processing of food orders and the interaction between food production and serving personnel during, at least, the busiest serving times.

OVERHEARD IN THE KITCHEN

Expediter—A person who serves as a liaison between food production and serving staff during busy serving times.

In many food service operations, kitchen managers provide a several-minute line-up training session to service staff before a meal period begins. This time can be used to explain daily specials, indicate menu items that may not be available, and emphasize the popular and profitable for which suggestive selling is important.

INFORMATION ON THE SIDE
Lots of Stress in the Kitchen!

Work demands during busy times can create stress for food production and serving personnel. These are times when voices can be raised, tempers can rise, and close cooperation and team work can be a challenge. The kitchen manager has a significant role to play in role-modeling the attitude and work actions that are required during these times.

Food production and service staff must recognize that, even in the best food service operation, honest mistakes can occur and, unfortunately, they can impact the work of others and the ability to meet guest service standards. However, front-and back-of-house professionals deal with these issues without letting personalities "get in the way." There is no favoritism ("Why did that order go out already when I have been waiting for my order for a longer time?"). At these times, it is very important for everyone to remember that they are all working together to serve the guests.

In some operations, kitchen managers visit with guests in dining areas to answer food-related questions, to assist guests with food allergies as they make ordering decisions, and, in general, to welcome the guests and thank them for visiting. They may also discuss food-related problems, make wine and food pairing suggestions, and answer questions that guests pose about their own at-home cooking activities.

Kitchen managers may, depending upon their property's practices and health department requirements, invite guests to view or tour kitchen areas. Some operations even have a "chef's table." In this special area invited guests can dine with the kitchen manager while observing some aspects of food preparation from a first-hand viewpoint. Other operations design kitchen areas with glass walls that enable guests in dining areas to view the kitchen. A more common design component is a broiling or other workstation located in part of the dining area. These and related efforts to turn kitchen areas into a show place please many guests and, at the same time, provide an incentive for the kitchen to remain clean and the work habits of food production personnel to be sanitary.

Banquet Operations

In this section of the chapter, you're learning how kitchen managers and their preparation teams assist food service personnel with beginning service tasks. However, now that we are discussing banquet operations, another team member in the food service operation must be considered. That team member is the **banquet services coordinator**, whose job it is to meet with clients to plan all aspects of the client's banquet.

The dining experience of these guests will, in large measure, relate to the production and serving skills of the kitchen manager and his/her team.

OVERHEARD IN THE KITCHEN

Banquet services coordinator—The person representing the food service operation who interacts with banquet clients to assure that the event being planned exactly meets the clients' needs; also called banquet sales coordinator; in large hotels, this responsibility might be part of the activities performed by a convention sales coordinator.

BANQUET PLANNING ACTIVITIES

Many properties that offer banquets provide **pre-set menus** for banquet guests. These menus can be produced and served as is or, alternatively, they can serve as a starting point with changes made to best suit the guests' needs. These menus have likely been planned by the kitchen manager and the menu planning team. Desired changes, if any, should be discussed with the kitchen manager to assure that the menu can be produced in a way that will meet the property's quality standards and the guests' expectations.

OVERHEARD IN THE KITCHEN

Menu (pre-set banquet)—A menu planned as an example of popular menus enjoyed by previous banquet guests that are suggested for other potential guests.

INFORMATION ON THE SIDE
Are Special Banquets Always Desirable?

"We want the best banquet possible, and money is no object!" Every banquet sales person would be happy to hear a customer make this statement. However, when these events are planned, it is always critical to assure that the property can deliver what is being promised. Few operations could properly offer table-side flambéing at an event for 1,000 people. Few properties would likewise have the oven capacity to provide fresh-baked appetizers, dinner rolls, baked entrées, and a baked dessert for that size of event. Therefore, it is always important to think about the property's reputation. Who could imagine, for example, the impact of 1,000 banquet guests leaving the property with "horror stories" about the food produced and service provided at their event?

A skilled banquet sales coordinator working closely with the kitchen manager may be able to suggest a creative banquet menu that can be produced without sacrificing quality standards. However, they must always know when to say "no" to customer suggestions or demands that may place the property's reputation in jeopardy.

The kitchen manager may attend one or more banquet planning sessions if questions arise, and/or if detailed information is required. As well, he or she may participate in after-event evaluation sessions designed to improve banquet planning, production, and delivery.

The final agreements between the banquet services coordinator and the event's host or hostess will be summarized in a **banquet event order**. This will include information that the kitchen manager must know such as the menu items to be served, number of servings to be prepared, service times, and special labor needs such as a buffet entrée carver.

OVERHEARD IN THE KITCHEN

Banquet event order—A form used by food sales, production, and serving personnel to detail all requirements for a banquet. Information provided by the sponsor is summarized on this document and becomes the basis for the formal agreement between the client and the hospitality operation; often abbreviated "BEO."

The responsibilities of kitchen managers in plating banquet meals depend upon the type of service being provided. These can include:

- **American service**—Menu items are portioned onto service plates that will be served to banquet guests.
- **Russian service**—An entrée such as beef tenderloin is thinly sliced in the kitchen and brought to the table by banquet personnel who then place the item on a plate with entrée accompaniments that has been set in front of the guest.
- **English service**—Menu items are placed in serving bowls or on serving platters, and the food is brought to the guest table for service in a "family-style" service; serving dishes are passed around the table by the guests.
- **Buffet service**—This service style has been discussed earlier in this chapter. Food preparation personnel may be responsible for bringing food to the "help yourself" buffet line and/or providing some portioning such as carving beef or ham on the buffet line.

OVERHEARD IN THE KITCHEN

American service (banquet)—Menu items are portioned onto service plates that will be served to banquet guests.

Russian service (banquet)—An entrée such as a beef tenderloin is thinly sliced in the kitchen and brought to the table by banquet staff who place the item on a plate with entrée accompaniments that has been set in front of the guest

English service (banquet)—Menu items are placed in serving bowls or on serving platters, and the food is brought to the guest table for service in a "family-style" service; serving dishes are passed around the table by the guests.

Buffet service—A service style in which guests select and portion menu items as they pass along one or more service counters. In some operations items such as omelets are made to order, and other items such as rounds of beef are carved to order.

BANQUET FOOD PRODUCTION CONCERNS

When preparing banquet food items it is probable that the kitchen manager will use the same recipes to prepare items of the same quality with the same ingredients purchased with the same specifications. Methods of food preparation might be the same, but quantities of menu items produced will likely differ. However, food production for the banquet operation in a typical restaurant will likely be more difficult than for the à la carte operation, especially if the kitchen was not planned for banquet production. One reason is that the restaurant kitchen has probably been designed to produce small volumes of numerous items rather than large volumes of specific items at one time.

Consider, for example, a typical restaurant's hot food production line consisting of a range oven, grill, deep fryer, and broiler. This equipment may be very appropriate for the variety of and volume of items produced for the à la carte dining room. However, it may be totally inadequate to produce, for example, 150 servings of steak or seafood fillet at one time to be served at a banquet. The production problem would be compounded significantly if à la carte "peaks" in guests' orders occur at the same time as the "big rush" for the banquet production. The results could be disappointed à la carte and banquet guests.

Unfortunately, this problem could occur if careful planning and analysis did not precede the decision to offer the banquet. The possible benefit of several thousand dollars in additional revenue from a banquet could be more than offset by significant negative word-of-mouth advertising which could lead to a reduction in the restaurant's core business (à la carte dining).

What can one learn from the above anecdote? One lesson is that the volume of items to be produced is a significant factor that may make it difficult for the typical restaurant to offer banquets for large groups unless the kitchen is capable of doing so.

BANQUET PORTIONING CONCERNS

Experienced kitchen managers know that it is one thing, for example, for a production employee to place a grilled steak, baked potato, and a vegetable on a single plate for immediate pick-up by a server. It is, however, another thing to preportion many plates at one time for banquet service. Where can one find the space required for this "assembly line?" How many employees will be needed? What type of equipment is required to keep hot food hot and cold food cold from the time of portioning through transport, holding and final banquet service to the guests? Space, personnel, and equipment/supplies are often unavailable in many restaurants for this specialized banquet-related task.

Figure 7.6 shows how a plating line might be planned for a banquet, and it provides an additional example of the planning that is required to assure that there are no "surprises" at a time when time is at a premium.

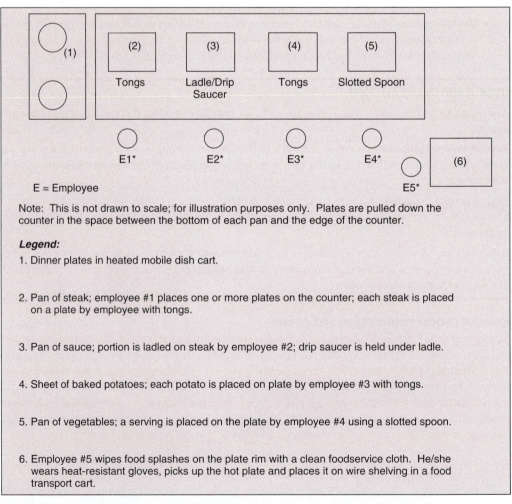

Note: This is not drawn to scale; for illustration purposes only. Plates are pulled down the counter in the space between the bottom of each pan and the edge of the counter.

Legend:

1. Dinner plates in heated mobile dish cart.

2. Pan of steak; employee #1 places one or more plates on the counter; each steak is placed on a plate by employee with tongs.

3. Pan of sauce; portion is ladled on steak by employee #2; drip saucer is held under ladle.

4. Sheet of baked potatoes; each potato is placed on plate by employee #3 with tongs.

5. Pan of vegetables; a serving is placed on the plate by employee #4 using a slotted spoon.

6. Employee #5 wipes food splashes on the plate rim with a clean foodservice cloth. He/she wears heat-resistant gloves, picks up the hot plate and places it on wire shelving in a food transport cart.

FIGURE 7.6 Diagram of Serving Line for Plating of Banquet Entrée Course (Steak w/Sauce, Baked Potato, and Vegetable)

When reviewing Figure 7.6, note that five staff members are required to portion this relatively simple entrée course. Notice also that specialized equipment (heated mobile dish cart and hot food transport warmer) are required. Note also that detailed information relating to the utensils that will be used for proportioning each item for this menu course is provided.

OFF-SITE CATERING

Restaurants, catering businesses, and hotels are among the hospitality operations that offer **off-site catering**.

OVERHEARD IN THE KITCHEN

Catering (off-site)—Food service in a location remote from the food service operation that requires the physical transport of food to an off-site location.

Off-site catering events are popular with business groups and also for individual social occasions such as birthdays, weddings, and anniversaries. Similar to planning for banquet operations discussed above, details leading to a formal agreement between the sponsor and the food service operation are required to help assure that there are no "surprises" on the day of service. This is especially important in off-site events since, by definition, kitchen managers and their employees must transport all of the food, serving utensils, paper supplies, and every other item required for the event. They do not have the ability to walk a few steps back to the kitchen or another area to retrieve items. Instead, careful planning is required to ensure that every single detail, including all food and nonfood items required for the event, will be available when needed.

A visit to the planned event site is typically undertaken before the menu is planned to determine what type, if any, of useable equipment is available and to assure that the location will accommodate the equipment that is necessary, including utility hook-ups. The kitchen manager and menu planning team has a basic menu planning limitation that also applies to room service operations (see the next section); the quality of food will deteriorate as time laps. This, in turn, places a large restraint on items that can be served if they must be produced on-site for delivery to the remote location. Note: This challenge might be lessened if the off-site location has some food preparation and holding equipment.

Very large catered events may require on-site work several days in advance of the event. This may be necessary, for example, when landscaping must be provided or altered and when tents must be constructed. Typically, the customer employs specialist sub-contractors to perform this work; the caterer's job is limited to food and beverage production and service-related activities. However, the caterer may employ special events planners to assume the responsibility for these and related tasks. More typically, however, smaller events do not require on-site work by the caterer before the day of the event.

On the day of the event, some work in the operation's kitchen will likely be needed. This includes food preparation and clean-up of the kitchen. As well, food, beverages, equipment, utensils, supplies, and numerous other items needed for the event must be counted and loaded on the transport vehicle(s). This is where attention to details is a must.

The Off-Site Location Inspection Review Form shown in Figure 7.7 can help to remind the kitchen manager about items that must be transported to the off-site facility. Also, packing sheets that identify everything to be shipped must be checked and rechecked (especially when several persons are involved in the packing process and when different persons pack equipment, food, and supplies). If washable dishes and flatware will be utilized, they also must be transported unless they are available at the off-site location.

During transport, sanitation concerns are important to minimize the time that **potentially hazardous foods** are kept within the temperature danger zone to minimize the possibility of a foodborne illness. Safety concerns are also important; for example, heavy equipment may shift during transport and cause injury to persons or damage to the delivery vehicle and/or its contents.

OVERHEARD IN THE KITCHEN

Potentially hazardous foods—Foods of animal origin or other items high in protein that are most frequently involved in cases of foodborne illness.

OFF-SITE LOCATION INSPECTION REVIEW FORM

Date of Visit: _____ Prospective Customer: _____ Event Date: _____ Event Time: _____

Location Contact:
Name: _____
Address: _____
Telephone: _____

Space to be Utilized for:
Reception: _____
Meal Service: _____
Other: _____

Access Times:
_____
_____
_____

Site Fees: _____

Site Access Time on Day of Event: _____

Access:
❏ Loading Dock ❏ Main Entrance Elevator: ❏ Yes ❏ No ❏ Not Needed ❏ Other: _____

Available Foodservice Equipment:
❏ Range Ovens _____
❏ Burner Tops _____
❏ Fryers _____
❏ Broilers _____
❏ Water/Sinks _____
❏ Preparation _____
❏ Pot Washing _____
❏ Ice Machine _____
❏ Work Tables _____
❏ Pots/Pans _____
❏ Fire Extinguisher _____

❏ Coffee Urns _____
❏ Refrigeration _____
❏ Heavy Duty Electric Lines _____
❏ Dishwashers _____
❏ Racks _____
❏ Microwave _____
❏ Work Space _____
❏ Portable Bars _____
❏ First Aid Kit _____
❏ Mops/Buckets/Brooms _____
❏ _____

Special Notes:
Is there adequate ventilation? ❏ Yes ❏ No   Is there adequate kitchen area? ❏ Yes ❏ No   Is there adequate dining area? ❏ Yes ❏ No
What is the smoking policy? _____
Is the gas or electricity turned on? ❏ Yes ❏ No   Where are the switches? _____
What is done with the dirty grease from the fryer, if used? _____
Where are the circuit breakers? _____ Is the box locked? ❏ Yes ❏ No   Is there a key? ❏ Yes ❏ No

Comments:

Dining Room Needs:

	Number	Size
Tables	_____	_____
Chairs	_____	_____
Buffet Tables	_____	_____

Dishes:

	Number
Dinner Plates	_____
Salad Plates	_____
Dessert Plates	_____
Coffee Cups/Saucers	_____
Water/Tea Glasses	_____

Flatware:

	Number
Knives	_____
Forks	_____
Spoons: Soup	_____
Spoons: Tea	_____
Spoons: Coffee	_____

Comments:

Alcoholic Beverage Service:
Does the establishment have a liquor license? ❏ Yes ❏ No   Who is responsible? _____
Can a one-day liquor license be obtained? ❏ Yes ❏ No   Who is responsible for getting? _____

Who has responsibility for bar?
_____

Who has responsibility for the bartenders?
_____

Bar hours: _____ to _____

Who can change this time period?
_____

Special Service with the alcoholic beverage service?

Who is responsible for getting? _____   Who is responsible for serving? _____

Restrictions on alcoholic beverage service: _____

Is bar set for keg beer? ❏ Yes ❏ No   Notes: _____

Who has responsibility for keg beer? _____   Who has responsibility for soft drinks? _____

FIGURE 7.7 Off-Site Location Inspection Review Form

Bar Needs:

	Number	Condition			Clean	
Type: _____	_____	❏ Good	❏ Ok	❏ Poor	❏ Yes	❏ No
Type: _____	_____	❏ Good	❏ Ok	❏ Poor	❏ Yes	❏ No
Wine: _____	_____	❏ Good	❏ Ok	❏ Poor	❏ Yes	❏ No
Champagne: _____	_____	❏ Good	❏ Ok	❏ Poor	❏ Yes	❏ No
Plastic: _____	_____	❏ Good	❏ Ok	❏ Poor	❏ Yes	❏ No
Beer Pitchers: _____	_____	❏ Good	❏ Ok	❏ Poor	❏ Yes	❏ No
Cork Screws: _____	_____	❏ Good	❏ Ok	❏ Poor	❏ Yes	❏ No

Other:
Trash Removal _____
AV Needs _____
Speaker Needs _____
Dance Floor _____
Guest Parking _____
Restroom (Guests) ❏ Yes ❏ No   Clean? ❏ Yes ❏ No   Who is responsible for upkeep? _____
Restroom/Lockers (Staff) ❏ Yes ❏ No   Clean? ❏ Yes ❏ No   Who is responsible for upkeep? _____
Handicap Access _____
Music/Band _____
Decorators _____
Facility staff to be available during event _____
Other _____
_____
_____

Special Areas:
How is the head table to be set? _____
    Special requests: _____
_____

Speaker podium layout? _____

Dining Area Diagram

Other Comments

FIGURE 7.7 *Continued*

Another concern: Everything must be carefully packed on the transport vehicle to reduce damage (jello molds, for example) and breakage (such as dishes). Location on the vehicle is also important. Light food items, for example, should be kept together and away from heavy non-food items.

At the off-site location, food items may need to be pre-prepared and held at the proper temperature until serving. The dining area must be set up, and a line-up meeting should be conducted after all staff are assembled at the off-site location and before they begin work. This session can be used to brief staff members about the event and its objectives and to review the menu, serving techniques, and work assignments. The kitchen manager in charge at the event's location must utilize all principles important in the art and science of supervision. This is necessary to assure that staff members work according to standard procedures, and that they are empowered to make on-the-spot decisions to make the event as enjoyable as possible for the customer and guests.

At the end of the event and back at the caterer's location, all items used off-site must be counted, cleaned, and replaced into inventory, if applicable.

As seen in the above "diary" of an off-site catered event, many of the necessary activities are very similar or identical to those required for a successful on-site food service event. However, some such as food transport and pre-preparation and preparation off-site, are very different. While careful attention to details is necessary in any type of food services, it is especially critical with off-site catering.

Room Service

Many **full-service hotels** offer room service, and some do so 24 hours each day, every day of the week. Guests of all types enjoy room service from business persons wanting a quick breakfast to small groups desiring a lunch during their meetings in a guest room to couples desiring a romantic meal.

OVERHEARD IN THE KITCHEN

Full-service hotel—A hotel that provides guests with extensive food and beverage products and services.

Large hotels may have a separate food preparation area to produce room service orders taken by order takers. There may also be a staging area used by room service attendants who prepare room service carts and trays for delivery to the guest rooms. In small properties, the kitchen manager may plan the room service menu which is prepared by the same food production personnel who prepare other meals for the property. These meals may be delivered to the guest room by a restaurant server according to an order written by the front desk clerk or dining room receptionist who takes the order.

PROFITABILITY

Guests noting the high prices on the room service menu often think that hotels make a lot of profit on this service. In fact, this is not so.

If room service is not profitable for the hotel, why is it offered? First, it is a service to guests. Some may select properties on the basis of its availability. Among these guests are those arriving on late airline flights and others wanting food/beverage services for small business meetings in guest rooms. Also, hotel rating services such as the American Automobile Association (AAA) assign their highest ratings to properties that offer room service (among other amenities).

Why does room service frequently lose money? High labor costs are one reason. Much time is needed to transport food from the kitchen to guest room areas. The capital costs incurred to purchase equipment such as delivery carts and warming devices can be significant. If costs were allocated for elevators to transport items, for staging areas to store room service carts and to prepare them for deliveries, and for similar costs, the expenses would even be greater. Finally, items such as glasses, cups, flatware, and serviceware increase room service costs. The need to return soiled room service items to kitchen areas often creates challenges. In many hotels, the question of "whose job is it?" arises. Housekeeping personnel, maintenance and security staff, and even managers may notice but not pick up and return these items, and this violates the concept of teamwork that is so important in the success of a hospitality operation.

In some hotels the room service department provides food and beverage service in **hospitality suites** and for other group functions in a guest room. In convention properties, vendors and exhibitors may invite customers to visit hotel rooms for **hosted events**. When these services are provided by room service rather than by banquet services, the likelihood of room service profitability increases because the relatively large number of persons generates revenue that more than offsets applicable costs.

OVERHEARD IN THE KITCHEN

Hospitality suite—A guest room rented by a supplier/vendor, usually during a convention/conference, to provide complimentary food and/or beverages to invited guests.

Hosted events—Functions that are complimentary for invited guests; costs are borne by the event's sponsor. A hosted bar may offer free beverages to wedding party guests, and a corporate sponsor may pay for a hosted reception in a hospitality suite.

MENU PLANNING

Special concerns are important when planning room service menus. As with any other food service alternative, quality is important. Room service menus should only offer items that can be transported relatively long distances from food preparation areas without decreases in quality.

As noted above, many guests perceive room service prices to be high, and they will demand that food quality requirements be maintained to help justify the prices. Unfortunately, some popular items (omelets and french fries, for example) are not ideal room service menu items because of quality problems that arise when they are held at serving temperatures for long periods of time during transport to guest rooms. Note: The kitchen manager can easily check food quality in a hotel restaurant or a banquet setting by sampling various items. However, managers have less access to products served in room service. Efforts to solicit feedback from guests are a critical way of determining whether quality requirements are consistently attained.

Cross-selling on room service menus is also possible. A room service breakfast menu can indicate that the hotel's Sunday brunch in the dining room is very popular. An invitation on the room service breakfast menu to call about daily dinner specials in the dining room can interest guests in thinking ahead about evening plans.

Room service orders, like those in à la carte dining operations, may be handwritten or, increasingly, are entered into a point-of-sale terminal (POS) by a food service employee. They may also be entered by the guests on their laptops and e-mailed to the hotel's Web site or entered into the TV set via the hotel's in-house channel provided by its satellite TV provider (example: Lodgnet). Orders can then be printed on hardcopy tickets given to the room service cook(s), and a copy is also given to the server when the order is transported to the guest room. Alternatively, the order can be transmitted to the cook(s) with an order printer. It is important for the room server to carefully note whether the items that have been plated (portioned) and placed on the cart for delivery are, in fact, the ones that were ordered.

Lobby Food Service

You've learned that most limited-service hotels offer a narrow range of food and beverage services. Most, however, do offer breakfast in their relatively small lobby areas and, therefore, a new term, lobby food services, has come into use.

While a highly-experienced and professionally trained kitchen manager is not usually required for a lobby food service operation offering a simple continental breakfast, some limited-service properties seek to build a competitive edge by offering a full hot breakfast with numerous "help yourself" menu items. These operations often require the services of a person with food production responsibilities, who must plan menu items and manage the breakfast staffing, production, service, and clean-up processes.

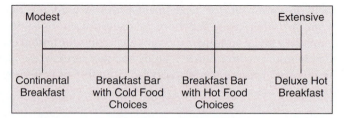

FIGURE 7.8 The Range of Limited-Service Hotel Breakfast Offerings

Figure 7.8 reviews a range of breakfast food service offerings from modest to extensive that can be offered in limited-service properties.

As you'll note in Figure 7.8, some properties offer a very limited continental breakfast that requires no cooking equipment and very little preparation or service space. A simple coffee maker and supplies (disposable cups, napkins, stir sticks, sugar/cream), a pitcher (or individual servings) of juice, a simple bread item with butter and, perhaps, jelly or a pastry (doughnut or sweet roll) illustrate the requirements for a limited continental breakfast with few guest choices.

A breakfast bar with cold food choices offers guests additional variety. This might, for example, include a selection of juices and several types of breads, rolls, and pastries along with coffee and milk. Other items (yogurts, fresh fruits, and assorted breakfast cereals) may also be available.

A breakfast bar with hot food choices expands the variety of menu items available to guests even further. Perhaps, for example, a toaster is available for bread, bagels, and prepared waffles and/or a waffle maker with preportioned batter available in portion cups can be used.

At the extreme range of Figure 7.8, some limited-service properties offer a **deluxe hot breakfast** with numerous food offerings. For example, there may be a buffet to allow guests to self-serve eggs (perhaps several styles), bacon, sausage, ham, potatoes, and other items that are prepared on-site in a small kitchen. In other properties, guests order desired items that have been prepared in advance or, alternatively, are prepared to order. In relatively few properties, a limited table service breakfast is available.

OVERHEARD IN THE KITCHEN

Deluxe hot breakfast—A breakfast with hot food choices offered by a limited-service hotel.

As the complexity of the breakfast food services increases, so does the amount of storage, equipment, preparation and service space, number of labor hours required, and skill levels of food service employees. In addition, associated operating expenses can rise dramatically. The decision about the type of food services to offer is critical and is an important part of the package marketed to the guests. Consider, for example, a new property being built or an existing facility being renovated. The space and equipment needs to offer a modest continental or a deluxe hot breakfast are vastly different. Significant financial consequences can occur if this space is included but not needed or if it is excluded and will later be required. As well, guests looking for value in their room rate will make personal decisions about the worth of the breakfast option for which they are paying. It is important to design food service needs into the property at the time it is constructed or when major renovation is done.

INFORMATION ON THE SIDE

Menu Planning and Limited-Service Hotels

Owners and kitchen managers of **independent hotels** can make their own decisions about what to offer guests. Corporate hotels owned by a multiunit hotel organization and franchise properties typically impose limitations on planners. For example, menus must be planned or, at least, breakfast components may be specified to standardize the breakfast within the hotel brand to meet the expectations of guests who visit different properties.

Standards may be established to specify items such as hot coffee and orange juice, and properties may be required to offer specific brands of items such as Kellogg breakfast cereals or Smucker's assorted jellies. There may also be requirements about the number of hours of breakfast operation and this, in turn, impacts the necessary serving equipment (how will milk be kept chilled and how could bread and pastries be kept from drying out?) as well as the labor hours that will be required.

A franchise company representative will include a review of the hotel's food service operations during inspection visits. Compliance with required standards, cleanliness and overall attractiveness of the serving and dining areas will be important parts of the property's evaluation.

Many of the factors used to plan menus in restaurants and full-service hotels also apply to menu planning in limited-service properties. For example, menus must consider the space required for storage, food preparation, service, dining and clean-up and sanitation, quality, and labor concerns will always be important.

SETTING-UP BREAKFAST SERVICE

A significant amount of effort is required to prepare for even a relatively simple breakfast for hotel guests. It is very unlikely that all (or even most) of the hotel's guests will want to have breakfast at the moment service begins. In fact, there may be only a few or even no guests present at the beginning of service. (If this is consistently the case, there may be a need to reevaluate the breakfast's start time.) However, the first guest should be able to select from the full variety of foods that will be available to those having breakfast later in the morning, and the reverse is also true. In other words, all the food items to be offered should be available during the entire service period. It is not appropriate to get the coffee ready and then begin preparing breakfast service for later-arriving guests. Hotel managers must carefully work out how long it takes to prepare for breakfast service, determine the most reasonable start and end times for service based upon guest desires, and then schedule labor accordingly.

INFORMATION ON THE SIDE

Who Ate the Doughnuts?

Doughnuts and other fresh pastries are delivered daily to many limited-service hotel properties for breakfast use. They may arrive before the food service attendants begin the work shift. Hopefully, these items will be properly received by the front desk clerk, night auditor, or other responsible employees and will then be quickly moved into a secure storage area. If this does not happen, the opportunity for employees and other nonguests to consume them is obvious.

Less-than-careful managers may have the philosophy that "Who cares about a few doughnuts?" In fact, the manager should care a great deal! Why? If each doughnut costs 25 cents and 10 doughnuts are consumed inappropriately each day, a property with a 10 percent bottom line (net income before taxes) must generate $25 each day to yield the $2.50 profit required to purchase the doughnuts.

(10 doughnuts @ $0.25 = $2.50 ÷ .10 profit = $25.00 in revenues to compensate for the cost)

If this consumption continued each day, the hotel would require revenues of $9,125 each year ($25/day × 365 days/year) just to pay for these unaccounted-for doughnuts. To continue with our example, if each hotel room was sold for $65.00, it would need to rent 140 rooms ($9,125 ÷ $65.00) just to compensate for the doughnut costs that would otherwise not need to be purchased.

No hotel (or any other business!) can afford to throw away more than $9,000 revenue annually on wasted expenses. In fact, doughnuts (and every other expense) add up quickly in the hotel business where the details are very important.

▋ NOW IT'S YOUR TURN

A PINCH OF THE INTERNET (7.2)

1. Technology can help food service personnel in à la carte operations to place orders from the guests' tables directly to food production areas. One system uses a palm device that sends a wireless signal to the main system through an access antenna. To learn about the "wireless waitress" system, go to:

www.accpal.com/wirelessrestaurantpos/index.htm

2. Customers can order food by phone and/or e-mail in some food service operations. To learn more about these opportunities, type "restaurant online ordering systems" into your favorite search engine.

3. Want to learn about equipment to transport banquet foods to dining areas? If so, type "banquet food transport equipment" into your favorite search engine.

4. Type "hotel room service equipment" into a search engine to learn about and view photos of room service transport and other equipment.

COMPLETING THE PLATE QUESTIONS (7.2)

1. Assume you were the restaurant manager and a guest had a concern about the temperature, serving size, ingredients, or other aspects of their meal. What should be your policy about who should address this concern: the restaurant manager, the dining room manager, or the kitchen manager? Defend your response.

2. What are several examples of issues that should be addressed (answered) by the kitchen manager rather than a banquet sales coordinator as an event for a customer is being planned?

3. Assume that you were a kitchen manager and your food service operation offered a "help yourself" salad bar. How would you decide whether food preparation or in-dining room food serving personnel should be responsible to keep the salad bar properly supplied during service, including the clean-up of food spills on and around the serving line? Defend your response.

4. In what ways are the position responsibilities the same or similar for a kitchen manager in a large-volume restaurant and a lobby food service operation serving a hot breakfast? In what ways are they different?

Kitchen Challenge Du Jour Case Study (7.2)

"We need to be team players; no one can agree with that more than me. However, there is a big problem brewing here that I mentioned to everyone that will listen, and no one seems to care or, at least, to take action about it" said Marco.

Marco, the kitchen manager at Vernon's Restaurant, was making some introductory remarks at a special managers' meeting he had requested. The meeting was attended by the property's manager, assistant manager, and all other department heads.

"It's just not fair to those of us in food production," Marco continued. "Its great to have banquet groups in here several nights a week, and I think our banquet sales staff does a great job in selling banquet events. We offer low prices that do make a difference and generate lots of business for us.

I also understand that the idea behind the pricing is that, first, banquet guests will get to know us and come back for à la carte dining. I'm also told that many of our guests arrive early and stay after the banquet event and use our cocktail lounge. The first gives us additional revenue over the long term, and the second tactic brings us immediate revenue on the day of the event."

"Yes," said Francisco, the restaurant manager, "and I'm sure you'll agree these are good things. Tell us once again exactly what problem you see with our pricing structure."

"Well sir," replied Marco, "the problem is, simply, the profit per meal."

"What do you mean," said Francisco, "You can't bank a percentage; we're interested in money that comes in that can be used to pay our bills including salaries and wages and to have something left over to put in the bank for the owners."

"Yes, that's true," replied Marco, "but what happens when we go over budget on our monthly income statements? People talk about the food cost percentage, and they say it is too high and that it should be lower. Also, bonuses for food preparation personnel are based in large measure upon obtaining budgeted food cost goals. When we sell banquet meals at very low cost, the food cost percentage is high. I don't think it's possible to have low selling prices to promote value in the banquet operation while, at the same time, enjoying a low food cost percentage. It's just not fair!"

Assume you were the Francisco, the restaurant manager:

a) How would you respond to Marco's concerns?

b) What are some things that you might do immediately?

c) What are some tactics that might be implemented over the longer term?

Overheard in the Kitchen Glossary

Serving (food)	Recipe management software	Order printer	Buffet service
Service (food)	File (computer)	Workstation	Catering (off-site)
Lobby food services (hotel)	Ingredient file	Work simplification	Potentially hazardous foods
Supply and demand (law of)	Standard recipe file	Expediter	Full-service hotel
Invoice	Menu item file	Banquet services coordinator	Hospitality suite
Steamship round (beef)	Base selling price (menu item)	Menu (pre-set banquet)	Hosted events
Purchase unit	Multiplier (selling price)	Banquet event order	Deluxe hot breakfast
Edible food yield	Pre-plate (banquet)	American service (banquet)	
Accompaniment (menus)	Limited-service hotels	Russian service (banquet)	
Costing (menu)	Continental breakfast	English service (banquet)	

KITCHEN MANAGEMENT SIMULATIONS
Where Content Meets Context!

LESSON 7

If you are reading this textbook as part of a formal class, your Instructor may want you to apply and practice what you have learned in this chapter by completing Lesson 7 of the Pearson Education Kitchen Management Simulation (KMS). If you are required to complete KMS Lesson 7; read the **About Lesson 7** below, then go to www.pearsonhighered.com/kms for instructions on how to access and complete it.

After you have successfully completed the lesson, think about the way you, as a professional kitchen manager, would answer the **For Your Consideration** questions that follow.

About Lesson 7

This lesson will teach you how to cost all of the individual ingredients in a recipe as well as how to cost menu items sold in various combinations. Then, you will be able to calculate costs for plates consisting of two or more individual menu items. Lastly, in this lesson you will learn how to calculate the cost of salad bars and buffets.

As you have learned in the KMS as well as this chapter, using standardized recipe costing aids kitchen managers in effectively controlling the expenses related to recipe production. Knowing how to cost individual recipe ingredients will also help you do a better job purchasing products to improve the operation's bottom line.

Accurately costing the food used for salad bars and for buffet style service allows kitchen managers to become better at forecasting food waste and controlling food production costs. This KMS lesson will show you exactly how they do it.

For Your Consideration

1. Why do you think it is important to accurately cost a recipe and all of its ingredients?
2. How do you think kitchen managers can best decide when a single ingredient's cost is too small to include in the calculation of the recipe's total cost?
3. How can kitchen managers accurately determine the value of food returned to the kitchen after a salad bar or buffet line has been closed for the day?

Kitchen Managers Use Effective Purchasing Practices

Learning Objectives

After studying this chapter, you will be able to:

1. Tell why effective purchasing procedures should be used and provide an overview of the purchasing process.
2. Explain important factors to consider when making purchasing decisions.
3. Describe basic concerns relating to other purchasing issues.

COMING RIGHT UP OVERVIEW

The menu is planned and the kitchen manager knows what items must be produced. Standard recipes have been selected and/or developed, and the food production team knows what ingredients are needed and how much each serving should cost. What's next? The required food products must be purchased.

Sounds easy? The way these activities are done in some food service operations, it is easy: Orders are simply called into the suppliers who have always been used. Perhaps the same quantity of products is ordered every time, and the purchasers obtain advice from suppliers about how much to order.

Hopefully, no kitchen manager uses these tactics but there are some persons who do not understand the importance of effective purchasing to the success of the food service operation and, therefore, do use unacceptable "short-cuts."

In this chapter, you'll learn about the importance of effective purchasing and review the critical elements in the process. Then the discussion will focus directly on the purchase decisions that must be made. Kitchen managers must think carefully about *what* must be purchased, the *quality* and *quantity* of products to purchase, *when* to purchase and, as importantly, *from whom* products should be purchased.

Decisions about the items to purchase and their required quality levels may not vary unless the menu changes. However, purchase quantities, delivery timing, and even supplier sources do change and can be different each time items are needed. Therefore, you'll learn that effective kitchen managers must make important decisions to ensure that their purchasing goals are consistently attained.

Several other purchasing-related concerns are also addressed in this chapter. The **purchase order** begins the formal process of communication that yields the right quality and quantity of items to be purchased from the best supplier at the best right time and price. You'll learn how to develop and use these important purchasing tools in this chapter. As well, kitchen managers desire a professional and ongoing relationship with their suppliers, and procedures that encourage this type of relationship will be explored.

Many people think that the most significant quality and finance-related problems occur during food production and service activities. In fact, all steps in the food/beverage management process, including those that occur before production and service, have a significant impact on the success of the food service operation. You will explore details about one of these activities—purchasing—in this chapter.

OVERHEARD IN THE KITCHEN

Purchase order—A document used to obtain prices from suppliers, to inform suppliers whose price proposal is accepted that a shipment should be delivered, and to explain any shipment or delivery requirements.

KITCHEN MANAGERS HAVE PURCHASING RESPONSIBILITIES

O B J E C T I V E

1. Tell why effective purchasing procedures should be used and provide an overview of the purchasing process:
   • Importance of effective purchasing
   • Overview of purchasing process

Menus dictate the food items to be offered, and standard recipes indicate the ingredients required to produce the items listed on the menu. These ingredients must be made available through a several-step process involving activities that are critical to assuring the ingredients available on-site will be of the appropriate quality and cost.

We presented an overview of the food management process in Chapter 1. Figure 1.3 in that chapter is shown again as Figure 8.1 below.

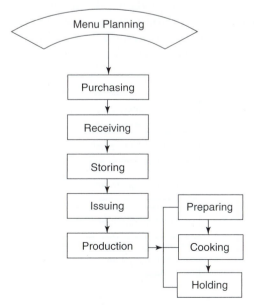

FIGURE 8.1   Overview of the Food Management Process

Figure 8.1 identifies each step in the food management process. In this chapter, we'll discuss purchasing activities, and procedures for receiving, storing, and issuing will be explained in Chapter 9.

Some very large food service operations have a purchasing department with personnel who are specialists in purchasing. As well, multi-unit restaurant and kitchen managers may receive some help from **centralized purchasing** personnel. By contrast, small-volume properties are unlikely to have these specialists. In these operations, purchasing may still be centralized (the owner/general manager purchases all necessary items) or, alternatively, a **de-centralized purchasing** system may be used. In a de-centralized purchasing system, the kitchen manager may purchase the food, the bar manager may purchase the beverages, and the dining room manager may work with the general manager to determine front-of-house linen, table decoration, and related needs. Regardless of the type of purchasing system, however, someone must do it, and the same basic principles are needed to attain the basic purchasing goal: to obtain the *right* quality of product in the *right* quantity from the *right* supplier at the *right* price and at the *right* time.

OVERHEARD IN THE KITCHEN

Purchasing (centralized)—The system in which purchasing is the responsibility of a specialist in a purchasing department in a large property, the owner/manager in a smaller property, or coordinated with persons outside the property in a multi-unit operation.

Purchasing (de-centralized)—The system in which purchasing is the responsibility of each department manager; for example, the kitchen manager purchases the food, and the beverage manager (head bartender) purchase the beverages.

A typical food service operation may require several hundred (or more) different food ingredients and, if alcoholic beverages are offered, many additional products must be purchased. Numerous decisions must be made to assure that the "right" products are purchased and are available when needed. Information helpful in making these decisions is the topic of this chapter's first section.

Importance of Effective Purchasing

The basic goal of purchasing noted above is critical for success. Unfortunately, it is very easy to state but much more difficult to attain. Figure 8.2 illustrates this goal and shows how, when it is attained, the guests and the food service operation benefit.

Let's look at each element in this goal to explain why purchasing is important:

- *Right quality.* The standard recipe indicates the products or ingredients needed to help ensure that the menu items are of consistent quality (which the guests desire) and consistent cost (which the kitchen manager requires). The concept of the right product in a kitchen manager's purchasing goal relates to quality. Consider, for example, the difference

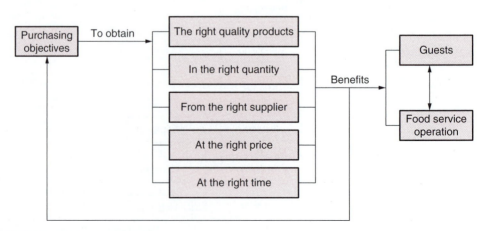

FIGURE 8.2 Purchasing Objectives

between ground beef with 10% and 20% fat content, and ground beef with no additives compared to and another ground beef product containing a nonfat dry milk or other type of extender. The menu item containing ground beef will be different when it is prepared with these different varieties of ground beef. Likewise, consider the menu description for an 8 ounce weight (as purchased) sirloin steak that is costed to help determine its selling price. If, instead, a 6 ounce serving is purchased, the guests will not receive the proper value for the dining dollars they spend. On the other hand, if a 10 ounce serving is purchased, the kitchen manager will be spending more than anticipated, and higher food costs will result in decreased profits.

- **Right quantity.** If too little product is purchased, **stock-outs** are likely; guests will be disappointed if their favorite item is not available, and the food production operation will likely be disrupted if substitute items must be produced. By contrast, if too much product is purchased, excess funds are tied up in inventory. Then there is an increased chance for spoilage, **pilferage** may occur, and there may be inadequate storage space.

OVERHEARD IN THE KITCHEN

Stock-out (inventory)—The condition that occurs when food products required for production are not available in storage.

Pilferage—The act of stealing small quantities of food product over a relatively long time period.

Kitchen managers purchase products and receive information from their suppliers.

- **Right supplier.** Kitchen managers in most locations have several sources of supply for most products. More than just a product is purchased when a purchase agreement is made. Information and service are also very important, and some suppliers do a better job of providing this assistance than do others. As well, a supplier offering a "good" price who does not deliver a product on time is not helping the food service operation.
- **Right price.** You have learned that guests are looking for value when they purchase menu items. In the same way, kitchen managers want value in the product purchase decisions they make. Price is important, but so are the other components in our purchasing goal.
- **Right time.** Products needed for Saturday night's banquet must be available on a timely basis. If they are received several days before the event, they will not be fresh. If they are received on the Monday after the event, they are of no use.

Is purchasing important to success? You have learned that it is and, in the next section, you will obtain a "big picture" overview of the purchasing process.

Overview of Purchasing Process

Effective purchasing involves more than waiting for the **distributor sales representative** (salesperson) to call for an order or talking to representatives when they call or visit. In fact, several steps are consistently followed in a properly planned purchasing system, and they are shown in Figure 8.3.

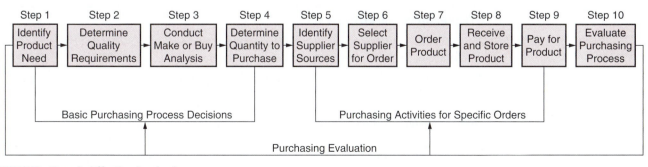

FIGURE 8.3 Steps in Effective Purchasing

OVERHEARD IN THE KITCHEN

Distributor sales representative—The representative of a supplier or distributor who sells products and provides information and services to food service operations; abbreviated DSR and often called "salesperson."

Let's briefly review the purchasing steps outlined in Figure 8.3

Step 1: *Identify Product Need*—Product need relates to what guests want. These needs are identified in the menu, and the ingredients required to produce them are specified in standard recipes.

Step 2: *Determine Quality Requirements*—You've learned that, when we are talking about purchasing, the term, "quality" relates to how suitable a product is for its intended purpose. For example, ground beef can be purchased with different percentages of fat content, and it can be purchased fresh or frozen. The kitchen manager must determine which product is best to meet the needs of the guests.

Step 3: *Conduct Make or Buy Analysis*—Some products can be prepared on-site or can be purchased partially or completely prepared. Should hamburger be purchased in bulk and then be portioned and shaped into patties by cooks, or should the product be purchased in a patty of specified weight? Decisions such as these must consider the availability of alternatives (first), quality concerns (second), and costs (last).[1]

Step 4: *Determine Quantity to Purchase*—Products can be purchased in large or small volumes. Important factors to consider when assessing how much to buy include available storage space and the possibility of product theft and/or loss of quality during long storage times. As well, **cash flow** issues may be important considerations.

Step 5: *Identify Supplier Sources*—Kitchen managers often have several suppliers who can provide each product they must buy. The kitchen manager's past experience, supplier references, and **trial orders** with potential suppliers can help to determine a "short list" of those suppliers who will be contacted when orders must be placed.

OVERHEARD IN THE KITCHEN

Cash flow—The total amount of money (cash) received and spent by a food service operation during a specific time period. Bills must be paid when they are due, and cash must be available to do so.

Trial order—A small order placed with a supplier to determine the quality of the product that will be received and/or to evaluate the quality of information and service provided by the supplier.

Step 6: *Select Supplier for Order*—Which potential supplier (Step 5) should provide the products needed for a specific order? The answer depends, in part, upon the type of purchasing system used. Supplier selection decisions may be based upon best prices determined through **price quotations** for each specific order, or pricing may be established in long-term **contracts** in which a supplier provides products for several months or longer at a price that is agreed upon before the first delivery is made.

OVERHEARD IN THE KITCHEN

Price quotation—A request made to a supplier for the current price of a product that meets the food service operation's quality requirements; also called "request for price quotation" (RFP).

Contract—An agreement made between two or more parties that is enforceable in a court of law.

Step 7: *Order Product*—Products can be ordered after the proper quality and quantity are known (Steps 2 and 4), and after the supplier has been selected (Step 6). Legal concerns then become important as does the possible need for **expediting**, to assure on-time delivery and to confirm that services meet the buyer's expectations.

OVERHEARD IN THE KITCHEN

Expedite (purchasing)—The act of following-up on the delivery schedule, quality, and/or other concerns that have been negotiated with suppliers.

Step 8: *Receive and Store Product*—Procedures are needed to assure that the proper quality and quantity of products are delivered. Then products must be properly stored to minimize quality or theft problems. Recordkeeping tasks applicable to product storage are also needed.

Step 9: *Pay for Product*—The timing of payments, concerns about **fraud** as payments are processed, and basic accounting concerns to identify and assign costs to the specific departments that incur them become important when payments are made.

OVERHEARD IN THE KITCHEN

Fraud—A crime that involves deceiving one or more persons for personal benefit; example: A supplier may claim that a product will be of very high quality but intentionally deliver a product of lower quality while charging the price of the higher-quality product.

Step 10: *Evaluate Purchasing Process*—Evaluation helps to assure that each step in the purchasing process is done correctly. This concern applies to the way that basic purchasing process decisions are made (Steps 1–4 in Figure 8.3) and to activities undertaken for specific orders (Steps 5–9 in Figure 8.3).

The purchasing overview just described justifies the commitment of time and effort required by the kitchen manager to consistently assure that purchasing achieves its intended goal.

Now that we have described the basic steps in the purchasing process, let's look at Figure 8.4 to review activities that are involved in the purchase of products for a specific order.

When you review Figure 8.4, remember that ingredients are used to produce menu items. In Step 1, production personnel obtain ingredients from storage. Quantities needed may be requested with an **issue requisition** (in large operations) and must be issued or transported to production areas. At some point the quantity of ingredients available in storage areas will be reduced, and additional products must be purchased.

In a large operation, a **purchase requisition** may notify purchasing personnel that additional quantities of products are required. In a smaller operation, the kitchen manager or other person with purchasing responsibility may simply note the quantity available in inventory and recognize the need for additional purchases.

One or more suppliers are contacted to learn about current product pricing and availability. In a large operation this is often done with a price quotation, and a purchase order is issued to the supplier who receives the order. The products are shipped to and received by the food service operation and placed in storage to rebuild inventory levels. The product usage, storage, purchasing, and receiving cycle is then repeated.

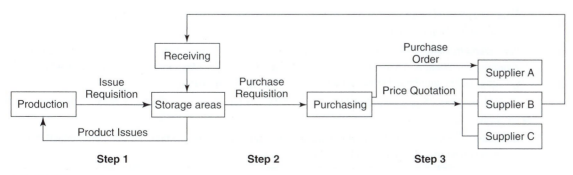

FIGURE 8.4 Purchasing Activities and Responsibilities

OVERHEARD IN THE KITCHEN

Issue requisition—A document used to identify the products and quantities that are removed from storage areas in a large volume food service operation.

Purchase requisition—A document used by food storeroom personnel in a large food service operation to inform purchasing employees when additional quantities of products are needed to build inventory levels to preestablished levels.

INFORMATION ON THE SIDE

What About "Paperless Purchasing?"

The extent to which kitchen managers use technology to help with purchasing varies between food service operations. At the one extreme, "old-timers" rely on manual (oral and written) systems for in-house purchasing tasks. At the other extreme are, increasingly, those properties in which "paper," if used, only helps storeroom personnel to remember what items must be issued as they collect products for transport to production areas. (Wireless technology, including notebook computers, can even eliminate "paperwork" for this step.)

Let's see how an "almost" paperless system might work: Production personnel send an electronic issue requisition to storeroom personnel. As noted above, a storeroom clerk prints a copy of the document to help him/her assemble products specified on the issue requisition or downloads the information on a handheld computer. The electronic issuing system automatically decreases the quantity of products in inventory until an **order point** is reached. What happens next depends upon the type of supplier selection process which is used. If, for example, a **prime supplier** system is in use, an order is electronically placed with the designated supplier. Alternatively, the purchaser may send an electronic price quotation request to several eligible suppliers requesting current prices for items of appropriate quality. Price quotations are electronically submitted by the suppliers, a supplier selection decision is made, and the order is electronically placed with the supplier.

If a **par inventory system** is used, the supplier delivers a specified quantity needed to re-build the inventory to the preestablished par. Alternatively, forecasts of future sales may be used to determine the quantity to be delivered when the order is placed. The supplier may then send an electronic confirmation of order "specifics" (items, quantity of items and delivery date, for example), and then products are delivered to the restaurant. At that time, receiving personnel use an **optical scanner** to read **bar codes** on packages of incoming products. Bar codes can even be printed at the property for incoming products without them. The quantity of products being added to inventory along with their purchase costs are then added to the food service operation's database of inventory information, and the cycle is repeated.

OVERHEARD IN THE KITCHEN

Order point—The number of purchase units of a specific product that should be in inventory when additional quantities of the product are ordered; see "purchase unit."

Prime supplier—The supplier chosen by a food service operation to provide products of a specified quality for a specified length of time.

Par system (inventory)—The normal quantity of purchase units of a product which should be available in inventory. For example, if a par of 10 cases of peaches should be in inventory and, if four cases are available, six cases will be purchased to build the inventory back to the par level.

Optical scanner—Equipment that can "read" data in a bar code on a product's label or package; see bar code.

Bar code—Lines of information that can be scanned into a computer system; bar code technology is used to update inventory information and for other purposes.

■ NOW IT'S YOUR TURN

1. The following Web site presents an excellent and simple overview of the features offered by a comprehensive food cost, recipe and inventory control system. Go to: www.foodtrak.com/ Click on "restaurants" and look at the case studies that are provided.

2. The hospitality industry has an association for persons interested in purchasing. The International Society of Hospitality Purchasers (ISHP) addresses a wide range of concerns of interest to industry professionals. To see its Web site, go to: www.ishp.org. At the site, you can learn about the society and review a statement of ethical purchasing practices and a code of professional conduct, among other information that is available.

3. "Green" purchasing refers to purchasing products that have a reduced negative impact on human health and/or the environment. To learn more about "green" purchasing, type the term "green food-service" in your favorite search engine.

1. Assume that you are the kitchen manager in a small restaurant with three departments: food production (your responsibility), dining room service, and lounge (beverage) operations. How might you organize the purchasing function for the property? In other words, "who would do what?"

2. What, if any, role do you think that the suppliers to a food service operation should have in helping the kitchen manager make purchasing-related decisions? What are examples of information and assistance that the suppliers might give to the kitchen manager?

3. What are some ways that effective purchasing can reduce costs for a food service operation without changing the quality of products that are purchased?

PURCHASING REQUIRES MANY DECISIONS

OBJECTIVE

2. Explain important factors to consider when making purchasing decisions.
   • Deciding what to purchase: quality concerns
   • Deciding from whom to purchase: supplier sourcing
   • Deciding how much to purchase: quantity concerns

Kitchen managers must implement systems to achieve the purchasing goal that you've learned: to obtain the *right* quality of product in the *right* quantity from the *right* supplier at the *right* price and at the *right* time. We will review important concerns about each of these topics in this section.

Deciding What to Purchase: Quality Concerns

The question, "What should be purchased?" appears easy to answer: The kitchen manager should purchase ingredients specified by standard recipes that are used to produce items required by the menu. However, this question is really more difficult to answer because the quality of necessary items must be considered. A primary concern relates to **suitability for intended use**. The best quality for an item relates to its use; the closer an item comes to being suitable, the better is its quality. For example, fresh whole tomatoes will likely be necessary for a chef's salad; canned tomato pieces may be "best" for use in a casserole item.

OVERHEARD IN THE KITCHEN

Suitability for intended use (quality)—This primary quality concern relates to considering the purpose for which an item will be used and then selecting the product determined to be "best" for that use.

The kitchen manager's concern about quality relates to value: the relationship between price and quality. While guests are the customers of the food service operation, kitchen managers

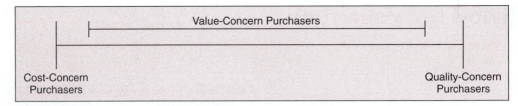

FIGURE 8.5 Purchasing and Value Concerns

are the customers of food suppliers. All customers, including guests and kitchen managers, look for value when they make purchase decisions. Figure 8.5 shows three types of purchasers:

- *Cost-concern purchasers.* These purchasers place the primary emphasis on cost; they want the lowest-possible cost products which are available. For example, some kitchen managers work for operations where guests want a lot of food for a very low cost, and these managers may place the highest priority on their product costs.
- *Quality-concern purchasers.* These buyers emphasize quality, and they want the highest-quality products that can be purchased. These purchasers are willing to pay whatever price is necessary and often work for high-check average "gourmet" restaurants. Their guests expect the very best and are willing to pay for it. These kitchen managers purchase the highest-quality products and pass the high food costs on to the guests in the selling prices that are charged.
- *Value-concern purchasers.* These buyers consider both cost and quality when making purchase decisions. They do so by, first, considering how the product will be used and, then, by purchasing the product which is most suitable for that use. Most kitchen managers work for food service operations where value (cost and quality) is the important purchasing concern.

Value-concern kitchen managers consider quality at all times. For example, they

- Incorporate quality standards into purchase specifications for the products they purchase.
- Provide purchase specifications to potential suppliers.
- Require that suppliers consider the quality standards incorporated into purchase specifications when product prices are quoted.

Kitchen managers should develop and use specifications for, at least, their **"A" items**: those relatively few products that cost the most to purchase. For example, 75% or more of all purchase dollars are likely used to purchase 25% or less of all products. These relatively few and most expensive products are the "A" items. The emphasis on purchasing "A" items should continue with focused control efforts at times of receiving, storing and issuing.

OVERHEARD IN THE KITCHEN

"A" Items (purchasing)—The relatively few products purchased by a food service operation that cost the largest percentage of the money spent to purchase all food products.

Figure 8.6 shows a simple purchase specification for a meat item. Meat products are expensive to purchase and are classified as "A" items by almost every kitchen manager. Therefore, it is reasonable that a purchase specification would be developed for meats.

Name of Product:	Strip Loin Steak, Boneless
Grade/Specification, if applicable:	IMPS 1178 Choice
Other Quality Information:	8 ounce serving with ½ ounce tare allowance; ¾ inch thick
Packaging:	Layer-packed between polyethylene sheets; 21 pound box (42 steaks per box)

FIGURE 8.6 Purchase Specification for Meat Item

When reviewing Figure 8.6, note that the purchase specification is for a boneless strip loin steak. The item requested is "IMPS 1178, Choice." This refers to the specification developed by the U. S. Department of Agriculture (USDA) in its **institutional meat purchasing specifications**, and "Choice" refers to the USDA quality grade. Note also that the specification requires an 8 ounce serving with a ½ ounce **tare allowance**. This indicates the actual weight which will be accepted. Acceptable steaks may vary in weight by no more than ½ ounce; an 8 ounce steak can weigh between 8¼ ounces and 7¾ ounces according to the specification. Note also that packaging specifications are provided.

The consistent quality of ingredients required for menu items is best ensured when purchase specifications are used.

OVERHEARD IN THE KITCHEN

Institutional meat purchasing specifications (IMPS)—Product standards for meat items developed by the U.S. Department of Agriculture.

Tare allowance (purchasing)—The weight range allowed for an item purchased on a per serving basis.

INFORMATION ON THE SIDE
Kitchen Managers and Quality Assurance

Some kitchen managers use the term, **"quality assurance,"** to refer to all activities that the food service operation undertakes to attain quality. In the context of purchasing, these include:

- Purchasing products that provide the best value for guests.
- Defining quality and developing purchase specifications that include quality standards.
- Evaluating suppliers to ensure they consistently deliver the proper products at a fair price.
- Emphasizing the importance of maintaining quality standards.
- Training purchasing personnel to accomplish purchasing activities.
- Inspecting products to ensure that quality standards are met when they are delivered.
- Implementing corrective actions to resolve purchasing defects.
- Obtaining **feedback** to improve purchasing.

OVERHEARD IN THE KITCHEN

Quality assurance—All activities that help a food service operation to attain quality.

Feedback—Information that allows kitchen managers to evaluate the effectiveness of processes or procedures.

Purchase specifications are important, but kitchen managers must also remember that:
- Information included in the specification must be measurable. Specifying "corn-fed beef" and the minimum butter fat content of ice cream is very easy to write into a specification, but these quality requirements are difficult to verify. If these concerns are important, it may be best to order, in the first instance, from a reputable supplier and, in the second example, by brand of ice cream. Note: Sometimes, hard-to-measure quality information, such as the fat content of ground beef, is important. Large-volume purchasers of this product should, on a routine but random basis, have in-coming samples analyzed by a qualified laboratory to confirm that the fat content requirement is met.
- It is likely that kitchen managers will pay for the quality of items required by purchase specifications even if they don't receive that quality. In other words, if an item of specified quality is ordered, the product must be inspected when it is received to ensure that the quality is correct. If it is not and the price charged is for the correct (higher) quality, the kitchen manager will have paid too much for the item. Therefore, effective receiving procedures are

required to ensure that incoming products meet quality requirements. Note: Tactics to do so will be discussed in Chapter 9.

Kitchen managers offering banquets may have an additional concern when determining what to purchase: Products not available on à la carte dining menus may be needed for a special banquet menu. If they are unfamiliar with a banquet menu item, it may help to obtain samples and evaluate products before final purchase decisions can be made.

Deciding from Whom to Purchase: Supplier Sourcing

Some would answer the question, "From whom should we purchase our products?" with the response, "Whoever gives us the lowest price!" However, this answer is short-sighted. First, you've learned that kitchen managers should not merely be looking for low price: They should be looking for value. Second, wise purchasers recognize the worth of service and information provided by their suppliers, and they are willing to pay for this assistance.

Kitchen managers' past experiences with suppliers are important and will likely influence their interest in continuing to buy from a specific supplier. Suppliers who always do what they promise are working to keep their customers happy in a way that is unlike their unreliable counterparts.

Decisions about those who will be asked to **bid** on the kitchen manager's orders result from **supplier sourcing** activities, and they impact the operation's ability to attain its purchasing goals.

Therefore, much more attention is required than a strategy expressed by "Let's purchase from our usual suppliers," or "Let's buy at the lowest price we can get." Both of these approaches may be part of the supplier sourcing decision, but they should not be the only or even the most important concerns. The best suppliers help kitchen managers to serve their guests, and that is why the supplier sourcing decision is so important.

OVERHEARD IN THE KITCHEN

Bid (competitive)—A supplier's response to a supplier's request for price quotation.

Sourcing (supplier)—Activities undertaken to determine which, often from among many, suppliers will be requested to quote prices for the products and services to be purchased by the food service operation.

Supplier sourcing involves decisions about which suppliers will be asked to submit prices for the products which are needed. It also involves developing relationships with other potential supply sources that may become important as the operation's product needs change or if the desired relationship with current suppliers cannot be maintained.

DESIRABLE SUPPLIERS

Many of the desired characteristics of suppliers are easy to define. Most kitchen managers would define a "good" supplier to be one who:

- Consistently provides the quality of products specified.
- Offers products at a reasonable price.
- Meets product delivery schedules.
- Provides useful support services.
- Offers useful information to the kitchen manager.
- Takes ownership of problems that occur and responds to the kitchen manager's needs.
- Informs the kitchen manager about order/delivery problems.
- Enjoys a stable financial position that is necessary to remain in business.
- Is mutually interested in providing value to guests and suggests how costs can be reduced without sacrificing quality requirements.
- Has similar values about the importance of maintaining ethical business relationships.
- Employs a highly motivated workforce to minimize problems from high employee turnover rates or union-related work stoppages.
- Has a genuine interest in helping the food service operation achieve its goals.
- Is accessible; communication between the kitchen manager and supplier is easy.

The above characteristics can be easily summarized: The best suppliers want to work cooperatively with kitchen managers so both parties can maximize the benefits from their relationship.

INFORMATION ON THE SIDE
The Best Intentions Are Not Always Sufficient

Kitchen managers know that "good" suppliers provide information and are **ethical**. However, problems can arise in spite of the best intentions of knowledgeable and honorable suppliers.

A "case study" from Florida shows how concerned suppliers can help kitchen managers. Fresh Florida grouper caught in the Gulf of Mexico wholesales for $10.00 per pound or more. Frozen grouper from Asia and South America sells for less than $5.00 per pound. A similar product (ponga) sells for less than $3.00 per pound.

A few years ago some seafood wholesalers received bulk shipping containers with contents labeled as "grouper" that really contained lower-quality and lesser-priced products. Kitchen managers who thought they were buying fresh grouper (and paying their suppliers a high price for it) were mislead. As well, their guests were misinformed because menu item descriptions were incorrect and, therefore, illegal. Even some seafood suppliers were unable to detect the problem.

What should be done to prevent future problems? At least one supplier now requires its seafood providers to provide **DNA certificates** with fish to identify their species. Then they have assurance about the products that are purchased, and they can then pass this assurance on to their hospitality customers.

Retrieved on 1/30/07 from: Stephen Nohlgren. State finds more grouper imposters. www.sptimes.com/2007/01/29/news

---

OVERHEARD IN THE KITCHEN

Ethical—Conforming to accepted standards of professional behavior.

DNA certificates—Documents that certify the species of the seafood product being sold. Note: "DNA" is the abbreviation of deoxyribonucleic acid, the material that contains information which tells cells how to function.

SUPPLIER SOURCING DECISIONS

You've learned that supplier sourcing relates to decisions made to determine which, often from among many, suppliers will be asked to quote prices for the products needed for the orders placed by the food service operation. How should these decisions be made? The answer involves learning as much as possible about potential suppliers to determine who are most likely to meet the needs of the organization.

There are numerous sources of information about potential suppliers. Learning about possible supply sources is an ongoing task and not just undertaken when there is an immediate and specific need for a new supply source. Supplier information sources include:

- *Reputation of supplier*—The kitchen manager's knowledge of and experience with those providing products to the local area is critical.
- *Trade publications*—The best kitchen managers keep up with industry-related information from various sources, including electronic and print magazines, news letters, and bulletins to learn about potential supply sources.
- *Electronic marketing information*—There are numerous buyers' guides available from industry publications, trade associations, and other sources that allow purchasers to search on the basis of, for example, a needed product, to identify possible sources.
- *Supplier representatives*—You've learned that "good" suppliers provide information to their **accounts**. Kitchen managers can ask their current suppliers for suggestions about other companies selling noncompetitive products.
- *Trade shows and other professional meetings*—Many **trade shows** offer opportunities for **qualified buyers** to learn about suppliers and their products. These professional meetings typically include time for attendees to visit exhibits, and to meet with and sample, if applicable, the exhibitor's (supplier's) products.

OVERHEARD IN THE KITCHEN

Accounts—A term used by suppliers to identify the organizations to whom they sell products.

Trade show—An industry-specific event that allows suppliers to interact with, educate, and sell to individuals and businesses that are part of the industry; also called exhibition.

Buyers (qualified)—Persons with the authority to make purchase decisions for their organization.

- *Other food service employees*—Staff members working at the kitchen manager's property and their peers in other properties (especially if the property is part of a multiunit organization) may have knowledge about potential products and suppliers.
- *Other information sources*—These include suppliers' catalogs, and files of hard copy or e-filed brochures and other information collected and cataloged by the kitchen manager.

The time and effort spent on assessing potential suppliers often relates to the financial importance of the relationship. Most of a food service operation's purchase dollars are spent with relatively few suppliers, and relatively few of the products purchased require the largest percentage of dollars spent for all product purchases. Not surprisingly, then, a priority effort to identify suppliers for these important purchases is required.

The quality of service provided by potential suppliers is an important concern. Unfortunately, service cannot be evaluated until after it is delivered. That is why a supplier's reputation is so important: Kitchen managers can probably assume that a supplier who has always provided excellent service will continue to do so. High-quality service occurs as the supplier provides timely and accurate price quotations, meets delivery schedules, makes it easy for purchasers to contact his/her representatives, and willingly assists in problem-solving.

You've learned that the quality of information provided by suppliers is another special concern, and it is an important factor when supplier sourcing decisions are made. Will high-quality technical advice be provided, and to what extent will a potential supplier provide information to help the food service operation address its ongoing challenges? Answers to these and related questions should help kitchen managers make supplier sourcing decisions, especially when a supplier enjoys that reputation with a large number of other purchasers.

Some kitchen managers conduct on-site inspections of a potential supplier's facilities to observe work methods, cleanliness, and the general organization of the facility. The condition of transport equipment is also important when, for example, highly **perishable** fresh produce, meats and seafood, and dairy products must be delivered during warm weather.

OVERHEARD IN THE KITCHEN

Perishable—The condition in which quality is reduced and spoilage occurs quickly when applicable products are not properly handled and stored.

Deciding How Much to Purchase: Quantity Concerns

Commercial food service operations with preplanned menus and their noncommercial counterparts with cyclical menus must purchase the same food products on a continuing basis. As well, catering businesses typically offer preplanned menu suggestions to event sponsors that feature entrées, salads, desserts, and other items that have been used in the past. These examples indicate the relationship between the estimated number of meals to be served and the quantities of items to be purchased.

Highly perishable items such as dairy products and fresh produce and bakery items cannot typically be purchased in quantities greater than what will be used over a several-day period. In contrast, frozen, canned, and **grocery products** can be purchased for usage over several months (or longer) if a kitchen manager wished to do so.

OVERHEARD IN THE KITCHEN

Grocery products—Items such as cereals, spices, and baking supplies that can be stored at about room temperature (70°F; 21°C) for a relatively long time period.

In all cases, however, effective kitchen managers remember the purchasing goal that includes the need to purchase the right quantity of food products each time an order is placed.

IMPROPER PRODUCT QUANTITIES CREATE PROBLEMS

Problems can occur when products are purchased in greater or lesser quantities than necessary. For example, purchasing too much:

- Ties up **capital** that could otherwise be used for something else.
- Impacts cash flow. Products held in inventory for excessive times must be paid for with money that could be used for other purposes.
- Affects flexibility. Kitchen managers may be less interested in taking advantage of special buys at significant discounts when excessive quantities are already on-hand.
- Requires more space to store products.
- Increases the risk of theft and pilferage.
- Creates quality problems for perishable products.
- Increases the risk of product damage or destruction.
- Increases handling costs. Examples: additional time needed to conduct inventories and perform storage area cleaning duties.

OVERHEARD IN THE KITCHEN

Capital—The amount of money invested in a food service operation by its owners.

Inadequate purchase quantities held in inventory can also create several problems:

- Inability to meet production requirements.
- Need to revise production plans because of inadequate amounts on hand.
- Possibility of disappointed guests who want to enjoy a favorite item which is unavailable.

Problems such as the above often occur when kitchen managers do not purchase the proper quantity of products. For reasons including convenience, cost, and practicality, kitchen managers do not usually purchase individual products when the quantities available reach an ideal order point. Instead, items are typically divided into several categories, and all (or most) products of the same type are ordered at the same time. For example, all fresh produce, fresh meats, and dairy products may be grouped into their specific categories. Then orders are placed for all items within these categories at the same time (and often from the same supplier for that order). This process means that the quantity of each product ordered may be different (more or less) than would be purchased if the order was being placed for just that product.

INFORMATION ON THE SIDE

Product Safety Levels Must Be Considered

The quantities of products ordered must consider **safety levels:** the amount of stock to be available in storage at all times. Reasons to maintain a safety level include:

- Assuring that products are available if there are problems with suppliers' delivery schedules.
- Guarding against errors that result in greater production volumes than planned.
- Replacing products that may become unusable.
- Considering mistakes in the counting of available inventory quantities.
- Allowing for product theft or pilferage.

The above concerns are important and should be considered. However, kitchen managers should not have safety levels that are excessively large because of cost, space needs, and quality problems.

OVERHEARD IN THE KITCHEN

Safety level (inventory)—The minimum quantity of a specific product that must always be available in inventory.

FACTORS AFFECTING PURCHASE QUANTITIES

Traditionally, the primary factors related to purchase quantity decisions have involved the estimated production needs based on business volume, volume purchase discounts (if any), available storage space, and cash flow.

Other important concerns include:

- *Minimum orders.* Many suppliers specify that a minimum dollar value of products be delivered to justify their delivery costs.
- *Anticipated increases or decreases in the product's price.* When product prices are increasing, kitchen managers may buy in larger-than-normal quantities. Also, when market prices are decreasing, they may purchase in smaller-than-usual quantities to take advantage of, hopefully, still lower prices in the future.
- *Special pricing.* Larger quantities may be purchased when, for example, suppliers or manufacturers offer "**close-outs**" such as short-term promotional discounts to introduce new products and/or to quickly sell products with outdated packaging.

OVERHEARD IN THE KITCHEN

Close-out—A tactic used by suppliers or manufacturers to quickly move (sell) an unwanted inventory item by reducing its selling price.

- *Special quantities required.* Trial orders, samples, or other unusually small quantities of products may be ordered at times when new menu items are being considered.

INFORMATION ON THE SIDE

Suppliers Can Help With Purchase Decisions

Good suppliers provide value by offering service and information that impacts a kitchen manager's decision about the quantity of products to be ordered. For example, they can alert buyers to close-out specials and help with trial orders and samples. Rigid definitions of minimum orders for delivery may be "bent" in some instances. Advanced information about changes in future market prices may be known by suppliers who keep up with changing market conditions. A suggestion: Kitchen managers should ask suppliers about how they (purchasers) can save purchase dollars without reducing quality. The answers they receive may be surprising and very useful.

PURCHASING METHODS

Purchasing methods vary based on the needs of each food service operation. However, they can be discussed in a general way be considering the types of food being purchased: perishable and less-perishable.

Purchasing Perishable Foods Perishable food products such as fresh produce, bakery, and dairy items must be purchased in small quantities that can be used within a few days. Decisions about the quantity of perishable products to purchase require knowledge about the amount of products on hand and an estimate of the quantity needed for the **order period**.

OVERHEARD IN THE KITCHEN

Order period (purchasing)—The time for which an order is placed. For example, produce may be purchased twice weekly and canned goods once every two weeks.

To illustrate, assume that Fredrico, a kitchen manager, estimates that 8 cases (24 heads each) of lettuce will be needed during the three days for which an order is being placed. He also notes that 1.5 cases of head lettuce are currently available in storage. It then becomes easy to determine the quantity of lettuce to purchase:

8.00 cases	(−) 1.50 cases	(=) 6.50 cases
Quantity Needed	(−) Quantity Currently	(=) Quantity needed
for Order Period	Available	
(3 days)		

Number of cases to order = 7.0

Fredrico knows that the price for each head of lettuce will increase if the supplier is asked for a **split case**, so it is an easy decision to "round up" and order 7 full cases to meet the property's needs for 6.50 cases. Note: Some suppliers will not even ship split cases.

OVERHEARD IN THE KITCHEN

Split case—A case of less-than-full purchase unit size sold by a supplier. Example: A supplier sells five #10 cans of peaches rather than a full case containing six #10 cans; also called a "broken case."

Higher charges for split case quantities are one reason that many small-volume food service operations buy from retail outlets such as buyer "clubs." These businesses may sell commercial-sized containers at a price lower than a wholesale supplier who prefers to sell in full-case sizes only.

The process used above to determine the quantity of lettuce to purchase can also be used to calculate the quantities of other perishable items needed for the order period. This process works well when purchasers can accurately estimate the quantity of items needed for the order period, and the general usage rates of these products are known.

Assume business is relatively slow during the first several days of the week (Monday-Thursday) and much busier for the weekend (Friday-Sunday). The kitchen manager may know the normal usage rates for perishable products during the slower first part of the week and uses the process just described to determine purchase quantities for orders placed on Friday or Saturday for Monday delivery. While the quantity of products that will be available at the end of the weekend will not be known when the order is placed, a conservative estimate (perhaps no on-hand inventory) may be factored into the quantity-to-purchase decision.

Continuing with our example, the purchaser will then also place an order for perishable goods on Thursday for delivery on Friday. The estimate of higher weekend usage will be known, and the quantity of product currently available when the order is placed can be determined and is factored into the purchase quantity decision.

The quantities of products routinely needed must be adjusted as business volume varies. Additional quantities will be needed when business volume is expected to increase because of celebrations, holidays, and other activities. Conversely, business volume estimates will be reduced at other times when business is slower because of, for example, periods of poor weather.

Purchasing Less-Perishable Foods   Less perishable items such as frozen foods and grocery items can be purchased for immediate use like their perishable counterparts, or they can be stored for longer-term use. They may be purchased in very small quantities if, for example, there is very little storage space available. Kitchen managers in other operations typically purchase in larger quantities to reduce the time spent on purchasing tasks and to enjoy lower prices from larger-volume purchases.

The **minimum-maximum system** is a popular one for use in purchasing nonperishable foods. It uses information generated by the property's inventory management system and is discussed in detail in Chapter 9.

OVERHEARD IN THE KITCHEN

Minimum-maximum (inventory system)—A system used to calculate product purchase quantities that considers the minimum quantity below which inventory levels should not fall, and the maximum quantity above which inventory levels should not rise.

PRODUCT YIELDS AFFECT PURCHASE QUANTITIES

The purchasing task would be much easier if all products purchased had a 100% **yield**, and some products do. For example, frozen pre-portioned eight ounce hamburger patties have an approximate 8 ounce (100%) yield. Note: The menu should indicate that the patty has a **serving size** weight of 8 ounces as purchased (AP), because there will be some cooking loss resulting in an edible portion (EP) weight of slightly less than 8 ounces.

OVERHEARD IN THE KITCHEN

Yield (Purchasing)—The amount (pounds or percent) of the as-purchased weight of a food item that is edible after it is processed; see "as-purchased."

Serving size—The quantity (weight, count, or volume) of a menu item to be served to a guest.

The quantity to purchase is relatively easy to determine when there is a 100% yield. Consider the eight ounce frozen servings of hamburger steak noted above:

Estimated servings required for order period	(−)	Number of servings in inventory	(=)	Quantity of eight ounce servings required

Kitchen managers typically buy preportioned meat products by the pound (1 pound = 16 oz.), and there are 2-8oz servings per pound (16 oz. ÷ 8 oz. = 2 servings). Standard packaging containers may be ten pound boxes or bags (10 pounds × 2-8 oz. servings per pound = 20-8 oz. servings per container) or 25 pound purchasing units (25 pounds × 2-8 oz. servings per pound = 50-8 oz. servings per container).

Some products, however, do not have a 100% yield, and then it is more difficult to determine the quantity of these items to purchase even when the number of servings required is known.

Example: Assume that Shasha, a kitchen manager for an upscale restaurant, is planning a banquet for 100 guests, and the host has requested that 6 oz. tenderloin fillets be served. Whole tenderloins weighing about ten pounds with an AP cost of $14.75 per pound are typically purchased. This entrée is a popular choice, and she has performed **yield tests** that reveal there is an approximate 60% yield for the desired product.

OVERHEARD IN THE KITCHEN

Yield test—A carefully controlled process to determine the amount (weight and/or percent) of the as-purchased quantity of a product remaining after production loss has occurred.

Shasha can use yield test information for numerous purposes. For example, she can calculate:

- *Production loss*—**Production loss** is the amount (weight and/or percent) of a product's AP weight which is not servable because of, for example, trim loss from fat and bones and from cooking shrinkage.

  In our whole tenderloin example, a ten pound (AP) loin will have a 40% production loss:

100%	(−)	60%	(=)	40%
AP weight	(−)	yield	(=)	production loss

- *Weight after processing and cooking*—The loin will weigh only six pounds after on-site trimming and cooking.

10#	(×)	[100% − 40%]	(=)	6#
AP weight	(×)	[AP yield − production loss]	(=)	Weight after processing

---

OVERHEARD IN THE KITCHEN

Production loss—The amount (weight and/or percent) of a product's as-purchased weight which is not servable.

- *Amount of product to purchase with no available inventory*—Shasha knows that only 60% of the amount of whole tenderloins purchased will be servable for the banquet. Therefore, the amount needed for the event assuming no product is currently available on-site can be easily calculated:

$$\frac{100 \text{ portions needed} (\times) 6 \text{ oz. per portion}}{60\% \text{ yield}} = \frac{600 \text{ oz.}}{.60} = 1{,}000 \text{ oz.}$$

$$\frac{1000 \text{ oz.}}{16 \text{ oz.}} = 62.5 \text{ pounds}$$

Since each tenderloin weighs approximately 10 pounds, Shasha must buy seven loins (62.5 pounds ÷ 10 pound loin = 6.25 rounded to 7 pieces).

- *Amount of product to purchase with some available inventory*—Assume Shasha has three whole 10-pound loins in storage that are not needed for another purpose. She must then purchase four additional loins to meet her banquet production requirements of 100 servings:

$$7 \text{ loins needed} (-) 3 \text{ loins available} = 4 \text{ loins to purchase}$$

- *Cost per servable pound*—The **cost per servable pound** is the cost of one pound of product which can be readily served to guests. In our example, the whole tenderloin costs $14.75 (AP) per pound and has a 60% yield. The cost per servable pound is $24.58:

$$\text{Cost per servable pound} = \frac{\text{AP price per pound}}{\text{Yield \%}} = \frac{\$14.75}{.60} = \$24.58$$

OVERHEARD IN THE KITCHEN

Cost per servable pound—The cost of one pound of a product in a form which will be served to guests.

- *Food cost for one serving*—Shasha will likely establish the selling price for the banquet based, at least in part, on the food cost that is incurred. Food costs for all items to be served must be determined and, for the tenderloin, it is:

$$\text{Food cost (one portion)} = \frac{\$24.58 \text{ (cost per servable \#)}}{16 \text{ oz.}} = 1.54 \text{ (cost per ounce)}$$

$$\$1.54 \text{ (cost per ounce)} \times 6 \text{ oz. (portion size)} = \$9.24 \text{ (portion cost)}$$

Note: The total serving cost of the tenderloin would increase if, for example, it was served bacon-wrapped and/or with a sauce.

NOW IT'S YOUR TURN

A PINCH OF THE INTERNET (8.2)

1. Want to learn about the U.S. Department of Agriculture's Institutional Meat Purchasing Specifications? If so, go to: www.usda.gov. Find the box titled "search" and type in "IMPS;" then click "go."

2. Kitchen managers can acquire much product information over the Internet. For example, go to: www.nestlefoodservices.com.au/ This site is similar to other food manufacturers/distributors, and you will find information about products, recipes, distributors, and other general information of interest to food/beverage purchasers.

3. Kitchen managers purchase numerous items besides food and beverage products. One of the country's largest nonfood distributors to the food service industry is Edward Don and Company. Check out their Web site at: www.don.com

   You can review detailed information and photographs of thousands of products in categories such as kitchen supplies, glassware, flatware, bar supplies, linens, disposables, and furniture. This information could, for example, be helpful to kitchen managers as they develop purchasing specifications for nonfood items.

4. Electronic buying guides can help kitchen managers obtain a significant

amount of information about products that can influence their purchasing needs, identify one of more specific manufacturers, and even locate several level supply sources for the product.

To learn how this process works, use the buying source for Restaurants & Institutions Magazine (www.foodservice411.com)

When you reach the site, click on "Food Service Equipment and Supplies." When you reach this page, click on "Products" and then "Product Knowledge Guide." You can then search for and learn about numerous types of food service equipment that kitchen managers may purchase.

COMPLETING THE PLATE QUESTIONS (8.2)

1. Some kitchen managers have purchase specifications but use them only when they request price quotations and they do not use them when receiving products to ensure that quality standards are met. Do you agree or disagree with this approach? Defend your response.

2. Assume that you were a kitchen manager trying to decide which suppliers you were going to buy from during the next several months. What is your definition of a "good" supplier who might earn your business? How would you evaluate the performance of an existing supplier to determine whether you should continue requesting price quotations from him or her?

3. If you were Shasha in the above example of determining the quantity of tenderloins to purchase, would you allow other employees to help you by assigning them the task of making the arithmetic calculations needed to determine yields? Why or why not?

Kitchen Challenge Du Jour Case Study (8.1)

"Don't we have enough work to do already?" Dean, a cook at the Columbia Grill was talking to Jose, another cook during a coffee break.

"We've not had any problems with the quality of our food products," Dean continued. "Sometimes products we need aren't available, and then we just substitute something else. At other times we get deals on products we don't normally use, and we find ways to incorporate them in the menu. Now that will all change because the new kitchen manager says we need to develop purchase specifications."

"Yes, I agree," said Jose, "we just haven't had any problems. Just yesterday some products were delivered that didn't seem to meet our quality requirements. I thought we could just negotiate lower prices for them so everybody would be happy."

"I think we realize some things that the new kitchen manager doesn't understand," said Dean. "We don't need detailed purchase specifications because we can handle any situation that arises. I'm not concerned if we have purchase specifications . . . as long as they don't affect me. However, it is going to be frustrating if the need to develop them affects my work."

a) What are some ways that purchase specifications can help the work of the cooks at the Columbia Grill? How, if at all, might their work tasks be negatively affected?

b) What can the kitchen manager do to address the negative feelings that these employees have about using purchase specifications at the restaurant?

c) How do you think the use of purchase specifications will improve the overall operation of the Columbia Grill?

OTHER PURCHASING CONCERNS

OBJECTIVE

3. Describe basic concerns relating to other purchasing issues.
   - Selecting suppliers and ordering products
   - Supplier relations

You might be thinking that a serious topic—obtaining products at the best price—has been omitted from our discussion about how kitchen managers should purchase food and other products.

That topic will now be explained, and then you'll learn about one other important concern: supplier relations.

Selecting Suppliers and Ordering Products

Basic principles required for effective purchasing are similar regardless of an operation's size. Buyers must always determine which suppliers from the list of potential suppliers will be used for specific orders and exactly what must be purchased.

Unfortunately, communication or other problems can occur when orders are placed. If this happens just once in a while, the kitchen manager and the seller will likely cooperate to resolve the problem. Then their relationship will improve, and the satisfaction that results encourages a continuing "partnership." However, if there are frequent problems which the kitchen manager believes are caused by the supplier, fewer or no additional orders will likely be placed with that supplier. As well, suppliers are less likely to provide value-added services for their "problem" accounts.

Kitchen managers can obtain important product information from their distributor sales representatives.

PRICING OVERVIEW

Price is the amount of money needed to purchase a product, and it is an obvious purchasing concern. However, obtaining the "lowest" price is *not* an objective of effective buyers. It is important to recognize that the "right" price is not necessarily the "lowest" price. Few kitchen managers think that the best meals are the cheapest meals, and a focus on lowest possible price usually indicates a buyer's misunderstanding about how prices are determined.

OVERHEARD IN THE KITCHEN

Price—The amount of money needed to purchase a product or service.

Four primary factors influence what kitchen managers pay for their products:

- *Product costs.* Assume you were selling a meal that costs you $10.00. To recover your costs, make a profit, and maintain your business, you must sell the meal for more than $10.00. If your guests do not value the meal enough to pay more than $10.00 for it, in the long term you cannot offer it.

    Key Point: A buyer and seller "partnership" is ideal. The kitchen manager should expect to provide a fair (reasonable) profit to the supplier in return for the products, services, and information received.

- *Prices reflect consumer demand.* Prices are influenced by consumer **demand**. When products are scarce and many buyers want them, the prices charged will generally be high. Sometimes (example: rare wines), the price reflects a limited supply. In other cases (example: expensive bottled waters), it is the guests' willingness to pay that most influences price.

    Key point: Kitchen managers should know when they are paying for product scarcity and when they are paying a premium price for product popularity. As well, kitchen managers should recognize when product popularity will last and when it may simply be a passing consumer fad.

OVERHEARD IN THE KITCHEN

Demand—The total amount of a product that buyers want to purchase at a specific price.

- *Prices reflect service features and enhancements.* Consider two buyers. One pays $100.00 for a case of fresh chicken but must pick it up at the supplier's location. The other pays $101.00 for the case, but it is delivered to the buyer's restaurant. Who received the best price? Despite the one dollar additional cost, the first buyer received a service (delivery) that would easily justify the price increase.

    Key Point: Kitchen managers know that they receive non-product benefits from their suppliers. Timely delivery, knowledge of the supplier's personnel, accurate invoicing, and ease of order placement are examples of service benefits reflected in a supplier's pricing structure.

- *Prices reflect supplier quality.* Food service operations with a reputation for quality food and outstanding service can charge more for their products as can suppliers who consistently provide excellent products and high-quality services.

  Key Point: Kitchen managers who focus only on purchase price without considering the supplier's reputation may receive neither quality nor value. Unethical suppliers who do not stand behind their products and services often cost kitchen managers much more than what they originally paid for the product.

Pricing Factors   Several factors directly affect the prices kitchen managers pay for products. In a **free market**, what kitchen managers pay for products is what they voluntarily agree to pay in a purchase contract.

OVERHEARD IN THE KITCHEN

Free market—An economic system in which businesses operate without government control in matters including pricing.

Contract pricing is common for many products and especially for services such as kitchen exhaust hood cleaning. The buyer may agree to a service provider's offer to clean the exhaust hood for a stated fee that will be paid each time the hood vents are cleaned.

OVERHEARD IN THE KITCHEN

Contract pricing—A pricing method in which the buyer and seller agree to a specific price for a defined product or service for a stated time period or until one party ends the agreement; also called fixed price contract.

Frequently, however, prices change each time products are ordered, and then a system to determine prices from alternative suppliers is required. Kitchen managers must decide whether to buy products from one or more suppliers. Generally, using more suppliers requires additional time for ordering, receiving, and invoice processing. These activities increase costs. However, a single-source supplier may charge higher prices if there is no competition. Therefore, kitchen managers often split their business among several suppliers.

The idea of using several suppliers appears sound, but sometimes it is not. Buyers who continually compare prices among competing suppliers and select, when quality is the same, the supplier offering the lowest price appear to be minimizing their costs. However, **cherry pickers** will likely be serviced last by suppliers because these buyers have not considered service levels, long-term relationships, dependability, or other non-pricing factors in their purchasing decisions.

OVERHEARD IN THE KITCHEN

Cherry picker—A buyer who purchases only a seller's lowest-priced products.

Buyers who do not pay their bills on time will likely pay more than their competitors for similar products. Suppliers often add the extra cost of carrying "slow-pay" accounts to the prices charged these buyers because, in effect, the supplier's funds are used to pay for the purchases.

Many suppliers offer **discounts** to buyers after prices are agreed upon. Suppliers are creative, and there are reasons for offering discounts. Kitchen managers should ask about all discounts offered by their suppliers because they might then pay a lower **net price**.

OVERHEARD IN THE KITCHEN

Discount—A deduction from the price buyers normally pay for products.

Net price—The total or per-unit amount paid for products after all discounts have been applied to the purchase price.

There may be several types of discounts available to kitchen managers, including

- *Prompt payment discount*—Discounts for prompt payment are common because suppliers want to reward accounts (customers) who pay their bills on time. Discounts typically apply when the entire amount owed is paid within a specified number of days or, in some cases, **cash on delivery (COD)** applies when products are received.

OVERHEARD IN THE KITCHEN

Cash on delivery (COD)—A transaction in which a buyer pays the full amount owed when products are delivered.

- *Quantity discount*—Many suppliers offer quantity discounts to encourage customers to increase their purchases. Buyers like the lower net prices, and sellers benefit because the cost of delivering additional products is generally marginal after the costs involved in delivering the initially purchased number of items is recovered. While quantity discounts can be significant, kitchen managers must be cautious because purchasing more than needed can create product waste, especially for perishable products. Additionally, there may be additional costs to finance and store excess products.
- *Customer status discount*—Preferred customer status is another reason discounts may be offered. Unlike food service operations that generally charge the same price to all of their customers, suppliers may offer status discounts to selected customers. These may result from the length of customer relationship, nonprofit business status, annual purchase volume, membership in a specific company, brand, or chain, and/or a supplier's desire to expand into a new industry segment or location.
- *Special discounts (promotions)*—Special discounts are often associated with holidays, seasons, or exclusive events with a desire to increase brand or product awareness being the motivation. Discounts may also be offered when a seller wants to clear inventories of older or discontinued products.
- **Rebates**—These are similar to discounts except discounts are deductions from normal selling prices, and rebates are discounts offered *after* a purchase has been made at the normal selling price. Manufacturers often use rebates to introduce new products or to increase awareness and sales volumes of existing products.

OVERHEARD IN THE KITCHEN

Rebate—An after-purchase discount; sometimes called a "cash back" offer.

INFORMATION ON THE SIDE
Impact of Discounts and Rebates

Assume a kitchen manager was able to negotiate a discount and a rebate on a case of six #10 cans of peaches. In this example, the lower net price is worth the effort:

Case (six #10 Cans):		
Normal Case Price		$42.00
Less Seller's "2% Prompt Payment" Discount	$0.84	
Less Manufacturer's After-Purchase Rebate	$3.00	
Less Total Discounts and Rebates		$ 3.84
	Net price	**$38.16**

If the kitchen manager in this example paid full price for the peaches, the cost for one can is $7.00 ($42.00 per case/6 cans per case). If the six cans are purchased for $38.16, the cost of one can is $6.36 ($38.16 per case ÷ 6 cans = $6.36). The difference in the price paid in this example is 10% ($7.00 − $6.36)/$6.36 = 10% (rounded). This lower per-can price can be compared among different suppliers when the competitive costs are evaluated.

Kitchen managers must know what they paid for the product in the serving size provided to guests. For example, four ounces (EP) of peaches are served at Vernon's Restaurant, and the drained weight of one can in the case of peaches is 76 ounces. Therefore, there are 19 servings of peaches per can (76 ounces ÷ 4 ounces) and 114 servings per case (19 servings per can (×) 6 cans per case).

In this example, one 4 ounce serving of canned peaches costs $0.33 ($6.36 per can/19 servings per can).

Knowledge of serving size is important because it impacts the food cost per serving, and it allows kitchen managers to compare suppliers' prices even if there is a difference in the package size, purchase unit, or market form of the products purchased.

COMPETITIVE BIDS

Many kitchen managers use competitive bids to determine the supplier offering the lowest costs for products of the required quality. However, isn't the use of competitive bids with its emphasis on lowest cost opposed to an emphasis on value (the relationship between price and the quality) because bidding stresses cost differences? Kitchen managers using competitive bids will *not* be emphasizing only the lowest cost when they have completed other activities including:

- Determining quality requirements for desired products and expressing them in purchase specifications distributed to prequalified suppliers.
- Considering the proper quantity of products needed and clearly communicating this information.
- Prequalifying suppliers using, when possible, the purchaser's experience and objective factors that assess the supplier's commitment to quality, value-added service, and provision of information.

When kitchen managers review responses submitted by suppliers in competitive bids, they should assure that the bid is for the same products in the same quantity specified in the price quotation. If there are no variations, the next concern relates to the quoted costs. Kitchen managers can evaluate costs and make supplier selection decisions in one of two basic ways:

- On the basis of the lowest total price for all items noted on each suppliers' quotation responses. In this case, a supplier quoting a price for only some products would be excluded. Advantages include the ability to purchase all items from one supplier and avoid the "paper work" required when multiple suppliers are used. A likely disadvantage to this supplier selection method is that the buyer may be paying a higher price for some products.
- On the basis of the prices quoted for each product in the quotation response. Supplier A may have submitted the lowest price for several products and would receive a purchase order only for those items. Supplier B may have submitted the lowest prices for other products, and these would be purchased from him/her. An advantage: The lowest price will be paid for every item. A disadvantage: additional time and expenses for order approval, receiving, and invoice processing will be required to interact with more than one supplier as orders for all products are placed.

Figure 8.7 shows a supplier competitive bid analysis for three items. Note that Supplier A submitted the lowest price for chicken. Chicken would be purchased from this supplier because

Analysis of Price Quotation No. 5736512

Product	Purchase unit	Supplier A	Supplier B	Supplier C
Ground beef	Pound	3.29	3.24	3.31
Tenderloin Steak	Pound	9.87	9.59	10.03
Chicken	2½ # bird	5.29	5.47	5.54

FIGURE 8.7 Sample Supplier Competitive Bid Analysis

of this low price bid, and Supplier B will be awarded the ground beef and tenderloin steak purchases. Kitchen managers may reserve the right to accept only specific products requested on an RFP. As well, many food service operations reserve the right to not award a bid to any supplier submitting a quotation.

Close Look At Purchase Orders   You've learned that purchase orders are used primarily by buyers in larger organizations to approve the purchase of products of a required quality in a specified quantity at an agreed-upon price and from a specific supplier. Figure 8.8 shows a purchase order which might be produced in a hardcopy or an electronic form.

When reviewing Figure 8.8, assume that the kitchen manager for Vernon's Restaurant has sent price quotation requests to several suppliers, including Acme Grocers who was selected to provide the items in the purchase order.

Note that (upper right hand corner) the purchase order (PO) number and date are included as is the preferred delivery date and property contact information if the supplier has questions. The purchase order also indicates that the "terms" are "Net 30." This means that the buyer will pay the total amount of the invoice ($783.17) within 30 days of the delivery date. Note: Sometimes buyers negotiate a discounted price for faster payment. For example, payment terms might be: "2/10; net 30." Then the buyer will receive a 2% discount if the total invoice is paid within 10 days; otherwise the total invoice amount is due within 30 days of the invoice date.

Purchase Order

From/Ship to:	Purchase from:		
Venon's Restaurant 1710 W. Summer Street SummerVille, NV, 00000 Telephone: 000-000-0000	Acme Grocers 2451 Elm Rd. Center Place, NV., 0000	PO No. PO Date: Delivery Date: Contact: Terms:	34X135 7/16/xx 7/20/xx John Davis Net 30

Item Purchased	Quantity Ordered	Quoted Price	Extended price	Spec #
Green beans	4 Case (#10 cans)	34.50	138.00	1715
Flour, All Purpose	3 Bag (50#)	22.17	66.51	18100
		Total	783.17	

Terms and conditions:
This purchase order expressly limits acceptance to the terms and conditions stated above and included on the following page. Any additional terms and conditions are rejected.

Buyer: _____ John Davis _____ Date: _____ 7/16/xx _____

Received by: _____ Date: _____

Delivery Instructions: _____
_____
_____

FIGURE 8.8   Sample Purchase Order

Procedures for issuing purchase orders typically include routing copies to the supplier and the property's receiving personnel. Additional copies may also be kept by the purchasing department and may be forwarded to accounting personnel. In most large properties, all orders except small purchases for which **petty cash** is used are authorized with a purchase order.

OVERHEARD IN THE KITCHEN

Petty cash—A cash fund used to make relatively infrequent and relatively low-cost product purchases.

Suppliers and purchasers typically require **terms and conditions** that apply to their transactions. For example, suppliers typically specify minimum purchase amounts that must be ordered before deliveries are made, and they may only deliver on specified days. Purchasers may have general concerns to be addressed in their supplier agreements. Often these are included in all purchase orders.

OVERHEARD IN THE KITCHEN

Terms and conditions—General provisions that apply to a supplier's price quotations and a buyer's purchase orders regardless of the specific products being purchased or sold.

Examples of terms and conditions include:

- *Purchase order to be exclusive agreement*—The purchase order specifically identifies all buyer's and seller's responsibilities.
- *Payment of invoices*—Buyer will pay the seller the amount agreed upon in the purchase order.
- *Sellers are independent contractors*—They cannot commit the buyer for obligations under another contract.
- *Confidentiality*—Information related to the product sale will not be shared with anyone.
- *Termination*—The buyer can terminate the purchase order if the seller fails to comply with it. As well, the seller can terminate the agreement if the buyer does not pay the seller within a specified time period.
- *Failure to perform*—Neither the buyer not the seller will be penalized for failing to perform for reasons beyond their control. Examples: fire and flood.
- *Invoice information*—Invoices should be sent to a specified location. Separate invoices are required for each purchase order, and invoices should indicate applicable purchase number orders.

Timing and Product Orders   You've learned that, when traditional purchasing systems are used, orders are placed when inventory levels must be increased for future production requirements. However, some kitchen managers use **standing orders** for some products because they typically involve minimal, if any, ordering time. A restaurant may have an agreement with a coffee or dishwashing chemical supplier to provide, respectively, coffee-related products and dishwashing chemicals. A route person may visit the property on a predetermined basis (example: every Tuesday morning) and replenish applicable products to a predetermined par level. A delivery invoice signed by and left with an authorized person at the property is used as the basis for payment.

OVERHEARD IN THE KITCHEN

Standing order—An agreement between a purchaser and a supplier that the same quantity of a specified product is required each time a delivery is made.

Expediting Procedures   Kitchen managers may sometimes need to expedite deliveries because, in spite of the best planning, problems can occur that affect orders. For example, purchase requisition problems can arise, and inventory management issues may misstate inventory

Challenge	Possible Expediting Tactic
1. Inadequate quantity at time of delivery.	1. Purchase product from another supply source.*
2. Improper product quality.	2. Purchase the product from retail source.
3. Purchaser error; product needed quickly.	3. Pick-up product at supplier's location; buy product from retail source.
4. Product shortage (multiunit property).	4. "Borrow" product (complete proper inter- property transfer form).
5. Product on back order (but available at the supplier's location before time of need).	5. Request that supplier make special delivery or that the product be delivered by a sales representative.

*A purchase order clause (terms and conditions) allowing the buyer to purchase the missing product in the marketplace with a credit to the amount owed the supplier for the difference between the quoted and actual price paid is useful.

FIGURE 8.9   Examples of Expediting Tactics

quantities. Weather conditions, strikes, and problems creating errors as delivery vehicles are loaded are examples of supplier-related reasons for product shortages.

Useful tactics to obtain products in "emergency" situations vary according to the situation, and several alternatives are noted in Figure 8.9.

Supplier Relations

The term, **supplier relations**, relates to how kitchen managers interact with their suppliers. A professional relationship is important, and the purchasing policies expressed in a **purchasing handbook** can help to enhance and maintain this relationship. These topics are discussed in this section.

OVERHEARD IN THE KITCHEN

Supplier relations—How purchasers interact with their suppliers.

Purchasing handbook — A document developed by the kitchen manager to inform suppliers about purchasing policies and procedures that must be followed at all times.

PURCHASER-SUPPLIER RELATIONSHIPS

How should kitchen managers interact with their suppliers? Figure 8.10 shows the range of possibilities.

As you review Figure 8.10, note that the traditional "I win; you lose" philosophy is on one end of the range and, at the other end, you'll note a "partnership" relationship: "We win together." A middle point along the range is labeled "Contemporary" and suggests "I win; you win."

Kitchen managers typically have differing relationships with each of their suppliers that may be noted at all of the points noted in 8.10. This is to be expected because purchasers do not (cannot) attempt to develop a "one size fits all" relationship with each supplier.

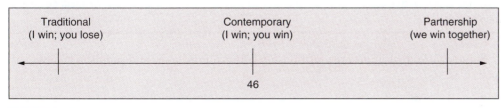

FIGURE 8.10   The Purchaser-Supplier Relationship

There are several general factors that often influence the relationship between the purchaser's organization and its suppliers:

- *Relative size (business volume) of both organizations*—A large food service operation is not likely to develop an extensive "partnership" with a supplier providing a tiny fraction of the purchaser's needs and the reverse is also true: A very large supplier is not likely to devote significant time and effort to develop an extensive relationship with a small-volume buyer.
- *Reliance on a supplier*—This can occur if, for example, a supplier is the only source of a very unique specialty item, and when a supplier has exclusive distribution rights to specific products sold in the purchaser's location.
- *Compatibility*—This concept relates to the extent to which the kitchen manager and supplier share cultural, moral, and ethical (among other) beliefs that help shape their businesses and impact their relationship. If there is not a good fit, one or both of the parties may wish to limit the purchaser/supplier relationship to a position on the more "traditional" end of the range noted in Figure 8.10 or the supplier might not be asked to submit price quotations.

IMPORTANCE OF PROFESSIONAL RELATIONSHIPS

Kitchen managers want their suppliers to treat them fairly and, hopefully, recognize the need to treat their suppliers the same way. Long-term relationships thrive when cooperative efforts that emphasize trust, flexibility, and innovation and not just product purchase costs are addressed. Both parties benefit from the improved communication and increased levels of trust that result.

What factors are typically among those that impact the relationship between the purchaser and supplier? These are the same concerns that were important when the decision to select the supplier was made. The kitchen manager considers:

- Consistency of product quality.
- "On-time" delivery schedules.
- Effectiveness of communication.
- Value pricing.
- Interest in addressing the purchaser's concerns.
- Level of service provided.
- Quality of information supplied.
- Payment processing procedures.

The kitchen manager's relationship with suppliers is likely to become stronger when few, if any, problems related to these concerns arise over time. Then they have a greater incentive to continue and expand upon their business relationships with their suppliers.

SUPPLIER-RELATED POLICIES

Kitchen managers working with other food service managers typically develop **policies** to help make decisions about important purchasing issues. These policies provide guidance about what to do if specific situations arise. Purchasing policies help to provide consistency because issues will always be addressed the same way, and problems will be resolved according to policy.

OVERHEARD IN THE KITCHEN

Policy—A (usually) written statement of principles or guiding actions that indicate what should be done in specific situations.

Some policies that impact the relationship between purchasers and suppliers involve concerns such as:

- Accepting gifts.
- No favoritism shown to any supplier.

- **Reciprocal purchases**.
- Use of local suppliers.
- **Conflicts of interest**.
- The need to obtain competitive bids.
- **Back-door selling** that occurs when a supplier attempts to contact and/or influence food production personnel without approval of the kitchen manager.
- Trial orders.
- Samples.
- Free meals/entertainment.
- Use of **sharp practices**.
- Taking advantage of suppliers such as, for example, when one supplier's price is given to a second supplier with the request to reduce the selling price.

OVERHEARD IN THE KITCHEN

Reciprocal purchases—A transaction in which a supplier agrees to purchase something from the purchaser if the purchaser agrees to purchase something from the supplier. Example: The purchaser makes an advertising commitment with a local newspaper and, in return, newspaper managers agree to spend a specified amount of money on food and beverage purchases at the property; also called bartering.

Conflict of interest (purchasing policy)—A business situation in which a food service employee has an interest in another organization that could (or does) compromise his/her loyalty to the hospitality employer.

Back-door selling (purchasing policy)—The act of a supplier attempting to contact or influence a food production employee without approval of the kitchen manager.

Sharp practice (purchasing policy)—Bargaining between the purchaser and potential seller in such a way that the purchaser unethically takes advantage of the seller.

Purchasing Handbooks   Kitchen managers in many, especially large, food service operations develop purchasing handbooks. These can be excellent communication tools to help inform new and to remind longer-term suppliers about the property's purchasing policies and procedures.

Topics that can be addressed in purchasing handbooks include:

- General information about the food service operation including a brief overview of its history, an organizational chart showing key positions, guest market descriptions, and mission statement.
- Basic purchasing procedures with an emphasis on contracts and communication between the organization and its suppliers. This may include statements about the need for competitive bidding, alternate supply sources, and procedures used to select suppliers.
- Procedures for product receiving including inspection.
- Payment policies and procedures.
- Purchasing policies.
- Details about electronic purchasing procedures.
- Copies of (or references to) purchasing forms.
- Information about preferences for "green" (environmentally preferable) products.

Once developed, the food service operation's purchasing handbook should be provided to all suppliers with whom the property does business. Hard or e-copies should also be given representatives of suppliers who make unannounced visits (**cold calls**) to purchasing staff, and they should be provided with price proposal requests sent to possible suppliers of one-time purchases.

OVERHEARD IN THE KITCHEN

Cold calls (purchasing)—A term relating to unannounced (unscheduled) visits by supplier representatives to hospitality purchasers.

■ NOW IT'S YOUR TURN

A PINCH OF THE INTERNET (8.3)

1. To see information about automated purchasing management systems, go to:
www.adaco.com
www.costguard.com

2. Want to learn how one large food service company addresses supplier relations? If so, check out the McDonald's Web site: www.mcdonalds.com
When you reach the site, click on "search" and then type in "supplier relations."

3. To learn more information about basic purchasing procedures, go to: www.restaurantreport.com Enter "purchasing" into the site's search box.

4. To see how kitchen managers can order products electronically from one supplier, go to: www.sysco.com and click on "place an order."

COMPLETING THE PLATE QUESTIONS (8.3)

1. What are three things that kitchen managers can do to learn about a possible supplier's reputation for providing quality products, information, and service?

2. What factors would you use to evaluate the performance of a supplier to whom you might send price proposal requests?

3. How would you determine the types of terms and conditions that you as a kitchen manager would want to use for purchase orders? What, if any, assistance would you request from your food service operation's manager or attorney?

4. What are the most important topics that you would include in a supplier handbook?

5. Assume you were a kitchen manager in a small food service operation without a full-time purchasing agent. What are additional purchasing-related tasks that you would need to do that would probably be done by the purchasing agent in a larger property?

Kitchen Challenge Du Jour Case Study (8.2)

"The price of seafood is increasing. This is partially a seasonal thing—and we're coming into the wrong season! However, I think we're still paying more for seafood than we should, and I want to find other seafood sources."

Joe, the manager of Vernon's Restaurant, was speaking to Michael, the kitchen manager, who replied, "I like our suppliers because they sell good products and give good service. They help us with our menu changes, and their ideas and product samples allow us to make some good decisions. You're the boss, but I would like to express our price concerns to the salespersons and then see what happens to our prices."

"Okay, Michael, let's try it," said Joe, "But, if prices keep increasing, I'm going to find some new suppliers."

Assume you were Joe:

a) What might you say to the seafood salespersons in efforts to reduce the costs of these products?

b) What, if anything, could you do to reduce your seafood costs?

c) What do you think about Michael's idea to speak with the salespersons as a tactic to reduce cost?

Overheard in the Kitchen Glossary

Purchase order	Cash flow	Issue requisition	Bar code
Purchasing (centralized)	Trial order	Purchase requisition	Suitability of intended use (quality)
Purchasing (de-centralized)	Price quotation	Order point	
Stock-out (inventory)	Contract	Prime supplier	"A" Items (purchasing)
Pilferage	Expedite (purchasing)	Par system (inventory)	Institutional meat purchasing specifications (IMPS)
Distributor sales representative	Fraud	Optical scanner	

Tare allowance (purchasing)	Capital	Cost per servable pound	Standing order
Quality assurance	Safety level (product	Price	Supplier relations
Feedback	inventory)	Demand	Purchasing handbook
Bid (competitive)	Close-out	Free market	Policy
Sourcing (supplier)	Order period (purchasing)	Contract pricing	Reciprocal purchases
Ethical	Split case	Cherry picker	Conflict of interest
DNA certificates	Minimum-maximum	Discount	(purchasing policy)
Accounts	(inventory system)	Net price	Back-door selling (purchasing
Trade show	Yield (purchasing)	Cash on delivery (COD)	policy)
Buyers (qualified)	Serving size	Rebate	Sharp practice (purchasing
Perishable	Yield test	Petty cash	policy)
Grocery products	Production loss (yield test)	Terms and conditions	Cold call (purchasing)

KITCHEN MANAGEMENT SIMULATIONS
Where Content Meets Context!

LESSON 8

If you are reading this textbook as part of a formal class, your Instructor may want you to apply and practice what you have learned in this chapter by completing Lesson 8 of the Pearson Education Kitchen Management Simulation (KMS). If you are required to complete KMS Lesson 8; read the **About Lesson 8** below, then go to www.pearsonhighered.com/kms for instructions on how to access and complete it.

After you have successfully completed the lesson, think about the way you, as a professional kitchen manager, would answer the **For Your Consideration** questions that follow.

About Lesson 8

This KMS lesson lets you practice the skills professional kitchen managers use when buying ingredients used to produce the menu items they sell. These essential skills include choosing the right products, determining the proper amounts to buy, and then creating Purchase Orders (POs) that provide vendors with details about what is to be purchased, when it is to be delivered, and the prices to be paid for the needed items.

Few kitchen management skills are more important or more complex than those related to buying food. This is true, in part, because the difference between as purchased (AP) quantities delivered

to the operation and the edible portion (EP) yields for food products delivered to guests can vary widely. Because that is true, kitchen managers must master the calculation of needed AP amounts, EP amounts, and various product yield percentages. In this lesson, you will practice those very skills. You will complete the lesson when you have shown you can perform all of these critical kitchen management tasks.

For Your Consideration

1. What advantages do foodservice operations that have minimal product specifications have over those whose menus require multiple product specifications? What advantages would those operations that utilize multiple product specifications have over those that use fewer specifications?

2. What effect do culinary-related training programs have on workers' skill levels and the ability of those workers to maximize the yield of ingredients that must be processed before being used in recipes?

3. Assume you placed a Purchase Order (PO) and in doing so erroneously ordered three times the amount of a needed perishable ingredient. Subsequently, the vendor delivers exactly what you ordered. How would your relationship with that vendor affect your ability to address and correct this problem?

Endnote

1. If you want to learn more about make or buy analysis, see: Ninemeier, J. and Hayes, D. Procurement of Hospitality Resources. Upper Saddle River, New Jersey. Prentice Hall. 2010.

9

Kitchen Managers Use Effective Receiving, Inventory Management, and Issuing Practices

Learning Objectives

After studying this chapter, you will be able to:

1. Review procedures to effectively receive products that have been purchased.
2. Explain basic procedures to manage products in storage.
3. Discuss the importance of and proper procedures for product issuing.

COMING RIGHT UP OVERVIEW

Several steps become important between the time when products are purchased and when food production begins. Kitchen managers must assure that plans are in place to effectively control products when they are received, while they are in storage, and as they are issued to production areas. The reason: If they do not quality can deteriorate and costs may increase.

Receiving is more that just allowing anyone who is closest to the back door when deliveries are made to "sign the paper work" and place products in storage. In this chapter you'll learn about basic receiving requirements, steps in product receiving, and we'll also review some special receiving concerns.

After products are received, they must be stored, and there are numerous inventory management practices that become important. We'll discuss quality, security, and record keeping concerns and how they should be best addressed. Also, it is important to know the quantity of products on-hand because, as you learned in the previous chapter, the amount available impacts the quantities that must be purchased. Therefore, you'll learn about the basics of the minimum-maximum inventory system that provides information to help determine purchase quantities. Another basic process, par inventory, will also be discussed because, with this system, inventory quantities must be known so the amount purchased can return product inventories to predetermined levels. A final study of inventory management will focus on how food cost (cost of goods sold) is calculated. You'll learn that the cost of products in storage is an important factor in the calculation, and we'll also review how food cost information, once calculated, is utilized.

A final section of this chapter reviews product issuing procedures. These become important because the correct quantity of products must be issued to meet estimated sales (production) requirements. Several steps are used in a well-controlled issuing process, and you will learn about them.

EFFECTIVE PRODUCT RECEIVING PRACTICES

O BJECTIVE

1. Review procedures to effectively receive products that have been purchased:
   - Receiving requirements
   - Steps in product receiving
   - Special receiving concerns

Receiving Requirements

Effective product receiving requires attention to personnel, the receiving area, and the tools and equipment needed for receiving activities. Our discussion of product receiving will begin with these topics.

RECEIVING PERSONNEL

Qualified and trained staff members should perform receiving tasks. The (unfortunately all-too-common) practice that allows almost anyone to sign the delivery invoice and move items to storage areas is not defensible.

Some receiving procedures are clerical or physical in nature; however, the ability to recognize the quality of incoming products and to confirm that they meet the property's standards requires training and experience. This is especially important for products such as fresh produce, meats, and seafood that are not typically purchased by a brand name that can be read on a package label. Careful observation and inspection of these items are essential to ensure that purchase specification requirements are met. Hopefully, those training for receiving positions can work shoulder-to-shoulder with experienced buyers, the kitchen manager, or other food production personnel to learn how to confirm that incoming products meet quality requirements.

Large-volume food service operations may have full-time receiving and storeroom clerks who have responsibilities for receiving and other before-food-production activities. In smaller-volume properties, staff members such as the kitchen manager or other members of the food production team may assume these duties. As you have already learned in our discussion about purchasing, however, the basic principles and practices required to effectively manage food products apply to operations of all size. Therefore, they must be performed by someone who is trained to do so regardless of whether these activities are an employee's only responsibility or just one of many required duties.

Successful receiving personnel:

- *Maintain sanitation standards*—Food safety and sanitation concerns are important aspects of quality, and they are incorporated in the property's purchase specifications.
- *Have knowledge of appropriate technology*—Technology can expedite receiving and storage procedures and yield accurate information if it is used properly. Technology is used by many large-volume operations today and will likely be increasingly used in properties of smaller size in the not-too-distant future.

- *Have the necessary physical strength*—Incoming cases of products can weigh 30 pounds or more. Flour and sugar are routinely packaged in 50 or even 100 pound bags, and packages of these sizes are often purchased because of lower purchase unit prices. Note: The **Americans with Disabilities Act (ADA)** prohibits discrimination against persons with disabilities. The ability to lift heavy or bulky containers may or may not be a **Bonafide Occupational Qualification (BOQ)**. Kitchen managers must know about and consider how to modify receiving tasks to accommodate otherwise qualified persons.

OVERHEARD IN THE KITCHEN

Americans with Disabilities Act (ADA)—Federal legislation that prohibits discrimination against people with disabilities in public accommodations, transportation, telecommunications, and employment. It applies to private employers, state and local governments, and certain other organizations with 15 or more workers.

Bonafide Occupational Qualification (BOQ)—A qualification that is judged to be reasonably necessary to safely or adequately perform all job tasks in a position.

- *Be able to resolve problems*—What should be done if incoming products do not meet quality requirements? What if incorrect quantities are delivered or products do not arrive when they should? Effective receiving personnel can answer these and related questions in a way that complies with applicable policies of the food service operation.
- *Maintain a concerned attitude*—The best staff members want to assist their organization. Concerned receiving personnel are committed to helping the food service operation move toward attaining its mission, and they recognize their role in helping to serve guests.

RECEIVING AREA

Ideally, the receiving area was considered as product flow concerns were initially planned. The best location is often close to the kitchen's back door but, in very large organizations such as hotels, they are often part of or close to a loading dock that is far from food storage and production locations. Small-volume properties with little space may use little more than a hallway or entry area (hopefully) close to the door where incoming products are received.

Adequate space to assemble all incoming products is necessary for counting and/or weighing products, and a receiving scale is needed. Space for transport equipment is likely required, and this can be significant if **pallet** loads of products are purchased.

OVERHEARD IN THE KITCHEN

Pallet—A platform (rack) typically constructed of wooden slats and used to store and/or move cases of products stacked upon it.

RECEIVING TOOLS AND EQUIPMENT

Receiving areas may require space for a desk, file cabinet, or other equipment and, often, computer access is needed because of the increasing use of technology during receiving tasks. Useful tools include pocket thermometers to determine the temperatures of perishable products and plastic tote boxes or other containers to transport ice for products such as fresh poultry and seafood. Increasingly, personal digital assistants (PDAs), notebook or laptop computers, and/or other wireless devices are used to access purchasing and inventory records required while receiving.

Steps in Product Receiving

Figure 9.1 reviews the steps required for effective receiving.

As you review Figure 9.1, note that the delivery invoice should be compared to the copy of the purchase order to help ensure that the quantity and price of products agreed upon when purchased are correct when they are delivered. Some items such as cases of canned goods can be counted, but other items such as fresh meats ordered by the pound must be weighed.

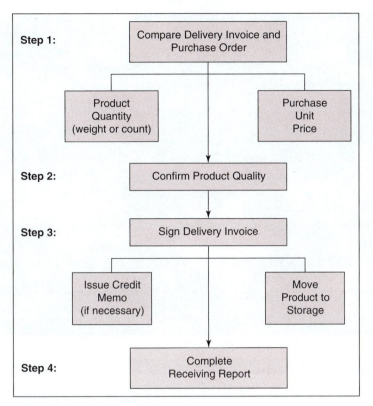

FIGURE 9.1 Steps for Effective Receiving

Figure 9.1 indicates that the second step in the receiving process involves confirming that the quality of the incoming products meets the purchase specifications. This step is very important and probably the most challenging. Standards incorporated into purchase specifications must be easily observable so that incoming products can be compared with the specifications. If receiving personnel have concerns about product quality, the kitchen manager and/or purchasing agent, if applicable, should be asked for assistance.

If no variations from product standards or other quality-related problems are observed, the delivery invoice can be signed (step 3 in Figure 9.1). However, if there are product shortages or other problems, a **credit memo** should be co-signed by the receiving employee and the supplier's delivery person to confirm that adjustments to the delivery invoice will be necessary. This is important because the signed delivery invoice is the basis for the payment that will be due to the supplier. Note: We'll discuss credit memos more fully later in this chapter.

OVERHEARD IN THE KITCHEN

Credit memo—A document used to revise (correct) information about product quantities and/or costs initially recorded on a delivery invoice.

After the delivery invoice has been signed, step 3 in Figure 9.1 also indicates that receiving personnel must quickly move products to their storage areas. Reasons include the need to help prevent loss of quality in refrigerated or frozen products and to reduce the possibility of product theft.

Figure 9.1 suggests a final step in product receiving: Complete a **receiving report**. This is used in food service operations that calculate food costs on a daily basis because it helps separate information on delivery invoices into the components required for daily food costing.[1]

OVERHEARD IN THE KITCHEN

Receiving report—A document that separates incoming food costs into components required for daily food cost calculations.

Special concerns are always required when purchasing and receiving fresh fruits and vegetables because they are highly perishable.

Special Receiving Concerns

Receiving procedures are impacted by concerns including those relating to quality, technology, and security. The management of credit memos is also important.

ENSURING QUALITY

It does little good to develop purchase specifications unless they are used when products are received to confirm that incoming products meet quality standards. An exhaustive list of ways to identify quality is difficult to develop and depends upon the specific items being purchased.

Effective receiving personnel can help to determine whether incoming products meet quality requirements. For example, sometimes this involves noticing that **slack-out seafood** is being represented as a fresh product. At other times, they can determine that the lengthy and sometimes confusing names of imported wines on shipping boxes do not match those on the purchase order. They can check expiration dates on applicable containers and should understand that produce in the center of a shipping container may not be of the same quality as products on the more visible top levels.

OVERHEARD IN THE KITCHEN

Slack-out seafood—Seafood that has been frozen and then thawed and represented to be a fresh item that can be sold at a higher price than if it was purchased frozen.

Experienced kitchen managers train their receiving employees so they know that it does little good to state necessary product quality requirements in purchase specifications unless these requirements are confirmed when products are received. They also ensure that receiving staff know that the food service operation is very likely to pay for the quality of products that have been ordered even if that quality is not received. It is much better for the receiving personnel to observe quality-related products before they are accepted than it is for the production employees to note the quality problem after foods have been issued for production.

IMPLEMENTING TECHNOLOGY

How can technology assist receiving personnel? First, "paperwork," can be eliminated and resulting "communication problems" can be reduced. Traditional hardcopy purchase orders identifying purchase commitments can be electronically routed to receiving personnel. Wireless technology allows receiving personnel to check incoming products without the need to print a copy of the purchase order. Those purchasing in large volumes can specify bar-code labels on incoming containers so quantity and cost information can be scanned and "automatically" entered into the property's inventory management system. Properties of all sizes with bar-code readers and accompanying software programs can use bar-code technology to assist with purchasing and inventory management.

Radio frequency identification (RFID) technology utilizes wireless transmitters affixed to the products in inventory. These systems enable wireless tracking of inventory in real time throughout the property.

OVERHEARD IN THE KITCHEN

Radio frequency identification (RFID)—An electronic wireless tracking system that uses a transmitter to provide noncontact and automatic location of stock throughout the food service operation.

Technology enables electronic versions of purchase specifications, delivery schedules, and communication between the food production, purchasing, accounting, and receiving department personnel to be more conveniently routed. Also, information from daily invoices can be electronically summarized on daily receiving reports that generate information used for daily food costing calculations or other purposes.

SECURITY

Security concerns at the time of receiving relate to problems that cause the food service operation to pay for products it does not receive. These problems can include:

- *Short weights or counts*—A carton containing, for example, 45 pounds of fresh steaks should be weighed. Ideally, steaks are removed from cardboard cartons for weighing. Container weight becomes more significant when fresh seafood or fresh poultry or seafood is packed in shaved ice in heavy, waxed cardboard containers. When incoming products are packed this way, they should be removed from the containers to determine the weight of the products actually received.
- *Assorted contents*—A carton containing 30 pounds of ground beef and 20 pounds of preportioned steaks will weigh the same (50 pounds) as a carton containing 20 pounds of ground beef and 30 pounds of fresh-cut steaks. However, the cost of the first container is much less than that of the second container so different items must be weighed separately.
- *Missing items*—A suggestion from the delivery person to, "Just sign the delivery invoice; I'll deliver additional products without putting it on the invoice next time," cannot be followed. First, the same receiving person may not be on duty or forget the missing item at the next delivery. Second, a delivery person is unlikely to have the authority to request that products not listed on delivery invoices should be placed on the truck for delivery.

Delivery personnel should not have access to nonpublic areas of the food service operation. Consider the possibility of theft when they are in storage areas (especially where liquor is stored) or, even worse, if they gain access to back-of-house corridors and employee-only elevators in hotels. Then access to other storage areas and even guest rooms may be possible, and employees or guests can be harmed by persons who are **trespassing**.

OVERHEARD IN THE KITCHEN

Trespassing—Unlawful (without the owner's permission) entry of a person onto the property of another person.

CREDIT MEMOS

Earlier in this chapter you learned that a credit memo must be issued when there is a difference such as weight or count in products included on a suppliers' delivery invoice and that actually received.

Date: _____   Credit Memo No.: _____

Supplier: _____

_____

_____

_____

_____

Issued to: _____

_____

_____

Account No. _____

For Invoice No.: _____

Item	Purchase Unit	Number Purchase Units	Price/Purchase Unit	Totoal price
			Total	$

Reason for Credit (Check):

☐ Back order ☐ Incorrect quality ☐ Incorrect Item

☐ Short start count/weight ☐ Incorrect price ☐ Not ordered

☐ Other: _____

Authorized Signatures:

Supplier's Representative   Purchaser's Representative

FIGURE 9.2 Sample Credit Memo

Figure 9.2 shows a sample credit memo. Note: The credit memo is typically offered by the delivery person but it is also wise to have a copy developed by the food service operation available in case the delivery person does not have one.

Credit memos indicate the amount of money recorded on the original delivery invoice that does not need to be paid because of a problem noted when products were delivered. In other words, it must be managed in the same way that money would be handled. For example, if the form is lost or, if the supplier's copy is fraudulently changed, the food service operation may need to pay for products that were never received. Credit memos are typically attached to the affected delivery invoice, and this document is routed with others in such a way that they promptly reach the food service operation's manager, kitchen manager, purchaser, accountant, or other authorized official. Managers in some operations even contact the supplier to confirm that they have a credit memo signed by both the supplier's and food service operation's representative.

NOW IT'S YOUR TURN

A PINCH OF THE INTERNET (9.1)

1. To see information about automated purchasing and receiving management systems; go to: www.adaco.com or www.costguard.com
2. Want to learn how one large food service company addresses supplier concerns? If so, check out the McDonald's Web site: www.mcdonalds.com When you reach the site, click "search" and type in "supplier relations."
3. To learn more information about product receiving, go to: www.restaurantreport.com Enter "receiving" into the site's search box.
4. To learn about food service receiving scales, visit www.webstaurantstore.com. When you reach the site, enter "food service receiving scales" in the site's search box.
5. To learn about the use of labels added to food products at time of product receiving to help with stock rotation, check out: www.daymarksafety.com

COMPLETING THE PLATE QUESTIONS (9.1)

1. Why do you think some food service operations do not permit product deliveries during busy food serving times?
2. Assume that you had been ordering meat products from a specific supplier for a long period of time. Would you require still require receiving personnel to weigh every incoming container of meat products? Why or why not?
3. Some distributors indicate that their delivery personnel will, at no extra cost, help to move incoming products from receiving to storage areas. If you were a kitchen manager, would you accept this assistance? Why or why not?
4. Assume that your property is part of a multiunit organization in which products are purchased and received at a central location and are then transported from that location to your property by employees of your organization. Would this impact the procedures you would use for product receiving? If "yes," what procedures would change? If "no," please defend your response.

Kitchen Challenge Du Jour Case Study (9.1)

"Hello Joe, how are you doing today?" asked Louis, an entry-level kitchen employee who sometimes received incoming products from suppliers. He was talking to Joe, a delivery person who worked for the Acme Town Provision Company, one of the largest fresh meat suppliers in the city. The two men were chatting while Joe was making a delivery to Vernon's Restaurant.

"Things are fine, Louis, and I hope they are with you. I just want you to know that I really enjoy working with you as we coach our sons' softball team. They're great kids and the team is doing well. We'll have quite a lot to celebrate at our upcoming end-of-season awards picnic.

"Your right, Joe, and I'm looking forward to it as well," said Louis. What's going to be on the menu?"

"Well Joe, I've been thinking about hamburgers for the kids and steaks for the adults. Just by coincidence, these are some of the items that I'm delivering to you today. I know that Vernon's Restaurant uses a lot of products, and you buy really good ones. Hey, what do you think about us taking a few for the event? It would almost be like your restaurant making a contribution to a great community cause."

"Do you mean I should just sign the invoice like they were received and then you could take them back with you and freeze them so we'll have them when we need them?" asked Joe.

"Yes, that's what I mean; the restaurant will never miss them, our families and friends will really enjoy them, and who will know the difference?" replied Joe.

Questions

a) Do you think that Louis is authorized to make a "donation" of meat products for his son's baseball awards dinner?

b) If you were the kitchen manager at Vernon's Restaurant, what procedures would you put in place to minimize opportunities for theft of food product at time of receiving?

c) Assume that Joe and Louis took the meat products in the manner they discussed. Assume also that you learned about it a few days later. As the kitchen manager, what, if anything, would you say to your employee? To the delivery driver? To Joe's employer, the meat provision company?

INVENTORY MANAGEMENT PRACTICES

O B J E C T I V E

2. Explain basic procedures to manage products in storage:
   • Overview of product storage
   • Management basics for products in storage
   • Minimum-maximum inventory system
   • Par inventory system
   • Calculation of food cost (cost of goods sold)

Experienced kitchen managers know that the quality of most food products will never be better than when they are received; they will not improve while they are in storage. However, product quality can be lowered if proper storage practices are not used. As well, the food service operation's financial goals are affected by storage practices. If for example, products are effectively stored, all of the products that have been purchased will be used to generate revenue. However, if they are not properly stored, food costs will increase if some products that have been purchased and paid for are then discarded, and more food will need to be purchased at additional cost. As this occurs, it will be more difficult for the food service operation to attain its financial goals.

The concerns about product quality and cost that began when products were purchased and continued as product-receiving tasks were undertaken must also be addressed while products are in storage awaiting use. Fortunately, the best procedures do not require excessive time or cost to implement and maintain, and they are discussed in this section.

Overview of Product Storage

There are three basic types of food storage with which kitchen managers must be familiar:

• *Dry storage (50°F−70°F; 10°C−21.1°C).* This is for grocery items such as canned goods, condiments, bakery products such as flour and sugar, and herbs and spices.
• *Refrigerated storage (less than 41°F; 5°C).* This is for items such as fresh meat, produce, seafood, and dairy products.
• *Frozen storage (less than 0°F; −17.8°C).* This is for items such as frozen meats, seafood, french fries, and other vegetables purchased in this market form.

Note: Some food service operations utilize other storage areas, including **broken case** rooms, and they may also have extensive storage space in work stations, including food preparation and serving areas.

OVERHEARD IN THE KITCHEN

Broken case (room)—A storage area used to store partial purchase units of food products that have been issued. For example, some operations issue products such as canned goods in full purchase units (cases) even if only partial units are needed. If two cans of vegetables are removed from a case containing six cans, the broken case has four cans remaining that are stored in a broken case room for quick access as needed.

Product **marking** can be an early step in the storage process. This involves printing information such as the date delivered and invoice cost on product containers entering storage. When this is done, kitchen managers and others can easily check stock rotation (products in storage the longest should be used first), and it is easy to include accurate product cost information on issue requisitions which will be discussed later in this chapter. Also, product cost information is needed when end-of-**fiscal period** inventory cost assessments are made. Note: This process will also be discussed later in the chapter. Some food service operations calculate food costs every day based, in part, on the value of issues, and if product cost information is included on cases and other containers this task is easy to do.

OVERHEARD IN THE KITCHEN

Marking (product storage)—The act of recording information about the date of product receipt and product cost on containers of products when they enter storage areas.

Fiscal period—An accounting period containing a specified number of months. Most fiscal periods are for 12 months, but they can begin on the first day of any month.

The location of storage areas is an important concern, and the ideal space is close to the receiving area and between the receiving and food production areas. Note: This ideal arrangement has at least one possible disadvantage; it may be easier for employees to steal items from storage when they exit the food service operation through the employee entrance (often the property's back door), if proper controls are not in place.

Storage areas are frequently affected by facility remodeling which can occur several times (or more) during the life of the building housing the food service operation. Sometimes, for example, frozen storage space is relocated to an outside area to convert interior space for other uses. Sometimes, as well, storage space is moved to remote locations, including on different levels of the building than those used for food preparation/service. Hopefully, kitchen managers recognize that storage space should be a critical part of the operation's **work flow** and should not just be located "wherever there is room."

OVERHEARD IN THE KITCHEN

Work flow—The movement of products through workstations in a food service operation; see workstation.

The decision about whether to purchase bread in a fresh or frozen market form has storage implications.

INFORMATION ON THE SIDE
More About Storage Locations

Food service operations using suppliers whose delivery personnel are unionized may encounter "inside back door" delivery limitations: The route persons can only move products from their delivery vehicle to just inside the building. This can be a concern when receiving and/or storage areas are located elsewhere.

Another storeroom location challenge arises when a large facility such as a hotel has several dining locations and/or kitchens. Then the within-property transport of food products to storage areas or within production areas create time and control issues that must be effectively addressed.

Management Basics for Products in Storage

This section discusses four aspects of inventory management: quality concerns, physical storage locations, record keeping issues, and security concerns.

QUALITY CONCERNS DURING STORAGE

Products can decline in quality even under the best environmental conditions if, for example, suggested storage times are exceeded, and/or if proper storage temperatures are not maintained. The recommended temperatures for different storage areas noted earlier in this chapter should be maintained, and they should be monitored with appropriate equipment.

Storage areas should be cleaned on a routine schedule, not just when someone "gets around to it." Shelving units should keep products off the floor and away from the walls and ceilings to help with cleaning and to improve air circulation. Kitchen managers who maintain the proper storage environment, minimize the time that products are in storage, and regularly monitor storage areas are taking important steps to manage product quality during times of storage.

PHYSICAL STORAGE LOCATIONS

Locations for product storage typically vary in food service operations of different sizes (production volumes).

Workstation Storage   Very small food service operations typically have one storage location for each type of food product. For example, they may have a workstation refrigerator in which all refrigerated items are stored. Kitchen personnel work out of this refrigerator as daily production evolves. Likewise, there may be a tall upright or chest-type freezer, and a small room or even an open-access shelving unit for dry storage may also be available. This limited storage works well when, for example, there are frequent deliveries of products, and dependable suppliers minimize the need for high inventory safety levels.

Workstation and Backup Storage Area   Larger food service operations are more likely to have workstation storage areas with additional backup storage because of the need for increased storage capacities. For example, there may be a workstation refrigerator for easy access during production, and there may be another two-, three-, or even four-door refrigerator located elsewhere in the property. A walk-in freezer may also be available, and more space will be needed for dry storage than in smaller food operations.

Centralized Storage   Still larger food service operations may have one or more walk-in refrigerators and freezers and a very large dry storage area. In addition, efficiently designed facilities will often have some refrigerated and, perhaps, frozen storage capacity in workstation and/or production line work areas.

These larger facilities utilize an inventory control system that differs from smaller-volume properties. First, issuing systems are often used to help track the movement of products from storage to production to service in a manner that allows the kitchen managers to match revenues with product usage. Second, when a centralized storage system is used, products remaining in workstation areas may be returned to centralized storage areas at the end of each shift. This increases control because there is less opportunity for theft or pilferage when products are under centralized inventory control than when they remain in more easily accessible workstation locations.

Type	Brief Description	Advantages	Disadvantages
Workstation storage	Food products are stored in the areas where food production personnel work. Example: Refrigerated products may be stored in the sandwich preparation area in a sandwich shop.	• Minimal storage space is required. • Increases employee productivity: no transport time is needed to move products from storage to production locations. • Reduced time to count inventory (only one location).	• Less control over products in storage. • Difficult to match product usage to production.*
Workstation and decentralized storage	Food products for several or more shifts are stored in workstation areas with additional storage in other areas close to food preparation areas.	• Additional on-site storage is available to minimize stock-outs. • Secure storage is available for the products that are not in workstation areas.	• Additional time is needed to count items in more than one storage location. • It is less likely that the quantity sold will be known.*
Centralized storage	Food products are primarily stored in central storage areas, and products are issued to workstations on an as-needed basis that considers estimated production volumes.	• Additional security of centralized storage can reduce theft and pilferage. • Knowledge of the quantities of products issued allows kitchen managers to determine expected revenues.* • Perpetual inventory control systems are easily implemented.**	• Additional space is required for larger-volume product storage. • Time is required for product issuing procedures, including transport time to production areas.***

*If the quantity of products available for production is known (the amount in storage), the difference between that amount and the quantity remaining after production is the amount produced; the amount produced (×) the selling price per item should equal the revenue that is generated. Example:

30	−	5	=	25	×	$10.00	=	$250.00
No. of steaks available (Beginning of shift)		No. of steaks available (End of shift)		No. of steaks sold		Selling price of each steak		Expected revenue from steak sales

** Perpetual inventory systems are discussed later in this chapter.
*** These procedures are judged cost-effective in operations that utilize them, but some labor time is required to move products from storage to the production location.

FIGURE 9.3 Three Types of Food Storage Areas

Storage Areas in Review   Figure 9.3 summarizes the three basic types of food storage areas and presents advantages and disadvantages to each.

RECORD-KEEPING CONCERNS DURING STORAGE

Record keeping concerns relating to inventory management include using a physical inventory system to determine the cost of products in inventory, maintaining a perpetual inventory process for, at least, "A" items, and determining inventory turnover rates.

Physical Inventories   Kitchen managers have several record-keeping concerns that should be addressed to best manage and control food products in inventory. For example, they must determine the cost of the products in inventory at the end of each month or other fiscal period.

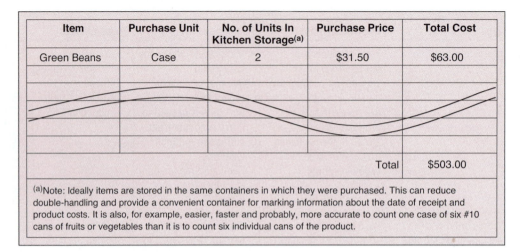

Item	Purchase Unit	No. of Units In Kitchen Storage(a)	Purchase Price	Total Cost
Green Beans	Case	2	$31.50	$63.00
		Total		$503.00

(a)Note: Ideally items are stored in the same containers in which they were purchased. This can reduce double-handling and provide a convenient container for marking information about the date of receipt and product costs. It is also, for example, easier, faster and probably, more accurate to count one case of six #10 cans of fruits or vegetables than it is to count six individual cans of the product.

FIGURE 9.4 Physical Inventory Form for Small Food Service Operation

That information is needed to determine the **food cost (cost of goods sold)** for the income statement. Note: We will discuss this process later in this chapter.

OVERHEARD IN THE KITCHEN

Food cost (cost of goods sold)—The cost of food that was purchased to produce the menu items that generated food revenue during a specified time period.

Many small volume food service operations make these calculations manually using forms similar to the one shown in Figure 9.4.

When you review Figure 9.4, you'll note that 2 cases of green beans were stored in the location used for dry storage. Each has a purchase price of $31.50 (this is easily determined because the price was marked on the case), so there is a total cost of $63.00. The process just described is used to determine the cost of all products in inventory. It is simplified because there is only one inventory location and because small operations typically carry reduced volumes of products in storage.

Physical inventory systems for mid-sized food service operations may utilize a physical inventory form similar to that illustrated in Figure 9.5. Note that it differs from Figure 9.4 because the kitchen manager must determine inventory quantities in storage and production areas.

When reviewing Figure 9.5, note that there are three cases of green beans in the storage area and one case in the production area. Each case has a purchase price of $31.50, so there is a total inventory cost of $126.00. Hopefully, the count of this item along with that related to all other items in storage has been obtained as a result of two persons doing the inventory. One, for example, could be the kitchen manager, and the second should be someone who is not involved with ongoing storage responsibilities such as a person from the accounting department. One person can count the number of inventory units and the second individual can complete the physical inventory form.

Item	Purchase Unit	No. of Units		Total Units	Purchase Price	Total Cost
		In Storage	In Production			
Green Beans	Case	3	1	4	$31.50	$126.00
					Total	$712.10

FIGURE 9.5 Physical Inventory Form for Mid-Sized Food Service Operation

Item	Purchase Unit	No. of Units In Centralized Storage	Purchase Price	Total Cost
Green Beans	Case	6	$31.50	$189.00
			Total	$1,390.04

FIGURE 9.6   Physical Inventory Form for Large-Volume Food Service Operation with Centralized Storage

Figure 9.6 shows a physical inventory form for a large-volume food service operation using centralized storage. Ironically, you'll note that the form is very similar to Figure 9.4 above for small operations because it is assumed that all food products to be counted for inventory purposes will be in one storage location. The difference: Small-volume properties store items in production-related areas, and their larger-volume counterparts store products in centralized areas that are (hopefully) close to food production spaces. Note: Large-volume operations may also use work station storage; however, they more typically use formal issuing systems, and the products unused after issue are returned to central storage areas.

When the physical inventory process is completed at the end of the month for food service operations of any size, the kitchen manager will have information needed to calculate the food costs for that month. Also, he/she will know the beginning inventory cost that will be used to calculate food costs for the next month.

INFORMATION ON THE SIDE

Technology to the Rescue!

Computerized systems are available to help with inventory counts and to determine inventory costs. For example, optical scanners can be used to read bar codes on containers of products in storage. This method provides a fast and accurate method to determine inventory costs, and "tomorrow" it may replace the manual system in use in most food service operations today.

Perpetual Inventory Procedures   Another record-keeping issue relating to storage involves the use of **perpetual inventory** information for selected products. When this is done, kitchen managers know, at any point in time, the quantity of products that should be available in inventory.

OVERHEARD IN THE KITCHEN

Perpetual inventory—An inventory management system that tracks all incoming and outgoing products so that kitchen managers know, on an ongoing basis, the quantity of product which should be available in inventory.

While it may not be practical or even useful for food service operations to maintain all products under a perpetual inventory system, this will likely be beneficial for the relatively few and expensive "A" items that are purchased and stored.

A perpetual inventory system works just like a person's checkbook: As money (food products) is deposited in the bank (brought into the storeroom), the balance on the checking account (food products in the storeroom) is increased. As money is withdrawn from the bank (food products are issued to production areas) the balance of money (food products) in the bank (storeroom) decreases. Therefore, at any point in time, one knows the amount of money (quantity of products) that should be in inventory.

Item:	Strip Steaks (6 oz.)		
Date	**No. of Purchase Units**		**Balance**
	In	**Out**	
			37
9/10/xx	-----	25	12
9/11/xx	35	20	27

FIGURE 9.7   Perpetual Inventory Form

Figure 9.7 shows the format for a perpetual inventory form, and the information collected is the same regardless of whether a computerized or manual system is in use.

When reviewing Figure 9.7, note that the kitchen manager considers strip steaks to be an "A" item because they are expensive and potentially theft-prone. Since they are valuable, they are included in the property's perpetual inventory system. There were 37 individual (6 ounce) servings of this item on hand when the new form was begun. On the first date (9/10), 25 steaks were issued leaving a balance of only 12 steaks in inventory (37 steaks − 25 steaks = 12 steaks). On the next date (9/11), 35 steaks were purchased, and 20 steaks were issued. This left a net balance of 15 steaks which increased the inventory balance to 27 servings (12 steaks + 35 steaks − 20 steaks = 27 steaks).

On a routine but random basis the kitchen manager should spot-check the number of strip steaks in the assigned storage area to assure that the number of servings available in inventory equals the balance noted on the perpetual inventory form.

INFORMATION ON THE SIDE

Who Uses What?

Must all food service operations use a physical and/or perpetual inventory system? The technically correct answer is "no," but commercial food service operations must report income profit or loss information to governmental agencies for tax purposes. Food cost is an expense that reduces profitability and, therefore, must be reported.

Some commercial properties operate on a **cash accounting system**. They assume their food cost is represented by the amount of checks written to pay for food purchases during the month or other accounting period. By contrast, other operations use an **accrual accounting system** to determine their food cost when income statements are prepared. To do so, they must use a physical inventory system to help determine food costs. Note: details about food cost (cost of goods sold) calculations are discussed later in this chapter.

What about the use of perpetual inventory systems? No food service operation is required by taxing authorities to maintain perpetual inventory balances. However, most would benefit from their use for, at least, the "A" items to manage and control these expensive products more closely.

Typically, as food service operations grow larger, they use accrual accounting systems and, as well, they take advantage of the benefits derived from the use of perpetual inventory methods.

OVERHEARD IN THE KITCHEN

Cash accounting system—An accounting system that considers revenue to be earned when it is received and expenses to have occurred when they are paid for.

Accrual accounting system—An accounting system that matches expenses incurred with revenues generated. This is done with the use of accounts receivable, accounts payables, and other similar accounts.

Inventory Turnover Rate   Another record-keeping concern applicable to storage involves the calculation of the **inventory turnover rate**. Inventory turnover rates measure how frequently food products are ordered and sold. They answer the question, "How many times each accounting period must the quantity of food available be purchased to generate the food and beverage revenues for the accounting period?"

OVERHEARD IN THE KITCHEN

Inventory turnover rate—The number of times in a specific period (example: month) that inventory is converted (turned into) revenue.

The basic formula for the inventory turnover rate is:

$$\text{Inventory Turnover Rate} = \frac{\text{Cost of Goods (Food) Sold}}{\text{Average Inventory}}$$

Let's see how the inventory turnover rate for food is calculated. Assume the kitchen manager takes a physical count of the food products in inventory and learns the following:

- Cost of food inventory at beginning of month = $29,500
- Cost of food purchases during month   = $76,000
- Cost of food inventory at end of month   = $27,500
- Food cost (cost of goods sold) during month = $78,000

The food inventory turnover rate equals:

$$\frac{\text{Food Cost (Cost of Goods Sold)}}{[\text{Beginning Food Inventory} + \text{Ending Food Inventory}] \div 2}$$

$$\frac{\$78,000}{[\$29,500 + \$27,500] \div 2}$$

$$\frac{\$78,000}{\$28,500}$$

$$2.74 \text{ turns}$$

If the inventory turns over approximately 2.75 times per month, the food products in inventory will last about 11 days (30 days in a month ÷ 2.75 turns).

The turnover rate, by itself, may not be especially helpful to the kitchen manager. Note: Some believe that a turnover rate below 1.00 time per month indicates excessive inventory levels, and turnover rates above 3.00 times may indicate that an inadequate quantity of food products are kept on hand and could yield product stock-outs. The ideal turnover rate for any food service operation, however, must be evaluated by considering the property's goals and the value of inventory that management determines should always be available. Note: These decisions are incorporated into the minimum-maximum inventory decisions discussed in the next section of this chapter.

Regardless of the target established for the operation, it is possible to note changes between fiscal periods when the inventory turnover rate is calculated each fiscal period. Why is the inventory turnover rate increasing or decreasing? What are the implications? What is the desired trend that the turnover rate should take? The answers to these and related questions can help to better control the food inventory and the costs associated with it.

SECURITY CONCERNS DURING STORAGE

The food products in storage locations have been purchased with the intent that they will be used to generate revenues. If, instead, they are stolen, money will have been spent and food expenses will be increased, but there will be no resulting revenue. Therefore, food costs will be greater than necessary, and profit levels will be lower than they should be.

Experienced kitchen managers consider their storage areas to be bank vaults, and their storage procedures address the question, "How should money be managed in a bank vault?" Simple procedures such as storing products in lockable areas with walls that extend to the ceiling and limiting access to storage areas can help reduce employee theft and pilferage. Differences between perpetual inventory quantities of "A" items and the quantities actually available in storage should be investigated. Some properties use employee **package inspection programs** to reduce the possibility of unauthorized "carry outs" of food or beverage products during acts of theft or pilferage.

OVERHEARD IN THE KITCHEN

Package inspection program (employee)—A policy that (a) discourages employees from bringing back-packs, shopping bags, and other large packages to work and (b) indicates that packages may be inspected when the employees leave work.

Some large-volume food service operations employ full-time storeroom clerks who, with few other employees, have access to storage areas. While this is not practical for most operations, small-volume properties can use several tactics to limit employee access to storage areas. For example, storage areas can be kept locked with scheduled times during which they are opened so the kitchen manager or other authorized persons can issue items from storage. Alternatively, "A" items may be kept locked and under perpetual inventory, and more general access is permitted to the storage areas used for other less expensive and less theft-prone items.

Wise kitchen managers know that problems can arise when employees have unlimited access to storage areas. They also understand that the problem is likely worsened when nonemployees are allowed to enter storage areas. This happens, for example, in food service operations that allow or even encourage delivery personnel to transport incoming items to storage areas. Unfortunately, there are few alternatives to this tactic when, for example, no or inadequate receiving area space is planned into the facility. As you learned, the ideal situation arises when products are formally received in a nonstorage area and transported to the storage area by the receiving clerk (in a large operation) or by a designated food service employee in smaller operations.

Minimum-Maximum Inventory System

The minimum-maximum inventory system requires the purchaser to determine, for each product in the system, the minimum and the maximum quantity below which inventory levels should not fall or rise.

Minimum-maximum inventory system procedures involve determining the quantity of each product that should be ordered to bring the existing inventory level back to the maximum point allowable when the order is received. The system is most often used to control the relatively few and most expensive "A" items, and it is not typically used to purchase inexpensive, low-volume-use, or perishable products.

Several terms must be understood as the minimum-maximum inventory system is discussed:

- *Purchase unit*—The standard size of the package or container in which the product is typically purchased.
- *Product usage rate*—The number of purchase units that are used during a typical order period.
- *Order period*—The time (number of days or weeks) for which an order is normally placed.
- *Lead time usage*—The number of purchase units typically used during the time between order placement and delivery. For example, if 3 cases (50# each) of frozen shrimp are normally used during the two days between product order and receipt, the lead time for this product is 6 cases (2 days $\times$ 3 cases used per day).
- *Safety level*—The minimum number of purchase units that must always remain in inventory because of late deliveries and unexpected increases in product usage rates.
- *Order point*—The ideal number of purchase units to be available in inventory when an order is placed.

OVERHEARD IN THE KITCHEN

Usage rate (minimum-maximum system)—The number of purchase units of a product used during a typical order period.

Lead time usage (minimum-maximum system)—The number of purchase units of a product typically used during the time between order placement and delivery.

Order point (minimum-maximum system)—The number of purchase units of a product hat should be available in inventory when an order is placed.

Assume that Vernon's Restaurant uses a large quantity of frozen shrimp of a specified size. It is an expensive "A" item included in the property's minimum-maximum inventory system. Let's further assume the following:

- Purchase Unit (frozen shrimp): Case—10 boxes (5# each; 50# total)
- Product usage rate—42 cases per order period
- Order period—2 weeks (14 days)
    Note: Daily usage rate = 3 cases (42 cases per order period ÷ 14 days)
- Product lead time = 4 days
    Note: number of cases used during lead time = 12 cases (3 cases used per day × 4 days)
- Product safety level = 12 cases.

The kitchen manager can now answer several questions about the purchase quantities for frozen shrimp.

Question #1—What is the maximum number of cases of shrimp that should ever be available in inventory? *Answer:* usage rate (+) safety level.

42	(+)	12 cases	(=)	54
Usage rate	(+)	Safety level	(=)	Maximum cases
(No. of cases)		(No. of cases)		

Question #2—What is the order point for the shrimp? *Answer:* lead time usage (+) safety level.

12 cases	(+)	12 cases	=	24 cases
Lead time	(+)	safety level	=	Cases at order point

Note: the order point (24 cases) can be verified:

No. of cases available when shrimp is ordered	24 cases
(−) No. of cases used before delivery (product lead time; 4 days × 3 cases/day)	(12 cases)
Number of cases available when shrimp is delivered (safety level)	12 cases

Question #3—How many cases of shrimp should be ordered at the order point (when there are 12 cases in storage)? *Answer:* usage rate.

42	(+)	12 cases	(=)	54
Usage rate	(+)	Order point	(=)	Cases to order
(No. of cases)		(No. of cases)		

Note: the number of cases to order at the order point can be verified:

Cases available	=	66 (24 cases [order point] (+) 42 cases [usage rate])
(−) Lead time cases	=	(12)
		54 cases (maximum inventory level; see question #1)

Question #4—How many cases of shrimp should be ordered if an order is placed when there are 30 cases in inventory? The order point for shrimp has not been reached, but the order is placed with other frozen seafood products, and all products will be purchased from the seafood supplier at the same time.

Step A: Calculate the number of cases of shrimp that exceed the order point:

30 cases	(−)	24 cases	(=)	6
No. of cases in storage	(−)	Order point	(=)	Excess cases
		(No. of cases)		

Step B: Calculate the number of cases to order:

42 cases	(−)	6	(=)	36
Order point	(−)	Excess cases	(=)	No. of cases to order
(No. of cases)				

Note: The need to order 36 cases of shrimp when there are 6 cases in excess of the order point can be verified:

36	(+)	30	(=)	66
No. of cases ordered	(+)	No. of cases in inventory	(=)	Total cases available when order is placed

66 cases	(−)	12 cases	(=)	54 cases
No. of cases available	(−)	Lead time (No. of cases)	(=)	Maximum number of cases

When reviewing the questions above, note that the kitchen manager can use information about product usage rate, order period, lead time, and safety level to determine:

- The minimum number of cases to be in inventory.
- The maximum number of cases allowable in inventory.
- The order point (number of cases)
- The number of cases that should purchased if an order will be placed before that product's order point is reached.

The safety level for the product represents the minimum number of purchased units below which product quantities cannot decrease. Factors to consider when establishing the safety level include:

- *The lead time required for re-orders*—As the frequency of deliveries decreases, the number of lead-time units should increase.
- *The product's usage rate*—As the volume of product usage increases, safety levels may need to be increased accordingly.

An ideal safety level will minimize the possibility of stock outs without the need to maintain excessive quantities of products in inventory.

Several factors also influence the decision about the lead times established for products. They can be established by considering the amount of time generally required for an order. Conditions that could increase the length of product delivery lead times include:

- When suppliers are not dependable. Note: This should be an important factor in deciding whether to continue to do business with them.
- When the food service operation is in a remote location and delivery delays are common.
- When market situations cause unpredictable conditions that affect the availability of products and the potential need for back orders of some items.

Par Inventory System

A par inventory system is similar to the minimum-maximum inventory system just discussed because the quantity of products to be purchased is that which will bring the inventory level to an allowable maximum (par). It is also similar because an effective inventory management system is needed to accurately determine the quantities available so that wise purchase decisions can be made. The par system is commonly used for dishwashing and other chemicals.

The quantity of product established for the par level is determined on the basis of experience, "trial and error," and other factors you learned about when safety stock levels and usage rates for the minimum-maximum inventory system were discussed.

Let's see how the par system works. The kitchen manager at Vernon's Restaurant has established a par level of 10 cases (24 heads per case) of lettuce. She orders the item on Tuesday for delivery on Thursday to maintain this par level. Before ordering, the manager counts the number of cases available and "rounds down" to the nearest full case. Example: This week she has 4 full cases and an opened case. Since only full cases are included in her par calculations, she notes 4 cases in inventory.

The manager also knows that she normally uses about one case each on Tuesdays and Wednesdays (the two days between order and delivery), and she also recalls the lettuce available in the open case. Therefore, she believes the estimate of two case usage for Tuesday and Wednesday will not create a stock-out.

Next, she determines the need to order 8 cases from her local supplier:

$$
\begin{array}{cccccc}
\text{(10 cases)} & (-) & \left(\begin{array}{c} 4 \\ \text{No. of cases} \\ \text{available} \end{array} \right. & \begin{array}{c} (-) \\ (-) \end{array} & \left. \begin{array}{c} (2) \\ \text{No. of cases} \\ \text{used before delivery} \end{array} \right) & \begin{array}{c} (=) \\ (=) \end{array} & \begin{array}{c} 8 \\ \text{No. of} \\ \text{cases to order} \end{array} \\
\text{Par level} & (-) & & & &
\end{array}
$$

If her usage estimate is correct, the par inventory level will be maintained when the delivery arrives:

$$
\begin{array}{ccccc}
4 & (-) & 2 & (=) & 2 \\
\text{No. of cases} & (-) & \text{No. of cases} & (=) & \text{No. of cases} \\
\text{available} & & \text{used} & & \text{available at delivery}
\end{array}
$$

$$
\begin{array}{ccccc}
2 & (+) & 8 & (=) & 10 \\
\text{No. of cases} & (+) & \text{No. of cases} & (=) & \text{No. of cases in par} \\
\text{available at delivery} & & \text{delivered} & & \text{inventory level}
\end{array}
$$

You'll notice that the kitchen manager was able to make an easy and fast determination about the number of cases of lettuce to order by considering:

- The established par level.
- The number of cases currently available.
- The number of cases likely to be used between when the product was ordered and when it was delivered.

The fast and simple advantages of the par inventory system must be countered with the potential disadvantage of stock-outs. These can occur if the par level is too low, the usage rate is higher than expected, and/or the purchaser is unable to expedite another delivery if unforeseen problems occur.

Par inventories do not typically create problems with excessive quantities on hand because wise kitchen managers decrease par levels if they notice that the quantities on hand are increasing. Also, decreased quantities available immediately before deliveries are made will likely be noticed, and estimated usage rates can be reconsidered so par levels can be adjusted. The process just described is a "trial and error" method that, over time, works well in many food service operations.

Calculation of Food Cost (Cost of Goods Sold)

What is a food service operation's actual food cost? The first response might be, "It is what the food service operation spent for food." However, as you will now learn, that response is too simple. Kitchen managers in most food service operations use an accrual accounting system, and they want to match the revenue generated during a specific accounting period with the expenses that were incurred to generate that revenue.

Figure 9.8 shows how a kitchen manager can compute the food cost (cost of goods sold) for a specific month.

Let's look at Figure 9.8 more carefully. First, note that the value of food inventory ($83,575 in line A) at the beginning of the accounting period (January) is added to the value of purchases ($187,615 in line B) during January. This indicates (in line C) the total value of food available during January ($271,190). Some of these products were used to generate January's food revenue and are no longer available in inventory. To determine that amount, the inventory value at the end of January ($89,540 in line D) is deducted to determine the unadjusted cost of food ($181,650 in line E) used during the period.

Some kitchen managers use the above calculations to determine the food cost that is reported in their income statement. Others, however, want to more closely match food revenue with food costs and they make some adjustments to the unadjusted food costs in line E. When looking at Figure 9.8, notice (in lines F and G #1) that the unadjusted food costs can be modified by adding **transfers** from and to the beverage operation.

Line No.				
A	Value of food inventory (beginning of period: January 1)	$ 83,575		
B	Value of food purchases during January	187,615		
C	Total value of food available during January			271,190
D	Value of food inventory (end of period: January 31)			(89,540)
E	Unadjusted food cost (cost of goods sold: January, 20xx)			181,650
F	Add adjustments: • Transfers *from* beverage operation			6,550
G	Deduct adjustments: 1. Transfers *to* beverage operation. 2. Transfers to labor cost (employee meals) 3. Transfers to marketing		(4,175) (8,900) (3,750)	
	Total deductions			(16,825)
H	Adjusted food cost (cost of goods sold: January, 20xx)			171,375
I	January food revenue:	$508,620		
J	• Food cost % (unadjusted) – line E	$181,650 $508,620	= 35.7%	
K	• Food cost % (adjusted) – line H	$171,375 $508,620	= 33.7%	

FIGURE 9.8   Calculation of Actual Food Costs with Adjustments for January, 20xx

---

OVERHEARD IN THE KITCHEN

Transfer (food cost calculation)—An adjustment made when food costs are calculated to better match food costs with the revenue generated by the sale of the food.

What are food and beverage transfers? Examples of transfers *from* the beverage operation (line F) include wine used in cooking and liqueurs used for tableside dessert flambéing. If these costs were not transferred from the beverage operation to the food operation, beverage costs would be overstated, and food costs would be understated. Examples of transfers *to* the beverage operation (line G #1) include produce such as lemons and oranges used for beverage garnishes and ice cream used as an ingredient in after-dinner drinks. If these costs were not transferred from the food operation to the beverage operation, food costs would be overstated and beverage costs would be understated. Remember that the intent of accrual accounting is to match revenues generated with expenses incurred to generate the revenue. This objective is better addressed when these transfers are made.

Figure 9.8 also shows that two other adjustments can be made to more accurately reflect food costs. These adjustments are made for labor costs and marketing expenses. Transfers of food costs to labor costs (line G #2) represent the cost of employee meals which are an employee benefit and, therefore, a labor cost rather than a food cost. Transfers from food to marketing (line G #3) represent the cost of free meals provided to potential guests looking for a site for a future function and/or dissatisfied guests who receive a "comp" meal. These are really marketing-related costs that did not generate food revenue and should, therefore, be removed from food costs and added to marketing costs.

When the above adjustments made, the adjusted food cost ($171,375 in line H) is known.

Do these calculations make any "real" difference? Let's continue to review Figure 9.8 and find out. In line J, the food cost % is calculated by using the unadjusted food cost: The January food revenue ($508,620) is divided into the unadjusted food cost for January ($181,650), and the result is 35.7%. In other words, 35.7% of all food revenue dollars in January were used to purchase the food that generated the revenue.

Now let's look at the food cost % in line K which is calculated using the adjusted food cost ($171,357 in line H). You'll note that the same January food revenue ($508,620 in line I) is divided into the adjusted food cost ($171,357). The result is 33.7%. Now the kitchen manager knows that only 33.7% of all food revenue dollars in January were used to purchase the food that generated the revenue.

The difference between the food cost percent calculated with unadjusted and adjusted food costs is 2.0% (35.7% − 33.7%). This percentage might seem small but, in operations of every size, each dollar counts. For example, the food service operation's revenue was $508,620 (see line I). If the kitchen manager did not make these adjustments, the food cost would have been overstated by $10,172.40 ($508,620 × .02). At the same time the expenses for beverages, labor costs, and marketing would be incorrect as well.

Kitchen managers must be consistent and always use the same (or no) adjustment factors when calculating food costs. In large operations with accountants/bookkeepers and in multiunit organizations where some accounting/control functions are managed off-site, it is important that all concerned parties "define" product costs in exactly the same manner.

INFORMATION ON THE SIDE

Petty Cash When There Is None In Inventory

Normally, food service operations minimize the use of cash payments for purchases. Checks allow for better control of expenses, and **audit trails** can be developed and more easily traced. However, some minor expenses such as "emergency" food purchases from grocery stores are best paid from a **petty cash fund** because it is more practical and less expensive to do so.

Petty cash funds must be maintained in secure locations and be administered by responsible managers. For example, a restaurant's petty cash bank might be kept in the property manager's office. A large hotel may have a petty cash fund administered by the kitchen manager, and one or more cash banks may be used by other departments as well.

Petty cash funds should be established on an **imprest** (cash advance) system:

- The amount of money in the petty cash fund should be based upon the normal value of petty cash purchases for a specific time period (example: two weeks).
- A check charged to "petty cash" is written and used to establish the petty cash fund.
- When purchases are needed, cash is removed from the cash bank. The change from the transaction and the purchase receipt is returned and, after confirming that the amount (cash change (+) receipt) equals the amount removed, both the cash (change) and receipt are placed in the cash bank. A **petty cash voucher** is attached to the receipt.
- When the petty cash fund must be replenished, a check is written to "petty cash" for the value of paid receipts in the fund. This check, converted to cash, replenishes the fund to its original value.

At any point in time, the actual value of the petty cash fund should equal the original amount of money allocated to petty cash: cash in the bank (+) paid receipts for all purchases.

OVERHEARD IN THE KITCHEN

Audit trail—A step-by-step record that allows financial data to be traced to its source.

Petty cash fund—A small amount of cash kept on hand for relatively low-cost purchases.

Imprest (petty cash system)—A petty cash fund in which payments to the fund are always in the amount required to bring its balance to the original amount. The petty cash balance is always maintained by cash and the receipts for cash payments.

Petty cash voucher—A slip signed by the person responsible for the petty cash fund that authorizes the withdrawal of cash from the fund for a specific purchase.

NOW IT'S YOUR TURN

A PINCH OF THE INTERNET (9.2)

1. Handheld wireless technology can help kitchen managers and their staff to quickly and effectively enter inventory counts and upload information into the property's inventory management system. To learn about one company's system, go to: www.culinarysoftware.com
2. To learn how the use of bar codes can assist with inventory management procedures, enter "inventory barcodes in restaurants" in your favorite search engine.
3. To review a blog dedicated to restaurant inventory management, go to: http://blog.intellitrack.net/
4. To review information about cost of goods sold calculations, enter "calculating cost of goods sold" into your favorite search engine.
5. Preserving food quality during storage is an important concern for all kitchen managers. To learn more about this topic, enter "food quality during storage" into your favorite search engine.

COMPLETING THE PLATE QUESTIONS (9.2)

1. Many food service operations have a policy requiring that no food can be discarded from storage areas without notifying the kitchen manager even if it is obviously and visibly spoiled. Do you agree with this policy? Why or why not?
2. What are three common ways that food service employees may steal food products from storage areas? What practical theft prevention procedures can be used by kitchen managers to reduce theft from occurring if these tactics are used?
3. How would you determine which food products should be classified as "A" items that require more record keeping and physical security?
4. Do you think that kitchen managers in small food service operations should calculate food cost (cost of goods sold) using the adjustments discussed in this chapter? Why or why not?
5. What are practical ways to monitor the temperature in refrigerated, frozen, and dry storage areas to best assure that food quality will be retained while products are stored in these areas?

Kitchen Challenge Du Jour Case Study (9.2)

"It's obvious that the food costs are higher than they should be," explained Ashley. Our new POS system tells me that we sold 425 portions of rib eye steaks last month. However, we purchased more than 600 portions, and I just did a physical count of the steaks in inventory, and there were only 25 steaks available. I don't know the number of steaks in inventory at the beginning of the month but whatever that number is it just means that more steaks that are unaccounted for."

Ashley is the kitchen manager of the Ponds Restaurant, and she is talking to its owner, Harrison. Harrison had inherited some money and had always wanted to own a restaurant. However, he had other business interests and hired Ashley who had been a manager in another industry for the last four years to assume responsibility for his new restaurant venture. Ashley began about three months ago after the previous kitchen manager quit, and Ashley was quickly learning about the restaurant's operation, including several "loopholes" in its control system.

"I'll bet your correct, Ashley," said Harrison, "It's getting more difficult to pay the bills with cash from operations, and my accountant tells me that the restaurant's profitability is decreasing each month."

Questions

a) How can the restaurant's new POS system help to correct the food cost problem? (Assume it shares capabilities with most POS systems on the market today.)
b) What are ideal food storage systems that should be in place at the Ponds Restaurant?
c) What, if anything, should Ashley do to involve existing staff members in the design of the revised control system? What suggestions do you have as she implements the system?

PRODUCT ISSUING PROCEDURES

OBJECTIVE

3. Discuss the importance of and proper procedures for product issuing.
   • Importance of effective issuing
   • Steps in product issuing

Importance of Effective Issuing

Do you think there should be some relationship between the quantity of food products produced and sold by the food service operation and the quantity of products removed from its storage areas? Of course there should be, but how can the kitchen manager match the quantity of issues with the amount of food produced and sold?

Some operations use an "open-door" approach to issuing: Whenever someone needs something, he or she simply goes to the proper storage area and removes it. When this tactic is used, every employee is really "in charge" of issuing. For example, production personnel retrieve food products, dining room servers may pick-up bus tubs of pre-prepared salad greens from the refrigerator, and buspersons have access to storage areas for condiments needed to re-stock the server's areas. An interesting observation: In many food service operations, storage areas are kept unlocked during the work day when employees are present and are then locked when the operation is closed and no employees are present. Shouldn't this storage practice be reversed to help reduce the possibility of theft?

Basic issuing procedures are necessary to continue the control concerns used when products are purchased, received, and stored. If they are not, food costs can increase with no offsetting revenues, and profitability will be lowered.

Storeroom handling time can be reduced if products can be stored and issued in their original packing cases.

Steps in Product Issuing

In food service operations using a perpetual inventory system, an issue requisition is typically used as authorization to remove items managed by the perpetual inventory system. Figure 9.9 shows a sample issue requisition used to obtain food products required by standard recipes.

When you review Figure 9.9, notice that rib eye steaks are considered "A" items, and they are included the food service operation's perpetual inventory records. When this system is used, an issue requisition is needed to authorize removal of the products from the storage area. The issuing process, then, reduces the quantity of items in inventory, and the applicable perpetual inventory records should also be adjusted to reflect the lower quantity of product in the storage area.

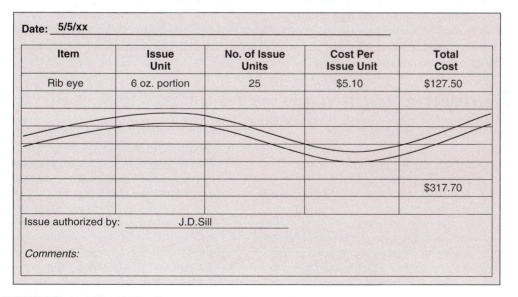

Date: 5/5/xx

Item	Issue Unit	No. of Issue Units	Cost Per Issue Unit	Total Cost
Rib eye	6 oz. portion	25	$5.10	$127.50
				$317.70

Issue authorized by: _____ J.D.Sill _____

Comments:

FIGURE 9.9 Issue Requisition Form

Figure 9.9 indicates that the issue unit for rib eyes is a 6 oz. portion and 25 issue units (6 oz. portions) are to be removed from inventory. Since the cost per purchase unit (6 oz. portion) is $5.10, the cost of the 25 steaks issued is $127.50 (25 portions × $5.10 per portion). At the end of the shift or day, the signed issue requisition form would be the authorization for the removal of the 25 steak servings, and the perpetual inventory form would be adjusted accordingly.

What if only 22 steaks were sold during the serving period for which they were issued? What would happen with the other 3 steaks that remain (25 servings issued [−] 22 servings sold [=] 3 servings)? In some operations, policies may require that these servings remain in workstation or production storage areas and be first-used during the next shift. In other properties, the applicable policy may require that the 3 portions be transferred back to central storage with the perpetual inventory quantity increased accordingly. Note: Regardless of the location of food storage areas (for example, in production areas, in workstations and other storage areas, or in centralized storage) the same concern about minimizing the potential for theft, errors, or misuse is important. Policies specific to the individual operation should be developed and consistently enforced.

INFORMATION ON THE SIDE
Technology and Product Issuing

Some food service operations utilize bar codes or even radio frequency identification (RFID) systems to help with food product control, including at time of issuing. For example, if bar codes have been attached to products in storage, product containers can be scanned when items are removed. When this is done:

- Inventory quantities are adjusted.
- Kitchen managers or other purchasers are alerted if the inventory level has been reduced to the order point.
- A report can be issued about the estimated revenue that should be produced by the items that are issued. (For example, if 10 steaks are issued with a sales value of $15.00 each, $150.00 in revenue should be generated: 10 steaks [×] $15.00 per steak.)

In our discussion of Figure 9.8, we assumed that only "A" items such as the steaks were included in the issuing system. This special control of expensive and theft-prone items would be considered to be practical in many food service operations. However, very large-volume food service operations using full-time storeroom personnel may require that all items be issued only if they are included on a signed issue requisition. In all operations, issue requisitions should be signed by the kitchen manager or other authorized employee, and the products and quantities issued should be based upon reasonable estimates of production needs.

Wise kitchen managers realize that food products must be effectively managed at every step through production and service to guests. These steps include those that occur immediately before food production begins, and the issuing process is just as important as those used for purchasing, receiving, and storing activities.

NOW IT'S YOUR TURN

A PINCH OF THE INTERNET (9.3)

1. To learn more about issuing, enter "food service issuing inventory control" into your favorite search engine.
2. Numerous companies offer software for inventory control, including food issuing. To view the Web sites of many of the organizations, type "food inventory software" or "restaurant inventory software" into your favorite search engine.

COMPLETING THE PLATE QUESTIONS (9.3)

1. Sometimes during "emergencies" (when food products are needed immediately), food production personnel remove products from inventory with the thought that "I'll complete the issue requisition later." What do you think about this idea? What are three practical procedures that you as a kitchen manager can implement to help reduce the occurrence of "food emergencies?"

2. What procedures should be in place to determine the order (sequence) in which food products received at different times should be removed from storage?

3. Sometimes a large number of food products must be issued (removed) from storage at the same time. If you were a kitchen manager, what would be your policy about when mobile transport carts should be used and/or how much (in weight) employee should be able to carry at one time?

4. What are two tactics that you might implement when decisions were made about where food products should be placed in storage areas that could help with product inventory and issuing?

5. Kitchen managers in some operations develop standardized recipes that indicate, for example, that all refrigerated products required for use in a recipe should be removed from the refrigerator at the same time. What would be one reason for this policy? What are your thoughts about it?

Overheard in the Kitchen Glossary

Americans with Disabilities Act (ADA)
Bonafide Occupational Qualification (BOQ)
Pallet
Credit memo
Receiving report
Slack-out seafood
Radio frequency identification (RFID)

Trespassing
Broken case (room)
Marking (product storage)
Fiscal period
Work flow
Food cost (cost of goods sold)
Perpetual inventory
Cash accounting system
Accrual accounting system

Inventory turnover rate
Package inspection program (employee)
Usage rate (minimum-maximum system)
Lead time usage (minimum-maximum system)
Order point (minimum-maximum system)

Transfer (food cost calculation)
Audit trail
Petty cash fund
Imprest (petty cash system)
Petty cash voucher

LESSON 9

If you are reading this textbook as part of a formal class, your Instructor may want you to apply and practice what you have learned in this chapter by completing Lesson 9 of the Pearson Education Kitchen Management Simulation (KMS). If you are required to complete KMS Lesson 9; read the **About Lesson 9** below, then go to www.pearsonhighered.com/kms for instructions on how to access and complete it.

After you have successfully completed the lesson, think about the way you, as a professional kitchen manager, would answer the **For Your Consideration** questions that follow.

About Lesson 9

You can take what you learned in this chapter and bring it to life when you complete KMS Lesson 9. This KMS lesson teaches you how to effectively count and calculate the value of inventory. You will first determine food and beverage quantity levels. When you know the amounts you have on hand you can calculate their monetary value. Then you will be ready to complete this multistep process by calculating the value of the product you have used and the cost of goods sold (COGS).

Applying proper inventory practices, such as knowing how much inventory is on hand, is one of your restaurant's key defenses against food waste and theft. It also protects your restaurant from stock outs; the running out of an item completely, which could mean dissatisfied customers.

Food and beverage products are one of the single largest cost expenditures restaurants encounter. By knowing how much inventory is on hand, its value, and the value of the food you have used, you are able to make well-informed purchasing decisions. When you complete this lesson you will show that you can analyze product usage, calculate your cost of goods sold, and improve your restaurant's profitability.

For Your Consideration

1. Many restaurants require two different people to verify inventory counts. Why do you think this practice is so common?
2. What would be the effect on cost of goods sold (COGS) if a kitchen manager bought excessive amounts of food that had to be discarded due to spoilage?
3. Assume you have an effective inventory system in place. However, each week your inventory count for steak shows you are missing an average of 5 steaks. What measures would you take to investigate the reasons for the missing product?

Endnote

1. For more information about the calculation of daily food costs, see: Jack Ninemeier. Planning and Control for Food and Beverage Operations. Seventh Edition. Lansing, Mi. Educational Institute of American Hotel & Lodging Association. 2009 (see Chapter 11).

10

Kitchen Managers Analyze Their Menus

Chapter Ingredients Outline

Learning Objectives

After studying this chapter, you will be able to:

1. Explain informal procedures that can be used to evaluate menus.
2. Describe detailed procedures helpful in determining the popularity and profitability of specific menu items when a formal menu engineering process is used.

COMING RIGHT UP OVERVIEW

You have learned that the menu is critically important to the success of every food service operation. For example, it must offer the items that guests like and will want to order. The ability to consistently produce these items according to quality requirements driven by standardized recipes will impact the guests' enjoyment and encourage them to return and to tell others about their positive experiences. This, in turn, creates an ongoing **revenue stream** that allows the operation to be profitable if the costs are effectively managed within the limitations posed by available revenues.

Kitchen managers and other members of the menu planning and design team do all that they can to best ensure that the menu meets its marketing and financial goals. However, the very best menu on the day it is implemented may not remain the best menu as time evolves. For example, the market characteristics of guests who visit the property may change, and, even if all or most of the guests are frequent visitors, food trends and fads may influence guest preferences. These are among the reasons that wise kitchen managers along with others on the food service operation's management team use informal and more formal procedures to regularly evaluate their menus.

This chapter begins by explaining the importance of menu analysis and then provides some examples of informal methods that every kitchen manager should use to learn about menu item challenges that require attention and resolution.

Not surprisingly, the first source of information about the menu is the guests who order and consume the items available on the menu. There are several fast, easy, and very inexpensive tactics that can be used for this purpose, and they will be discussed in detail.

Kitchen managers should never forget about the experts working on their food production teams. Hopefully, those who produce menu items were asked about suggestions when the menu was planned, and their opportunities for making suggestions should continue when the menu is in use. It should not be surprising that the professionals who produce the items may have suggestions about production improvements, and kitchen managers who ignore the opportunity to gain this information are losing a great potential resource.

Service personnel typically have much greater face-to-face time with guests than do kitchen managers and their employees. Therefore, the dining room manager and all front-of-house staff members can provide at least informal input to address the question, "What do our guests like and dislike about our menu and menu items?" Opportunities to obtain input from service personnel will also be discussed in this chapter.

Restaurant reviews are available in the news media in many communities, and local, regional, and even national data bases of restaurant review information are available online. Persons posing as guests hired by the food service operation who complete a **shopper's report** provide additional sources of information that can be helpful in menu analysis, and these will be described as will review sites to which guests and other members of the public have contributed.

The second part of this chapter will focus on a more formalized method of menu evaluation called menu engineering. While the term suggests a complicated process, it really is not. Kitchen managers use menu item sales and cost information to classify menu items into categories based upon the popularity (number of items purchased) and profitability (contribution margin: menu item selling price [−] cost of food). After each menu item's popularity and profitability is known, kitchen managers and others on the food service operation's management team can make decisions about ways to increase sales of the most profitable items. You'll learn that the use of menu engineering tactics can help to increase the base of revenues needed to meet your food service operation's financial goals.

OVERHEARD IN THE KITCHEN

Revenue stream—The flow of money that comes into the food service operation that is generated from the sale of products and services to guests.

Shopper's report—Information provided by persons hired by the food service operation to pose as guests to closely observe and report on their dining experiences at the property. Observations typically include those related to service, sanitation and cleanliness, the menu and menu items, and many other observable aspects of the operation, experience, and environment.

INFORMAL MENU ANALYSIS PROCEDURES

OBJECTIVE

1. Explain informal procedures that can be used to evaluate menus.
   - Importance of menu analysis
   - Input from guests
   - Input from production personnel
   - Input from service personnel
   - Input from other sources

Kitchen managers and other members of the menu planning and design team have invested significant time and effort to develop menus that please the guests. Did they make the right decisions? Do guests' preferences for menu items change over the life of the menu? Can the menu be improved? These and related questions identify the concerns that all kitchen managers should have about their menus. There are numerous informal and easy-to-use methods that can be used to analyze menus, and they will be discussed in the beginning section of this chapter.

Importance of Menu Analysis

Diners in most communities have numerous dining-out alternatives. They can, in effect, "vote with their feet" as they decide where they would like to enjoy a meal away from their homes. As well, consumers in schools and universities and some other noncommercial food services often have dining alternatives and/or are eager to inform responsible administrators about dining difficulties that they encounter. Complaints can range from those related to food production, service, sanitation, value, and others. However, the availability of the products that are served clearly impact their perceptions of the food service operation.

INFORMATION ON THE SIDE

Service Personnel Know!

One of the authors of this book recently visited a popular seafood restaurant and ordered a pan-fried seafood entrée. The server immediately replied, "Since you have a taste preference for a pan-fried entrée, could I please suggest a similar item that all of our guests really enjoy?" Based on the well-written and enticing menu description, he thanked the server for the suggestion but ordered the original entrée.

When the item was served, it became clear why the server had suggested another item. The seafood serving was very small, was highly salt-seasoned, and was excessively fried leaving a greasy and not-very-tasty batter coating.

At the end of the meal, the server returned to the table to remove the soiled dishes and noticed that little of the entrée had been consumed. Her response, "I'm sorry that you didn't seem to enjoy the meal, sir," seemed genuinely apologetic and not "I told you so!"

Upon leaving, the guest asked to speak to the manager who explained in a fairly insincere response that "We have a new cook working tonight; he's still learning how to do things."

Needless to say, that manager did not realize that guests do not care about inexperienced staff, the condition of food production equipment, or other operating problems. Instead, their concern focuses on value: The quality of the food and dining experience compared to the price that was paid. It appears that the kitchen manager and on-duty manager of this property did not know and/or did not care about the food being served and the guest experience that was received.

Professional kitchen managers do not place service personnel in the position of having to inform guests about which items are "good and bad." Instead, they should make an effort to assure that all items consistently meet property standards and, if they do not, they should not be on the menu.

Professional kitchen managers want to do their best to please all of their guests all of the time. They consider menu-related problems that are identified to be improvement challenges and welcome the opportunities to make changes. They also use numerous methods to determine what their guests really think about the menu of available items and, as you'll learn, there are many ways to do this.

Input from Guests

Have you ever finished your meal at a restaurant, walked up to the cashier area to pay the bill, and passed by a manager who asked the question, "How was everything?" Most of us have had this experience, and many of us probably think that the question is more of a "goodbye" than a sincere request for information that can lead to better guest experiences in the future. These managers do not consider the fact that each guest who has a positive experience can help confirm that the food service operation is using the correct procedures. As well, every negative experience (and, unfortunately, even the best operations have them) provides an opportunity for the operation to improve. Food service employees who ask the question, "How was everything?" without really caring if there is a response or what it might be are missing significant opportunities to learn, to show guests that their opinions are valued, and to improve.

Let's look at common methods used to obtain guests' input about the menu and other aspects of their dining-out experiences:

All of us at Vernon's Restaurant want you to enjoy your dining experience with us, and we are anxious to learn your comments. Please take a moment to let us know how we did and how we might improve.

Date:_____   Name of Server: _____

	Poor	Acceptable	Perfect	Comments
Greeting when you entered	❏	❏	❏	
Quality of service	❏	❏	❏	
Quality of food	❏	❏	❏	
Restaurant cleanliness	❏	❏	❏	
Menu prices	❏	❏	❏	
Food presentation	❏	❏	❏	
Overall experience	❏	❏	❏	

Other Comments:

If you would like to be added to our mailing list for news about upcoming events, meal specials, and dining coupons, please provide the information below:

Name: _____   or E-mail address: _____

Address: _____

Thank you for answering our questions!

FIGURE 10.1   Sample Guest-Comment Card

GUEST COMMENT CARDS

Many food service operations provide hard-copy comment cards for guests to provide information about their meal and other aspects of their experience. Perhaps the comment cards are readily available on the guest table, or they may be printed on guest checks, or the questionnaire may be brought to the table with the guest check. A sample comment card is shown in Figure 10.1.

When reviewing the sample guest-comment card in Figure 10.1, note that it allows guests to provide a rating of specific aspects of their dining experience and to provide general comments as well.

Hopefully, this information is collected, carefully analyzed, recorded, and used for improvement purposes. Sometimes, however, the information provided is dismissed by kitchen managers and others who take negative comments personally: "The guest doesn't know what he is talking about." "Well, we did have a problem during that shift, but it doesn't happen very often." "I think I know who that guest was; he complains all the time!"

It is always important to remember that the purpose of guest comment information is to improve the operation. It is not provided to make employees defensive, to identify who should be "punished," or to place blame on one or more employees.

Some food service operations develop a standard such as "We can't please everyone all the time; therefore, we'll take immediate action when more than 10% (or another target number) of guests complain about something." However, every food service operation would be better if kitchen managers investigated and worked to resolve every problem identified by every guest. While this might not always be possible, managers know that dissatisfied guests may not return, and that these guests may also inform numerous persons about their negative experiences.

INFORMATION ON THE SIDE

"Electronic Comment Cards"

Increasingly, food service operations use social media such as Twitter and Facebook to learn their guests' opinions about dining experiences. Guests can send comments (even while they are still visiting the food service operation!) to their families, friends, and contacts that complement or complain about a food service operation. Sometimes this feedback can be received before the guest leaves the property, and then corrective actions may be taken to better assure that guests leave with the problem resolved rather than with an unsatisfied complaint.

"MANAGE BY WALKING AROUND"

In some food service operations, dining room or other managers visit each guest table after the entrée is served to personally thank the guests for visiting and to determine if they are enjoying their meal and overall experience. When this tactic is used, the best information will not be learned from a "How is everything?" greeting such as that described earlier. Instead, a polite statement such as "Good evening, we're genuinely pleased that you are visiting us this evening. I would like to know if I can assist you with anything." Then, if a guest response indicates an improvement opportunity, a corrective action can be taken. As well, comments relating to the menu and food items can be logged into a hardcopy or electronic record that can be later shared with the kitchen manager.

PROPERTY WEB SITE INFORMATION

Increasingly, restaurants include a "review" or "guest comments" section on their Web sites. Guests are encouraged to access the Web site, learn about "what's new" at the property, and provide comments about recent dining experiences. Again, those related to the menu and specific food items can be logged and shared with food production personnel.

These Web sites are also used by persons wanting to learn more about local dining alternatives. Positive comments about the menu items, service, and other aspects of interest to most guests may encourage them to visit and, hopefully, their satisfaction will yield repeat business for the food service operation.

Input from Production Personnel

While some members of the kitchen manager's food production team will likely be eager to share their ideas, others must be asked to do so. Hopefully, the kitchen manager conducts regularly scheduled staff meetings. Discussions about the menu and menu items should be a regular part of these sessions. Assume, for example, that several guests have recently complained that vegetable accompaniments are over-cooked. Some food production personnel have likely worked in other food service operations and can bring suggestions, about what has and has not worked in other properties, to the discussion table.

Suggestions to resolve this problem can be requested during the meeting, discussion can follow, and potential resolution tactics can be implemented. As this is done, new procedures for cooking and holding vegetables will be those suggested by the food production team—not by the kitchen manager alone. This will bring satisfaction to the staff members who will think "the new process is our idea, and we really work together as a team."

Input from Service Personnel

As you know, service personnel probably have more opportunities for direct observation and interaction with the guests than do any other employees in the food service operation. If there are menu-related problems, they will likely know about them.

How can service employees make this information available? First of all, they should be requested and urged to do so. Second, they will likely only make comments a single time if, for example, they speak directly to the kitchen manager who, then, becomes angry, defensive, and/or even abusive.

Kitchen managers working for multi-unit food service operations have an additional source of information helpful with menu planning and analysis: they can talk to kitchen managers in other units.

A better approach: The dining room manager can implement a system in which service staff provide their observations at the end of each shift. This information can then be recorded and shared with the kitchen manager. Another alternative: The information can be discussed at each front-of-house staff member meeting, and the kitchen manager can attend this part of the meeting.

Input from Other Sources

Other sources of information about guest acceptance of the menu include restaurant reviewers and shoppers' reports.

RESTAURANT REVIEWERS

Some persons, especially in large cities, have a job that many people would like to have: They review restaurants for a living. Even television stations and newspapers in relatively small communities often employ someone whose responsibility, in part, includes the conduct of restaurant reviews. Their recorded or written observations will likely be of interest to many viewers/readers and should also be of concern to the kitchen manager and other members of the food service operation's management team.

Increasingly, Web sites (**blogs**) are available that post reviews from volunteers who contribute observations about their dining-out experiences. Some kitchen managers believe that persons are more likely to post these reviews if they are dissatisfied with some portion of their experience than if they are fully satisfied with all of it. This may or may not be correct. However, these reviews will be in the public domain, they cannot be controlled by the food service operation, and they will be read by persons who have not visited the property. Kitchen managers should routinely review the Web sites of which they are familiar to learn what is being said and to determine if helpful improvement suggestions about the menu or other aspects of the operation are made.

OVERHEARD IN THE KITCHEN

Blog—A Web site containing a list of entries in reverse order of posting (most recent entries at the top of the list) that provide personal insights about a common theme such as restaurants or travel.

SHOPPERS' REPORTS

You learned above that some food service operations hire "shoppers" who pose as guests and visit the property to learn what typical guests experience on a visit to the property.

It is very likely that the menu and specific menu items will be a significant aspect of a shopper's visit to a food service operation. If there is more than one shopper, each will likely order a different menu item, and they may want to try several items and share them with each other.

Kitchen managers and all others in the property should understand that the purpose of a shopper's visit is not to "catch people doing something wrong"; instead, it is to identify areas of excellence and improvement potential. Information provided from shoppers may be no more or no less important than that received from other guests. Instead, combined input from all menu evaluation sources should be carefully reviewed and should be used to make decisions about improvement alternatives.

INFORMATION ON THE SIDE
Use Meetings to Communicate

Many people believe that kitchen managers and other busy managers attend too many meetings and, as a result, must neglect important work. However, in a busy food service operation, menu and menu item improvement suggestions may come from several sources. Therefore, it is easy to see how information could be lost, de-emphasized because of current operating problems, and/or "filed for future action."

As suggested in this chapter, a special menu evaluation meeting may not be necessary. Instead, time can be spent on the topic at a meeting scheduled for another purpose. Example: A weekly food production meeting can include a brief discussion of the menu. If applicable, dining room managers can make brief visits to a food production meeting and present menu-related information provided by members of the food servers' team.

As is true with any improvement plan, a time frame for completion is generally advised. Finding a problem and resolving it "when we get around to it" is not a useful tactic. Instead, it is better to identify a problem, discuss alternatives, and determine and implement an improvement tactic. Then someone can be assigned to evaluate whether the planned change has, in fact, resolved or reduced the problem.

▮ NOW IT'S YOUR TURN

A PINCH OF THE INTERNET (10.1)

1. Want to learn more about guest comment cards, see examples, and read about guests' dining-out experiences? If so, type "restaurant guest comment cards" into your favorite search engine.
2. Many restaurants allow guests to post comments about recent dining experiences on their Web sites. Type in the names of some local or other restaurants that you like or have heard about to see whether guests' comments are posted.
3. Zagat Survey, LLC, is one of the largest and most popular organizations that review restaurants. Check out its Web site (www.zagat.com) to see some of this organization's restaurant reviews.
4. Dine.com advertises itself as "the world's largest restaurant guide written by you." Check out its site (http://dine.com) and then review some of the restaurants in your area.
5. To learn about restaurant mystery shoppers and the services they can provide to restaurant owners and kitchen managers, type "restaurant shoppers" into your favorite search engine.

COMPLETING THE PLATE QUESTIONS (10.1)

1. If you visit a food service operation and experience a problem with a menu or menu item, do you typically discuss your concerns with a management employee? Why or why not?
2. What are three examples of menu item evaluation information that you might want to ignore if you were a kitchen manager reviewing input from guests?
3. How would you determine restaurant review sites that you, as a kitchen manager, might routinely want to review for feedback about your operation?
4. If you were a kitchen manager, would you want your property to employ a shopper's service for routine but random visits to your property? Why or why not?
5. What are the five most important things that you as a kitchen manager would like to include on a guest comment card about your menu and menu items?

Kitchen Challenge Du Jour Case Study (10.1)

"Ladies and gentlemen, we may have a problem, and I would like to share it with you," said Raoul, the kitchen manager at Vernon's Restaurant, in a regularly scheduled food production meeting. "It seems that an increasing number of guests are complaining about the temperature of the entrées they are served. For example, during the first three months of this year, we received, on average, about two complaints per week. Of course, this is not good, and we were sometimes able to determine what specifically caused the problem on a specific visit."

"Lately, however, the problem appears to have worsened. For example, we received about five negative remarks about food temperature during each week of the last month. What do you think about this and, more importantly, what can we do about it?" asked Raoul.

"I'll tell you what the problem is," said Jasmine, a line cook at the restaurant.

"It's the servers, of course," she continued. "We have some new ones, we have some untrained ones, and we have others that just don't care. They don't know when to put the orders in, they claim to get overloaded with too many guests, and the food sometimes remains on the pick-up counter and ready to serve long before some of the servers pick it up. This happens all the time and then the untrained servers make us food production professionals look bad. It's all their fault!"

Questions

a) If you were Raoul, what would you say to Jasmine and others about these remarks during the meeting?

b) Would you discuss concerns with the dining room manager? Why or why not?

c) Would you invite the dining room manager to one of your food production team's meetings? Why or why not?

d) What are your thoughts about the use of a cross-functional team comprised of food production and food serving personnel to address this problem?

MENU ENGINEERING PROCEDURES

O B J E C T I V E

2. Describe detailed procedures helpful in determining the popularity and profitability of specific menu items when a formal menu engineering process is used:
   • All about popularity and profitability
   • Menu engineering worksheet
   • Menu engineering in action
   • Evaluation of menu revisions

Menu engineering can be used by kitchen managers and others on the food service operation's management team to determine the menu items that they want to sell: Those that are the most popular and the most profitable.

You learned in Chapter 5 that menu engineering is a method of menu evaluation that focuses on the sale of these popular and profitable items. It allows kitchen managers to use sales information to determine how frequently guests select specific menu items. They can also cost the ingredients in standardized recipes (see Chapter 7) and use this information to determine the profitability of each item.

All About Popularity and Profitability

Menu engineering identifies the popularity and profitability of competing menu items to help kitchen managers know how to manage them. These concepts are discussed in this section.

POPULARITY

What is a good definition of a popular menu item? While all kitchen managers can probably answer the question, "What are your most popular menu items?" the factors they consider as they respond may differ.

For example, the single item that sells more than any other competing item is the most popular. Which of the remaining items are "popular?" Some kitchen managers might indicate three, four, five (or other number) best-selling items, and others might say that any menu item that sells more than the "average" item is popular.

Menu engineering has a very specific definition of **popularity**. It assumes that a popular menu item is one that sells 70% of what it would be expected to sell if all items were equally popular.

Assume a menu has ten **competing menu items**. If all items were equally popular, then each menu item would be ordered 10 percent of the time (100% divided by 10 items = 10%). Since menu engineering assumes an item to be popular if it sells only 70% of what is expected, an item on a ten-item menu would be popular if it sold 7% or more of total sales (100% divided by 10 items) × .70 = 7%).

OVERHEARD IN THE KITCHEN

Popularity (menu engineering)—A factor along with profitability that describes menu items that kitchen managers want to sell. A menu item is popular if it sells 70% of expected sales (100% ÷ number of competing menu items × .70); see competing menu items (menu engineering).

Competing menu items (menu engineering)—The range of menu items within one menu category from which guests make their menu selection decisions. For example, children's menu selections and desserts would not normally compete with entrée selections on most menus, and they would not be included in a menu engineering analysis of entrées.

Let's look at three examples of how menu item popularity is determined for competing menu items using a simple two-step process to determine popularity. Step 1 involves calculating the percentage of total menu sales generated by one menu item if all menu items were equally popular. Step 2 involves determining 70% of the expected sales percentage discovered in Step 1.

EXAMPLE 1   **10 Item Menu**

$$\text{Step 1: } \frac{100\%}{\text{All menu item sales}} \div \frac{10}{\text{No. of competing menu items}} = \frac{10\%}{\text{\% of total menu item sales if all items are equally popular}}$$

$$\text{Step 2: } \frac{10\%}{\text{Item sales \% if all items are equally popular}} \times \frac{70\%}{\text{Menu engineering popularity goal}} = \frac{7\%}{\text{\% of total sales required for a popular menu item}}$$

As you review Example 1 above, note (in Step 1) that the percentage of total sales required if all items were equally popular (sold the same amount) is determined. This is done by dividing 100% (all menu item sales) by 10 (the number of competing menu items). Then (in Step 2), 70% of that equal sales percentage is calculated. The result, 7%, is the popularity goal for a ten-item menu. In other words, an item on a menu containing ten items is considered popular when menu engineering is done if the menu item sells 7% or more of menu item sales.

Now let's calculate the required popularity of menu items on menus of two additional sizes:

EXAMPLE 2   **20 item menu**

$$\text{Step 1: } \frac{100\%}{\text{All menu item sales}} \div \frac{20}{\text{No. of competing menu items}} = \frac{5\%}{\text{\% of total menu item sales if all items are equally popular}}$$

$$\text{Step 2: } \frac{5\%}{\text{Item sales \% if all items are equally popular}} \times \frac{70\%}{\text{Menu engineering popularity goal}} = \frac{3.5\%}{\text{\% of total sales required for a popular menu item}}$$

EXAMPLE 3   **25 item menu**

$$\text{Step 1: } \frac{100\%}{\text{All menu item sales}} \div \frac{25}{\text{No. of competing competing menu items}} = \frac{4\%}{\text{\% of total menu item sales if all items are equally popular}}$$

$$\text{Step 2: } \frac{4\%}{\text{Item sales \% if all items are equally popular}} \times \frac{70\%}{\text{Menu engineering popularity goal}} = \frac{2.8\%}{\text{\% of total sales required for a popular menu item}}$$

Kitchen managers can easily determine the number of each menu item sold by reviewing existing sales information. They might, for example, review point of sale (POS) information for the previous one or two months (the longer time period, the better!). With most POS systems, menu item sales information can be carried from month-to-month, and there are few, if any, arithmetic calculations required to determine the total number of each competing menu item that is sold.

Now that you learned how to calculate the popularity of menu items using the menu engineering process, let's turn our attention to the second factor: profitability.

PROFITABILITY

Menu engineering requires kitchen managers to pay attention to a menu item's **profitability**. As was true in our discussion of popularity above, some background information is needed to fully understand what profitability means when it is used in menu engineering.

OVERHEARD IN THE KITCHEN

Profitability (menu engineering)—A factor along with popularity that describes menu items that kitchen managers want to sell. A menu item is profitable if its contribution margin is equal to or greater than the weighted average contribution margin of all competing menu items.

When reviewing the definition above, note that profitable menu items have contribution margins (CMs) that are equal to or greater than the weighted average CMs of all competing menu items. In Chapter 5, you learned how to calculate a CM: menu item selling price (−) the menu item's food cost.

Traditionally, when kitchen managers considered the profitability of their menu items, they focused on each item's **food cost percentage**: menu item food cost ÷ menu item selling price. They believed that items with a lower food cost percentage would provide more profit than their higher food cost percentage counterparts. The reason: A lower percentage of revenue was required to purchase the food that generated the revenue. Therefore, more revenue would be "left over" to pay for nonfood costs and to contribute to the operation's profit.

OVERHEARD IN THE KITCHEN

Food cost percentage (menu item)—The food cost of a menu item divided by its selling price.

Figure 10.2 shows the difference between the contribution margin emphasized in the menu engineering process and the food cost percentage that has been the traditional profit goal. Note: Figure 10.2 assumes the food service operation offers only three menu items to simplify our discussion.

Let's look at Figure 10.1 more closely:

- Item A has a food cost of $3.50 (Column 1) and a selling price of $10.95 (in Column 2). Its food cost percentage is 32.0% (Column 3: $3.50 ÷ $10.95), and its contribution margin (Column 4) is $7.45 ($10.95 [−] $3.50).
- Item B has a food cost of $8.00 (Column 1) and a selling price of $18.25 (in Column 2). Its food cost percentage is 43.8% (Column 3: $8.00 ÷ $18.25), and its contribution margin (Column 4) is $10.25 ($18.25 [−] $8.00).
- Item C has a food cost of $12.50 (Column 1) and a selling price of $26.50 (in Column 2). Its food cost percentage is 47.2% (Column 3: $12.50 ÷ $26.50), and its contribution margin (Column 4) is $14.00 ($26.50 [−] $12.50).

Menu Item	Menu Item			
	Item Food Cost (1)	Item Selling Price (2)	Item Food Cost Percentage (3)	Item Contribution Margin (4)
Item A	$ 3.50	$10.95	32.0%	$ 7.45
Item B	$ 8.00	$18.25	43.8%	$10.25
Item C	$12.50	$26.50	47.2%	$14.00

FIGURE 10.2 Maximize the Contribution Margin

A review of all three items indicates that item A has a lower food cost percentage (32.0% in Column 3) than either Item B (43.8% in Column 3) or Item C (47.2% in Column 3). If the food service operation's profit goal is to minimize its food cost percentage, Item A is clearly the best. Item C, by contrast, has the highest food cost percentage (47.2% in Column 3). According to the traditional approach, it is the least profitable item.

Now let's look at the contribution margins of the three items. Item A with the lowest food cost percentage (32% in Column 3) also has the lowest contribution margin ($7.45 in Column 4). By contrast, Item C with the highest food cost percentage (47.2% in Column 3) has the highest contribution margin ($14.00 in Column 4).

Remember that the contribution margin is the amount of revenue that remains from an item's selling price after deducting its food cost. Therefore, Item C is the best item to sell because its contribution margin is $6.55 higher than item A:

$$\begin{array}{ccccc} \$14.00 & - & \$7.45 & = & \$6.55 \\ \text{contribution margin} & - & \text{contribution margin} & = & \text{additional contribution} \\ \text{(Item C)} & & \text{(Item A)} & & \text{margin} \end{array}$$

In other words, there is $6.55 more remaining from the revenue generated from the sale of Item C than from the sale of Item A after product costs are deducted from selling price. This additional $6.55 can be used to pay for all nonfood costs and to make a "contribution" to the operation's profit goals.

It should be clear, then, that the kitchen manager's goal should be to *maximize* the contribution margin and *not* to *minimize* the food cost percentage.

INFORMATION ON THE SIDE

"You Can't Bank a Percentage!"

You've learned that reliance on a food cost percentage to yield profit is less valuable than recognizing contribution margin dollars to be a measure of profit. Which would you rather have: a 90% profit on sale of $1.00 ($.90) or a 10% profit on a sale of $100.00 ($10.00)?

Wise kitchen managers realize that dollars—not percentages—should be considered when management decisions are made.

The emphasis on contribution margin instead of food cost percentage also applies when kitchen managers consider the **menu mix**: All of the servings of a menu item that are sold compared to the total sale of all competing menu items. For example, if 100 servings of beef stew are sold on a day when 500 total meals were served, the menu mix for the beef stew is 20% (100 beef stew servings ÷ 500 total meals served).

OVERHEARD IN THE KITCHEN

Menu mix—The total number of servings of a menu item that are sold compared to the total sale of all competing menu items.

Let's see how the food cost percentages and contribution margins can vary depending upon the sales mix. We'll do so by, first, reviewing Figure 10.3.

Let's see what Figure 10.3 tells us. First, note (in Column 1) that this food service operation sells three items and (in Column 2) the number of each item sold and the total number of items sold (1,300 meals) is shown.

Column 3 indicates the food cost for each item. For example, item A has a total food cost of $4.00 per meal, and item C has a food cost of $9.00 per meal. Note: Recall the emphasis in Chapter 7 that the only time a menu item's food cost can be assured is when standardized recipes are used and when each ingredient in the standardized recipe is costed with current market costs.

Column 4 indicates the total food cost to produce the number of each menu item that is served. For example, 600 servings of item A were sold (Column 2) and, since each serving cost $4.00 (in Column 3) the total food cost (Column 4) is $2,400.00 (600 servings of item A × $4.00 per serving = $2,400.00).

Menu Item (1)	Menu Mix (2)	Item Food Cost (3)	Total Food Cost (4)	Item Selling Price (5)	Total Revenue (6)	Contribution Margin (7)
A	600	$4.00	$2,400.00	$12.00	$7,200.00	$4,800.00
B	400	$7.00	$2,800.00	$15.50	$6,200.00	$3,400.00
C	300	$9.00	$2,700.00	$19.00	$5,700.00	$3,000.00
Total	**1,300 meals**		**$7,900.00**		**$19,100.00**	**$11,200.00**

$$\text{Food Cost Percentage} = \frac{\text{Total Food Cost (col. 4)}}{\text{Total Revenue (col. 6)}} = \frac{\$7,900.00}{\$19,100.00} = 41.4\% \text{ (rounded)}$$

$$\text{Average Contribution Margin} = \frac{\text{Contribution Margin (col. 7)}}{\text{Total Meals (col. 2)}} = \frac{\$11,200.00}{1,300 \text{ Meals}} = \$8.62$$

FIGURE 10.3   Menu Mix Week One—Food Cost Percentage and Contribution Margin

The selling price for each menu item is shown in Column 5, and the total revenue generated by each item is indicated in Column 6. For example, 600 servings of item A were sold (Column 2) and $12.00 was charged for each serving (Column 5). Therefore, the total revenue from the sale of all servings of item A is $7,200.00 (Column 6: 600 servings × $12.00 per serving)).

Column 7 indicates the contribution margin for each item. For example, item A generated total revenue of $7,200.00 (Column 6) and had a total food cost of $2,400.00 (in Column 4). Therefore, its contribution margin is $4,800.00 (Column 7: $7,200.00 revenue [−] $2,400.00 food cost).

Figure 10.3 also indicates that the total food cost for all 1,300 meals served was $7,900.00 (total of Column 4), and the total revenue generated from the sale of all items was $19,100.00 (total of Column 6). Therefore, the total contribution margin generated by all 1,300 items sold was $11,200.00 (Column 7: $19,100.00 revenue [−] $7,900.00 food cost).

Now that the total food cost, revenue, and contribution margin are known, it is possible to calculate the food cost percentage and the weighted average contribution margin for all 1300 meals that were sold. You'll note the procedures to do this and the resulting information at the bottom of Figure 10.3. During the time period covered by this menu mix analysis, the food service operation had a total food cost percentage (all menu items) of 41.4% (rounded), and it had an average contribution margin (all menu items) of $8.62.

Let's assume that the menu mix changed and the new menu mix and resulting financial information are shown in Figure 10.4.

When you review Figure 10.4, notice that 1,300 meals were again served, but the menu mix for the three menu items changed (see Column 2). Also notice that each menu item's food cost (in Column 3) and the selling price (in Column 5) remain the same as in Figure 10.3.

Since the menu mix changed, the total food cost, total revenue, and contribution margin for each item also changed from the menu mix data in Figure 10.4. For example, Figure 10.4 indicates that only 400 servings of item A was served (in Column 2) instead of the 600 servings noted in Figure 10.3. Therefore, the total food cost of item A (Column 3) is now $1,600.00: 400 servings (Column 2) × $4.00 per serving (Column 3), and the total revenue that was generated also changed: 400 servings of item A (Column 2) × $12.00 selling price (Column 5) = $4,800.00 (Column 6).

Since the food cost and revenue changed, the contribution margin (Column 7) also changed: $4,800.00 revenue (Column 6) [−] $1,600.00 food cost (Column 4) = $3,200.00. You'll also notice that the total food cost ($9,100.00 in Column 4) increased significantly from the total food cost in Figure 10.3 ($7,900.00 in Column 4 of that Figure). Also, the total revenue (Column 6: $20,850) in this Figure for the menu mix in week two increased slightly from $19,100.00 in Figure 10.3 for the menu mix in week one (Column 6). Finally, note that the contribution margin in this Figure for the menu mix in week two increased to $11,750.00 (Column 7) from $11,200.00 (Column 7) in the menu mix for week one in Figure 10.3.

Menu Item (1)	Menu Mix (2)	Item Food Cost (3)	Total Food Cost (4)	Item Selling Price (5)	Total Revenue (6)	Contribution Margin (7)
A	400	$4.00	$1,600.00	$12.00	$4,800.00	$3,200.00
B	300	$7.00	$2,100.00	$15.50	$4,650.00	$2,550.00
C	600	$9.00	$5,400.00	$19.00	$11,400.00	$6,000.00
Total	1,300 meals		$9,100.00		$20,850.00	$11,750.00

$$\text{Food Cost Percentage} = \frac{\text{Total Food Cost (col. 4)}}{\text{Total Revenue (col. 6)}} = \frac{\$9,100.00}{\$20,850.00} = 43.6\%$$

$$\text{Average Contribution Margin} = \frac{\text{Contribution Margin (col. 7)}}{\text{Total Meals (col. 2)}} = \frac{\$11,750.00}{1,300 \text{ Meals}} = \$9.04 \text{ (rounded)}$$

FIGURE 10.4   Menu Mix Week Two—Food Cost Percentage and Contribution Margin

The most important comparison, that of the total food cost percentage and the total contribution margin for the week one menu mix (Figure 10.3) and the week two menu mix (Figure 10.4) are repeated below:

Menu Mix	Food Cost %	Contribution Margin
Week Two (Figure 10.4)	43.6 %	$9.04
Week One (Figure 10.3)	(41.4%)	($8.62)
	2.2 %	$0.42

The comparison of food cost percentage and contribution margin information for the menu mix in week two and the menu mix in week one above reveals two important factors: The total food cost percentage for week two *increased* by 2.2 %, and the average contribution margin for week two *increased* by $0.42.

As you've learned, the traditional belief would be that the week one menu mix is most profitable because it produced a food cost percentage that is 2.2 % lower than menu mix in week two. However, you've also learned that, in reality, the week two menu mix is better because it has generated an average contribution margin that is $0.42 higher than the earlier sales mix. Note: The significance of a $0.42 increase in contribution margin is easier to recognize when you understand that it really represents the increase of $546.00 (1,300 meals $\times$ .42 cent per meal = $546.00) that remains after total food cost is deducted from total revenue, and that amount ($546.00) is available to pay for nonfood costs and to contribute to the operation's profits.

A careful review of menu mix information for weeks one and two reveals that the menu mix has changed, and more servings of the higher-priced item C were sold, and fewer servings of the lower-priced item A were ordered by guests. Your first thought might be that this change in menu mix is very difficult to achieve because many guests prefer lower-priced items. Therefore it will be difficult to increase the sale of higher-priced items and reduce the sale of the lower-priced menu items. If you believe this, you are correct; It is difficult to do. However, the purpose of menu engineering is to identify the popularity and profitability of competing menu items. When this information is known, there are numerous ways to influence the sale of the preferred items. Both of these topics will be discussed in detail in the remainder of this chapter.

Menu Engineering Worksheet

Kitchen managers can use a menu engineering worksheet to determine the popularity and profitability of competing menu items, and a sample is shown in Figure 10.5.

Note: This worksheet allows kitchen manages to manually evaluate the menu. While menu engineering software is available, it is important to understand the basic concepts, and procedures to evaluate the menu are the same even when an automated system is used.

At first, the menu engineering worksheet may appear difficult to complete. However, if you look at each column separately, understand what information is included in each column, and

Restaurant: _____   Date of Analysis: _____

Meal Period: ❐ Breakfast   ❐ Lunch   ❐ Dinner

(A) Menu Item	(B) Number Sold	(C) Menu Mix %	(D) Food Cost	(E) Sales Price	(F) Item CM	(G) Total Food Cost	(H) Total Revenues	(L) Item CM	(P) CM Type*	(R) Menu Mix Type**	(S) Menu Item Classification
Tuna Salad Plate	270	14.3	3.25	7.25	4.00	877.50	1957.50	1080.00	Low	Low	Dog
Beef Stew	490	25.9	4.25	8.50	4.25	2082.50	4165.00	2082.50	Low	High	Plow Horse
Fried Chicken	810	42.9	5.15	9.75	4.60	4171.50	7897.50	3726.00	High	High	Star
Sirloin Steak	320	16.9	8.25	13.50	5.25	2640.00	4320.00	1680.00	High	Low	Puzzle
	N					I	J	M			
Column Total	1890					9771.50	18,340.00	8568.50			
Additional Computations:						O = M/N (average CM) $4.53	Q (Popularity) = 100% / No. items × 70% 17.5%				

* Profitability
** Popularity

FIGURE 10.5 Menu Engineering Worksheet

know where to find the information, you'll see that it is easy to complete. The task will be worth the effort because of the help it provides in menu evaluation.

Let's see how the menu engineering worksheet in Figure 10.5 is completed:

- *Column A (Menu Item)* lists competing menu items. The menu being studied has only four competing items. Note: Few, if any, food service operations offer only four competing items. However, this simplified example illustrates all of the major concepts involved in menu engineering. Since menu engineering analyzes competing items, operations with different menu categories for breakfast, lunch, and dinner should perform a separate analysis for each menu. You'll note that the specific meal period for which the menu engineering review is being done can be indicated at the top of the worksheet.

INFORMATION ON THE SIDE

Menu Engineering Evaluates Competing Menu Items

You've learned that the term, "competing menu items," in menu engineering refers to menu items that normally "compete" with each other when guests make menu selection decisions. Most typically, kitchen managers are interested in evaluating their entrée selections although they could evaluate desserts, salads, soups and other à la carte-priced items that are listed in separate categories on the menu.

The evaluation of competing entrées should include its food cost and also the food costs for accompaniments such as salad or vegetable choice, bread and butter, and any other items that are included in each entrée's selling price.

Since only competing items are studied, items such as those on a "children only" section of the menu should be excluded. Specials concerns may apply to other items. Examples: If the operation features a "dinner for two" or a large pizza that is known, on average, to serve three guests, the number of these items sold will need to be adjusted accordingly when the menu mix is determined.

- *Column B (Number Sold)* reports the number sold of each item in Column A. Data is taken from sales history information that compiles sales over a previous time period. Increasingly, food service operations use point-of-sale (POS) systems that tally this information, and it will be found in POS system records. Alternatively, some properties may still use manual guest check systems, and this will require a hand tally of sales information unless it has been collected for other purposes such as purchasing or to verify revenue collection.

  If there is not a great variation in volume count, the history information for 4-6 weeks may be sufficient. However, if there is large variation in the menu mix on different days, a longer sales period will likely provide more helpful information.

- *Box N* reports the total number of all competing menu items sold during the sales analysis period. Note that 1,890 portions of the four menu items listed in column A were sold during the time period being studied on the menu engineering worksheet in Figure 10.5

- *Column C (Menu Mix %)* indicates the percentage of total sales (Box N) represented by each menu item in column A. For example, 270 portions of Tuna Salad Plate were sold (see Column B). This represents 14.3% (see Column C) of the total items sold during the period (1890 servings in Box N); 270 portions ÷ 1,890 total servings equal 14.3%.

- *Column D (Food Cost)* is the per-serving cost for every ingredient in each menu item in Column A when (a) items are prepared according to standardized recipes and when the recipes have been costed with current ingredient costs. We'll assume that the Beef Stew (Column A) includes a salad, biscuit, and butter portion. These items have a total per-serving food cost of $4.25 (Column D) when they are prepared according to currently costed standardized recipes.

- *Column E (Sales Price)* is the selling price listed on the menu for each menu item. The selling price of Fried Chicken (Column A) is $9.75 on the menu, and that price is listed for the item in Column E.

- *Column F (Item CM)* reports the contribution margin (item's selling price [−] food cost) for each item in Column A. For example, the Sirloin Steak has a contribution margin of $5.25 (Column F): $13.50 (selling price in Column E) − $8.25 (food cost in Column D).

- *Column G (Total Food Cost)* indicates the total food cost to produce all servings of each menu item that were sold. For example, 270 servings of Tuna Salad Plate were sold (see Column B). Each serving has a $3.25 food cost (see Column D). Therefore, the total food cost for all servings of Tuna Salad Plate that were sold was $877.50 (in Column G): 270 servings × $3.25 = $877.50.

- *Box I* indicates the total food cost incurred to produce all servings of all menu items. The total food cost to produce all 1,890 items sold during the menu evaluation period (Box N) is $9,771.50: the sum of the food costs for all menu items in Column G.

- *Column H (Total Revenues)* tells the total revenue from the sale of each menu item. For example, since 270 servings of Tuna Salad Plate were sold (Column B) at a per-serving selling price of $7.25 (Column E), the total revenue generated was $1,957.50: 270 servings × $7.25 = $1,957.50.

- *Box J* tells the total revenues generated from the sale of all menu items. For example, $18,340.00 was generated from the sale of all 1,890 menu items (Box N).

- *Column L (Item CM)* indicates the total contribution margin from the sale of each menu item. For example, Fried Chicken generated a total contribution margin of $3,726.00: $7,897.50 revenues (Column H) − $4,171.50 food costs (Column G) = $3,726.00.

- *Box M* indicates the total contribution margin from the sale of all menu items. For example, the 1,890 menu items sold (Box N) generated a total contribution margin of $8,568.50 (total of Column L).

- *Box O* indicates the weighted average contribution margin generated from all menu items: $8,568.50 total menu contribution margin (Box M) ÷ by 1,890 total meals (Box N) = $4.53.

  The kitchen manager now has determined the item-profitability goal for this menu: He/she wants to sell those items that have a contribution margin of $4.53 or more. Note: This is often referred to as the "**seat tax**."

OVERHEARD IN THE KITCHEN

Seat tax (contribution margin)—A slang term indicating the contribution margin of a menu item or (in menu engineering) the weighted average contribution margin for all items sold during the period under study.

- *Box Q (Popularity)* is used to calculate the popularity goal for each menu item. Note: You've learned that traditional menu engineering model defines item popularity to be 70% of expected sales.

   The menu engineering worksheet in Figure 10.5 has four menu items. If each was equally popular, it would represent 25% of all sales (100% ÷ 4 = 25%), and 70% of this expected sales percentage is 17.5% (25% × .70% = 17.5%). The kitchen manager now knows the most popular items on the menu: Those with a menu mix (Column C) of 17.5% or higher.
- *Column P (CM Type)* indicates whether the contribution margin of each item in Column A is lower or higher than the average contribution margin stated in Box O. For example, Tuna Salad Plate has an item contribution margin of $4.00 (Column F). This is lower than the average contribution margin ($4.53 in Box O), so it is listed as a low contribution margin item in Column P. By contrast, Fried Chicken has an item contribution margin of $4.60 (Column F). This is higher than the average contribution margin ($4.53 in Box O), and it is listed as a high contribution margin in Column P.
- *Column R (Menu Mix Type)* indicates whether the popularity of each menu item is higher or lower than the menu's popularity goal. For example, Tuna Salad Plate has a menu mix percent of 14.3% (Column C). This is lower than the menu's popularity goal (17.5% in Box Q), and it is reported to have a low menu mix percent in Column R. By contrast, Fried Chicken has a menu mix percent of 42.9% (Column C). This is higher than the menu's popularity goal (17.5% in Box Q), and it is reported to have a high menu mix percent in Column R.
- *Column S (Menu Item Classification)* gives a name to each menu item listed in Column A. The traditional names for menu items in each menu engineering classification are described in Figure 10.6.

When kitchen managers complete a menu engineering worksheet such as that shown in Figure 10.5, they will know how each competing item on their menu is classified. With this knowledge, they can begin to make decisions about how to best manage each menu item. In effect, then, the menu engineering process really begins *after* a menu engineering worksheet (Figure 10.5) is completed.

Menu Engineering in Action

What can kitchen managers do once they have learned about the popularity and profitability of their menu items? The answers to this question are very important because, as just suggested, the menu can only be improved if the knowledge gained from menu engineering analysis is used to make improvements. You'll learn about the challenges posed by and the tactics to effectively manage each of the four menu item classifications in this section.

PLOW HORSES

The challenge: Guests like these items and may visit the restaurant to order them. If this is the case, they cannot be removed from the menu even though they are not profitable.

Kitchen managers must discover how to increase the profitability of plow horses. One tactic involves considering how the item's food cost can be reduced because, as this occurs, the profitability (contribution margin) will increase. One obvious way to do this is to reduce the serving size. However, large portions that provide guest value may be one reason that plow horse items are popular.

Name	Profitability		Popularity	
Plow Horse	**Low**		**High**	
(Beef Stew)	A plow horse has a contribution margin that is less than the average contribution margin for all menu items.	Example: Beef Stew has a low profitability because its contribution margin ($4.25 in Column F) is less than the average contribution margin ($4.53 in Box O).	A plow horse has a popularity % that is equal to or higher than the menu's popularity goal.	Example: Beef Stew has a high popularity because its menu mix % (25.9% in Column C) is higher than the menu's popularity goal (17.5% in Box Q).
	Profitability		**Popularity**	
Dog	**Low**		**Low**	
(Tuna Salad Plate)	A dog has a contribution margin that is less than the average contribution margin for all menu items.	Example: Tuna Salad Plate has a low profitability because its contribution margin ($4.00 in Column F) is less than the average contribution margin ($4.53 in Box O).	Dogs have a popularity % that is lower than the menu's popularity goal.	Example: Tuna Salad Plate has a low popularity because its menu mix % (14.3% in Column C) is lower than the menu's popularity goal (17.5% in Box Q).
	Profitability		**Popularity**	
Star	**High**		**High**	
(Fried Chicken)	Stars have a contribution margin that is equal to or higher than the average contribution margin for all menu items.	Example: Fried Chicken has a high profitability because its item contribution margin ($4.60 in Column F) is higher than the average contribution margin ($4.53 in Box O).	Stars have a popularity % that is equal to or higher than the menu's popularity goal.	Example: Fried Chicken has a high popularity because its menu mix % (42.9% in Column C) is higher than the menu's popularity goal (17.5% in Box Q).
	Profitability		**Popularity**	
Puzzle	**High**		**Low**	
(Sirloin Steak)	Puzzles have a contribution margin that is equal to or higher than the average contribution margin for all menu items.	Example: Sirloin Steak has a high profitability because its item contribution margin ($5.25 in Column F) is higher than the average contribution margin ($4.53 in Box O).	Puzzles have a popularity % that is lower than the menu's profitability goal.	Example: Sirloin Steak has a low popularity because its menu mix % (16.9% in Column C) is lower than the menu's popularity goal (17.5% in Box Q).

FIGURE 10.6   Names of Menu Engineering Classifications in Figure 10.5

While each kitchen manager must consider how their specific food service operation might reduce food costs for low-contribution-margin menu items, two useful alternatives may be to:

- Replace expensive garnishes with less-expensive items.
- Replace high-cost menu item accompaniments such as a twice-baked potato with lower-cost alternatives, and re-price the more expensive items as à la carte. In other words, guests would have a choice of several accompaniments with each entrée, but they would pay an additional cost for more expensive items.

The profitability of plow horses will also increase if the selling price is increased, although the relatively low price may currently represent a value to guests and contribute to the item's popularity. This tactic may meet with the least guest resistance if the item is unique to the food service operation and is not available at competing properties. Unfortunately, there are probably few menu items for which this competitive edge is enjoyed.

If prices are increased, it might be better to do so in several stages rather than all at the same time. One interesting idea that involves an increase in selling prices is to add an additional menu item accompaniment at the same time. For example, consider a complementary dessert with a $1.00 food cost that is added to a plow horse meal with the selling price increased by $1.50. This might appear to be a good value for a guest while, at the same time, the profitability (contribution margin) will increase by 50 cents: $1.50 increased selling price − $1.00 increased food cost).

Other tactics to manage plow horses include shifting demand to more desirable items. For example, you learned about a menu's prime real estate in Chapter 5: Those areas of a menu that guests will likely view more often than others while they are deciding what to order. If the goal is to reduce the sale of plow horse items, they should not be located in these high-profile menu areas. Guests, especially frequent visitors, will still know about the item, and others will search it out. However, wise kitchen managers will place the items they want to sell (stars and puzzles) in the prime real estate areas of their menu.

Kitchen managers can work with their dining room manager counterparts to help shift guest demand to the desirable items. For example, servers can be trained to use suggestive selling techniques to recommend items that the food service operation wishes to sell (puzzles and stars), and plow horse items would not be on this list. Table tents and other **advertising** tools can be used to shift demand away from plow horses to more profitable items.

OVERHEARD IN THE KITCHEN

Advertising—The communication of a message about a product or service offered by a food service operation which is directed at a specific market of potential guests.

Another concern in managing plow horses relates to the labor cost required to produce them. You'll recall that food cost (not labor cost) is the only factor considered as contribution margins are determined with the traditional menu engineering process. Therefore, plow horses that require a significant amount of production labor to produce such as a made-from-scratch beef stew with "home-made" biscuits will cost the operation much more than a plow-horse counterpart made from a convenience item that requires little production labor (example preportioned hamburger patties). Kitchen managers may be able to justify plow horse items with little production labor since less revenue from the item's sale will be necessary to cover labor cost.

PUZZLES

The challenge: These items are profitable, and their sales should be increased because they are not popular.

You've learned that puzzles are items that the food service operation likes (they are profitable) but that guests do not frequently order (they are not popular). Tactics to manage puzzles, then, are almost the opposite of those you learned about above how to manage plow horses. Kitchen managers want to decrease the sale of plow horses and increase the sale of puzzles.

One basic approach is to make puzzles more attractive by adding value. For example, perhaps a larger serving size can be offered, especially if the current small size is judged to hurt its sales. More expensive meal accompaniments can be added, or another menu item such as a complimentary dessert or a fresh-baked loaf of bread might be included without an increase in selling price. These tactics will increase the food cost and, therefore, decrease the contribution margin. However, done effectively, the contribution margin might still be high enough to classify the item as profitable. Then, they will generate higher profit (contribution margin) levels if they are more frequently selected by the guests.

Puzzles should be located in high-profile locations on menus so that guests are more likely to see them. The use of suggestive selling tactics by servers and point-of-sale advertising should be directed at puzzles. Other examples of effective strategies include the use of badges on server uniforms ("The chef loves our pork chops!") and placing these items on menu boards in entrance areas where guests wait for tables.

The concept of guest value must always be considered when tactics to manage puzzles are planned. For example, perhaps puzzles are over-priced from the guests' perspectives. If they are, that could be one reason why they have high contribution margins but are not popular. It may be possible, therefore, to reduce the selling price to some extent, so that it will provide greater value that will drive higher guest sales while still maintaining profitability.

STARS

The challenge: Don't do anything that will impact the profitability or popularity of these items.

You know that star menu items are those that the food service operation really likes to sell because they are profitable, and guests like them because they are popular.

Star menu items present one time that the kitchen manager's best tactic is probably to do nothing! For example, applicable purchase specifications must indicate the quality of ingredients and then should not be changed. Serving sizes are probably of the correct size, and the standardized recipes used to prepare them are probably the best for the items.

Perhaps the strategy to use with stars is to encourage increased sales. As you learned above, this might be done by suggestive selling, by the use of point-of-sale advertising, and by assuring that these items are included in prime menu locations.

Some kitchen managers consider price increases for their star items. This may not be a good idea if the selling price represents a value that will decrease as the price rises. On the other hand, perhaps the item is not available elsewhere (example: The kitchen manager's property has a dining room overlooking a beautiful ocean seascape). Kitchen managers will likely need advice from the property's management team before making selling price decisions about stars.

DOGS

The challenge: It may be easy to remove dogs from the menu, but there could be some problems in doing so.

Menu items that are dogs are not liked by the food service operation because they are not profitable. Likewise, they are not of interest to guests because they are seldom ordered. It is often an easy decision to remove dogs from the menu. However, there may be times when this is difficult to do.

Consider, for example, a frequent guest who always orders this item and brings others to the food service operation for business lunches. Won't this guest be frustrated when the item is no longer available? Depending upon the item and how labor-intensive it is to prepare, perhaps the guest can be told that, "While the items is being removed from our menu, it will be available for your special order." As well, there may be little short-term harm in leaving a dog on the menu if it is made-to-order (there will be no left-overs), it uses only ingredients used in other dishes, it is made from convenience food products, and all its ingredients have a relatively long storage shelf life.

INFORMATION ON THE SIDE
You Can Go Broke Selling Only Stars!

There are few things that are certain in the food service industry, and this includes menu engineering. The use of this menu evaluation process can be very helpful but it, alone, cannot ensure success.

Food service operations are comprised of closely related subsystems and, as kitchen managers change a procedure in one subsystem, this can affect other subsystems. For example, assume that menu engineering is used to improve the sales of high contribution margin puzzles and stars. Assume also that only ten guests visited the property during the week, and each one of them ordered a star item. It is very unlikely that the total amount of revenue generated from the sale of these ten menu items will be sufficient to pay the food service operation's costs and the owner's profit requirements. Therefore, menu engineering cannot replace the need for marketing tactics to alert potential guests to the property and to encourage repeat guests to return to the property.

Menu planning and design, purchasing, receiving, storing, and issuing procedures, and other subsystems in the food service operation are all useful tactics, but they cannot guarantee success unless all the other subsystems are being used and effectively managed.

Evaluation of Menu Revisions

You've learned how the menu engineering process can be used to determine menu item classifications which, then, can drive the use of tactics to improve the food service operation's profitability. Menu engineering can also be used to objectively evaluate menu changes.

Let's consider a food service operation in which the menu has gone through revisions without using menu engineering procedures. Assume the kitchen manager is asked, "Is the new menu better than the old one?" The common response might include observations such as, "Yes, our guests seem to like it," and "The cooks haven't complained about the need to prepare some new menu items," and "Our revenues have increased somewhat with our new menu."

Now let's consider the response to this question about whether a menu change has brought about improvements when the kitchen manager has used menu engineering: "Our new menu is better than our previous one because we have increased our average contribution margin from $6.25 to $7.10 without a decrease in guest count." This kitchen manager recognizes that contribution margin is a very important factor in profitability. His/her counterpart in the above example only knew that revenues have increased. However, if food costs also increased with the revised menu there may not be higher profitability because the higher cost of food purchases may offset the revenue increases.

The kitchen manager has made the job of this food server easier because guests enjoy the menu items featured on the revised menu.

INFORMATION ON THE SIDE

"Menu Engineering and Banquet Menus"

This chapter has discussed how menu engineering can be used to improve à la carte restaurant menus. However, its use can also be expanded to banquet menus. For example, many food service operations offering banquet services make preplanned menus available to banquet planners. These menus may be those which have been popular with previous guests and which can be produced within the limitations of the food service operation's labor, equipment, and available production space.

The menu engineering process can be used to identify which banquet menus are the most profitable and popular. This information can, then, guide the banquet sales staff as they interact with potential function hosts. For example, they will know which menus should be suggestively sold. As well, they might offer a complementary menu item accompaniment as an incentive for specific menus to be selected. As a final example, banquet menus can be designed so their prime real estate is used for placement of the most profitable and popular menu items.

NOW IT'S YOUR TURN

A PINCH OF THE INTERNET (10.2)

1. To learn more about the basic menu engineering process and how it can be used to improve menus, type "menu engineering" into your favorite search engine.
2. You've learned that service staff can use suggestive selling techniques to influence their guests' purchases of preferred menu items. Type the term, "restaurant suggestive selling" into your favorite search engine to learn about this topic. Also, if you work in a restaurant, consider sharing the ideas you have learned with the dining room manager and using them in your work if you are a food server.
3. To learn more about menu item contribution margins, type the term, "restaurant contribution margin" into your favorite search engine.

COMPLETING THE PLATE QUESTIONS (10.2)

1. What are some factors that you as a kitchen manager would consider when deciding what time period for menu item sales should be studied when you complete a menu engineering worksheet?

2. What would you say to a kitchen manager who stated, "I don't need menu engineering to know the items on my menu that do and don't sell: My production records tell me everything I need to know"?
3. Some of the tactics that can be used to implement the results of menu engineering require assistance from the dining room manager and his/her service staff. What tactics might you as a kitchen manager use to share menu engineering information and to urge that suggestive selling and related tactics be used to improve the food service operation?
4. How would you as kitchen manager, who is also a member of the operation's menu planning and design team, use menu engineering results when the menu was revised?
5. Assume you were a kitchen manager in a multiunit food service organization that had two other properties in the same town. Assume also that all three properties used exactly the same menu. Would you suggest that menu engineering procedures be used for each of the three properties' menus? Why or why not?

Kitchen Challenge Du Jour Case Study (10.2)

"I think I've heard of everything now!" said Roger as he spoke to Yolanda during a coffee break on the morning shift of Vernon's Restaurant. Both were cooks who had worked together at the restaurant for several years.

"What are you talking about, Roger," replied Yolanda.

"Well," said Roger, "I'm talking about our new kitchen manager and all the changes she is making on our operation even though I don't think there's anything wrong with how things work now. Why do you think we are making so many changes in lots of our menu items? We've had no trouble with our menu—the guests all seem to like it, and they keep coming back, and we cooks have no problem preparing everything needed in the quantities required for each day's production."

"And now look what's happening," Roger continued. "First, we were told that we're going to make fruit pies and give away slices to guests that order a couple of our menu items. We've also increased the serving sizes of some items and reduced the sizes for others. We've added more potato choices, and some are included as part of the cost of the meal and others are priced separately. We've changed garnishes and have added and taken off several items from our daily soup and sandwich board offerings. Examples can continue, but you get the point I'm making: Lots of changes are going on around here when there was no need to make them, and I think they disrupt our operation."

Assume that you were the new kitchen manager at Vernon's Restaurant:

a) What are some things that you could have done to involve Roger, Yolanda, and other food production personnel when you began to do menu engineering and as you discovered that some changes were necessary?

b) What are some things that you could do now that you know that at least some of the cooks are upset about the changes?

c) How, if at all, could your food production team help you to determine what changes might be helpful as you implemented the results of the menu engineering process?

Overheard in the Kitchen Glossary

Revenue stream	Competing menu items (menu engineering)	Menu mix
Shoppers' report		Seat tax
Blog	Profitability (menu engineering)	Advertising
Popularity (menu engineering)	Food cost percentage (menu item)	

LESSON 10

If you are reading this textbook as part of a formal class, your Instructor may want you to apply and practice what you have learned in this chapter by completing Lesson 10 of the Pearson Education Kitchen Management Simulation (KMS). If you are required to complete KMS Lesson 10; read the **About Lesson 10** below, then go to www.pearsonhighered.com/kms for instructions on how to access and complete it.

After you have successfully completed the lesson, think about the way you, as a professional kitchen manager, would answer the **For Your Consideration** questions that follow.

About Lesson 10

This KMS lesson lets you practice the skills professional kitchen managers use when they analyze their menus for the purpose of making the menus perform better. These essential skills include determining which menu items are the most popular and which are the most profitable.

After you have determined the most popular and profitable menu items you sell, you can use the menu engineering process to make informed decisions about how to improve your current menu.

The results of applying menu engineering to your menu allow you to make specific changes in menu items that can lead to increased sales revenue and an improved bottom line. In this important lesson you will practice doing just that.

When you have completed the lesson you will have shown you understand how kitchen managers evaluate and improve their menus using a variety of menu management-related skills and strategies.

For Your Consideration

1. Some menu items are not very popular, but still remain on a kitchen manager's menu through many menu revisions. Why would a kitchen manager elect to retain such menu items? What are some specific steps kitchen managers can take to increase the number of times such items are selected by guests?

2. Some menu items have below average levels of weighted contribution margin (CM) but remain on a kitchen manager's menu through many menu revisions. Why would a kitchen manager elect to retain such menu items? What are some specific steps kitchen managers can take to increase CM of these menu items?

3. The menu engineering techniques you learned are generally applied to menus that have already been placed into use. What are some important menu engineering principles you think could be applied to menus being developed for restaurants that have not yet opened for business?

Kitchen Managers Analyze Sales and Control Revenue

Chapter Ingredients Outline

Learning Objectives

After studying this chapter, you will be able to:

1. Explain how effective kitchen managers use basic financial information to control their food service operations.
2. Discuss basic back-of-house procedures to control food revenue.
3. Recognize activities used by kitchen managers to assist the property's management team as they analyze sales information and control revenue.

COMING RIGHT UP OVERVIEW

As we begin the last chapter in this book, it is helpful to state something you've learned in the earlier chapters. Effective kitchen managers have many responsibilities that extend beyond menu planning, food purchasing and production, and managing their back-of-house staff. While these activities are of critical importance to every food service operation, today's professional kitchen managers also must know about and be comfortable with financial management concerns. Examples include the discussions of labor cost control in Chapter 3, the calculation of food costs in Chapter 9, and menu engineering analysis in Chapter 10.

This chapter focuses on two additional financial management concerns shared by kitchen managers: analyzing sales information and controlling revenue.

At first, these topics may seem strange in a book written for kitchen managers. Aren't these topics those which most concern dining room managers, who supervise food servers, and property managers, who prepare money for bank deposits?

The answers to the above questions are "yes;" revenue must be controlled at these times. However, the kitchen manager, as an important member of the food service operation's management team, also has responsibilities to forecast, control, and take corrective actions to manage revenues, and these tasks are discussed in this chapter.

The first part of the chapter will examine the basic process of management control. Too often, some managers think of control as involving only physical tasks such as locking the storeroom door or requiring the use of portion control tools. While these are examples of control, there is also an organized process to "managing numbers," and steps in that process will be discussed in detail. It is one thing, for example, to know how many meals were *served* and how much revenue was generated from those sales. It is, however, another thing to know how many meals were *produced* and how much revenue was generated from their sale. When the difference between the number of meals served and the number of meals produced is large, costs are increased and profits are reduced. These concerns are addressed in this chapter.

The chapter's second major focus is on specific back-of-house practices that impact revenue control. What types of revenue information are important to kitchen managers? How can kitchen managers use accurate revenue information to better manage their operations? These are among the questions to be addressed in our discussion of revenue control procedures that are important to all kitchen managers.

The chapter (and the book!) concludes with a case study about revenue control that shows how professional kitchen managers can work with others on the management team to determine and resolve revenue-related challenges. It will make the point that what happens in the front of the house is impacted by those managing food production activities.

CONTROLLING BY THE NUMBERS

OBJECTIVE

1. Explain how effective kitchen managers use basic financial information to control their food service operation.
   - Kitchen managers must know the numbers
   - The management control process
   - More about variance analysis
   - Close look at corrective action procedures
   - Implementing change

The term, "numbers," is a slang term that refers to money (financial) aspects of the food service operation. Perhaps, for example, you've heard the expression, "Accountants crunch numbers." They collect and interpret financial information. For example, if a restaurant offers à la carte and banquet dining, it is important to know the revenue that has been generated from **sales** in each **revenue center**. Recordkeeping systems generate information about total revenues for each of these operations, and that information may be compared to other data and used for planning purposes. These tasks are examples of "number crunching" performed by managers and/or accountants and others.

OVERHEARD IN THE KITCHEN

Sales—The number of menu items that are sold. Example: If ten hamburgers are sold, the sales of that menu item are ten.

Revenue center—A department within a food service operation that generates revenue. Example: A restaurant may have à la carte dining, beverage, and off-site catering departments (revenue centers).

Kitchen Managers Must Know the Numbers

Wise kitchen managers know that it doesn't do much good to know the amount of revenue collected unless that amount can be compared against expected revenues to determine if there is a difference. Note: You learned in Chapter two that the difference between an amount of expected revenue or expense (for example, from the budget) and the actual amount of revenue generated or expenses incurred is called a variance. **Corrective actions** must be taken to reduce undesirable variances.

OVERHEARD IN THE KITCHEN

Corrective action—A tactic implemented in efforts to reduce an undesirable variance between expected and actual revenues or expenses.

The process we are discussing is called management control, and there is much to learn about the process.

INFORMATION ON THE SIDE

Be Careful with Accounting Terms to Avoid Confusion

Three accounting terms are sometimes used to mean the same thing but really have different meanings. Kitchen managers should carefully avoid "communication problems" when they discuss financial information with other managers:

- *Sales*—The number of units (such as the number of hamburger sandwiches) that have been sold.
- *Revenue*—The amount of money generated from the sale of menu items. If a food service operation sells ten hamburgers at $5.00 each, it has *sales* of 10 and *revenues* of $50.00 (10 sandwiches × $5.00 each)
- *Income*—Another term for *profit*; the amount of money that remains from revenue after the expenses required to generate the revenue have been deducted.

OVERHEARD IN THE KITCHEN

Income—Profit; the amount of money that remains from revenue after the expenses required to generate the revenue have been deducted.

INFORMATION ON THE SIDE

Two Assumptions = One Fact!

Estimated revenue levels are of significant importance to kitchen managers and their peers on the management team as budgets are planned. Because most budgets begin with an estimate of revenue, a common tactic involves using the current year's revenue as a base and making adjustments for the next year.

Assume, for example, that the food revenue for the current year will likely approach $655,000. Assume also that the property management team plans to implement some marketing tactics and a new menu that they assume will increase the next year's revenue by 5%. They can, then, estimate next year's revenue level:

$$\underset{\textit{Current} \text{ year's revenue}}{\$655,000} \quad (\times) \quad \underset{\text{Percentage increase}^*}{105\%} \quad = \quad \underset{\text{Next year's budget estimates}}{\$687,750}$$

With estimated revenue determined, budget planners can next estimate the number of guests if they forecast the check average by using the following formula:

Estimated revenue (÷) by Estimated check average = Estimated number of guests.

In this example, if the check average is estimated at $26.50, the restaurant will serve 24,717 guests during the budget year:

$687,750 revenue (÷) $26.50 check average = 25,953 guests (rounded).

As you can see, assumptions about revenue levels and check averages yield information about the estimated number of guests. This information will be used by the kitchen manager to develop staffing plans, determine whether changes may be necessary to accommodate the number of meals to be served, and allow the kitchen manager to negotiate food purchase unit prices if **definite quantity contracts** are negotiated.

*Next year's budget will be the same as this year's budget (100%) plus an increase of 5%: 100% + 5% = 105%.

OVERHEARD IN THE KITCHEN

Definite quantity contracts—A purchasing method in which a buyer agrees to purchase a specific quantity of products over a specified period of time with a lower purchase unit price than if individual orders were placed during that time period.

The Management Control Process

One of the most important steps in management involves the **control** of resources such as revenue and food and labor costs.

OVERHEARD IN THE KITCHEN

Control—The multi-step management activity that involves (1) estimating the amount of revenue or expense, (2) determining the actual amount of revenue or expense, (3) making a comparison between the estimated and actual amounts, (4) taking corrective action if there is an undesirable variance, and (5) determining the results of the corrective actions that were taken.

Figure 11.1 shows the steps in the control process and provides an example of each. Let's review the control process illustrated in Figure 11.1:

- *Step 1*—The first step in the control process is to establish expected revenue levels. In Figure 11.1, the dining room manager, probably working with the restaurant's manager, establishes a forecasted or expected goal of $85,000 in food revenue for January, 20xx.
- *Step 2*—At the end of January, the actual amount of revenue generated in Dining Room A is determined. That amount was taken from point-of-sale (POS) records and is reported on an **income statement schedule** that indicates the amount of total revenue generated by each revenue center. Note: The amount of total revenue will be reported on the food service operation's income statement.

OVERHEARD IN THE KITCHEN

Income statement schedule—A supplement to the food service operation's income statement that shows financial details for each revenue center.

Step	Example
1. Estimate Expected Revenue	The operating budget establishes a revenue goal of $85,000 for Dining Room A for January, 20xx.
2. Determine Actual Revenue	The income statement indicates that the actual revenue is $79,000 for Dining Room A.
3. Assess the difference (variance) between expected revenue (Step 1) and actual revenue (Step 2)	The $6,000 negative variance ($85,000 − $79,000 = $6,000) is determined by the kitchen manager to be excessive and must be investigated.
4. Implement corrective actions to reduce the variance	Decision-making (problem-solving) tactics are used to generate and select alternatives to reduce the problem, and two tactics are implemented. First, managers will ensure that all food orders are entered into the POS system to help prevent collusion between server and production personnel. Second, they will establish a system to match the number of portion-cut steaks and other "A" items issued from storage with the number actually sold or left-over at the end of each meal period to account for all issued items.
5. Evaluate corrective actions taken to assess success (reduced variance)	Estimated and actual revenue in Dining Room A for the next month has a reduced variance but it is still greater-than-desired. Tactics addressing server revenue theft detection are then implemented and will be evaluated.

FIGURE 11.1 Steps in the Control Process

This kitchen manager is talking with a cook about a new procedure to address a problem identified by the management control process.

- *Step 3*—The difference between expected revenue (Step 1) and actual revenue (Step 2) is calculated and indicates a negative (undesirable) difference of $6,000. In other words, the revenue from Dining Room A should have been approximately $6,000 more than it was, if Dining Room A's revenue were accurately estimated in the budget.

- *Step 4*—Corrective actions must be implemented to reduce the variance. Two tactics involving food production personnel will be implemented. First, procedures will be used to ensure that servers enter guest orders into the POS system and, second, a system will be used to accurately determine the number of expensive "A" items that were actually produced and served. Note: information can then be matched with POS information to "double-check" that revenue was generated for all items sold.

- *Step 5*—The results of corrective actions must be evaluated to determine if they have been successful. In Figure 11.1, the new food production-related procedures were helpful, but there is still an undesirable difference between estimated and actual revenue in Dining Room A. The management team must believe that their revenue estimates are reasonable because they decide to implement additional server-related tactics to better assure that revenue collection is not compromised.

INFORMATION ON THE SIDE

Be Careful About the Food Cost Percent!

Many managers use food cost percentage information to evaluate their performance. Consider, for example, a manager who estimates a 33% food cost in the operating budget and then determines that the actual food cost was 35%.

Many managers would think that this 2% negative variance (35% actual ($-$) 33% forecast = 2% negative variance) is caused by higher-than-necessary food costs that relate to food production problems. However, recall how a food cost percentage is calculated:

$$\text{Food cost percentage} = \text{Food cost} (\div) \text{Food revenue}.$$

If the food cost percentage is higher than it should be, the above equation indicates that one reason may be because the food cost is higher than it should be. However, the equation also indicates another possibility: The food cost percentage is higher-than-expected because the revenue is too low! Managers attempting to discover causes for unacceptable variances must analyze control procedures in the back- and front-of-house. That is why this chapter on the kitchen manager's responsibility for revenue control has been included.

More About Variance Analysis

You have learned that the revenue control process involves estimating anticipated revenues, determining actual revenues, and comparing the two to determine if there is an undesirable difference between the two. This managerial process is called **variance analysis**.

OVERHEARD IN THE KITCHEN

Variance analysis (revenue)—The process of studying differences between estimated and actual revenue levels to determine if there are problems that require corrective action.

INFORMATION ON THE SIDE

"Let the Numbers Talk to You"

Numbers on a computer screen or printed on a computer print-out can't talk, or can they? Of course they can't "talk" in the way we do. However, when knowledgeable kitchen managers and other members of a property's management team look at operating data such as revenue levels, it can sometimes seem that the numbers are "shouting" about the financial status of the operation.

Managers who can "hear" the numbers speak have developed careful budgets or other plans that serve as benchmarks against which they compare actual financial results. They compare these statistics, and they understand ratios that show how a number such as food revenue compares to another number such as food cost. They don't look at the numbers "when they get around to it"; instead, they recognize the need for financial analysis to be among their most important duties.

After these managers "listen to the numbers," they make decisions that answer questions such as "Are there any problems and, if so, where are they occurring?" They also have the knowledge, experience, and "common sense" to know potential reasons why revenue and cost levels might be out of line. They know how to implement a decision-making process to establish priorities for corrective actions, to implement procedures designed to reduce variances, and to evaluate the results of their newly-implemented procedures.

Experienced kitchen managers really do let "the numbers speak to them," and their food service operation benefits from their ability to listen.

Variances between budgeted (estimated) and actual revenues are easy to calculate:

$$\text{Actual Revenue} - \text{Forecasted Revenue} = \text{Revenue Difference}$$

These differences can be positive (favorable) or negative (unfavorable).
Let's look at an example of dollar variance and percentage variance:

Dollar Variance (unfavorable)

$$\underset{\text{Actual Revenue}}{\$10,000} - \underset{\text{Forecasted Revenue}}{\$11,000} = \underset{\text{Revenue Difference}}{-\$1,000}$$

In this example, there is a negative (unfavorable) revenue difference because budget planners estimated that they would generate more revenue than they actually did. Note: Some managers use brackets to express a negative variance. For example, they would write ($1,000) rather than −$1,000 when expressing a negative (unfavorable) variance of $1000.

Dollar Variance (favorable)

$$\underset{\text{Actual Revenue}}{\$10,000} - \underset{\text{Forecasted Revenue}}{\$9,000} = \underset{\text{Revenue Difference}}{-\$1,000}$$

In this example, there is a positive (favorable) revenue difference because the actual amount of revenue generated was *greater* than the amount budget planners estimated.

Revenue variances can be calculated as a percentage difference using the following equation:

$$\text{Revenue \% Variance} = \frac{\text{Actual Revenue (\$)} - \text{Forecasted Revenue (\$)}}{\text{Forecasted Revenue (\$)}}$$

To illustrate, assume the following:

- Forecasted Revenue = $9,500
- Actual Revenue = $10,450

The revenue percentage variance is calculated as follows:

$$\frac{\text{Actual Revenue} - \text{Forecasted Revenue}}{\text{Forecasted Revenue}} = \frac{\$10,450 - \$9,500}{\$9,500} = 10\%$$

The food service operation generated a 10% positive (favorable) difference in revenue because the actual revenue was 10% greater than the forecasted revenue.

Now let's look at a second example:

- Forecasted revenue = $11,000
- Actual revenue = $9,500

In this example, there is a 13.6% negative (unfavorable) difference because the actual revenue is less than the forecasted revenue:

$$\frac{\text{Actual Revenue} - \text{Forecasted Revenue}}{\text{Forecasted Revenue}} = \frac{\$9,500 - \$11,000}{\$11,000} = (13.6\%)$$

DO ALL VARIANCES REQUIRE CORRECTIVE ACTION?

What factors influence whether a difference between estimated and actual revenue levels should be investigated so corrective action can be taken? Two special concerns involve the amount of the difference and whether the reason for the difference is understandable.

Assume that Vernon's Restaurant has estimated a food revenue goal of $70,000 for meals. At the end of the month the actual revenue of $60,000 is $10,000 less than the budget estimate: $70,000 − $60,000 = $10,000.

Is the $10,000 negative variance significant, and does it require investigation to determine reason for lower revenue? Only the management team at Vernon's Restaurant can answer this question. They, like all restaurant management teams, are confronted with numerous challenges, and they should know whether revenue analysis should receive a priority for their limited available time. Certainly, as the revenue difference increases and as it continues over a number of months, this concern will receive a higher priority.

INFORMATION ON THE SIDE

Which Variance Is Most Significant?

Experienced kitchen managers know that problems represented by the largest variance between expected and actual revenues should receive the priority for corrective action. Look at the information below to determine which variance is creating the greatest problem for the property's management team:

Revenue Source	Variance Between Estimated and Actual Revenue
Dining Room (à la carte)	(3%)
Banquet operations	(7%)

It is easy to see that the banquet operation has the largest *percentage* variance between estimated and actual revenue. In other words, revenue from the banquet operation should have been 7% more that it was if the estimated revenue goal was achieved. By contrast, revenue for the dining room was only 3% less than anticipated.

There is an old saying that, "You cannot bank a percent." To determine which of these two revenue sources should receive a priority for corrective action, it is much more important to know the *dollars* of variance rather than the *percentage* of variance, and this information is shown below:

Revenue Source	Revenue Goal	Revenue Variance %	Revenue Difference
Dining room	$89,500	(3%)	($2,685)
Banquet	$12,400	(7%)	($868)

The above information suggests the opposite of the information presented earlier. In fact, the reduced revenue generated by the dining room is a much more serious problem than the unrealized banquet revenue. The amount of lost revenue ($2,685) in the dining room is almost three times that of the lost revenue from banquet operations (only $867).

Kitchen managers contributing input to their food service operation's management team must recognize that priority concerns relate to bankable dollars not calculated percentages.

EXPLAINABLE AND UNEXPLAINABLE VARIANCES

In addition to the dollar and percentage amount of variance, management teams can make a distinction between **explainable variances** and **unexplainable variances**.

OVERHEARD IN THE KITCHEN

Variance (explainable)—A variance caused by one or more factors that managers understand.

Variance (unexplainable)—A variance caused by one or more unknown factors.

As the names imply, an unexplainable variance is one which requires investigation to determine the cause. For example, if the management team at Vernon's Restaurant does not understand why the à la carte dining room revenue variance exists, perhaps it should be investigated, and this task will be given a priority if the amount is considered significant. In contrast, if there was a lower-than-expected guest count for two days caused by severe weather, this may be an

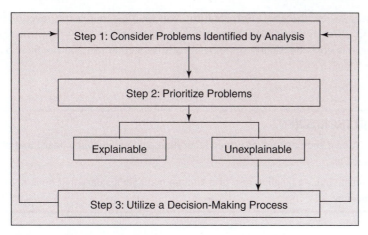

FIGURE 11.2   Steps in Corrective Action Process

easily explainable reason for the lower revenue. Then, investigation and subsequent corrective action is likely unnecessary.

Close Look at Corrective Action Procedures

After problems (significant variances between planned and expected revenue) are identified, they must be "managed." Figure 11.2 outlines a three-step process to do this. Let's look at these steps more closely.

STEP 1: CONSIDER PROBLEM(S) IDENTIFIED BY ANALYSIS

The management team must have a professional concern that it is their responsibility to address problems causing revenue variances. This philosophy of "being in control" may seem obvious. However, some managers think they are already doing the best possible job and they cannot, therefore, improve still further. Others, especially those with extensive experience in the restaurant business, may believe that there is a "short cut" to being successful ("Just take care of the guests," or "Only worry about food costs"). Then they focus their attention on only one part of the operation. Today's managers recognize that "every penny counts," and they challenge themselves to progress on their improvement journey toward **zero defects**.

OVERHEARD IN THE KITCHEN

Zero defects—A goal of no deviations from standards; there are instances where production, service, financial, and other goals are not met.

STEP 2: PRIORITIZE PROBLEMS

All members of the food service operation's management team are busy, and none of them can do everything they would like to. They must apply effective principles of time management to their work and address their most important concerns first. For example, which is more important: controlling revenue or controlling costs? If this question was asked of students taking an examination, the correct answer would probably be "both of the above"; however, busy managers must set priorities.

Assume a management team could develop corrective action tactics to increase revenues by $2,000 or to decrease costs by $2,000. Which would have the most positive input on the food service operation? To illustrate the answer, assume the following:

	Current	Increase Revenue by $2,000	Decrease Variable Costs by $2,000
Revenue	$ 12,000.00	$ 14,000.00	$ 12,000.00
Variable Costs (70%)	(8,400.00)	(9,800.00)	(6,400.00)
Fixed Costs (20%)	(2,400.00)	(2,400.00)	(2,400.00)
"Profit"	$ 1,200.00	$ 1,800.00	$ 3,200.00

When you review the above information, you see that increasing revenue by $2,000 only yields a $600 increase in profit ($1,800 profit − $1,200 profit = $600 profit increase). However, decreasing variable costs by $2,000 increases profit by $2,000 ($3,200 profit − $1,200 profit = $2,000 profit).

OVERHEARD IN THE KITCHEN

Cost, variable—A cost such as food or waged labor (that paid on an hourly basis) that changes in direct proportion to revenue.

Cost, fixed—A cost such as building rent or a kitchen manager's salary that does not change in direct proportion to revenue.

In other words, a revenue increase is offset by the additional variable costs needed to generate the revenue. By contrast, a variable cost decrease falls completely to the "bottom line."

This example suggests that, when possible, a priority should be given to cost control rather than revenue increases if the variances between estimated and actual amounts of both (costs and revenues) are similar. However, this can be much easier to talk about than to actually do.

For example, consider a restaurant with a large labor-cost variance and a smaller revenue variance. The management team decides that the best way to reduce the labor cost is to **negotiate** with the labor union about a change in job descriptions. This will, at best, involve a complicated and time-consuming process. However, little time may be required to train dining room managers to randomly use the **open check** feature on the POS system to verify that all items served to a specific table have been entered into the POS system to assure revenue collection. In these two examples, the significant labor-cost problem cannot be resolved immediately but the smaller problem can be addressed very quickly.

OVERHEARD IN THE KITCHEN

Negotiate—The process by which two or more parties determine the course of action that is best for each of the parties.

Open check (POS system)—Information contained in POS systems about food and beverage items on guest checks that have been opened but not closed; guests have ordered some food or beverage items but have not yet paid for them.

As suggested by Figure 11.2, the issue of explainable and unexplainable problems is important as priorities for corrective action are considered. Consider, for example, problems created by inoperative equipment. Higher-than-planned labor costs may be incurred for the additional labor hours that are needed until new equipment is purchased or the parts on order by the repair service are received. There is no further need to consider possible corrective actions in this instance because the kitchen manager knows about the problem and is addressing it.

In contrast, if labor costs are excessive and the reason is unknown (unexplainable), a well-thought-out decision-making process will be required to identify potential causes so they can be corrected. The amount of excessive costs created by problems with unexplainable causes will be a very important factor in establishing the priority for problem resolution.

UTILIZE A DECISION-MAKING PROCESS
After the management team has determined which unexplainable problem to address, a decision-making process to do so can be used. Figure 11.3 shows steps that can be used to reduce problems identified in the analysis process.

Step	Example
Step 1: Define the Problem	Guest check average for food has been declining for each of the last three months.
Step 2: Generate Alternatives	• Need to use suggestive selling. • Need to evaluate menu (food items available and design of the menu) to determine if changes can increase revenues. • Errors in procedures used to calculate check average information. • Theft of revenue by **collusion** between food servers and food production personnel.
Step 3: Evaluate Alternatives	• Guest shoppers did not observe suggestive selling; training is needed to implement suggestive selling program. • Menu recently re-designed; guest counts are up slightly. • An auditor has found no "bookkeeping problems" suggesting employee theft.
Step 4: Select the "Best" Alternative	Implement a suggestive selling program.
Step 5: Implement the Alternative	Train service staff; implement a contest in which all servers with a specified minimum guest check average win complimentary meals and sweatshirts.
Step 6: Evaluate the Effectiveness of the Solution	Determine the extent to which the guest check average increases after the suggestive selling training program has been implemented.

FIGURE 11.3   Basics of the Decision-Making (Problem-Solving) Process

OVERHEARD IN THE KITCHEN

Collusion—An agreement between two or more people to commit fraud.

Let's look at the decision-making process more closely:

- *Step 1: Define the Problem.* Sometimes a problem is obvious, and lower revenue volumes and/or increases in food costs may be examples. Sometimes, however, it is much more difficult to identify the problem. Consider, for example, the view of some kitchen managers that an increasing number of job applicants enter the workforce with a lowered work ethic than did those in previous years, and this contributes to high employee turnover rates. There are, probably, numerous societal, cultural, and other components of this issue that make problem identification difficult and its solution impossible.

  Some managers ask themselves, "What would the situation be like in the absence of the problem?" to help define and clarify the concern they want to correct.

  Unfortunately, in the real world, problems do not occur on a one-at-a-time basis. Instead, managers are typically confronted with many problems at the same time. They must, then, set their problem solving priorities using procedures such as those noted above.

- *Step 2: Generate Alternatives.* What can be done to address the problem? The management team should have "answers" to this question, but the food service operation's employees may have suggestions as well. The use of cross-functional teams can often help to identify potential solutions. For example, the problem that "some guests complain about slow service," may be addressed by the kitchen manager, dining room manager and servers, food production personnel and, perhaps, others who can provide ideas to help resolve the problem.

- *Step 3: Evaluate Alternatives.* Factors, including the ability to resolve the problem, costs, ease of implementing a solution, and the impact on other work processes are among those which can help to evaluate the solution alternatives generated in Step 2 above.

- *Step 4: Select the "Best" Alternative.* Often, the "best" solution involves utilizing aspects of several possible alternatives developed in Step 2.

- *Step 5: Implement the Alternative.* Employee training, purchase of necessary equipment/tools, **process revisions**, and trial study are among the tactics that may be helpful as solution alternatives are implemented.

OVERHEARD IN THE KITCHEN

Process revisions—Changes to work methods to reduce defects and increase opportunities to please the guests.

- *Step 6: Evaluate the Effectiveness of the Solution.* If the management team has considered what the situation would be like if the problem no longer existed (Step 1), this step becomes easier. Often, it is difficult to find solutions that totally eliminate the problem. In fact, a problem may still exist but, as a result of the decision-making process, its impact on the organization can be lessened. If the problem is still significant relative to others confronting the food service operation, the management team may decide to repeat the problem-solving process and to identify and implement new alternatives designed to reduce the impact of the problem still further.

Implementing Change

Perhaps the corrective action process will determine that an existing procedure which should be used has not been used consistently. This problem might be easily addressed with training and closer supervision. Perhaps, however, the decision-makers will conclude that new and different procedures are needed to keep revenues in line with budget estimates. Then the managers must become experts in implementing change.

One of the first obstacles that must often be overcome occurs when affected employees resist the changes. Employees who are used to doing something one way may not like changes in standard operating procedures. They may believe that "We have always done it this way!" or "We have never done it that way!"

They may be uncertain about how they will be affected by the change, and they may not want to take time, if necessary, to learn "new ways of doing things." They may also be concerned about the closer coaching and supervision interactions which may be used as the change is implemented and evaluated. If this human nature to resist change is understood and addressed, managers are much more likely to be successful in their change efforts.

OVERCOMING RESISTANCE TO CHANGE

There are several tactics that managers can use to overcome resistance to change. All will be more effective if, first, the manager has had a history of involving employees, explaining, defending and justifying why changes are necessary, and if the manager has historically been correct: The situation is "better" after the change than before it was made.

Let's look at some of these tactics:

- Involve employees in the decision-making process. You learned in Chapter 3 that use of a **participative management** style improves the quality of the decision-making process. It also makes the implementation of corrective actions easier because employees consider the decision to be "ours" rather than a decision made solely by the kitchen manager.
- Inform employees in advance about changes that will impact them.
- Select the best time to implement the change. For example, "trying something new" during an extremely busy shift is never a good idea.
- Share past successes; review other changes that have benefited the employees and the food service operation.
- Reward employees for sharing ideas in the decision-making process which benefit the restaurant and themselves.

OVERHEARD IN THE KITCHET

Participative management—A leadership method that increases the quality of the decision-making process by involving employees in the decision: use of this method can also improve the employees' job satisfaction.

CHANGE MUST BE MANAGED

Management teams who truly believe in the quality management process will be leading their staff members through **continuous quality improvement (CQI)** efforts.

OVERHEARD IN THE KITCHEN

Continuous quality improvement (CQI)—On-going efforts within the food service operation to better meet or exceed guests' expectations and to define ways to perform work with better, less-costly, and faster methods.

These teams recognize that, regardless of how small a change may be, the food service operation is improved because of any change that helps the organization to better meet its mission and goals. Employees working within a CQI environment look forward to it because they know about its benefits, and they will be active participants in it. Another advantage: CQI typically works "from the bottom up" because the employees closest to the situation are very likely to have improvement ideas about the areas of their responsibilities. Their suggestions about increasing revenues, for example, can be very creative and of great assistance. When a CQI philosophy is in place, kitchen managers are really facilitators who define a problem and then use a team approach to analyze, take corrective action, and implement necessary changes.

NOW IT'S YOUR TURN

A PINCH OF THE INTERNET (11.1)

1. Managers of food service operations may need qualified consultants to help with problem identification/resolution in the event that on-site managers cannot address the concerns. To learn about food service consultants and what they do, check out the Web site of the Food Service Consultants Society International: www.fcsi.org

2. How about an online library of great information to help you learn more about decision-making? Go to: www.bettermanagement.com

   Under the Topic Menu click on "Performance Management." The basic principles of decision-making and leadership discussed in many of these popular articles are applicable to food service managers as well as to leaders of other businesses.

3. To learn basic information about and see business plans for restaurants, go to: www.bplans.com

4. To learn how to use Microsoft Office Excel for variance analysis, go to: www.office.microsoft.com

   Enter "variance analysis" in the site's search box.

5. To learn basic information about revenue management in restaurants, go to: www.entrepreneur.com

   Enter "restaurant revenue management" in the site's search box.

COMPLETING THE PLATE QUESTIONS (11.1)

1. Many hotels and some, especially large, food and beverage operations form "executive committees" comprised of higher-level managers from each department. Among other responsibilities, these groups serve as cross-functional teams to provide diverse input about operating challenges that confront their organization. A restaurant utilizing this approach will likely include the kitchen manager on the committee. What are the advantages to the organization and the kitchen manager when this tactic is used? What are potential disadvantages?

2. The chapter makes the point that some food production managers are more comfortable when they consider their role to be limited to management of food and labor. Others recognize the importance of these concerns but also understand the importance of management control and analysis processes such as those discussed in this chapter. What is your view, and how do you defend it?

3. If you were a food production employee in an operation "rolling out" new operating procedures to better control revenue, would you like to be involved in the decision-making process? Why or why not? Do you think other staff members would have the same view that you do? How, if at all, would your responses to these questions impact how you would manage back-of-house employees?

4. Assume you were a kitchen manager and discovered that one of your food production employees was colluding with a food server to steal revenue and/or food products from the restaurant. What would you do?

5. The chapter provides details about steps that could be used to control revenue. How could these same steps be used to control food or labor costs or other resources that are the responsibility of most kitchen managers?

Kitchen Challenge Du Jour Case Study (11.1)

Billy was one of the most popular students in the high school located in Specialville, a small community in the Midwest. He was busy with activities that included being the captain of his school basketball team and a grill cook at a local restaurant. He dated Janet, another popular student who, coincidentally, was a food server at the same property.

One of the reasons that Billy and Janet were so popular was that they were worked together to provide free meals to their friends when those friends visited the restaurant while Billy and Janet were at work.

The process was very simple. Sally would enter, for example, an order for a soup and dessert in the POS system. When picking up the soup she would tell Billy that one of their friends was in the dining room and wanted a grilled hamburger steak or pork chop. Billy would, then, prepare this item, and Janet would take it to their friend when she picked up something else for another guest.

Billy and Janet talked about this plan before they began to steal from the property. Billy had commented, "What's the big deal; the restaurant is always busy, and I'll bet the owner makes 95 cents for every dollar he collects." Janet agreed and countered with her justification; "Restaurant owners and managers know that some employees steal, and some guests leave without paying. They just build this cost into their budget and always make out okay."

a) Indentify at least one thing that is wrong with the statements that Billy and Janet made to each other to justify their thefts.

b) What are two signs that the restaurant owner, manager, and/or bookkeeper should notice that would indicate a potential theft of product and lower-than-appropriate revenue levels?

c) Assume you were the restaurant manager and you discovered the problem:
   - What would you do about Billy and Janet?
   - What changes would you make in the existing food ordering/pick-up procedures to best ensure that this theft method could not be used by other food production/service personnel in the future?

KITCHEN MANAGERS AND REVENUE CONTROL

OBJECTIVE

2. Discuss basic back-of-house tactics to control food revenue.
   - Role of technology in revenue control
   - Revenue calculations and analysis procedures
   - Revenue calculations and production planning

When many persons think about revenue control in food service operations, they first think about the general manager who develops revenue control procedures and dining room managers who develop and monitor revenue collection procedures used by food servers, cashiers, and any other cash-handling staff members. However, kitchen managers are important members of the property's management team. They have responsibilities that impact revenue control as well.

Role of Technology in Revenue Control

Few areas within food service operations have undergone more technological change in the last fifteen years than those related to revenue control. Managers know that quality information is a key ingredient in decision-making, and those who use advanced technology revenue collection and control systems do so because they:

- Desire assurance that all revenue that is owed is collected
- Want a faster and more convenient method of collecting revenue information
- Prefer to undertake a more detailed analysis of the revenue information that is generated

Enhancements to already advanced hardware and software technology make the gathering of important management information easier-to-use than ever before.

TECHNOLOGY HARDWARE

The technology available in modern point-of-sale (POS) systems continues to expand. Management teams must assess which technological developments can truly help their operations. Once known and purchased, they can reduce operating costs while providing high-quality information useful for decision-making. **Hardware** advances in POS systems come rapidly.

OVERHEARD IN THE KITCHEN

Hardware (computer)—Physical equipment such as the input/output device, central processing unit, and external storage device required for a computerized system.

Common hardware items include:

- *Monitors.* **Monitors** can serve two functions. They can be used as input and/or display devices. In the kitchen, monitors display guest orders in the sequence they are received, and they can highlight order revisions. They must be designed to withstand the extreme heat, smoke, and humidity conditions that exist in many kitchens. In dining areas, monitors often feature touch screen entry and are designed to maximize server effectiveness by thoughtful placement of data entry functions, easy-to-view content displays, and efficient print functions.

OVERHEARD IN THE KITCHEN

Monitor (computer)—A computer system output component that displays text and graphics.

- *Input Devices.* Input devices allow servers to place orders. Traditionally this has been done by entering orders onto a keypad or touch screen. Recently, however, new input devices have been developed that are handheld for wireless connection to the main POS terminal. This allows servers to enter guest orders without having to return to a central POS station or to wait in line while other servers manually enter orders into a POS terminal. Typically, these devices use a touch pad for information entry, but new models can be programmed to recognize an individual server's handwriting.
- *Receipt Printers.* Receipt printers serve two functions. In the kitchen, they can provide production personnel with hard copy orders even in the extreme temperatures in many preparation areas. In the dining room, they allow servers to quickly and quietly print guest receipts with speed, accuracy, and reliability.
- *Charge Card Readers.* Card readers that allow servers to authorize credit, debit, and other types of charge cards have advanced in speed and ease-of-use. They have historically been designed as an integral part of the POS system to eliminate the need to connect separate card readers with the POS system. Increasingly, these devices are wirelessly connected to an operation's POS to allow for easy at-the-table guest payment.

TECHNOLOGY SOFTWARE

Today's sophisticated **software** programs are designed either as stand-alone personal computer programs or are included as part of a larger POS system. The choice of these programs depends greatly upon the type of food service operation in which it will be used. For many managers, however, helpful software packages related to revenue collection and control include those that:

- Maintain revenue totals from different POS locations within one restaurant.
- Maintain revenue totals from different POS locations within a restaurant chain or group.
- Compare products produced from sources of information entered in POS systems to actual inventory reductions.
- Reconcile guest check totals with total revenue collected.

Kitchen managers use revenue and sales data entered by servers into point-of-sale (POS) systems to help forecast production needs.

- Identify the amount of revenue generated by the restaurant, day, menu item, shift and/or server.
- Separate revenue generated by type of guest (dine-in, carry-out, drive-through, delivery, private party banquets, off-site catering, and bar/lounge).
- Reconcile credit card deposits with credit card sales.
- Maintain **accounts receivable** records.
- Create the revenue portion of the income statement after reconciling bank deposits, charge card sales deposits, returned checks, and bank deposits.

OVERHEARD IN THE KITCHEN

Software—Programs that instruct (control) a computer system's hardware components.

Accounts receivable—Money that is owed to a food service operation that has not been received. Example: revenue owed by a company with an account at the property that pays its outstanding bill at the end of each month.

Those who select a food service operation's software programs understand that connecting the various programs will be very important. For example, a software program that computes total server gratuities (tips) for a specific payroll period is good. One that interfaces those server gratuity totals with the food service operation's own payroll-generating software is better! Software programs that connect (interface) with the property's current software is preferable to a new program that does not.

INFORMATION ON THE SIDE
Work Station Printers and Display Units Enhance Communication

Technology makes it easy for busy food servers to communicate with food production personnel. The older method of food servers shouting "order!" in a noisy food production/server pick-up area is being replaced by silent **work station printers** that transmit food order information after entry into a POS system to the food production area or even to a specific space within it (examples: grill or salad area). As the name implies, this equipment issues a print-out that corresponds to the items ordered by guests that must be produced in the kitchen.

For operations that do not need work copy output, **kitchen display units** provide the same information on a computer monitor, and there is no need to handle pieces of paper.

Both of these hardware items accomplish two objectives: They make communication easier and more accurate and assure that all orders prepared in the kitchen have, first, been entered into the POS system.

OVERHEARD IN THE KITCHEN

Work station printer—A remote printing device in a kitchen area that prints a food order that has been entered into the POS system.

Kitchen display unit—A video display monitor that shows orders entered into a POS system on a monitor in a kitchen workstation area.

Revenue Calculation and Analysis Procedures

While technology makes revenue data available on, literally, a real-time basis, management teams in many food and beverage operations typically analyze revenue data at the end of each month. Then, revenue data from the POS system is used to help develop income statements and, as discussed earlier in this chapter, initial revenue information reported on the income statement can be compared with budget estimates during the control process.

In addition to monthly analysis, revenue information can be compared more frequently. For example, several key indicators such as guest check average might be reviewed every day, and the guest check average for each week might also be noted. The reason: The management team desires to take corrective actions on a timely basis, and a one-time review at the end of each month does not allow this to occur.

Special situations such as the introduction of a new menu or an advertising campaign highlighting specific menu items will also likely cause managers to review POS system information more frequently than they might do otherwise.

INFORMATION ON THE SIDE

Revenue Information Is Available; It Does Not Need to Be Calculated!

Modern POS systems can manipulate financial information in almost anyway desired without the need for manual calculations. Why, then, should busy managers know how to make arithmetic calculations to yield the same information generated by their POS systems?

There are three reasons for this, and all relate to the fact that knowledgeable food service managers are "smarter" than technology. First, the managers must decide what information should be collected, and how it should be reported. Then the POS system can be programmed to "do what the managers want." For example, could the management team make better decisions if revenues were separated for different meal periods (breakfast, lunch, and dinner)? If so, managers must identify the specific information required and then program the POS with the hours that each type of meal is served. Then they must develop and implement operating procedures so, for example, information about breakfast revenue concludes when the last guest during that time period is served and information for lunch begins to be collected when the first guest orders a mid-day meal.

A second example occurs when the managers decide how the guest check average should be calculated. Should, for example, revenue from food sales be separated from alcoholic beverage sales? The POS system can do it either way (or many other ways). However, the system used must be driven by what the management team wants, and this should consider the information that is best for decision-making.

A third reason that managers must be able to make manual calculations arises when budget estimates and other operating standards are developed. POS systems use actual operating results to generate ratios and other desired information. Managers should consider the impact of menus, check averages, and budgeted labor costs on staffing schedules, for example, and information entered into POS systems relating to historic sales will be helpful. Therefore, "while the machine can do it," managers must also have knowledge and skills required for the most basic calculations that impact and report the results of their food service operation

There are several common ways that revenue information is evaluated, and we'll discuss some of them in this section.

CALCULATION OF TOTAL REVENUE

Management teams in all food service operations want to know the total amount of revenue generated during the month, week, and day, and they may also want that information for the **day-part** or even by the hour.

OVERHEARD IN THE KITCHEN

Day-part—A segment of the day that represents a change in menu and customer response patterns; for example, the time during which breakfast or lunch menus are offered.

The following examples show what information is required, and how managers can calculate revenue information to help their decision-making.

Note: Each of the calculations described below can be made for a month, week, day, or any other time period.

A) **Total Revenue from Food Service Operations.** These calculations separate revenue by products/services sold:

	Example
Food revenue	$780,000
Beverage revenue	210,000
Other Revenue*	35,000
Total revenue	$1,025,000

*Examples may include banquet room rental or audio/visual charges for meetings conducted at the property.

B) **Total Revenue by Location.** These calculations separate the revenue generated in separate areas within the food service operation:

	Example
À la carte dining room	$ 97,000
Banquet room	40,000
Lounge/bar	19,000
Total revenue	$156,000

Note: In this example, revenues in the à la carte dining room include those generated from the sale of food and beverages.

C) **Total Revenue by Type of Guest.** These calculations separate revenue by the type of food services purchased by the guests:

	Example
Dine-in	$47,500
Carry-out	8,200
Drive-through	16,800
Banquet	14,000
Bar/lounge	$ 9,500
Total revenue	$96,000

Total revenue calculations can sometimes be easier to understand when the *percentage* of revenue generated by a specific revenue source such as dine-in operations is calculated, and this is easy to do.

The formula used to calculate the percentage of total revenue from each source is:

Revenue Source Sales ÷ Total Revenue = Revenue Source Contribution Percent

For example, to determine the percentage of total revenue generated from dine-in operations in (C) above:

$$\frac{\text{Revenue \%}}{\text{Dine-In Operations}} = \frac{\text{Revenue from Dine-In Operations}}{\text{Total Revenue}} = \frac{\$47,500}{\$96,000} = 49.5\% \text{ (Rounded)}$$

CALCULATION OF CHECK AVERAGE

Revenue analysis can also focus on and make use of check average information. You'll recall from our discussion in Chapter 3 that check average (also called "guest check average") is the average amount of money spent a guest during one visit.

Calculation of the check average is simple: total revenue from sale of foods and beverages divided by the total number of guests served.

EXAMPLE

Assume the total à la carte dining room revenue in (B) above is for the month, and 6,065 guests were served. The check average for the month is:

$$\frac{\text{Total Food \& Beverage Revenue}}{\text{Number of Guests Served}} = \frac{\$96,000}{6,065 \text{ Guests}} = \$15.85 \text{ (rounded)}$$

A) **Check Average Time of Day: Meal**

Let's assume the following information applies to one week, and we'll use the above equation to calculate the check average:

Meal Period	Total Revenue	Number of Guests	Check Average
Breakfast	$ 9,500	985	$ 9.64*
Lunch	$18,400	1,225	$15.02
Dinner	$27,095	1,231	$22.01

*Example: total revenue ($9500) ÷ number of guests (985) = $9.64 check average

B) Check Average by Location

To calculate the check average by location, use the following equation:

$$\text{Location Check Average} = \frac{\text{Revenue Per Location}}{\text{Number of Guests Served}}$$

Assume the following for one day:

Location	Total Revenue	Number of Guests	Check Average
À la carte dining room	$1,710	120	$14.25*
Banquet room	$1,112	65	$17.10

*Example: total revenue ($1710) ÷ no. of guests (120) = $14.25 check average

Note: A review of the above information indicates that check average data based on location (example: à la carte dining room) may not be very helpful to decision-making when food is served for more than one meal period in the location. The reason: The check average is likely to differ between each of these meal periods. Therefore, it is typically most useful to calculate check average by time of day (by meal) such as in (A) above.

C) Check Average by Type of Customer

Want to know the check average of each guest based upon the food services they purchased? The calculation to do so is easy:

$$\text{Type of Guest Check Average} = \frac{\text{Revenue By Guest Type}}{\text{Number Of Guests Served}}$$

Assume the following for one month:

Type of Guest	Total Revenue	Number of Guests	Check Average
Dine-In	$30,375	2,250	$13.50*
Carry-Out	$11,288	1,050	$10.75
Banquet	$17,100	1,200	$14.25

*Example: total revenue for dine-in guests ($30,375) ÷ number of guests (2250) = $13.50

CALCULATION OF REVENUE VARIANCES

You learned about the importance of calculating variances between budgeted and actual revenues earlier in this chapter, and this section explores how the process can be used for specific categories of revenue information.

A) Calculation of Revenue Variance by Location

Assume forecasted and actual revenues for Vernon's Restaurant were as follows for February, 20xx;

	Forecasted Revenue	Actual Revenue	Variance ($) (4)	Variance (%) (5)
À la carte Dining Room	$90,000	$94,000	$ 4,000	4.4%
Banquet Room	$54,000	$48,000	$−6,000	−11.1%

The differences (dollars) for both locations can be easily calculated:

$$\text{Actual Revenue} - \text{Forecasted Revenue} = \text{Revenue Difference}$$

- For the à la carte dining room: $94,000 − $90,000 = $4,000 (column 4)
- For the banquet room: $48,000 − $54,000 = [−] $6,000 (column 4)

The revenue percentage differences for both locations are calculated by the following:

$$\frac{\text{Acutal Revenue} - \text{Forecasted Revenue}}{\text{Forecasted Revenue}}$$

- For the à la carte dining room:

$$\frac{\$94,000 - \$90,000}{\$90,000} = 4.4\% \ (\text{column } 5)$$

- For the banquet room:

$$\frac{\$48,000 - \$54,000}{\$54,000} = -11.1\% \ (\text{column } 5)$$

Note: Each of the calculations described above can be made for a day, week, month, year or other time period, if revenue forecasts for the time period are available.

B) Calculation of Revenue Variance by Time of Day: Meal

Assume forecasted and actual revenues for Vernon's Restaurant (which is open for lunch and dinner) were as follows for March, 20xx:

| | Revenue | | Variance | |
	Forecasted (2)	Actual (3)	($) (4)	(%) (5)
Lunch	$28,500	$24,900	−$3,600	−12.6%
Dinner	$42,500	$44,500	$2,000	4.7%

Remember the equation to calculate dollar and percentage variances noted above:

$$\text{Actual Revenue} - \text{Forecasted Revenue} = \text{Revenue Difference}$$

- For lunch: $24,900 − $28,500 = −$3,600 (column 4)
- For dinner: $44,500 − $42,500 = $2,000 (column 4)

The equation to calculate revenue percentage differences for both meal periods was also reviewed above:

$$\frac{\text{Acutal Revenue} - \text{Forecasted Revenue}}{\text{Forecasted Revenue}}$$

- For lunch:

$$\frac{\$24,900 - \$28,500}{\$28,500} = -12.6\%$$

- For dinner:

$$\frac{\$44,500 - \$42,500}{\$42,500} = 4.7\%$$

Note: Each of the calculations described above can be made for a day, week, month, year, or other time period, if revenue forecasts for the time period or available (column 4).

C) Calculation of Revenue Variance by Type of Customer

Assume forecasted and actual revenues for Vernon's Restaurant, which offers dine-in and carry-out food services were as follows for the week (seven days) of 7/16/xx:

| | Revenue | | Difference | |
	Forecasted (2)	Actual (3)	($) (4)	(%) (5)
Dine-In	$8,400	$8,150	−$250	−3.0%
Carry-Out	$2,700	$2,400	−$300	−11.1%

By now, you should be able to apply the equation used to calculate the dollar difference in forecasted and actual revenues for dine-in and carry-out customers:

$$\text{Actual Revenue} - \text{Forecasted Revenue} = \text{Revenue Difference}$$

- Dine-In:

$$\$8,150 - \$8,400 = -\$250$$

- Carry-Out:

$$\$2,400 - \$2,700 = -\$300$$

As well, you should be able to calculate the % difference:

- Dine-In:

$$\frac{\text{Actual Revenue} - \text{Forecasted Revenue}}{\text{Forecasted Revenue}} = \frac{\$8,150 - \$8,400}{\$8,400} = -3.0\%\,(\text{column 5})$$

- Carry-Out:

$$\frac{\text{Actual Revenue} - \text{Forecasted Revenue}}{\text{Forecasted Revenue}} = \frac{\$2,400 - \$2,700}{\$2,700} = -11.1\%\,(\text{column 5})$$

Each of the calculations described above can be made for a year, month, week, day, or any other time period.

Revenue Calculations and Production Planning

How do kitchen managers know the quantity of food to produce for a specific shift? In some operations, production planning is relatively simple because guest counts are steady, and there are few surprises, for example, about the number of guests to expect for lunch on Tuesday or dinner on Saturday evening. These properties are even more fortunate when there is little variation in the popularity of each menu item.

Let's assume that Vernon's Restaurant serves approximately 250 customers on an "average" Saturday night. Different guest counts occur when there is a community event (guest counts will likely increase) or problems such as inclement weather (when guest counts will likely decrease). Assume further that the POS system information suggest that 10% of the guests typically order a 6 oz. sirloin steak entrée. In this case, the number of steaks the kitchen manager will need to have available each Saturday is easy to calculate: 250 guests × 10% = 25.

The kitchen manager knows that a few extra steaks must be available in case there is a "run" on them, and this is no problem because the steak is on the menu, and the product is always available.

CASE STUDY: KITCHEN MANAGERS AND REVENUE CONTROL

Objective

3. Recognize activities used by kitchen managers to assist the property's management team as they analyze sales information and control revenue.
   - The situation at Vernon's Restaurant
   - The kitchen manager's team
   - The shopper's report
   - Case study wrap-up

This book and especially this chapter has emphasized that concerned professional kitchen managers are responsible for more than back-of-house food production and related duties. They should be an important member of the cross-functional property-wide management team. In total, all of the managers with their different duties and experiences can provide creative input to challenges confronting their food service operations. They know that a problem confronting any manager really affects all managers because success of the food service operation—their employer—can be impacted by how well the challenge is addressed. This concluding section provides a review of revenue control as it impacts kitchen managers.

The Situation at Vernon's Restaurant

The executive management team at Vernon's Restaurant was not surprised when Vernon, the restaurant owner and general manager, opened the weekly meeting with the following remarks:

"Business has been pretty good here the last four months if the definition of 'pretty good' is the parking lot full of cars and our dining room full of customers. It is not pretty good, however, if the term means that the revenues are similar to or even higher than they were during the same four months last year and if it means we are exceeding our budgeted revenue goals for these four months."

"How can our revenues be lower if our guest counts are not down? Well, our POS system suggests some clues. First, our check averages are lower by about $2.00 per person. Second, and even worse, the items we really want to sell the most based on our ongoing menu engineering analysis are losing popularity. Third, we have had an increase, although only a slight one, in negative customer comments about food quality and portion sizes."

"We are a closely-knit management team, and we have never had comments from service personnel that, if the cooks would prepare better food we could sell it, nor have we had comments from kitchen managers that we could sell food products we want, including appetizers and desserts, to increase the check average if only the servers would do a better job of selling the items."

"I know we are all very busy resolving current operating problems, but these are unusual times. We must give an additional priority to determining what is wrong and to fixing it. Here's what I want you to do:

- The kitchen manager should meet with the production team to carefully consider the situation I just described: lower check averages, reduced sales of our most profitable items based on menu engineering results, and food quality and portion size complaints.
- The dining room manager should meet with the front-of-house staff to discuss the same three concerns.
- Both the food production and the dining room teams should identify potential problems and suggest how they can be resolved.
- The kitchen and dining room managers should then meet, discuss each team's recommendations, and develop a proposal to be presented at our next executive management meeting, which will be in about ten days."

"If you have any questions, or if I can help in any way while your teams address these concerns, let me know. I do want to invite a shopper's team to visit several times during these coming ten days. Otherwise, I want to learn your suggestions and then our executive management team can consider what to do."

The Kitchen Manager's Team

After an initial meeting to discuss challenges, the kitchen manager's team met a total of three times.
The Kitchen Manager's Report:

We think several things should be done:

- *Increase the check average*—We can offer a value-priced special dessert and appetizer-of-the-day that will contribute money above the contribution margin to increase our check average. Maybe we can begin a "dessert club" with a free dessert or appetizer after a specified number is purchased.
- *Management of the menu*—Our most profitable items are often, but not always, our highest priced items. As the sale of our profitable items decrease, the check average also decreases. However, the financial problem is worsened because the contribution margin that is "buried" in the check average also goes down. We could re-do our menu engineering analysis to confirm which items are currently the most popular, although study of our POS system will also indicate this. In fact, our problem with the sale of profitable items probably relates, in part, to some guests' comments about food quality and portion size.
- *Assure food quality and portion size*—I admit that our food quality has suffered a little in recent months. The reasons, while explainable, are not defensible. They include the need to purchase many of our products from a new supplier since the previous one who provided many ingredients for our entrées has gone out of business. Unfortunately, we have paid a little less attention to food purchase specifications for our "A" items, and the reduced quality of some ingredients affects some of our menu items, including those which are most profitable. They are, then, not re-ordered by our regular guests, and these ingredient issues relate to the food quality complaints. Needless to say, an emphasis on suppliers following purchase specifications has already begun.

We can't determine why there are complaints about portion size. Our production employees consistently follow standard recipes, including the use of the required portion control tools. I work with the food production line staff on most of our busy nights, and I have not noticed any problem with portion size.

The Dining Room Manager's Report:

- One reason the check average may be low is that we have discontinued our suggestive selling contest in which all servers who have a check average above a specified amount for five shifts receives a gift certificate for use at several local retail stores. Suggestive selling training along with the reimplementation of this program should increase the check average. As well, the same tactic (suggestive selling) should help to increase the sale of our profitable items as identified by menu engineering.
- Our team doesn't have any comments about food quality or portion sizes. Our servers say they are receiving some negative feedback from the guests compared to the past. However, they don't notice a significant trend. As well, our team thinks that issues about food quality and portion size would best be addressed by the kitchen manager and his team.

The Shopper's Report

The two shopper's reports were much more positive than negative but did suggest two findings:

- On both visits the shoppers indicated that, when servers were asked about suggestions, comments such as "generous servings" and "We can provide you with a doggy bag" were mentioned, and they could also hear these comments being made at a near-by table.
- During one visit, the shopper's team was seated close to the server station and parts of conversations between servers could be overheard. At one point, the server mentioned to a peer that she was going out with a person as soon as he finished cooking. The name of the cook was the same as one who was working that shift.

Case Study Wrap-Up

In just ten days, the Vernon's Restaurant executive management team had generated several ideas about the three challenges that confronted them:

- Lower check averages could be caused by the lack of suggestive selling by servers. This might be resolved by suggestive selling training, implementation of a server check average contest, and the offering of daily special value-added appetizers and desserts.
- The lower popularity of profitable menu items could be caused by lack of suggestive selling and guests' concerns about food quality and portion size.
- Food quality complaints may be due to a failure to follow through on the use of food purchase specifications because of a supplier change, and portion size complaints might stem from more-aggressive servers who exaggerated when they explained menu item portions.

The shopper's report comment about a potential relationship between a food server and a cook made the owner/manager think about revenue security issues. He didn't suspect that the server was colluding with the cook and bypassing the POS system. On the other hand, he did recognize the need to review cash handling procedures for all service personnel. After all, he reasoned, one reason that the check average had decreased may be because revenue is low due to a service security issue.

After the reports with recommendations about each of the problems were given, Vernon's owner/manager summarized the experience "There is an old saying that food service is comprised of a number of closely-related subsystems, and as one subsystem is affected so are all the others."

"I think that this concept was proven in the problem resolution process we just experienced. Production staff can cause problems for service staff and the restaurant. As well, service employees may create issues for production personnel and the restaurant. We really do need to be a team. We cannot separate revenue control and food production by convenient ideas such as 'servers are responsible for revenue, and kitchen personnel are responsible for food production.' In fact, we are all responsible for every activity that impacts our operation because we are all affected by it."

This kitchen manager is proud because he knows he can identify and resolve operating challenges as he moves forward on the journey towards culinary excellence.

NOW IT'S YOUR TURN

A PINCH OF THE INTERNET (11.2)

1. New computer software related to restaurant revenue collection and control appears frequently. To stay abreast of new products, go to: www.foodsoftware.com

   Bookmark the Web site and return to it regularly for updates.

2. Some new input devices have been designed to read a food server's handwriting and send requested orders directly to the kitchen or bar. To see one handwriting recognition program, go to: www.actionsystems.com

3. Point-of-sale (POS) system hardware and software are becoming increasingly sophisticated. To view a Web site developed exclusively for the selling of advanced technology POS products, go to: www.posworld.com

COMPLETING THE PLATE QUESTIONS (11.2)

1. What are three ways that activities of the kitchen manager and his/her team can impact the food service operation's check average?

2. What are several information items generated by POS systems that you, as a kitchen manager, would like to know about each day?

3. What kind of information would you, as a kitchen manager, be interested in learning from food servers? How would you obtain this information?

4. What would you do if you were a kitchen manager and several guest comments were made about poor food quality, and you just didn't believe they could be true?

5. Servers often relay guests' requests about special order items to kitchen managers. If you were a kitchen manager, what factors would you use to determine whether the special order items would be prepared? Would you permit special orders? Why or why not? If you would, what special factors would you consider?

Kitchen Challenge Du Jour Case Study (11.2)

Kevin was the kitchen manager at "We've Got What You Want" restaurant. It offered a fairly standard soup, salad, and entrée menu with a twist: every item was priced as à la carte so customers could purchase and pay for only those specific items that they wanted.

After two months of operation, the restaurant manager met with Kevin to discuss a problem: "Our revenue is not on forecast, and I've been trying to figure out why for several weeks. One thing I've noticed is that, especially when we're busy, some of our service staff take the preportioned dinner salads from the salad-pick-up refrigerator in the kitchen without entering the sale in the POS system. As you know, servers don't need to order this item from the production crew; they can just walk in to the kitchen and get these salads."

"I really don't think they are stealing," the manager continued." Most of our sales are by credit or debit card, and there is no way they can receive cash. What I think is happening is that they become rushed, take the salads to their guests, and think to themselves that they will enter the item into the POS system for printing on the guest check before the guests leave. Then, of course, they often forget to do so."

"Well, that's interesting," said Kevin, "I wonder if the same thing is happening with our loaves of freshly baked bread and our selection of desserts. Those items which are also selected by service staff rather than being passed over the hot food counter by production personnel."

"Yes," replied the manager, "I've thought of that as well, and it's easy to consider the significant revenue loss that we could be encountering."

"Well," said Kevin, "What do you think we should do about it?"

"That's why I wanted to talk to you Kevin. I think there is a simple solution and I want to get your input. Basically, I want to ask you and your staff to keep a running count of the number of each of the salads, loaves of bread, and desserts that are taken to the servers' pick-up areas. For example, if the meal period begins with 24 bowls of salad and 24 more salad bowls are added during the shift that means 48 salads were placed in the refrigerator during the shift. If, for example, our POS system says we sold 42 during the shift, we should have 6 salads remaining at the end of the shift."

"Well," replied Kevin, "I guess that's one way to handle the problem, and I think it would work. The bad news is that it is one additional task that we in the kitchen don't need, especially in the middle of the busiest time periods when majority of these self-select items would be sold."

"I understand that, Kevin," said the owner, "However, it seems logical that the counting should be done by someone back here because that's where the pick-up area is. Do you have any other suggestions?"

a) Can you think of any other solutions that Kevin could suggest to the owner?
b) Assuming you cannot think of any alternative tactics, what are the biggest problems that Kevin would have in revising procedures for this counting task to be done?
c) How exactly should Kevin design the procedures to count these products? Be specific.
d) What opportunities do both the owner and Kevin have to explain to everyone in the restaurant that the food production staff are really partnering with service staff to help the restaurant meet its financial goals?

Overheard in the Kitchen Glossary

Sales	Variance analysis (revenue)	Open check (POS system)	Monitor (computer)
Revenue center	Variance (explainable)	Collusion	Software
Corrective action	Variance (unexplainable)	Process revisions	Accounts receivable
Income	Zero defects	Participative management	Work station printer
Definite quantity contracts	Cost, variable	Continuous quality	Kitchen display unit
Control	Cost, fixed	improvement (CQI)	Day-part
Income statement schedule	Negotiate	Hardware (computer)	

KITCHEN MANAGEMENT SIMULATIONS
Where Content Meets Context!

LESSON 11

If you are reading this textbook as part of a formal class, your Instructor may want you to apply and practice what you have learned in this chapter by completing Lesson 11 of the Pearson Education Kitchen Management Simulation (KMS). If you are required to complete KMS Lesson 11; read the **About Lesson 11** below, then go to www.pearsonhighered.com/kms for instructions on how to access and complete it.

After you have successfully completed the lesson, think about the way you, as a professional Kitchen Manager, would answer the **For Your Consideration** questions that follow.

About Lesson 11

This KMS lesson lets you practice the skills professional kitchen managers use every day to analyze their sales and contribute to the effective control of the revenue generated in their operations.

Effective kitchen managers understand that the more they know about how their operations' revenue is generated, the better decisions they can make about how to manage their kitchens. For that reason, this lesson shows how kitchen managers carefully assess their revenue generation based on the physical location in which the revenue was generated, by the time of day the revenue was generated, and by the type of customer making food and beverage purchases.

Because a food operation's total revenue is dependent on both the number of guests served and how much each guest spends, the lesson also allows you to practice calculating guest check averages based on location, time of day and the type of guest served.

The lesson concludes by showing how kitchen managers compute the differences (both in amount of money and by percentage) between the revenues that were forecasted to be achieved during a specific period of time and the actual revenue generated during that same period.

You will have completed this lesson (and the entire Kitchen Management Simulation!) when you have performed all of the calculations critical to a kitchen manager's assessment of revenue generation.

For Your Consideration

1. Why is it important that kitchen managers know exactly how much revenue has been generated in their operations on a daily basis? On a weekly basis? On a monthly basis?
2. Food service operations can achieve revenue increases by attracting more customers (increasing guest counts) or by selling more food to each guest visiting their operation (increasing check average). Which approach to growing revenues do you feel would be easiest to implement? Which approach would generate the most profits? Explain your answers.
3. Forecasting future food and beverage revenue generation in an operation is an important, but sometimes difficult, task. What specific pieces of information identified in this lesson could be used by a kitchen manager to help increase the accuracy of his or her revenue forecasts? How would their use increase the accuracy of the forecast?

PROFESSIONAL KITCHEN MANAGEMENT GLOSSARY

"A" Items (purchasing)   The relatively few products purchased by a food service operation that cost the largest percentage of the money spent to purchase all food products.

Accompaniment (menu)   An item such as a salad, potato, and/or other choices that are offered with and included within the price charged for an entrée.

Accounts   A term used by suppliers to identify the organizations to whom they sell products.

Accounts receivable   Money that is owed to a food service operation that has not been received. Example: revenue owed by a company with an account at the property that pays its outstanding bill at the end of each month.

Accrual accounting system   An accounting system that matches expenses incurred with revenues generated. This is done with the use of accounts receivable, accounts payables, and other similar accounts.

Advertising   The communication of a message about a product or service offered by a food service operation which is directed at a specific market of potential guests.

Aesthetic   Relating to one's sense of beauty.

Aficionado (wine)   A person who knows a great deal about wine.

À la carte menu   A menu in which each food item served during the meal is sold at a separate price, and the total guest charge depends upon the items selected.

Allergy (food)   An unusual response to a food triggered by the body's immune system. Allergic reactions to food can cause serious illness and even death.

American service (banquet)   Menu items are portioned onto service plates that will be served to banquet guests.

Americans with Disabilities Act (ADA)   Federal legislation that prohibits discrimination against people with disabilities in public accommodations, transportation, telecommunications, and employment. It applies to private employers, state and local governments, and certain other organizations with 15 or more workers.

Appetizer   A food item served as the first course in a meal to stimulate one's appetite; sometimes called starter course.

Application form   An early step in the employee selection process in which applicants provide job-related information that helps kitchen managers determine whether they are suitable for the position.

As-purchased (weight)   The weight of a product before it is prepared or cooked; also called "AP weight."

Attrition   A reduction in the workforce caused by voluntary separation.

Audit trail   A step-by-step record that allows financial data to be traced to its source.

Authority   Power; the ability to do something including to make decisions.

Autocratic (leadership style)   A leadership approach in which decisions are typically made and problems are resolved without input from affected staff members.

Back-door selling (purchasing policy)   The act of a supplier attempting to contact or influence a food production employee without approval of the kitchen manager.

Backflow   The backward flow of contaminated water into a drinking water supply that is caused by back pressure in a building's plumbing system.

Background check   A review of a job applicant's criminal history, credit, driving record, or other information that relates to an applicant's suitability for employment.

Back-of-house   An industry term for employees, positions, and/or departments that have little direct guest contact.

Banquet   An event in which all or most guests are served items on a pre-selected menu.

Banquet event order   A form used by food sales, production, and serving personnel to detail all requirements for a banquet. Information provided by the sponsor is summarized on this document and becomes the basis for the formal agreement between the client and the hospitality operation; often abbreviated "BEO."

Banquet services coordinator   The person representing the food service operation who interacts with banquet clients to assure that the event being planned exactly meets the clients' needs; also called banquet sales coordinator; in large hotels, this responsibility might be part of the activities performed by a convention sales coordinator.

Bar code   Lines of information that can be scanned into a computer system; bar code technology is used to update inventory information and for other purposes.

Base selling price (menu item)   The benchmark selling price of a menu item calculated by the use of an objective pricing method. After its calculation, kitchen managers may modify the actual selling price based upon marketing issues, competitive pricing structures, and the "psychology" of pricing.

Batch-cooking   The preparation of food needed in large quantities in small volumes (batches) to maximize food quality by reducing holding times until service.

Benchmark   The search for the best ways to do things and then comparing these ways to how a food service operation does them to learn how well the operation is doing.

Benchmark (standard)   A standard against which to compare and improve one's products or services.

Benefits (employee)   Indirect financial compensation paid to attract and retain employees or to meet legal requirements. Some benefits are mandatory (example: social security taxes) while others are voluntary (example: vacation days).

Bid (competitive)   A supplier's response to a supplier's request for price quotation.

Bin number (wine)   A number telling the location in a wine cellar where a specific wine is stored. Bin numbers are often provided to allow guests to order wines by number rather than their name.

Blind tasting   The process of evaluating food items in a way that raters are not aware of the recipe's ingredients, preparation methods, or other information when they sample the food items.

Blog   A Web site containing a list of entries in reverse order of posting (most recent entries at the top of the list) that provide personal insights about a common theme such as restaurants or travel.

Body language Nonverbal communication, including gestures and eye movements, that send information about a person's intentions to another person.

Bonafide Occupational Qualification (BOQ) A qualification that is judged to be reasonably necessary to safely or adequately perform all job tasks in a position.

Boutique (brewery) A small-volume business that produces very high quality beer that is typically distributed within a small area.

Brainstorming A method to gain ideas from group members in which each person makes suggestions without comment by other members of the group.

Broken case (room) A storage area used to store partial purchase units of food products that have been issued. For example, some operations issue products such as canned goods in full purchase units (cases) even if only partial units are needed. If two cans of vegetables are removed from a case containing six cans, the broken case has four cans remaining that are stored in a broken case room for quick access as needed.

Broth A clear liquid soup made by simmering meaty cuts in water until the desired flavor, body, and color are developed.

Budget (Operating) A plan that estimates revenues and expenses for a specific period of time.

Buffet A style of food service in which menu items are generally selected and portioned by guests as they pass along one or more serving counters. Some buffets use food production personnel to carve roast beef or ham and to make omelets or other items to order.

Buffet service A service style in which guests select and portion menu items as they pass along one or more service counters. In some operations items such as omelets are made to order, and other items such as rounds of beef are carved to order.

Bureaucratic (leadership style) A leadership approach that involves "management by the book" and the enforcement of policies, procedures, and rules.

Buyers (qualified) Persons with the authority to make purchase decisions for their organization.

Calibrate To check or verify. For example, the thermostat of an oven should be calibrated (verified) on a routine basis to confirm that the internal temperature is that for which the thermostat has set.

Call brand (liquor) A specific brand of liquor requested by a guest. Typically, these brands are more expensive and of a higher quality than the brands that would be served if no specific brand was requested.

Call-in The term for employees who, when they are scheduled to work, notify managers that they will not work.

Capital The amount of money invested in a food service operation by its owners.

Carafe A glass bottle used to serve wine or water.

Career ladder A plan that shows how one can advance to more responsible positions within a food service operation. Kitchen managers develop career ladders to plan and schedule training or other educational activities to help employees be promoted.

Cash accounting system An accounting system that considers revenue to be earned when it is received and expenses to have occurred when they are paid for.

Cash flow The total amount of money (cash) received and spent by a food service operation during a specific time period. Bills must be paid when they are due, and cash must be available to do so.

Cash on delivery (COD) A transaction in which a buyer pays the full amount owed when products are delivered.

Casserole An entrée that can include combinations of meat or seafood and pasta such as lasagna or spaghetti or cheese and pasta such as baked macaroni and cheese.

Catering The process of selling a banquet event and interacting with the banquet client.

Catering (off-site) Food service in a location remote from the food service operation that requires the physical transport of food to an off-site location.

Center of the plate The concept that the entrée should be positioned on a plate by placing the entrée in the center of the plate. Then other menu items should be slightly overlapped moving toward the plate's rim so there is no center area of the plate that is not covered with food.

Chain of command The path by which authority (power) flows from one management level to the next lower level within the food service operation.

Chain recipe A recipe that produces an ingredient used in another recipe.

Check average The average amount spent by a guest at a food service operation. The formula for check average is: Revenue/Number of Guests Served = Check Average. For example, if 100 guests are served during the evening meal period, and revenues of $1500.00 are received, the check average is $15.00 ($1500.00 revenue ÷ 100 guests = $15.00 check average).

Cherry picker A buyer who purchases only a seller's lowest-priced products.

Cleaning The removal of soil and pieces of food from the items being cleaned.

Clip-on (menu) A menu insert or attachment that advertises daily specials or emphasizes other menu items.

Close-out A tactic used by suppliers or manufacturers to quickly move (sell) an unwanted inventory item by reducing its selling price.

Coaching Efforts made by kitchen managers to encourage proper job behavior.

Code of ethics A formal statement developed by a food service operation that defines how its employees should relate to each other and the persons and groups with whom they interact.

Cold calls (purchasing) A term relating to unannounced (unscheduled) visits by supplier representatives to hospitality purchasers.

Collusion An agreement between two or more people to commit fraud.

Commercial food service operations Food services in hotels, restaurants, and other businesses that want to make a profit.

Compensation package The money and other valuable items (fringe benefits) provided in exchange for the work employees do.

Competency Standards of knowledge, skills, and abilities required for successful job performance.

Competing menu items (menu engineering) The menu items that normally "compete" with each other when guests make menu selection decisions. For example, children's menu selections and desserts would not normally compete with entrée selections on most menus.

Competitive edge Something desired by guests that is not offered by competitors. Examples may include an ocean view, special entertainment, or a food item requiring specialized skill in its preparation or equipment for its production.

Conflict of interest (purchasing policy)   A business situation in which a food service employee has an interest in another organization that could (or does) compromise his/her loyalty to the hospitality employer.

Consomme   A clear soup made by combining a flavored stock or broth with other ingredients to produce a soup that has no fat.

Continental breakfast   A breakfast that typically includes a bread item such as a roll or pastry, fruit juice, and coffee or tea but no hot food items.

Continuous quality improvement (CQI)   On-going efforts within the food service operation to better meet or exceed guests' expectations and to define ways to perform work with better, less-costly, and faster methods.

Contract   An agreement made between two or more parties that is enforceable in a court of law.

Contract pricing   A pricing method in which the buyer and seller agree to a specific price for a defined product or service for a stated time period or until one party ends the agreement; also called fixed price contract.

Contribution margin   Product selling price ($-$) product cost. For example, assume a bottle of wine is purchased for $9.50 and sells for $16.99: Contribution margin = $7.49 ($16.99 selling price − $9.50 cost).

Control   The multi-step management activity that involves (1) estimating the amount of revenue or expense, (2) determining the actual amount of revenue or expense, (3) making a comparison between the estimated and actual amounts, (4) taking corrective action if there is an undesirable variance, and (5) determining the results of the corrective actions that were taken.

Controller   The person who records, classifies, and summarizes a food service operation's business transactions. This person develops financial statements and provides suggestions about what they mean to the property owner/managers; also called accountant or bookkeeper.

Convenience food   Food that has some labor built-in that otherwise would need to be added on-site. Examples include presliced meats, frozen vegetables, and baked desserts.

Cooking   Applying heat to food to make it more enjoyable.

Coordinated Pest Management Program (CPMP)   A five-step program of inspection, identification, sanitation, application of pest management procedures, and evaluation to control and eliminate pests in food service operations.

Corrective action   A tactic implemented in efforts to reduce an undesirable variance between expected and actual revenues or expenses.

Cost minimization   A financial goal of non-commercial food service operations that exist for reasons other than making a profit but that want to keep expenses low; abbreviated "cost min."

Cost per servable pound   The cost of one pound of a product in a form which will be served to guests.

Cost percentage   Product cost ÷ by selling price. For example, assume a bottle of wine is purchased for $9.50 and sells for $16.99: Cost percentage = 55.9% ($9.50 ÷ $16.99)

Cost, fixed   A cost such as building rent or a kitchen manager's salary that does not change in direct proportion to revenue.

Cost, variable   A cost such as food or waged labor (that paid on an hourly basis) that changes in direct proportion to revenue.

Cost-effective   A situation in which time and money benefits gained are greater than the costs that are incurred.

Costing (menu)   The process of determining the food cost required to produce all menu items that make up a meal (plate cost) offered at a set selling price when standard recipes for all menu items are utilized.

Costing (recipe)   The process of determining the cost to produce all (or one) serving of a recipe by considering the recipe's ingredients, current ingredient costs, and the number of servings which the recipe yields.

Credit memo   A document used to revise (correct) information about product quantities and/or costs initially recorded on a delivery invoice.

Critical control point (CCP)   Something that can be done in the movement of food from the times of receiving to service to help prevent, eliminate, or reduce hazards to those who consume the food.

Critical control point limit (HACCP program)   Boundaries (maximum/minimum limits) which define the extent to which a critical control point must be controlled to minimize risks of food-borne illness.

Cross-contamination   The transfer of germs between food and/or nonfood items by direct contact or indirect contact such as with equipment or utensils.

Cross-functional team   A group of employees from different departments who work together to resolve problems.

Cross-selling (menu)   Tactics used to advertise other products and services offered by the hospitality operation in addition to those noted on a specific menu.

Cuisine   A style or manner of preparing food.

Culture (food service operation)   The beliefs, values, and norms shared by persons in the food service operation that are considered valid and are passed on to new employees as they work within the operation.

Cyclical (cycle) menu   A menu in which the food items rotate according to a planned schedule such as every twenty-eight days.

Day-part   A segment of the day that represents a change in menu and customer response patterns; for example, the time during which breakfast or lunch menus are offered.

Defect   Any output such as a food product that does not meet the standard set for it.

Definite quantity contracts   A purchasing method in which a buyer agrees to purchase a specific quantity of products over a specified period of time with a lower purchase unit price than if individual orders for the products were negotiated during that time period.

Delegate   The process of assigning authority (power) to subordinates to allow them to do work that a higher level manager would otherwise need to do.

Deluxe hot breakfast   A breakfast with hot food choices offered by a limited-service hotel.

Demand   The total amount of a product that buyers want to purchase at a specific price.

Democratic (leadership style)   A leadership approach in which staff members are encouraged to participate in the decision-making process.

Desktop publishing systems   A personal computer and specific software used to create high-quality page layouts and documents that otherwise would need to be developed by a professional printer.

Die-cut (menu)   A menu that has been punched or cut into a special shape with a metal tool called a die.

Discount   A deduction from the price buyers normally pay for products.

Discrimination   Treating persons unequally for reasons that do not relate to their legal rights or abilities including race, nationality, creed, color, religion, age, sex, or sexual orientation.

Distributor sales representative   The representative of a supplier or distributor who sells products and provides information and services to food service operations; abbreviated DSR and often called "salesperson."

Diversity   The concept that people are unique with individual differences that result from variations in their race, ethnicity, gender, socioeconomic status, age, and physical abilities, among others.

DNA certificates   Documents that certify the species of the seafood product being sold. Note: "DNA" is the abbreviation of deoxyribonucleic acid, the material that contains information which tells cells how to function.

Dry heat   A cooking method in which the food to be cooked is exposed directly to heat or flame. Examples: broiling and frying.

Du jour menu   A menu in which some or all food items are changed daily.

Edible food yield   The useable amount of a food ingredient that can be prepared from a given purchase unit of that ingredient. Example: one pound (16 ounces) of fresh mushrooms yields 6 cups of cleaned sliced mushrooms or 5 cups of cleaned chopped mushrooms.

Edible portion   The amount of a food item that can be served to guests after the product is cooked. For example, a hamburger patty that weighs four ounces when placed on the grill may only weigh 3.6 ounces after it is cooked; often abbreviated "EP."

Electrocution   Being killed by an electric shock.

Employee handbook   A manual given to employees that explains employment policies, including those relating to employment issues and compensation, including benefits, operating concerns, and legal requirements.

Employer of choice   A business with a reputation for being a desirable place to work and whose recruiting efforts are easier because of its good name.

Empower   The act of giving authority (power) to employees to make decisions within their areas of responsibility.

English service (banquet)   Menu items are placed in serving bowls or on serving platters, and the food is brought to the guest table for service in a "family-style" service; serving dishes are passed around the table by the guests.

Entrée   A food item served as the primary (main) course in a meal; sometimes call main course.

Ethical   Conforming to accepted standards of professional behavior.

Ethics   Concerns relating to what is right and wrong when dealing with others.

Excessive price spread   The concept that, as the range in menu item selling price increases, there is a decrease in check average.

Exit interview   A meeting held between a kitchen manager and an employee leaving the food service operation conducted to learn why the employee is leaving and what can be done to improve the organization.

Expedite (purchasing)   The act of following-up on the delivery schedule, quality, and/or other concerns that have been negotiated with suppliers.

Expediter   A person who serves as a liaison between food production and serving staff during busy serving times.

Expenses   Costs incurred by a food service operation to generate its revenues.

Fad   A short-lived interest in something like a food item.

Fast-track employees   Employees who meet the quantity and quality standards for all tasks in their existing position and who participate in a planned professional development program designed to quickly advance them within the food service operation.

Feedback   Information that allows kitchen managers to evaluate the effectiveness of processes or procedures.

File (computer)   A block of information containing a program, document, or collection of data.

Fire suppression system   A ventilation system containing chemicals that are sprayed on equipment below if a fire begins beneath it.

Fiscal period   An accounting period containing a specified number of months. Most fiscal periods are for 12 months, but they can begin on the first day of any month.

Flavor   A food quality factor that affects how it tastes and smells.

Food cost (cost of goods sold)   The cost of food that was purchased to produce the menu items that generated food revenue.

Food cost percentage (menu item)   The food cost of a menu item divided by its selling price.

Foodborne illness   A sickness caused by eating food that has been contaminated by germs, chemicals, or physical hazards.

Forecast (labor cost control)   An estimate of the number of guests to be served or the amount of revenue to be generated for a specific meal period or day.

Fraud   A crime that involves deceiving one or more persons for personal benefit; example: a supplier may claim that a product will be of very high quality but intentionally deliver a product of lower quality while charging the price of the higher-quality product.

Free market   An economic system in which businesses operate without government control in matters including pricing.

Free pour (alcoholic beverages)   A manual system of making cocktails and other alcoholic drinks which relies on the bartender to control the quantity of alcohol in the drink without use of a portioning tool such as a jigger or shot glass.

Front-of-house   An industry term for guest-contact employees, positions, and/or departments.

Full-service hotel   A hotel that provides guests with extensive food and beverage products and services.

Fusion (cuisine)   Foods that blend the traditions of more than one cuisine. Example: Many Hawaiian menu items include ingredients and use cooking methods popular in the culture of numerous ethic or regional traditions.

Garbage   Food waste that cannot be recycled.

Garnish   An edible decoration used to make a menu item attractive.

Grapevine   An informal channel of communication throughout an organization.

Grocery products   Items such as cereals, spices, and baking supplies that can be stored at about room temperature (70°F; 21°C) for a relatively long time period.

Guest count   The number of guests to be served during a specific time period.

Halal (food)   Foods that meet Muslim dietary laws.

Half-bottle (wine)   A bottle holding one-half of the amount of a standard full bottle of wine. Half-bottles contain 0.375 liters.

Harassment   Unwanted and annoying actions, including threats or demands, by one or more persons.

Hardware (computer)   Physical equipment such as the input/output device, central processing unit, and external storage device required for a computerized system.

Haute cuisine   Food that is elaborately or skillfully prepared, especially that of France.

Hazard (food contamination)   Microorganisms, chemicals, and physical objects which can contaminate food.

Hazard Analysis Critical Control Points (HACCP)   A practical system using proper food-handling procedures along with monitoring and record keeping to help ensure that food is safe for consumption.

Herb   A leaf of an aromatic (fragrant) plant used to add flavor to foods being cooked.

Holding   The task of keeping food items at the proper serving temperature until they are prepared.

Hospitality industry   Organizations that provide lodging and/or food services to people when they are away from their homes.

Hospitality suite   A guest room rented by a supplier/vendor, usually during a convention/conference, to provide complimentary food and/or beverages to invited guests.

Hosted events   Functions that are complimentary for invited guests; costs are borne by the event's sponsor. A hosted bar may offer free beverages to wedding party guests, and a corporate sponsor may pay for a hosted reception in a hospitality suite.

Imprest (petty cash system)   A petty cash fund in which payments to the fund are always in the amount required to bring its balance to the original amount. The petty cash balance is always maintained by cash and the receipts for cash payments.

Income   Profit; the amount of money that remains from revenue after the expenses required to generate the revenue have been deducted.

Income statement   A summary of how much profit, if any, the food service operation earned. It shows the revenues, expenses, and profits during a specific time period such as month or year; also called "profit and loss" ("P&L") statement.

Income statement schedule   A supplement to the food service operation's income statement that shows financial details for each revenue center.

Induction   Activities that provide general information about the specific department in which the new staff member will work.

Ingredient file   A computerized record that contains information about each ingredient purchased, including purchase unit size and cost, issue unit size and cost, and recipe unit size and cost. Interestingly, each of these units can differ. For example, prepared applesauce may be purchased in a case of six #10 cans (purchase unit size), issued one can at a time (issue unit = #10 can) and used in recipe by the cup (recipe unit = cup).

Ingredients   The individual elements in a menu item. For example, flour and sugar are two ingredients in bread (a menu item).

Inspection (sanitation)   An on-site review of a food service operation that is made to help assure that sanitation regulations are being followed.

Institutional meat purchasing specifications (IMPS)   Product standards for meat items developed by the U.S. Department of Agriculture.

Interview questions (direct)   Specific questions typically organized in advance and followed to learn specific information about job applicants.

Interview questions (indirect)   Open-ended questions asked to learn about a job applicant's opinions and attitudes.

Intranet   A network consisting of computers for a single food service organization that can be at the same or different locations.

Inventory turnover rate   The number of times in a specific period (example: month) that inventory is converted (turned into) revenue.

Investment   The amount of money that an owner has used to start and operate the business.

Invoice   A statement (bill) from a supplier that indicates the products, quantities, and resulting charges that must be paid by the food service operation that receives them.

Issue requisition   A document used to identify the products and quantities that are removed from storage areas in a large volume food service operation.

Issuing   The process of moving products from storage areas to the place of production.

Job description   A list of the tasks that must be performed by a person working in a specific position.

Job offer   An invitation, made by a kitchen manager to the most qualified job applicant, which outlines the terms and conditions under which employment will be offered.

Kitchen display unit   A video display monitor that shows orders entered into a POS system on a monitor in a kitchen workstation area.

Kosher (food)   Food that is prepared according to Jewish dietary laws.

Labor cost percentage   The percentage of food revenue used to pay for the labor cost incurred to generate the food revenue. The basic calculation is:

$$\frac{\text{Labor Cost}}{\text{Food Revenue}} = \text{Labor Cost \%}$$

Labor-intensive   A job situation in which technology cannot be used to replace employees.

Laissez-faire (leadership style)   A leadership approach that minimizes directing employees and, instead, maximizes the delegation of tasks to staff members.

Law suit   A legal action by one person or organization against another person or organization.

Lead time usage (minimum-maximum system)   The number of purchase units of a product typically used during the time between order placement and delivery.

Limited service hotel   A lodging property that offers very limited food service or none at all; sometimes a complementary breakfast is served, but there is not a table-service restaurant.

Line-level employees   Staff members whose jobs are considered entry-level or nonsupervisory and who are paid an hourly rate rather than a salary.

Line-up (training)   A brief information training session held before the work shift begins.

Lobby food services (hotel)   Food services typically offered by limited-service hotels; those lodging operations that offer few, if any, food and beverage services.

Make or buy analysis   The process of deciding whether a menu item should be prepared on-site or purchased as a convenience food.

Management company-operated (noncommercial food services) A noncommercial food service operation that is managed and operated by a food service management company.

Manager A staff member who directs the work of supervisors.

Market All of the people with the desire and ability to purchase the products and services offered by a food service operation.

Market form Different ways that food products can be purchased. For example, frozen bread dough or baked sliced bread can be used, fresh hamburger (ground beef) is available in bulk or preportioned patties, and hamburger can also be purchased frozen in bulk or preportioned patties. Each of these alternatives is a market form.

Marking (product storage) The act of recording information about the date of product receipt and product cost on containers of products when they enter storage areas.

Mark-up factor (pricing) The number of times by which a product's cost is multiplied to arrive at a selling price.

Material Safety Data Sheets Written statements that provide information about a chemical substance including hazards and the best ways to handle them.

Menu A list of all the food items that a food service operation has available for consumers.

Menu (pre-set banquet) A menu planned as an example of popular menus enjoyed by previous banquet guests that are suggested for other potential guests.

Menu category A group or list of alternative menu items such as entrées, salads, and desserts.

Menu design The process by which the planning team develops a format for the menu that will be presented to guests to inform them about the items available.

Menu engineering A method of menu evaluation that focuses on the goal of selling as many as possible of the menu items that are the most popular for guests and the most profitable for the food service operation.

Menu item file A computerized record about information relating to menu items tracked with the operation's point-of-sale (POS) system.

Menu items Specific food items that are available at the food service operation.

Menu layout A term relating to the placement of menu item categories on the menu.

Menu mix The total number of servings of a menu item that are sold compared to the total sale of all competing menu items.

Menu rationalization The menu planning tactic that involves using the same main ingredient in several different menu items.

Merchandising The act of promoting certain menu items in efforts to encourage guests to select them.

Minimum-maximum (inventory system) A system used to calculate product purchase quantities that considers the minimum quantity below which inventory levels should not fall, and the maximum quantity above which inventory levels should not rise.

Mission statement A planning tool that generally explains what the organization wants to accomplish and how it intends to do so.

Moist heat A cooking method in which food is cooked by extended exposure to steam or hot liquids. Examples: stewing and braising.

Monitor (computer) A computer system output component that displays text and graphics.

Morale The total of an employee's feelings about his/her employer, workplace, and other aspects of the food service operation.

Motivate The act of providing an employee with a reason to do something. Employees are motivated when their supervisor offers them something they want (example: higher pay rate) in return for something the supervisor wants (example: work in a higher-level position).

Multiplier (selling price) The mark-up by which the plate cost of a menu item must be multiplied to determine the item's base selling price; see plate cost.

Negotiate The process by which two or more parties determine the course of action that is best for each of the parties.

Net price The total or per-unit amount paid for products after all discounts have been applied to the purchase price.

Noncommercial food service operations Food service operations whose financial goal does not involve making profit from the sale of food and beverage products.

No-Show The term for employees who, when they are scheduled to work, do not notify managers that they will not work and do not report for their assigned shift.

Open check (POS system) Information contained in POS systems about food and beverage items on guest checks that have been opened but not closed; guests have ordered some food or beverage items but have not yet paid for them at the end of their visit.

Optical scanner Equipment that can "read" data in a bar code on a product's label or package; see bar code.

Order period (purchasing) The time for which an order is placed. For example, produce may be purchased twice weekly and canned goods once every two weeks.

Order point The number of purchase units of a specific product that should be in inventory when additional quantities of the product are ordered; see "purchase unit."

Order point (minimum-maximum system) The number of purchase units of a product hat should be available in inventory when an order is placed.

Order printer Equipment that transmits food service orders from point-of-sale equipment to the order pick-up area and prints or electronically displays orders in that area; also called kitchen printers or remote printers.

Organic foods Foods that are produced, processed, and packaged without using chemicals such as antibiotics or growth hormones in animals and without pesticides, fertilizers or radiation, among other polluting chemicals and practices, while growing fruits and vegetables.

Organization chart A chart that shows how positions in an organization relate to each other.

Orientation The act of providing basic information about the food service operation that must be known by all employees in all departments.

Overtime (budget standard) The number of labor hours actually worked in excess of the number of labor hours that were scheduled.

Overtime (legal) The number of hours of work after which an employee must receive a premium pay rate (usually 1.5 times the basic hourly rate).

Package inspection program (employee) A policy that (a) discourages employees from bringing backpacks, shopping bags, and other large packages to work and (b) indicates that packages may be inspected when the employees leave work.

Pairing (food and wine) The notion that some wines go better with food than others, and that the wine should be selected after the food item to match the food with which it will be consumed.

Pallet   A platform (rack) typically constructed of wooden slats and used to store and/or move cases of products stacked upon it.

Par system (inventory)   The normal quantity of purchase units of a product which should be available in inventory. For example, if a par of 10 cases of peaches should be in inventory and, if four cases are available, six cases will be purchased to build the inventory back to the par level.

Participative management   A leadership method that increases the quality of the decision-making process by involving employees in the decision: use of this method can also improve the employees' job satisfaction.

Perishable   The condition in which quality is reduced and spoilage occurs quickly when applicable products are not properly handled and stored.

Perpetual inventory   A system that tracks all incoming and outgoing products so that kitchen managers know, on a continual basis, the quantity of product which should be available in inventory.

Pesticide   A chemical used to kill pests such as rodents or insects.

Petty cash   A cash fund used to make relatively infrequent and relatively low-cost product purchases.

Petty cash fund   A small amount of cash kept on hand for relatively low-cost purchases.

Petty cash voucher   A slip signed by the person responsible for the petty cash fund that authorizes the withdrawal of cash from the fund for a specific purchase.

Physical hazard (food)   Objects such as glassware and metal shavings in food that can cause illness and injury if they are eaten.

Pilferage   The act of stealing small quantities of food product over a relatively long time period.

Point-of-Sale (POS)   An electronic system that collects information about revenues and guest counts, among numerous other data.

Policy   A (usually) written statement of principles or guiding actions that indicate what should be done in specific situations.

Popularity (menu engineering)   A factor along with profitability that describes menu items that kitchen managers want to sell. A menu item is popular if it sells 70% of expected sales (100% ÷ number of competing menu items × .70); see competing menu items (menu engineering).

Position analysis   A process to identify each task in a position and how the task should be done.

Potentially hazardous foods   Foods of animal origin or other items high in protein that are most frequently involved in cases of foodborne illness.

Premium brand (liquor)   The most expensive brands of quality liquor available at a food service operation.

Preparation   The steps involved in getting an ingredient ready for cooking or serving. For example, celery is cleaned and chopped before cooking in a stew.

Pre-plate (banquet)   The portioning of menu items onto plates that will be served to banquet guests. These plates are frequently covered to keep hot foods hot or placed in heated transport equipment to move the food to banquet service areas.

Preportion   Menu items that have been divided into the proper weight or size before being purchased by the food service operation.

Price   The amount of money needed to purchase a product or service.

Price quotation   A request made to a supplier for the current price of a product that meets the food service operation's quality requirements; also called "request for price quotation" (RFP).

Prime real estate (menu design)   The areas on a menu most frequently viewed by guests and which, therefore, should contain the items that menu planners most want to sell.

Prime supplier   The supplier chosen by a food service operation to provide products of a specified quality for a specified length of time.

Process revisions   Changes to work methods to reduce defects and increase opportunities to please the guests.

Production   The process of getting food products ready for service.

Production loss   The amount (weight and/or percent) of a product's as-purchased weight which is not servable.

Productivity   The quality and quantity of output compared to the amount of input such as labor hours needed to generate the output. For example, if it takes 1.25 hours to prepare a recipe, and changes are made to reduce the preparation time to 1.0 hour, productivity has increased. This 15 minutes (.25 hours) can then be used for other tasks.

Professionals   Persons working in an occupation that requires extensive knowledge and skills.

Profit   The difference between the amount of money that a food service operation earns and spends.

Profit maximization   A financial goal of commercial food service operations that exist to make a profit; abbreviated "profit max."

Profitability (menu engineering)   A factor along with popularity that describes menu items that kitchen managers want to sell. A menu item is profitable if its contribution margin is equal to or greater than the weighted average contribution margin of all competing menu items.

Purchase order   A document used to obtain prices from suppliers, to inform suppliers whose price proposal is accepted that a shipment should be delivered, and to explain any shipment or delivery requirements.

Purchase requisition   A document used by food storeroom personnel in a large food service operation to inform purchasing employees when additional quantities of products are needed to build inventory levels to preestablished levels.

Purchase specification   A description of the quality requirements that must be met by the products purchased by the food service operation.

Purchase unit   The unit weight, volume, or container size in which a product can be purchased. For example, salad oil can be purchased in pint, quart, or gallon-sized containers.

Purchasing   The process of deciding the right quality and quantity of items that should be purchased and selecting a supplier who can provide them at the right price and right time.

Purchasing (centralized)   The system in which purchasing is the responsibility of a specialist in a purchasing department in a large property, the owner/manager in a smaller property, or coordinated with persons outside the property in a multi-unit operation.

Purchasing (de-centralized)   The system in which purchasing is the responsibility of each department manager; for example, the kitchen manager purchases the food, and the beverage manager (head bartender) purchase the beverages.

Purchasing handbook   A document developed by the kitchen manager to inform suppliers about purchasing policies and procedures that must be followed at all times.

Quality   The consistent delivery of products and services according to expected standards.

Quality assurance   All activities that help a food service operation to attain quality.

Questions (open-ended)   A question that cannot be answered with a "yes" or "no." Open-ended questions require a thoughtfully considered response.

Quick-service (restaurant)   A food service operation that provides a limited menu and limited service (generally self-serve at counters or through vehicle drive-through windows) at low prices; also called a QSR, or "fast-food" restaurant.

Radio frequency identification (RFID)   An electronic wireless tracking system that uses a transmitter to provide noncontact and automatic location of stock throughout the food service operation.

Rebate   An after-purchase discount; sometimes called a "cash back" offer.

Receiving   The transfer of ownership from a supplier to the food service operation which occurs when products are delivered.

Receiving report   A document that separates incoming food costs into components required for daily food cost calculations.

Recipe (chained)   A recipe that yields an ingredient used in another recipe.

Recipe conversion factor (RFC)   A factor (number) that is used to adjust ingredients in a standard recipe when the number of servings and/or serving size of a current recipe must be changed because they differ from those in a desired recipe. The calculation required to determine this factor is:

$$\frac{\text{Desired Recipe Yield}}{\text{Current Recipe Yield}} = \text{Recipe Conversion Factor}$$

Recipe Evaluation   A formal process in which evaluators determine the extent to which a standard recipe is acceptable by considering the product it yields according to several predetermined factors.

Recipe management software   Written programs, procedures, instructions, or rules relating to the operation of a computer system that involves or impacts standard recipes.

Reciprocal purchases   A transaction in which a supplier agrees to purchase something from the purchaser if the purchaser agrees to purchase something from the supplier. Example: the purchaser makes an advertising commitment with a local newspaper and, in return, newspaper managers agree to spend a specified amount of money on food and beverage purchases at the property; also called bartering.

Recruiting   The search for persons who may be interested in vacant positions.

Recruiting (external)   Activities used to inform persons who do not work for the food service operation that new staff members are needed.

Recruiting (internal)   The use of existing employees to help fill position vacancies. Current employees may be promoted from within to fill positions with greater responsibility, or they may refer friends, neighbors, and others to the property.

Refuse   Solid waste such as cardboard and glass that is not removed through the sewage system.

Regular (guest)   An industry term referring to a guest who frequently visits a food service operation.

Repeat business   Guests who return to the food service operation because they enjoyed a positive experience during earlier visits.

Resources   What the kitchen manager has available to attain goals. Examples include people, food products, time, and money.

Responsibility   The need for a person to do the work that is included in a specific position.

Retention rate (employee)   The number of employees who remain during a specific period of time divided by the number of employees who worked in the kitchen during that same period. The retention rate is generally stated as a percentage. One calculation for annual retention rate % is:

Number of Employees Who Remain ($\div$) Total Number of Employee = Annual Retention Rate %

Return on Investment (ROI)   An accounting calculation that relates profit with the investment made to generate the profit. The formula for ROI is: Annual Profit $\div$ Investment = ROI. Example: if an owner invests $500,000 in a restaurant that has a $40,000 profit in one year, its ROI is 8% ($40,000 $\div$ $500,000 = 8.0%).

Revenue   The amount of money generated from the sale of food and beverage products.

Revenue center   A department within a food service operation that generates revenue. Example: a restaurant may have à la carte dining, beverage, and off-site catering departments (revenue centers).

Revenue stream   The flow of money that comes into the food service operation that is generated from the sale of products and services to guests.

Role play   A group training activity in which trainees assume different roles (examples: cook and server) to apply information presented in the training session.

Russian service (banquet)   An entrée such as a beef tenderloin is thinly sliced in the kitchen and brought to the table by banquet staff who place the item on a plate with entrée accompaniments that has been set in front of the guest

Safety   The protection of a person's physical well-being and health.

Safety level (inventory)   The minimum quantity of a specific product that must always be available in inventory.

Salary   Money paid to an employee for work performed that is calculated on a weekly, monthly, or annual basis.

Sales   The number of menu items that are sold; example: if ten hamburgers are sold, the sales of that menu item is ten.

Sanitizing   The elimination of germs that remain after cleaning.

"Scratch" (food products)   An industry term for foods made with raw ingredients on-site.

Seat tax (contribution margin)   A slang term indicating the contribution margin of a menu item or (in menu engineering) the weighted average contribution margin for all items sold during the period under study.

Selection   The process to evaluate job applicants to assess their suitability for a position.

Self-operated (noncommercial food services)   A noncommercial food service operation that is managed and operated by the organization's employees.

Separation   The term for employees who leave the operation for voluntary or involuntary reasons.

Service   The process of helping guests by meeting their wants and needs with respect and dignity in a timely manner.

Service (food)   The process of transferring food and beverage products from service staff to the guests.

Service charge   A labor-related fee added by the management of a food service operation that must be paid by the guests. Service charges are typically computed as a percentage of a guest's food and beverage expenditures.

Serving (food)   The process of moving prepared food items from production staff to service personnel.

Serving costs   The cost to produce one serving of a menu item when it is prepared according to the standard recipe.

Serving size   The quantity (weight, count, or volume) of a menu item to be served to a guest.

Sharp practice (purchasing policy)   Bargaining between the purchaser and potential seller in such a way that the purchaser unethically takes advantage of the seller.

Shopper's report   Information provided by persons hired by the food service operation to pose as guests to closely observe and report on their dining experiences at the property. Observations typically include those related to service, sanitation and cleanliness, the menu and menu items, and many other observable aspects of the operation, experience, and environment.

Signature item   A food or beverage item that guests associate with a specific food service operation. Examples may include a "one-pound pork chop" or an "oyster boat:" (a loaf of French bread hollowed and filled with deep-fried oysters).

Slack-out seafood   Seafood that has been frozen and then thawed and represented to be a fresh item that can be sold at a higher price than if it was purchased frozen.

Smallwares   Pots, pans, measuring and portioning devices, and other utensils used for food production and service.

Sneeze guards   A see-through barrier used to protect foods in self-service counters from other guests who might sneeze or cough on the food.

Software   Programs that instruct (control) a computer system's hardware components.

Sourcing (supplier)   Activities undertaken to determine which, often from among many, suppliers will be requested to quote prices for the products and services to be purchased by the food service operation.

Spice   A seasoning obtained from the seeds, fruit, roots, bark, or other nonleaf part of a plant.

Split (wine bottle)   A bottle holding a single serving of wine. Splits contain .1875 liters or 1/4 of a standard full wine bottle.

Split case   A case of less-than-full purchase unit size sold by a supplier. Example: A supplier sells five #10 cans of peaches rather than a full case containing six #10 cans; also called a "broken case."

Split-shift   A work schedule in which an employee works a certain number of hours during a shift, leaves the work site, and then returns later in the same day for a second work shift.

Standard   Something that can be used to compare one thing against another. For example: A labor cost standard indicates how many labor dollars or hours should be used. The actual number of labor dollars or hours spent can be compared to this standard to determine how well labor was controlled.

Standard of identity   A detailed description of ingredients to be included in a specific food product. For example, "fruit cocktail" must have a specified percentage of maraschino cherries and other fruits. If it does not, the product must be called "mixed fruit."

Standard recipe   Instructions to produce a food or beverage item that, if followed, will help assure that the food service operation's quality and quantity standards for the product are met. Standard recipe information should include the type and amount of ingredients, preparation procedures including equipment and tools, yield (number of servings and serving size), garnishes, and any other information needed to properly produce and serve the item.

Standard recipe file   A computerized record that contains the recipes for the menu items produced. Data includes each recipe's ingredients, preparation method, yield (number of serving and serving size), and ingredient costs along with each item's selling price and food cost percentage (food cost ÷ selling price).

Standing order   An agreement between a purchaser and a supplier that the same quantity of a specified product is required each time a delivery is made.

Steamship round (beef)   A large beef roast that consists of the whole round with rump and heel.

Steward   An employee who washes pots, pans, dishes, and cleans the food and beverage facility.

Stock-out (inventory)   The condition that occurs when food products required for production are not available in storage.

Storing   The process of holding products under the best storage conditions until they are needed.

Subordinate   A term referring to an employee (associate or staff member) in a lower organizational level.

Suggestive selling   The tactic of insuring that guests are aware of the products/services offered by the food service operation. Successful suggestive selling benefits the guests who can try new products/services, the employees (if they are tipped on revenues generated) and the hospitality operation because revenues are increased.

Suitability for intended use (quality)   This primary quality concern relates to considering the purpose for which an item will be used and then selecting the product determined to be "best" for that use.

Supervisor   A staff member who directs the work of entry-level employees.

Supplier relations   How purchasers interact with their suppliers.

Supply and demand (law of)   A belief about the supply (availability) of an item and its price compared to its demand. Often, as the price of an item increases, demand for that product decreases; the reverse is also true.

Table d'hôte menu   A menu in which food items comprising a meal are sold at a fixed price, and the total guest charge does not depend upon the items selected.

Table tent   A printed advertisement placed directly on the guests' tables that is used to promote menu specials.

Table turn   An industry term relating to the number of times a dining room table is used during a dining period.

Tare allowance   An adjustment feature on a scale that excludes the weight of a pot or pan placed on the scale to hold food ingredients being measured.

Tare allowance (purchasing)   The weight range allowed for an item purchased on a per serving basis.

Task   A duty or responsibility that is part of a job position.

Task breakdown   A position analysis tool that indicates how each task identified in the task list should be done.

Task list   A position analysis tool that indicates all tasks included within a position.

Taste Test   A process to learn the opinions of managers, employees, and guests about the food items being considered for the menu.

Temperature danger zone   The temperature range between 41°F (5°C) and 135°F (57°C) in which many harmful germs multiply quickly.

Terms and conditions   General provisions that apply to a supplier's price quotations and a buyer's purchase orders regardless of the specific products being purchased or sold.

Texture   A description of how a food feels that is an important factor in food quality.

Toxin   A poisonous chemical produced by germs or other living things.

Trade puffing   The tactic of boasting about a product when advertising. A "Mile-High Pie" is obviously not one mile tall, and the "best hamburger in the world" is probably more of a merchandising statement than it is a provable fact.

Trade show   An industry-specific event that allows suppliers to interact with, educate, and sell to individuals and businesses that are part of the industry; also called exhibition.

Training   The process of developing one's knowledge and skills to improve job performance.

Training lesson   The information and methods used to present one session in a training plan.

Training plan   An overview of the content and sequence of an entire training program.

Trans fats   A form of fat that has been shown to raise blood cholesterol levels.

Transfer (food cost calculation)   An adjustment made when food costs are calculated to better match food costs with the revenue generated by the sale of the food.

Transformational (leadership style)   A leadership approach in which leaders interact with employees in a way that permits both the leaders and their associates to raise one another to a higher level of motivation.

Trend   A gradual change in guests' food preferences that is likely to continue for a long time in the future.

Trespassing   Unlawful (without the owner's permission) entry of a person onto the property of another person.

Trial order   A small order placed with a supplier to determine the quality of the product that will be received and/or to evaluate the quality of information and service provided by the supplier.

Truth-in-menu   The requirements (and laws in some locations) that menu descriptions honestly tell the quantity, quality, point of origin, and other information so that readers will understand the items being described; for example, "fresh gulf shrimp" cannot be frozen shrimp from the Indian Ocean.

Turnover rate (employee)   The number of employees who leave during a specific period of time divided by the number of employees working during that same period. The turnover rate is generally stated as a percentage. One calculation for annual turnover rate % is as follows:

Number of Employees Who Leave (÷) Total Number of Employees = Annual Turnover Rate %

Umami (taste)   A term that describes a savory, brothy, or meaty taste.

Usage rate (minimum-maximum system)   The number of purchase units of a product used during a typical order period.

Value   Guest views about what they pay for something in comparison to what they receive for the payment.

Variance (budget)   The difference between an amount of revenue or expense indicated in the budget and the actual amount of the revenue or expense.

Variance (explainable)   A variance caused by one or more factors that managers understand.

Variance (unexplainable)   A variance caused by one or more unknown factors.

Variance analysis (revenue)   The process of studying differences between estimated and actual revenue levels to determine if there are problems that require corrective action.

Vegetarian   A person who eats no meat or fish and, often, no other animal products. Their diets are chiefly comprised of fruits, grains, and nuts.

Vegetarian (menu item)   Food items that do not contain meat or animal products.

Vintage (wine)   Wine grown from grapes one vineyard during one growing season.

Viticultural   Relating to wine production.

Wage (hourly)   Money paid to an employee for work performed during a one-hour time period.

Wine list   A special menu that indicates the wine selections offered by a food service operation along with their selling prices. Brief descriptions of the wines are also often included.

Work flow   The movement of products through workstations in a food service operation; see workstation.

Work simplification   The design of a work process such as producing food on a cooks' line in a way that requires a minimal number of steps or motions that will yield products meeting the property's quality requirements.

Workstation   An area with necessary equipment in which closely-related work activities are performed by persons working in similar positions. For example, food preparation personnel may work in a cooks' line that houses several items of food equipment used to hold or produce food items that have been ordered by service staff.

Workstation printer   A remote printing device in a kitchen area that prints a food order that has been entered into the POS system.

Yield (Purchasing)   The amount (pounds or percent) of the as-purchased weight of a food item that is edible after it is processed; see "as-purchased."

Yield (recipe)   The number of servings and the size of each serving that are produced when a standard recipe is followed. For example, a standard recipe may yield fifty 3 oz. servings of a specified food item every time it is correctly used.

Yield test   A carefully controlled process to determine the amount (weight and/or percent) of the as-purchased quantity of a product remaining after production loss has occurred.

Zero defects   A goal of no deviations from standards; there are instances where production, service, financial, and other goals are not met.

Zero tolerance   A policy that allows no amount or type of harassing behavior.

INDEX

Page references followed by *f* and *b* indicate figures and boxes respectively.